MERCEDES-BENZ

230
230S
230SL
1963-1968

WORKSHOP MANUAL

A Floyd CLYMER Publication by:
www.VelocePress.com
Copyright 2024 Veloce Enterprises

PREFACE

TRADEMARKS & COPYRIGHT

Mercedes-Benz ® is the registered trademark of Mercedes-Benz AG. This publication is not sponsored by or endorsed by the trademark owner. We recognize that some words, model names and designations, for example, mentioned herein are the property of the trademark holder. We use them for identification purposes only. This is not an official publication however; it may include non-copyright works of the trademark holder.

INTRODUCTION

Welcome to the world of digital publishing ~ the book you now hold in your hand was printed using the latest state of the art digital technology. The advent of print-on-demand has forever changed the publishing process, never has information been so accessible and it is our hope that this book serves your informational needs for years to come. If this is your first exposure to digital publishing, we hope that you are pleased with the results. Many more titles of interest to the classic automobile and motorcycle enthusiast, collector and restorer are available via our website at www.VelocePress.com. We hope that you find this title as interesting as we do.

NOTE FROM THE PUBLISHER

The information presented is true and complete to the best of our knowledge. All recommendations are made without any guarantees on the part of the author or the publisher, who also disclaim all liability incurred with the use of this information.

INFORMATION ON THE USE OF THIS PUBLICATION

This manual is an invaluable resource for those interested in performing their own maintenance. However, in today's information age we are constantly subject to changes in common practice, new technology, availability of improved materials and increased awareness of chemical toxicity. As such, it is advised that the user consult with an experienced professional prior to undertaking any procedure described herein. While every care has been taken to ensure correctness of information, it is obviously not possible to guarantee complete freedom from errors or omissions or to accept liability arising from such errors or omissions. Therefore, any individual that uses the information contained within, or elects to perform or participate in do-it-yourself repairs or modifications acknowledges that there is a risk factor involved and that the publisher or its associates cannot be held responsible for personal injury or property damage resulting from the use of the information or the outcome of such procedures.

WARNING!

One final word of advice, this publication is intended to be used as a reference guide, and when in doubt the reader should consult with a qualified technician.

CONTENTS

Basic troubleshooting & tools	5
Engine	17
Fuel	33
Ignition	49
Cooling	55
Clutch	61
Manual gearbox	69
Automatic transmission	79
Prop-shaft, rear axle & suspension	91
Front suspension & hubs	107
Steering	117
Brakes	129
Electrical	143
Body	153
Technical data	165
Torque wrench settings	175
Lubrication chart	178
Wiring diagrams	180
Conversion chart	186

BASIC TROUBLESHOOTING AND TOOLS

(NOTE: Detailed troubleshooting can be found at the end of each appropriate chapter)

Troubleshooting can be relatively simple if done logically. The first step is to define symptoms as closely as possible. Subsequent steps involve testing and analyzing areas which could cause the symptoms.

Procedures in this chapter are not the only ones possible. There may be several approaches to solving a problem, but all methods must have one thing in common—a logical, systematic approach.

TROUBLESHOOTING EQUIPMENT

The following equipment is necessary to properly troubleshoot the engine and its components.

1. Voltmeter, ammeter, and ohmmeter
2. Hydrometer
3. Compression tester
4. Vacuum gauge
5. Tachometer
6. Dwell meter
7. Timing light
8. Exhaust gas analyzer

Items 1 through 7 are essential. Item 8 is necessary for exhaust emission control compliance. The following is a brief description of the function of each instrument.

Voltmeter, Ammeter, and Ohmmeter

For testing the ignition and electrical systems, a good voltmeter is required. The range of the meter should cover from 0 to 20 volts, and have an accuracy of $\pm \frac{1}{2}$ volt.

The ohmmeter measures electrical resistance and is required to check continuity (open- and short-circuits), and to test fuses and lights.

The ammeter measures electrical current. One for automotive use should cover 0-10 amperes and 0-100 amperes. An ammeter is useful for checking battery charging and starting current. The starter and generator procedures use an ammeter to check for shorted windings.

Hydrometer

A hydrometer gives an indication of battery condition and charge by measuring the specific gravity of the electrolyte in each cell.

Compression Tester

The compression tester measures pressure buildup in each cylinder. The results, when properly interpreted, can indicate general cylinder and valve condition. To perform the compression check, proceed as follows:

1. Run the engine until normal operating temperature is reached.

2. Block the choke and throttle in the wide open position.

3. Remove all spark plugs.

4. Connect compression tester to one cylinder, following manufacturer's instructions.

5. Have an assistant crank the engine for at least 4 turns.

6. Remove the tester and record the reading.

7. Repeat the above steps for each cylinder.

If the compression readings fall within the appropriate range shown in the Technical Data specifications, and do not differ from each other by more than 20 psi (40 psi for diesel engines), the rings and valves are in good condition. If all cylinders are uniformly low or high, the compression tester may be inaccurate. The important point is the difference between the readings.

Compression Defects

1. *Low Compression in One Cylinder*. If a low reading (see above) is obtained on one cylinder, this indicates valve or ring trouble. To determine which, pour about a teaspoon of engine oil through the spark plug hole onto the top of the piston. Turn the engine over once to clear some of the excess oil, then take another compression test and record the reading. If the compression returns to normal, the valves are good but the rings are defective on that cylinder. If compression does not increase, the valves require servicing.

2. *Low Compression in Two Adjacent Cylinders*. This may indicate that the head gasket has blown between the cylinders and that gases are leaking from one cylinder to the other. Replace the head gasket as described in Chapter One.

To isolate the trouble more closely, compare the compression readings with vacuum gauge readings as described below.

Vacuum Gauge

The vacuum gauge is easy to use, but difficult for an inexperienced mechanic to interpret. The results, when considered with other findings, can provide valuable clues to possible trouble.

Connect the vacuum gauge with a T-connector in the hose from the carburetor to the vacuum advance on the distributor. Vacuum reading should be steady at 18-22 in. Subtract 1 in. from reading for every 1,000 feet of altitude. **Figure 1** shows numerous typical readings with interpretations. Results are not conclusive without comparing to other test results, such as compression readings.

Fuel Pressure Gauge

This instrument is vital for evaluating fuel pump performance. Often a vacuum gauge and fuel pressure gauge are combined into one instrument.

Tachometer

A tachometer is essential for tuning engines with exhaust emission control systems. Ignition timing and carburetor adjustments must be performed at specified idle speeds. The best instrument for this purpose is one with a range of 0-1,000 or 0-2,000 rpm. Extended range (0-6,000) instruments lack accuracy at lower speeds. The instrument should be capable of detecting changes of 25 rpm.

Dwell Meter

A dwell meter measures the distance in degrees of cam rotation that the distributor breaker points remain closed while the engine is running. Since this angle is determined by breaker point gap, dwell angle is an accurate indication of point

①

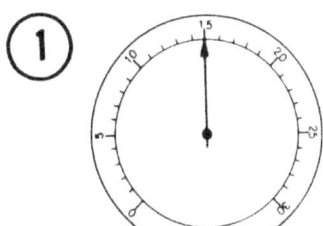

1. NORMAL READING
Reads 15 in. at idle.

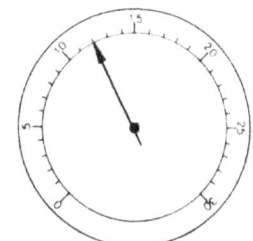

2. LATE IGNITION TIMING
About 2 inches too low at idle.

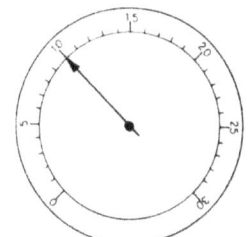

3. LATE VALVE TIMING
About 4 to 8 inches low at idle.

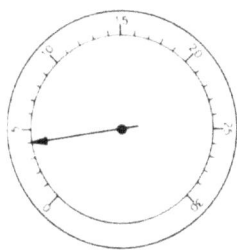

4. INTAKE LEAK
Low steady reading.

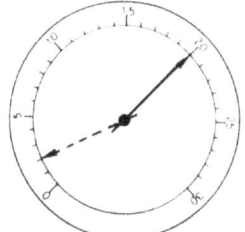

5. NORMAL READING
Drops to 2, then rises to 25 when accelerator is rapidly depressed and released.

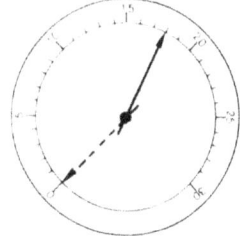

6. WORN RINGS, DILUTED OIL
Drops to 0, then rises to 18 when accelerator is rapidly depressed and released.

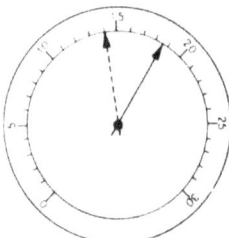

7. STICKING VALVE(S)
Normally steady. Intermittently flicks downward about 4 in.

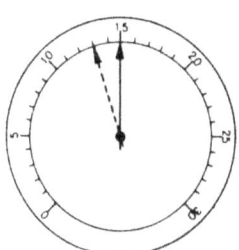

8. LEAKY VALVE
Regular drop about 2 inches.

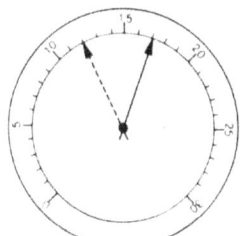

9. BURNED OR WARPED VALVE
Regular, evenly spaced down-scale flick about 4 in.

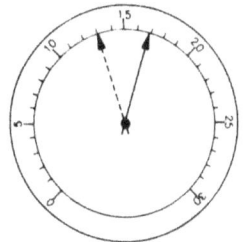

10. WORN VALVE GUIDES
Oscillates about 4 in.

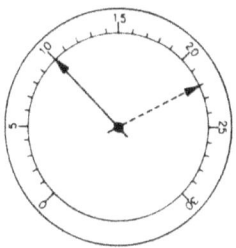

11. WEAK VALVE SPRINGS
Violent oscillation (about 10 in.) as rpm increases. Often steady at idle.

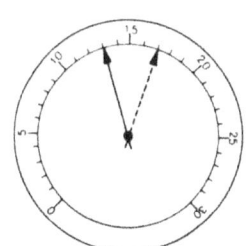

12. IMPROPER IDLE MIXTURE
Floats slowly between 13-17 in.

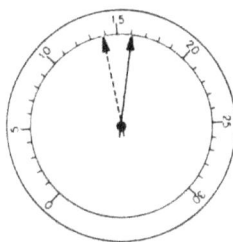

13. SMALL SPARK GAP or DEFECTIVE POINTS
Slight float between 14-16 in.

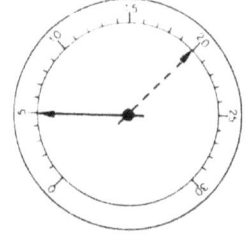

14. HEAD GASKET LEAK
Gauge floats between 5-19 in.

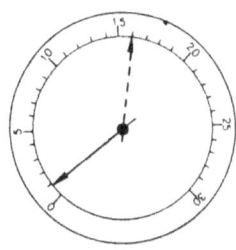

15. RESTRICTED EXHAUST SYSTEM
Normal when first started. Drops to 0 as rpm increases. May eventually rise to about 16.

gap. Many tachometers incorporate a dwell meter as well. Follow the instrument manufacturer's instructions to measure dwell.

Stroboscopic Timing Light

This instrument permits accurate engine timing. By flashing a light at the precise instant that cylinder No. 1 fires, the position of the crankshaft pulley at that instant can be seen. Marks on the pulley are lined up with the crankcase pointer to time the engine.

Suitable lights are neon bulb and xenon strobe types. Neon bulb timing lights are difficult to see and must be used in dimly lit areas. Xenon strobe timing lights can be used in bright sunlight. Use the light according to the manufacturer's instructions.

Exhaust Analyzer

Of all instruments, this is the least likely to be owned by an amateur mechanic. The most common type samples exhaust gases from the tailpipe and measures thermal conductivity. Since different gases conduct heat at varying rates, thermal conductivity is a good indication of gases present.

STARTER TROUBLESHOOTING

Starter system troubles are relatively easy to isolate. The following are common symptoms.

Engine Cranks Very Slowly or Not At All

Turn on the headlights; if the lights are very dim, the battery or connecting wires most likely are at fault. Check the battery with hydrometer. Check wiring for breaks, shorts, and dirty connections. If the battery and wires are all right, turn the headlights on and crank the engine. If the lights dim drastically, the starter is probably shorted to ground.

If the lights remain bright or dim slightly when cranking, the trouble may be in the starter, solenoid or wiring. If the starter spins, check the solenoid and wiring to the ignition switch. To isolate the trouble, short the large battery solenoid terminal to the small solenoid ignition lead (not to ground). If the starter still fails to crank properly, refer the problem to a dealer or automotive electrical specialist.

Starter Turns, But Does Not Engage With Engine

Usually caused by defective pinion or solenoid shifting fork. The teeth on the pinion, flywheel ring gear, or both may be worn too far to engage properly.

Starter Engages, But Will Not Disengage When Ignition Switch Is Released

Usually caused by sticking solenoid, but occasionally the pinion may jam on the flywheel. The pinion can be temporarily freed by rocking the car in fourth gear.

Loud Grinding Noises When Starter Runs

The teeth on the pinion and/or flywheel are not meshing properly or the overrunning clutch mechanism is broken. Remove the starter and examine gear teeth and pinion drive assembly.

CHARGING SYSTEM TROUBLESHOOTING

Charging system troubles may be in the generator (alternator), voltage regulator, or drive belt. The following symptoms are typical.

Dashboard Indicator Shows Continuous Discharge

This usually means that battery charging is not taking place. Check drive belt tension. Check battery condition with hydrometer and electrical connections in the charging system. Finally, check the alternator and/or voltage regulator.

Dashboard Indicator Shows Intermittent Discharge

Check drive belt tension and electrical connection. Trouble may be traced to worn alternator brushes or bad slip rings.

Battery Requires Frequent Addition of Water or Lamps Require Frequent Replacement

Alternator may be overcharging the battery or the voltage regulator is faulty.

Excessive Noise from the Alternator

Check for loose mountings and/or worn bearings.

ENGINE TROUBLESHOOTING

These procedures assume the starter cranks the engine over normally. If not, refer to the *Starter* section.

Engine Won't Start

Could be caused by the ignition system or fuel system. First, determine if high voltage to spark plugs occurs. To do this, disconnect one of the spark plug wires. Hold the exposed wire terminal about ¼ to ½ in. from ground (any metal in the engine compartment) with an insulated screwdriver. Crank the engine. If sparks don't jump to ground or the sparks are very weak, the trouble may be in the ignition system. If sparks occur properly, the trouble may be in the fuel system.

Engine Misses Steadily

Remove one spark plug wire at a time and ground the wire. If engine miss increases, that cylinder is working properly. Reconnect the wire and check the other. When a wire is disconnected and engine miss remains the same, that cylinder is not firing. Check spark as described above. If no spark occurs for one cylinder only, check distributor cap, wire, and spark plug. If spark occurs properly, check compression and intake manifold vacuum.

Engine Misses Erratically at All Speeds

Intermittent trouble can be difficult to find. It could be in the ignition system, intake system, or fuel system. Follow troubleshooting procedures for these systems to isolate the trouble.

Engine Misses at Idle Only

Trouble could be in ignition or carburetor idle adjustment. Check idle mixture adjustment and check for restrictions in the idle circuit. Check for inlet manifold and vacuum leaks.

Engine Misses at High Speed Only

Trouble is in the fuel system or ignition system. Check accelerator pump operation, fuel pump delivery, fuel line, etc. Check spark plugs and wires.

Low Performance at All Speeds, Poor Acceleration

Trouble usually exists in ignition, fuel system, or exhaust system.

Excessive Fuel Consumption

Could be caused by a number of seemingly unrelated factors. Check for clutch slippage, brake drag, defective wheel bearings, poor front end alignment, faulty ignition, leaky gas tank or lines, and carburetor condition.

Low Oil Pressure Indicated by Oil Pressure Gauge

If the oil pressure gauge shows low oil pressure with the engine running, stop the engine immediately. Coast to a stop with the clutch disengaged. The trouble may be caused by low oil level, blockage in the an oil line, defective oil pump, overheated engine, or defective oil pressure gauge. Check the oil level and drive belt tension. Remove and clean the oil pressure relief valve. Do not re-start the engine until you know why the low indication was given and are sure the problem has been corrected.

Engine Overheats

Usually caused by trouble in the cooling system. Check the level of coolant in the radiator, condition of the drive belt, and water hoses for leaks and loose connections. Check the operation of the electric cooling fan. Can also be caused by late ignition or valve timing.

Engine Stalls As It Warms Up

The choke valve may be stuck closed, the manifold heat control valve may be stuck, the engine idling speed may be set too low, or the emission control (PCV) valve may be faulty.

Engine Stalls After Idling or Slow-Speed Driving

Can be caused by defective fuel pump, overheated engine, high carburetor float level, incorrect idle adjustment, or defective emission control valve.

Engine Stalls After High-Speed Driving

Vapor lock within the fuel lines caused by an overheated engine is usually the cause of this trouble. Inspect and service the cooling system. If the trouble persists, changing to a different fuel or shielding the fuel line from engine heat may prove helpful.

Engine Backfires

Several causes can be suspected; ignition timing, overheating, excessive carbon, wrong heat range spark plugs, hot or sticking valves, cracked distributor cap, a hole in the exhaust system, excessively rich fuel/air mixture.

Smoky Exhaust

Blue smoke indicates excessive oil consumption usually caused by worn rings or valve guides. Black smoke indicates an excessively rich fuel mixture.

Excessive Oil Consumption

Can be caused by external leaks through broken seals or gaskets, or by burning oil in the combustion chamber. Check the oil pan and the front and rear of the engine for oil leaks. If the oil is not leaking externally, valve stem-to-guide clearances may be excessive, piston rings may be worn, cylinder walls may be scored, PCV may be plugged.

Engine Is Noisy

1. *Regular Clicking Sound*—Valves and/or tappets out of adjustment.

2. *Ping or Chatter on Load or Acceleration*—Spark knock due to low octane fuel, carbon buildup, overly advanced ignition timing, and causes mentioned under engine backfire.

3. *Light Knock or Pound With Engine Not Under Load*—Indicates worn connecting rod bearings, worn camshaft bearings, misaligned crankpin, and/or lack of engine oil.

4. *Light Metallic Double Knock, Usually Heard During Idle*—Worn or loose piston pin or bushing and/or lack of oil.

5. *Chattering or Rattling During Acceleration*—Worn rings, cylinder walls, low ring tension, and/or broken rings.

6. *Hollow, Bell-like Muffled Sound When Engine Is Cold*—Piston slap due to worn pistons, cylinder walls, collapsed piston skirts, excessive clearances, misaligned connecting rods, and/or lack of oil.

7. *Dull, Heavy Metallic Knock Under Load or Acceleration, Especially When Cold*—Regular noise: worn main bearings; irregular noise: worn thrust bearings.

IGNITION SYSTEM TROUBLESHOOTING

The following procedures assume the battery is in good enough condition to crank the engine at a normal rate.

No Spark to One Plug

The only causes are defective distributor cap or spark plug wire. Examine the distributor cap for moisture, dirt, carbon tracking caused by flashover, and cracks. Check spark plug wire for breaks or loose connectors.

No Spark to Any Plug

This could indicate trouble in the primary or secondary ignition circuits. First, remove the coil wire from the center post of the distributor. Hold the wire end about ¼ in. from ground with an insulated screwdriver. Crank the engine. If sparks are produced, the trouble is in the rotor or distributor cap. Remove the cap and check for burns, moisture, dirt, carbon tracking, cracks, etc. Check rotor for excessive burning, pitting, and cracks, and check its continuity with a test light.

If the coil does not produce any spark, check the secondary wire for a break. If the wire is good, turn the engine over so the breaker points are open. Examine them for excessive gap, burning, pitting, or loose connections. With the points open, check voltage from the coil to ground with a voltmeter or test lamp. If voltage is present, the coil is probably defective. Have it checked or substitute a coil known to be good.

If voltage is not present, check wire connections to coil and distributor. Disconnect the wire leading from the coil to the distributor and measure from the coil terminal to ground. If voltage is present, the distributor is shorted. Examine breaker points and connecting wires carefully. If voltage is still not present, measure the other coil terminal. Voltage on the other terminal indicates a defective coil. No voltage indicates a broken wire between the coil and battery.

Weak Spark

If the spark is so small it cannot jump from the wire to ground, check the battery. Other causes are bad breaker points, condenser, incorrect point gap, dirty or loose connection in the primary circuit, or dirty or burned rotor or distributor. Check for worn cam lobes in the distributor.

Missing

This is usually caused by fouled or damaged plugs, plugs of the wrong heat range, or incorrect plug gap.

FUEL SYSTEM TROUBLESHOOTING

Fuel system troubles must be isolated to the carburetor, fuel pump, or fuel lines. The following procedures assume the ignition system has been checked and is in proper working order.

Engine Will Not Start

First, determine that fuel is being delivered to the carburetor. If fuel is delivered to the carburetor, check the carburetor and choke system for dirt and/or defects.

Engine Runs at Fast Idle

Misadjustment of fast idle screw or defective carburetor, vacuum leak, intake manifold leak, carburetor gasket leak.

EXHAUST EMISSION CONTROL TROUBLESHOOTING

Failure of the emission control system to maintain exhaust output within acceptable limits is usually due to a defective carburetor, general engine condition, or defective exhaust control valves.

CLUTCH TROUBLESHOOTING

Several clutch troubles may be experienced. Usually the trouble is quite obvious and will fall into one of the following categories:

1. Slipping, chattering, or grabbing when engaging.

2. Spinning or dragging when disengaged.

3. Clutch noises, clutch pedal pulsations, and rapid clutch disc facing wear.

Clutch Slips While Engaged

Improper adjustment of clutch linkage, weak or broken pressure spring, worn friction disc facings, and grease or oil on clutch disc.

Clutch Chatters or Grabs When Engaging

Usually caused by misadjustment of clutch linkage, dirt or grease on the friction disc facings, or broken, worn clutch parts, warped or burned flywheel.

Clutch Spins or Drags When Disengaged

The clutch friction disc normally spins briefly after disengagement and takes a moment to come to rest. This sound should not be confused with drag. Drag is caused by the friction disc not being fully released from the flywheel or pressure plate as the clutch pedal is depressed. The trouble can be caused by clutch linkage misadjustment, defective or worn clutch parts, or a warped flywheel.

Clutch Noises

Clutch noises are usually most noticeable when he engine is idling. First, note whether the noise is heard when the clutch is engaged or disengaged. Clutch noises when engaged could be due to a loose friction disc hub, loose friction disc springs, and misalignment or looseness of engine or transmission mountings. When disengaged, noises can be due to a worn release bearings, defective pilot bearing, or misaligned release lever.

Clutch Pedal Pulsates

Usually noticed when slight pressure is applied to the clutch pedal with the engine running. As pedal pressure is increased, the pulsation ceases. Possible causes include misalignment of engine and transmission, bent crankshaft flange, distortion or shifting of the clutch housing, release lever misalignment, warped friction disc, damaged pressure plate, or warped flywheel.

Rapid Friction Disc Facing Wear

This trouble is caused by any condition that permits slippage between facings and the flywheel or pressure plate. Probable causes are "riding" the clutch, slow releasing of the clutch after disengagement, weak or broken pressure spings, pedal linkage misadjustment, warped clutch disc or pressure plate, faulty master or slave cylinders, blocked cap vent or flex hose.

TRANSMISSION TROUBLESHOOTING

Hard Shifting Into Gear

Common causes are the clutch not releasing, misadjustment of linkage, linkage needing lubrication, detent ball stuck, or gears tight on shaft splines.

Transmission Slips Out of First or Reverse Gear

Causes are gearshift linkage out of adjustment, gear loose on main shaft, gear teeth worn, excessive play, insufficient shift lever spring tension, or worn bearings.

Transmission Slips Out of Second, Third, Fourth, or Fifth Gear

Gearshift linkage is out of adjustment, misalignment between engine and transmission, excessive main shaft end play, worn gear teeth, insufficient shift lever spring tension, worn bearings, or defective synchronizer. Gear may be loose on main shaft.

No Power Through Transmission

May be caused by clutch slipping, stripped gear teeth, damaged shifter fork linkage, broken gear or shaft, and stripped drive key.

Transmission Noisy in Neutral

Transmission misaligned, bearings worn or dry, worn gears, worn or bent countershaft, and excessive countershaft end play.

Transmission Noisy in Gear

Defective clutch disc, worn bearings, loose gears, worn gear teeth, and faults listed above.

Gears Clash During Shifting

Caused by the clutch not releasing, defective synchronizer, or gears sticking on main shaft.

Oil Leaks

Most common causes are foaming due to wrong lubricant, lubricant level too high, broken gaskets, damaged oil seals, loose drain plug, and cracked transmission case.

DIFFERENTIAL TROUBLESHOOTING

Usually, it is noise that draws attention to trouble in the differential. It is not always easy to diagnose the trouble by determining the source of noise and the operating conditions that produce the noise. Defective conditions in the universal joints, wheel bearings, muffler, or tires may be wrongly diagnosed as trouble in the differential or axles.

Some clue as to the cause of trouble may be gained by noting whether the noise is a hum, growl, or knock; whether it is produced when the car is accelerating under load or coasting; and whether it is heard when the car is going straight or making a turn.

1. *Noise during acceleration*—May be caused by shortage of lubricant, incorrect tooth contact between drive gear and drive pinion, damaged or misadjusted bearings in axles or side bearings, or damaged gears.

2. *Noise during coasting*—May be caused by incorrect backlash between drive gear and drive pinion gear or incorrect adjustment of drive pinion bearing.

3. *Noise during turn*—This noise is usually caused by loose or worn axle shaft bearing, pinion gear too tight on shafts, side gear jammed in differential case, or worn side gear thrust washer and pinion thrust washer.

4. *Broken differential parts*—Breaking of differential parts can be caused by insufficient lubricant, improper use of clutch, excessive loading, misadjusted bearings and gears, excessive backlash, damage to case, or loose bolts.

A humming noise in the differential is often caused by improper drive pinion or ring gear adjustment which prevents normal tooth contact between gears. If ignored, rapid tooth wear will take place and the noise will become more like a growl. Repair as soon as the humming is heard so that new gears will not be required. Tire noise will vary considerably, depending on the type of road surface. Differential noises will be the same regardless of road surface. If noises are heard, listen carefully to the noise over different road surfaces to help isolate the problem.

BRAKE SYSTEM TROUBLESHOOTING

Brake Pedal Goes to Floor

Worn linings or pads, air in the hydraulic system, leaky brake lines, leaky wheel cylinders, or leaky or worn master cylinder may be the cause. Check for leaks and worn brake linings or pads. Bleed and adjust the brakes. Rebuild wheel cylinders and/or master cylinder.

Spongy Pedal

Usually caused by air in the brake system. Bleed and adjust brakes.

Brakes Pull

Check brake adjustment and wear on linings and disc pads. Check for contaminated linings, leaky wheel cylinders, loose calipers, lines, or hoses. Check front end alignment and suspension damage such as broken front or rear springs and shock absorbers. Tires also affect braking; check tire pressures and tire condition.

Brakes Squeal or Chatter

Check brake and pad lining thickness and brake drum and rotor condition. Ensure that shoes are not loose. Clean away all dirt on shoes, drums, rotors, and pads.

Brakes Drag

Check brake adjustment, including handbrake. Check for broken or weak shoe return springs, swollen rubber parts due to improper brake fluid or contamination. Check for defective master cylinder. Also check the brake pedal-to-master cylinder clearance.

Hard Pedal

Check brake linings for contamination. Check for brake line restrictions and frozen wheel cylinders and calipers.

High Speed Fade

Check for distorted or out-of-round drums and rotors and contaminated linings or pads.

Pulsating Pedal

Check for distorted or out-of-round brake drums or rotors. Check for excessive disc runout.

COOLING SYSTEM TROUBLESHOOTING

Engine Overheats

May be caused by insufficient coolant, loose or defective drive belt, defective thermostat, defective water pump, clogged water lines, incorrect ignition timing, and/or defective or loose hoses, defective thermoswitch or fan motor. Inspect radiator and all parts for leaks.

Engine Does Not Warm Up

Usually caused by defective thermostat or extremely cold weather.

Loss of Coolant

Radiator leaks, loose or defective hoses, defective water pump, leaks in cylinder head gasket, cracked cylinder head or engine block, or defective radiator cap may be the cause.

Noisy Cooling System

Usually caused by defective water pump bearings, loose or bent fan blades, or defective drive belt.

STEERING AND SUSPENSION TROUBLESHOOTING

Trouble in the suspension or steering is evident when any of the following occur:

1. Hard steering
2. Car pulls to one side
3. Car wanders or front wheels wobble
4. Excessive play in steering
5. Abnormal tire wear

Unusual steering, pulling, or wandering is usually caused by bent or misaligned suspension parts. If the trouble seems to be excessive play, check wheel bearing adjustment first. Next, check steering free-play and kingpins and balljoints. Finally, check tie rod ends by shaking each wheel.

Tire Wear Analysis

Abnormal tire wear should always be analyzed to determine the cause. The most common are incorrect tire pressure, improper driving, overloading, and incorrect wheel alignment. **Figure 2** identifies wear patterns and their most probable causes.

Underinflation — Worn more on sides than in center.

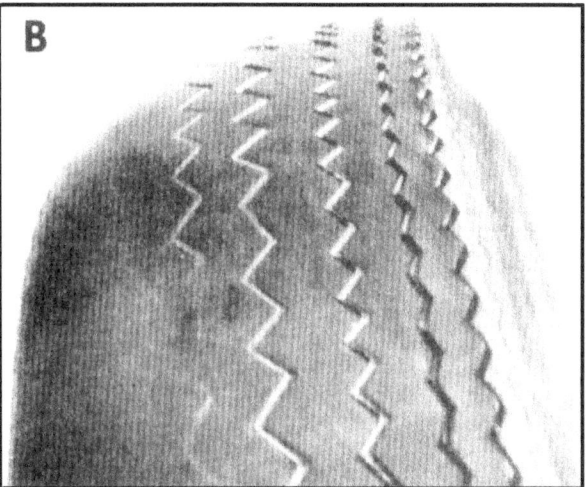

Wheel Alignment — Worn more on one side than the other. Edges of tread feathered.

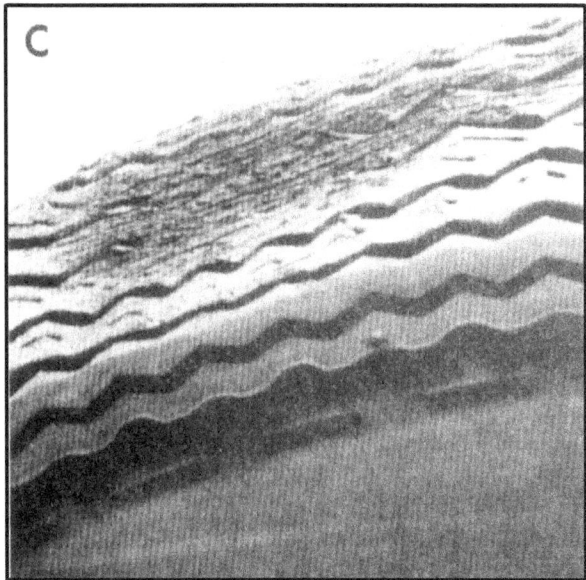

Road Abrasion — Rough wear on entire tire or in patches.

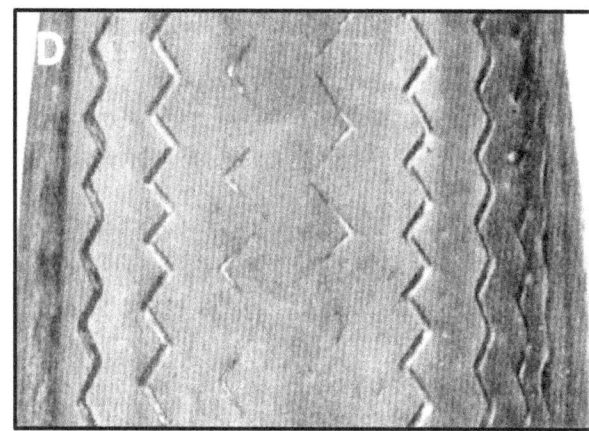

Overinflation — Worn more in center than on sides.

Wheel Balance — Scalloped edges indicate wheel wobble or tramp due to wheel unbalance.

Combination — Most tires exhibit a combination of the above. This tire was overinflated (center worn) and the toe-in was incorrect (feathering). The driver cornered hard at high speed (feathering, rounded shoulders) and braked rapidly (worn spots). The scaly roughness indicates a rough road surface.

Wheel Balancing

All 4 wheels and tires must be in balance along 2 axes. To be in static balance (**Figure 3**), weight must be evenly distributed around the axis of rotation. (A) shows a statically unbalanced wheel. (B) shows the result—wheel tramp or hopping. (C) shows proper static balance.

To be in dynamic balance (**Figure 4**), the centerline of the weight must coincide with the centerline of the wheel. (A) shows a dynamically unbalanced wheel. (B) shows the result—wheel wobble or shimmy. (C) shows proper dynamic balance.

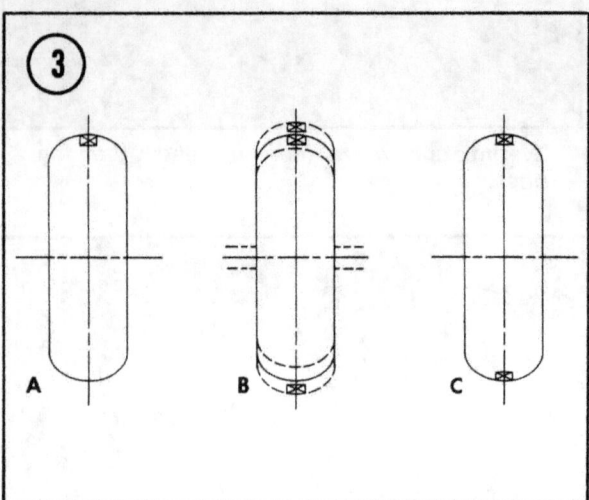

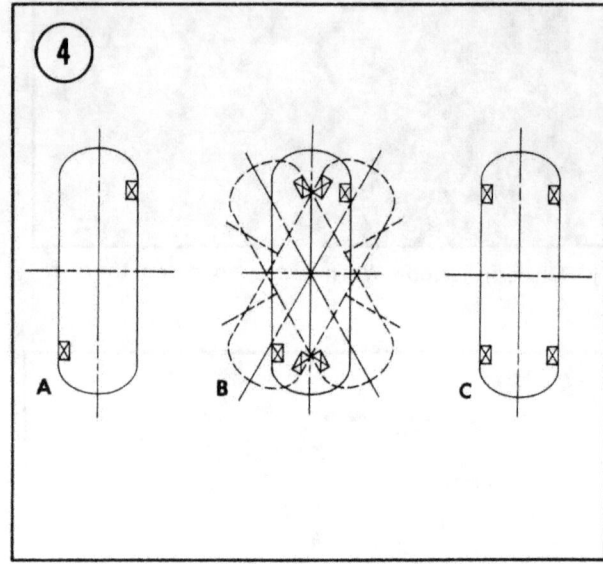

CHAPTER 1—ENGINE

1 Description
2 Engine and gearbox removal
3 Removing the cylinder head
4 The camshaft
5 Valves and valve clearances
6 Decarbonizing
7 The valve timing gear and distributor drive
8 The sump and oil pump
9 The oil filter and relief valves
10 The clutch and flywheel
11 The jointing flange
12 Pistons and connecting rods
13 The crankshaft
14 Reassembling a stripped engine
15 Fault diagnosis

1 Description

All the models covered by this manual are fitted with six-cylinder engines. The valves are mounted vertically in the cylinder head and operated from a single overhead camshaft. The valves are arranged in two in-line banks, one bank being inlet valves and the other bank exhaust valves, with the inlet valves nearest to the carburetter side of the engine. Normally overhead camshafts require shimming to adjust the valve clearance and it is difficult for the owner to have a sufficiently large selection of shims to adjust all the valves correctly. The Mercedes engine overcomes this difficulty by using short rocker arms pivoting on special ballpins. The cam acts on a curved surface of the rocker and the end of the rocker operates the valve. The adjustment is set by altering the height of the pivot ballpin. A schematic layout of the valve gear is shown in **FIG 1**. It should also be noted that seals are fitted to the valve guides to prevent oil running down the valve stems and into the combustion chambers.

The camshaft is fitted with a timing sprocket at its front end and is driven by a duplex chain from another sprocket on the front of the crankshaft. The chain is tensioned by a hydraulic tensioner which presses a small sprocket firmly against the timing chain and the chain is prevented from thrashing by slipper pads. The timing chain also drives an idler sprocket and shaft from which the drive for the distributor, oil pump and mechanical fuel pump (on carburetter type engines) is taken. The parts of the 230SL timing gear are shown in **FIG 2**.

The crankshaft is of conventional design, running in four main bearings. Sealing at the rear end is by a special fabric seal but at the front end a conventional type oil seal is fitted. A damper is also fitted to the front end of the crankshaft to absorb torsional vibrations.

Cooling is by water circulation, round the engine and through a conventional radiator. On all engines the internal oil circulation also helps to cool the bearings and pistons. Normally this heat is then radiated or taken by the air flow from the sump, though some sports cars are fitted with an oil cooler, similar to the water radiator, where the passage of air cools the oil. Mercedes models are fitted with an oil/water cooler on the lefthand side of the engine. Instead of using air to cool the oil the heat is taken from the oil by the coolant. On start-up the coolant rapidly heats up as it is prevented from passing through the radiator by the thermostat, and heat is then transferred from the coolant to the oil, ensuring that the whole engine

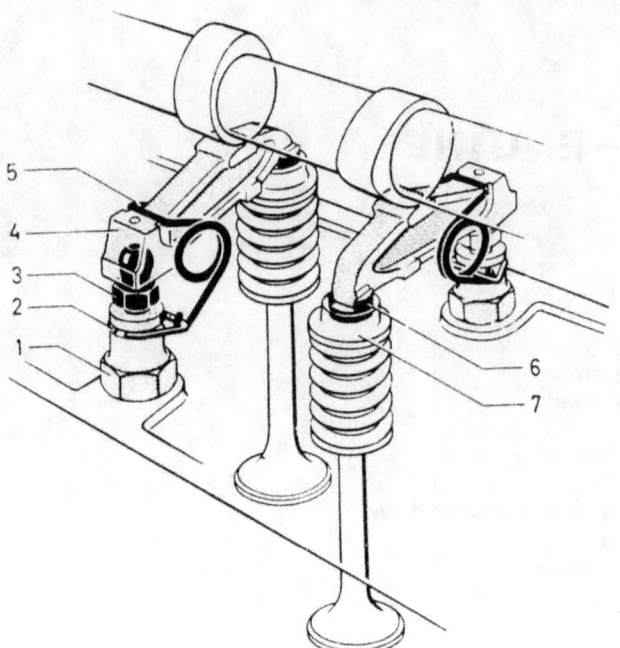

FIG 1 Schematic view of the valve gear

is rapidly warmed up. Once the engine is hot the oil is at a higher temperature than the coolant, so heat is transferred from the oil to the coolant and then lost in the radiator. As a further assistance in cooling at hot spots the exhaust valves are sodium-filled. At running temperature the sodium melts and heat is transferred from the hot head of the valve to the stem and from there to the crankcase. **Do not saw open old exhaust valves and remember that worn valves must be safely disposed of and not dumped.** Some engines are fitted with molybdenum-filled piston rings to lower the friction and prevent overheating.

Aluminium alloy is used extensively in the engine for its light weight and good heat-transferring properties. **The alloy is softer than steel or iron and overtightening bolts or studs can easily lead to the threads being stripped from the casting.** Heli-Coil inserts can be used to rectify stripped threads.

2 Engine and gearbox removal

The engine and gearbox are supported on three rubber mountings. The front mountings attach to bearers mounted onto the crankcase approximately at the centre of gravity and their lower ends are fixed to the lateral support member of the front suspension. The third and rear mounting is attached to the rear cover of the transmission and acts on a support member bolted to the chassis.

On earlier models a one-piece cast sump is fitted. This sump can be removed from the engine with the engine fitted to the car so that access to the big-ends and oil pump is possible without removing the engine from the car.

After November 1965 the design of the sump was changed to a two-piece construction. An alloy casting is bolted directly to the crankcase and a sheet-metal lower part is bolted to the casting. Only the sheet-metal portion can be removed when the engine is fitted to the car so the engine must be removed from the car for attention to the big-ends or oil pump.

The transmission can be removed from the car leaving the engine in place. For the manual gearbox see **Chapter 6, Section 2** and for the automatic transmission see **Chapter 7, Section 5**. The attachments of the transmission will be only lightly dealt with in this chapter and the owner is advised to check the appropriate chapter for fuller details. Similarly different types of propeller shaft are fitted to different age models and the owner should refer to **Chapter 8, Section 2** for further details.

On all models decarbonizing and top overhaul can be carried out with the engine fitted. For attention to the crankshaft or main bearings the engine should be removed from the car.

If the owner is not a skilled automobile engineer it is suggested that while they will find much useful information in this manual they should read it very carefully before starting work. In addition, it is of critical importance the owner pays particular attention to the safe supporting of the car if a ramp or pit is not available.

1 Disconnect the battery. Remove the bonnet (see **Chapter 13, Section 5**). Drain the cooling system (see **Chapter 4, Section 2**) retaining the coolant if the inhibitor or antifreeze is still fresh. Remove the radiator (see **Chapter 4, Section 3**).

2 Remove the carburetter air cleaner and its bracket. Disconnect the carburetter controls and disconnect the fuel supply pipe to the mechanical fuel pump. On the 230SL disconnect the controls and fuel pipe to the fuel injection pump. Further details are given in **Chapter 2**.

3 Disconnect the electrical leads to the starter motor and generator (or alternator on later models). Disconnect the low-tension lead to the distributor and the high-tension lead between the distributor and ignition coil. Disconnect any other electrical leads connecting the engine to the car. It is most advisable to label each lead as it is disconnected otherwise by the time the engine is refitted there will be uncertainty as to the correct connections. Very carefully unscrew the water temperature gauge bolt from the cylinder head and lay the capillary tube out of the way.

4 From underneath the car; slacken the bolts that secure the exhaust pipe bracket to the transmission and disconnect the speedometer drive. On cars fitted with a manual transmission remove the two nuts (bolts on earlier models) that secure the clutch slave cylinder. Lift off the slave cylinder and wire it safely out of the way so that the flexible hose is neither kinked nor strained. There is no need to disconnect the flexible hose. On cars fitted with automatic transmission disconnect the leads to the unit and disconnect the oil pipes that lead to and from the oil cooler. The oil pipes must be plugged to prevent the ingress of dirt. Disconnect the propeller shaft from the drive flange of the transmission.

5 Disconnect the exhaust pipes from the exhaust manifolds. Slide the exhaust pipes outwards to free them from the manifold. Disconnect the gear selector linkage. On the manual gearbox with steering column mounted selector remove the lockwashers and free the pushrods from the ball ends on the levers of the bearing assembly at the base of the steering column. When a floor mounted gearlever is fitted, the shift rod and both the pushrods must be disconnected from the top cover

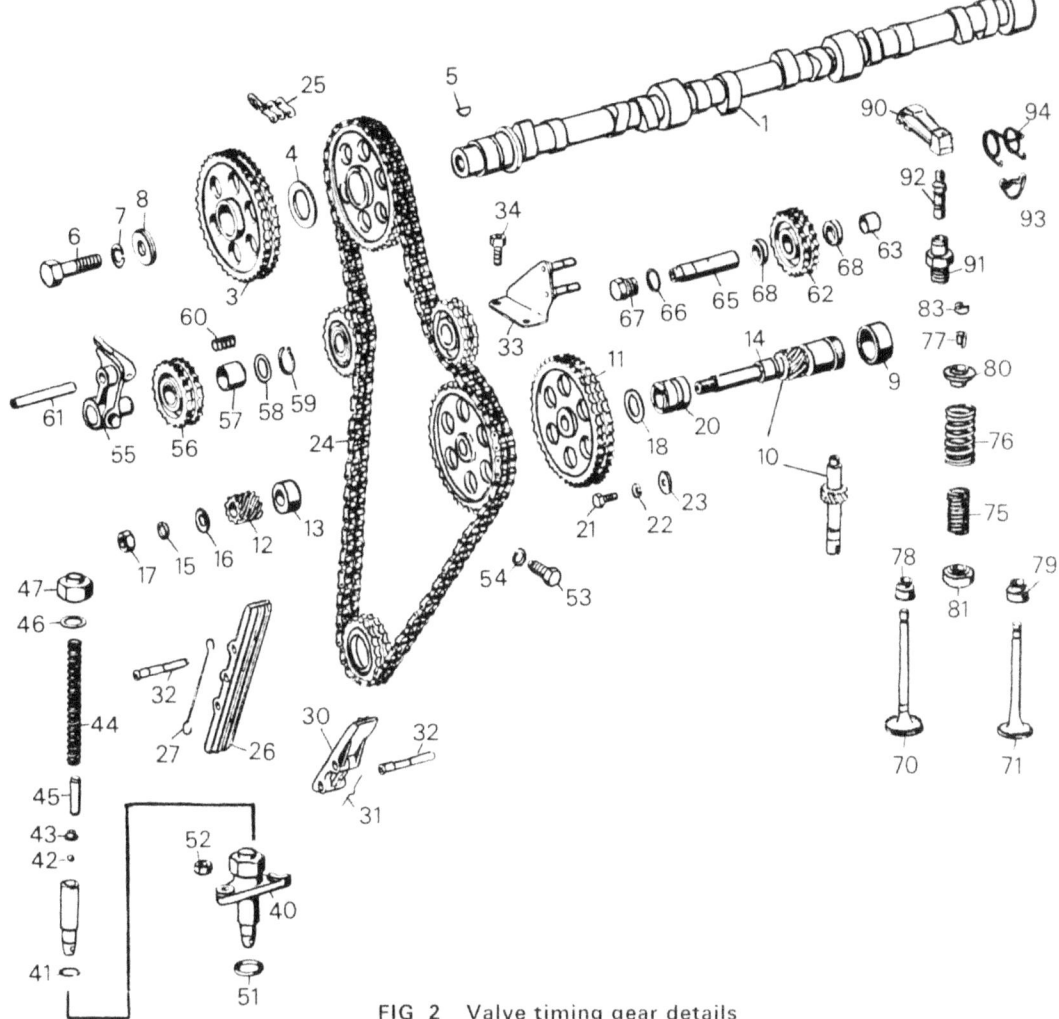

FIG 2 Valve timing gear details

of the gearbox. Further details are given in **Chapter 6**, while the details of the linkage fitted to the automatic transmission are given in **Chapter 7, Section 4**. **In all cases it is vital that the rods are laid out of the way so that they do not catch and become damaged as the engine is removed or refitted.**

6 Take the weight of the engine with a jack and block of wood under the gearbox. Raise the jack until the load is just taken off the rear mounting. Remove the support member, after marking its position and remove the mounting from the rear cover of the transmission by undoing the securing nuts.

7 Support the engine with slings as shown in **FIG 3**. Take off the locknuts and unscrew the bolts that secure the front two rubber mountings to the bearers on the engine. Check that all connections between engine/transmission and the car are disconnected. Also make sure that the reverse light switch is disconnected as on some models the leads connect the transmission to the car. Lay thick pads of rag or sacking over the wings and other vulnerable parts to protect them from damage. Raise the engine very slightly on the slings and draw it forwards, taking care that the sump does not foul on the steering linkage. Swivel the transmission downwards, so that the unit makes an angle of 45 deg. with the horizontal, and lift the unit out of the car.

The engine is refitted in the reverse order of removal but note the following points.

1 Keep the engine supported on the slings until all the mounting bolts have been refitted. It will be much easier to move the engine while it is partially suspended than to try moving the dead weight to align the bolt holes.

2 Make sure that the rear mounting is correctly fitted to the aligning marks and the correct clearance is set (see **Chapter 6, Section 2**).

3 The front mountings should be set with a small clearance. Screw the mounting bolts fully in and then back them out by one full turn before locking them with the locknuts.

4 Use new gaskets when reconnecting the exhaust pipes to the exhaust manifolds.

5 When the engine is in place and all connections are made, fill up and check all oil and coolant levels. Check for leaks both before and after starting the engine.

3 Removing the cylinder head

The cylinder head details are shown in **FIG 4** and the timing gear details are shown in **FIG 2**.

FIG 3 Position of the slings for removing/replacing the engine

1 Drain the cooling system, noting that **the engine must be cold before the cylinder head is removed.** Disconnect the water hoses to the cylinder head. Take out the two banjo bolts that secure the water pump vent pipe in place. Remove the air cleaner. Take out the temperature gauge bulb from the cylinder head, **being extremely careful not to bend, twist or kink the capillary tube.** Remove the distributor complete with its bearing from the engine (see **Chapter 3, Section 4**).

2 Free the vent pipe 60 from the valve cover 50. Take out the bolts 56 with their washers 57 and lift off the valve cover 50 complete with its gasket 55. Only if the gasket 55 is in very good condition should it be left in place but if it is at all damaged or permanently compressed it should be removed and discarded, and a new one fitted on reassembly.

3 It is advisable to free the manifolds from the cylinder head. They are secured in place with bolts and clamping pieces. If the manifolds are left in place then disconnect the exhaust pipes from the exhaust manifolds and disconnect the carburetter controls. On fuel injection models disconnect the injection pipes, labelling them for reconnection. Disconnect the high-tension leads from the sparking plugs, making sure that they are labelled for order.

4 It is most advisable, though not absolutely essential, to remove the valve rocker arms, as this will ensure that all the valves are fully closed and that they will not hit the pistons or become damaged when the head is removed. The method is removal is shown in **FIG 5**. Turn the engine, using a suitable spanner on the bolt that secures the crankshaft pulley, until the base circle of the appropriate cam is against the rocker arm. Lift the spring clamp 2 out of its slot and move the spring outwards to free it from the rocker 3. Insert the special tool No. 111.589.01.61 as shown and use it to press the valve firmly down into the head. Lift the rocker off its ballpin and store all the rockers in the correct order for reassembly.

5 Refer to **FIG 2**. Unscrew the bolts that secure the hydraulic tensioner and withdraw the unit from the engine. Take out the bolt 6 that secures the camshaft sprocket 3 to the camshaft 1 removing the washers 7 and 8. Use a suitable two-legged puller to draw the

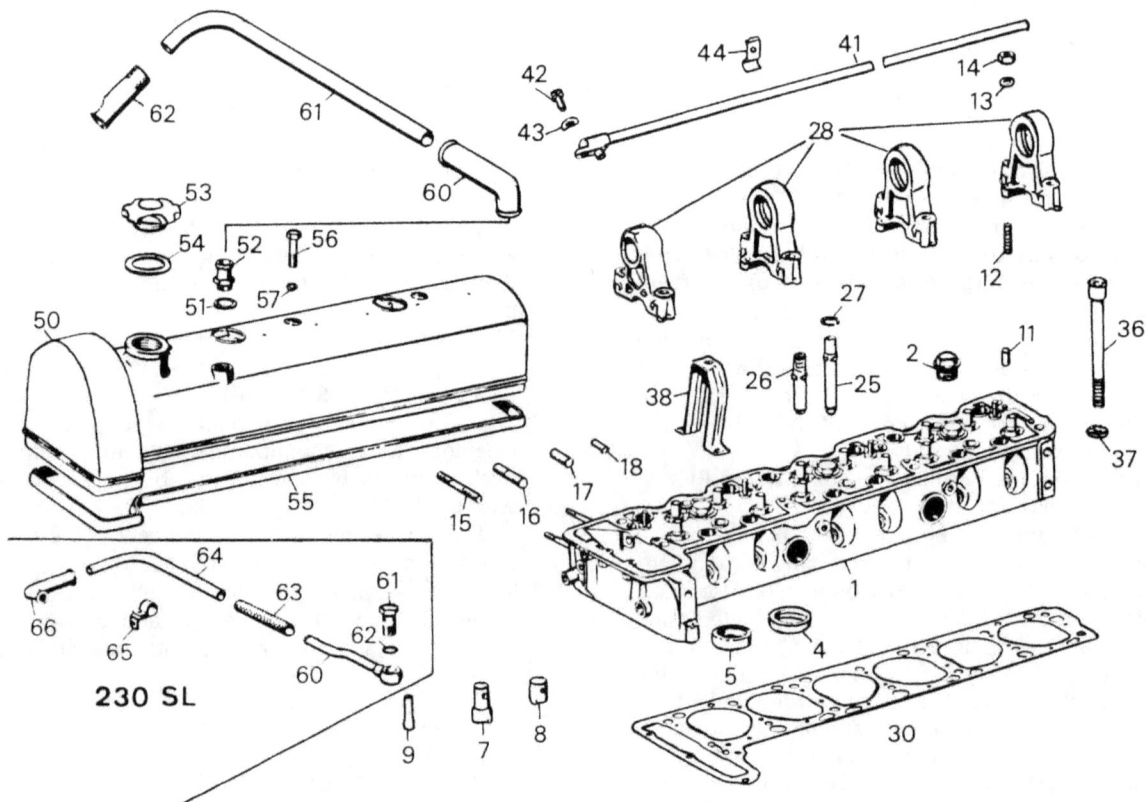

FIG 4 Cylinder head details, the inset shows the vent pipes for the 230SL model

sprocket 3 from the camshaft 1, collecting the compensating washer 4 that is behind the sprocket. Normally the key 5 is straight but offset keys are used to adjust the valve timing. **If the key is offset then the direction of the offset must be carefully noted and the key refitted correctly otherwise the valve timing will be incorrect.**

6 Slacken the cylinder head bolts, part of a turn at a time, in the reverse order to that shown in **FIG 6**. When all the bolts are slack unscrew them fully and remove them. Undo the other four bolts 'a' shown in the figure. The cylinder head can now be lifted off the engine.

The cylinder head is refitted in the reverse order of removal but note the following points:

1 The mating faces of the block, cylinder head and manifolds must all be perfectly clean and free from specks of dirt. Old jointing compound should be softened with carbon tetrachloride and then carefully scraped off. Check the surfaces for truth with a long steel straightedge or by using engineer's blue on a surface table or plate glass. High spots or slight distortion can be cleaned off using a scraper or by careful filing with a smooth file. Excessive distortion requires the cylinder head to be machined true by a specialist firm.

2 Always fit a new cylinder head gasket and manifold gasket. Jointing compound is not required on the cylinder head gasket but a thin film of grease will help to seal it.

3 Check that the threads on the block are clear and not partially filled with dirt and make sure that the bolts turn freely in the threads. Lay the gasket and cylinder head back into place. Liberally coat the threads of the bolts and under their heads with graphited-oil, and screw the bolts in finger tight. Tighten the bolts, progressively in the order shown in **FIG 6**, in four separate stages. First to 4 kgm (29 lb ft) then to 6 kgm (44 lb ft) and finally with the engine cold to 8 kgm (58 lb ft). Reassemble the remainder of the engine and start it up. Run it for five minutes longer after the coolant has reached a temperature of 80°C and tighten the bolts to the last stage of 9 kgm (65 lb ft) with the engine hot.

4 Refit the timing chain in the reverse order of removal. Turn the engine until it is exactly at TDC on No. 1 cylinder (front). Fit the timing chain over the sprocket and refit the timing parts and compensating washer so that the mark on the compensating washer exactly aligns with the mark on the front camshaft bearing pedestal, as shown in **FIG 7**. Secure the sprocket in place with the bolt and washers. If there is any doubt as to the accuracy of the timing or the position of the offset key, then the car should be taken to an agent who will have the necessary gauges to check the valve timing.

5 **The chain tensioner must be fitted empty of oil and then filled and bled when it is fitted.** Bolt the tensioner back into place and use a screwdriver to press it fully tight, as shown in **FIG 8**. Fill the pocket in the cylinder head with warm engine oil and slowly release the tensioner pressure, keeping the pocket filled with warm oil. **Repeat the operation until no air bubbles appear when the tensioner is**

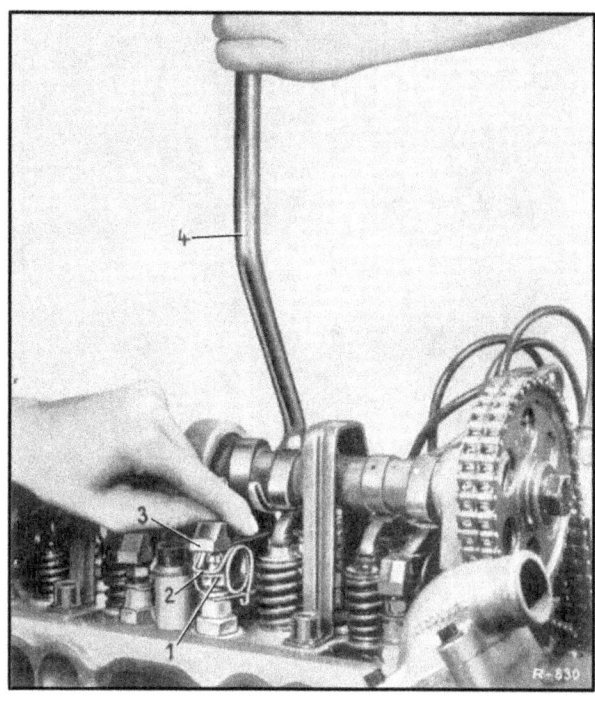

FIG 5   Removing a rocker arm

1 Ballpin head
2 Clamping spring
3 Rocker arm
4 Removal and installation tool
112 589 08 61 00

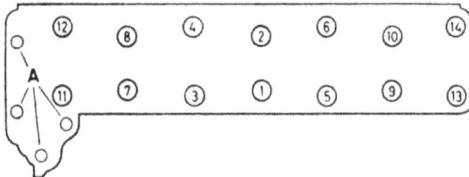

FIG 6   Sequence for tightening the cylinder head bolts, the four bolts 'A' should not be overtightened

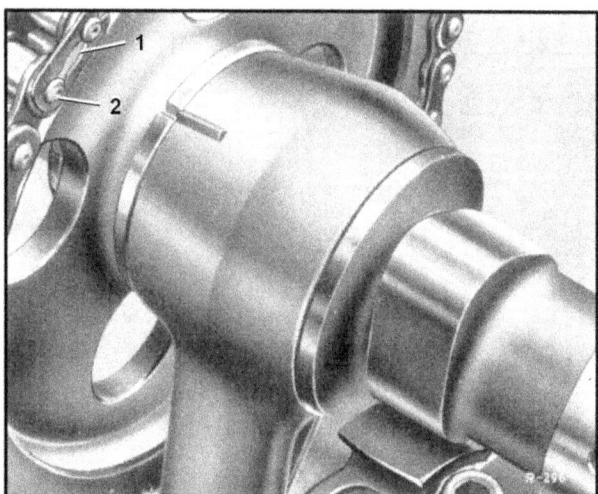

FIG 7   Valve timing marks aligned with engine at TDC. Note the method of fastening the jointing link

1 Spring lock   2 Connector link (chain lock)

FIG 8 Bleeding the chain tensioner

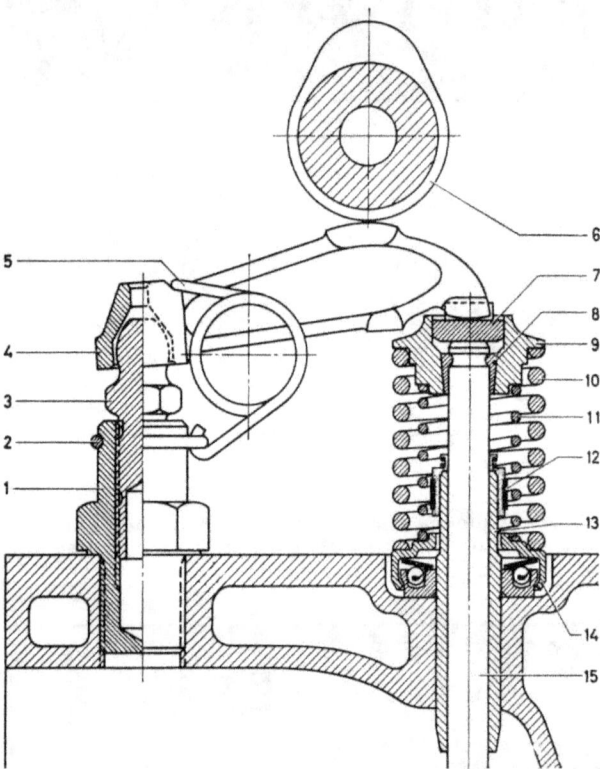

FIG 9 Sectioned view of the valve train

1 Ballpin base
2 Annular spring
3 Ballpin head
4 Rocker arm
5 Clamping spring
6 Camshaft
7 Pressure piece
8 Valve cone half
9 Valve spring retainer and sealing ring retainer
10 Outer valve spring
11 Inner valve spring
12 Valve sealing ring
13 Valve guide
14 Valve rotator
15 Valve

pressed in. It will be extremely difficult to move the tensioner even with heavy pressure when it is correctly filled and bled. If the bleeding is not carried out then the tensioner will always be loose and the chain will rattle.

6 The remainder of the engine is reassembled in the reverse order of dismantling. When the car has been driven for 300 to 1000 kilometres (150 to 600 miles)

the torque of the cylinder head bolts should be rechecked with the engine hot. Slacken back each bolt in turn and then tighten it to the correct torque load of 9 kgm before checking the next bolt in the order shown in **FIG 6**. The bolts should not be checked by attempting to tighten them with a torque spanner without slackening them first, as they may already be too tight, or deposits are holding the bolt giving a false reading.

4 The camshaft

The camshaft and its attachments are shown in **FIG 4**.

Removal:

The pedestal bearings 28 should not be removed from the cylinder head unless it is essential to have them off, as in machining the head or fitting new bearings. For this reason the camshaft should only be removed after the cylinder head has been removed from the engine. Take off the camshaft sprocket with the compensating washer and the camshaft can then be withdrawn rearwards from the four pedestal bearings.

Refit the camshaft in the reverse order of removal. When refitting the cylinder head check that the camshaft rotates freely after the cylinder head bolts have been tightened to each stage. If the camshaft sticks then the pedestal bearings should be tapped into alignment using a plastic-faced hammer on their bases.

End float:

With the camshaft fitted use feeler gauges to measure the end float of the camshaft between the rear face of the compensating washer and the front face of the front pedestal bearing. The correct end float is .05 to .128 mm (.002 to .005 inch). If the end float is outside these limits then the front face of the camshaft will have to be reground to bring the end float within the correct limits.

The radial play of the camshafts should be checked at the same time using a DTI (Dial Test Indicator). If the radial play exceeds the limits of .025 to .057 mm (.001 to .002 inch) the camshaft and bearings should be measured and the camshaft reground with new bearings fitted.

Bearings:

The design of the camshaft and bearings was changed and the lubrication to the camshaft was also changed. The earlier version of the camshaft had oil grooves machined around 2, 3 and 4 journals. Later camshafts do not have these oil grooves and instead a crescent groove is machined into the bearings, joining the upper and lower oil cases in the bearings. The earlier type of parts are no longer available as spares, so if they are worn then the later type will have to be fitted and the lubrication modified.

If the bearings have been removed make sure that the mating surfaces are scrupulously clean and that the bearings fit flush to the cylinder head. Align the bearings by tapping their bases with a plastic-faced hammer so that the camshaft turns freely.

5 Valves and valve clearances

A sectioned view of a typical valve and its operating gear is shown in **FIG 9**. Not all the models are fitted with the valve rotator 14 shown in the figure but they will then have a sealing ring under the lower cap. The valve rotator shown in the figure requires no maintenance and it should be renewed if it does not rotate smoothly.

Valve seals:

The seals 12 around the valve guide have been altered slightly from time to time, though their basic design is still similar and it is mainly the dimensions which vary. If the seals fail they can be renewed without removing the cylinder head from the engine.

Turn the engine over until it is on the firing stroke with both valves closed. Remove the two rocker arms, as shown in **FIG 5** and operation 4 of **Section 3**. Take out the appropriate sparking plug and fit a suitable adaptor in its place using the adaptor and a compressor to pressurize the combustion chamber to approximately 5 kg/sq cm (70 lb/sq in). This pressure will keep the valves closed. Use a spring compressor to press down the valve springs and remove the pressure piece and valve collets. If the magnetic lifting device shown in **FIG 10** is not available use a pair of tweezers instead. Once the collets have been removed the pressure on the springs can be released and they can be lifted off together with the retainer 9. Prise off the old seals from the valve guides and press on new seals, using a tool made up to the dimensions shown in **FIG 11**. When the seals have been fitted refit the remainder of the parts in the reverse order of removal.

Valve guides and seats:

These are steel inserts held in by an interference fit in both cases and they are also renewable with oversizes available. It is not advisable for the owner to attempt to renew either a worn seat or guide as, apart from the heating of the head that is required, accurate machining may also be necessary, as well as the cutting of the seat to the correct thickness while still being concentric with the valve guide. The work is best left to an agent who will have all the equipment necessary.

Checking the valves:

Use a valve spring compressor to take the pressure off the valve springs and remove the collets as described earlier. The valves can then be removed from the cylinder head.

The valves may be cleaned by mounting them in the chuck of an electric drill or lathe and using emerycloth to remove the deposits. Take great care not to damage or score the seat or the machined portion of the valve stem.

Check the seats for pitting and wear. Minor wear can be removed using grinding paste but deeper damage should be removed using garage equipment which grinds the valve seat. If, after machining, the thickness of the un-machined portion of the head above the seat is less than 1 mm (.04 inch) for the inlet valves and 1.5 mm (.06 inch) for exhaust valves, then the valves should be scrapped and new ones fitted.

Use a steel straightedge to check the valve stems and renew any valves that have bent stems.

Grinding-in valves:

The valves must be ground in to the mating seats in the head and they must be fitted into their original positions.

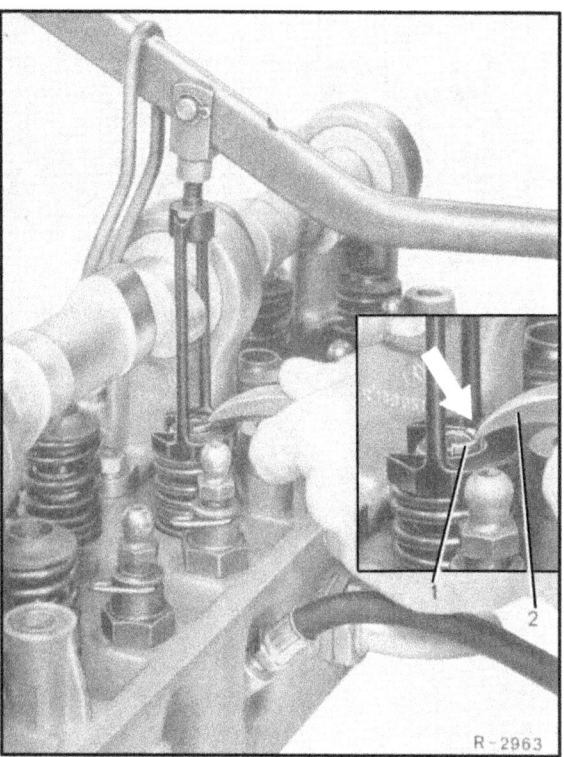

FIG 10 Removing the valve springs with the cylinder head fitted to the engine

1 Valve collet   2 Magnetic lifter 108 589 09 63 00

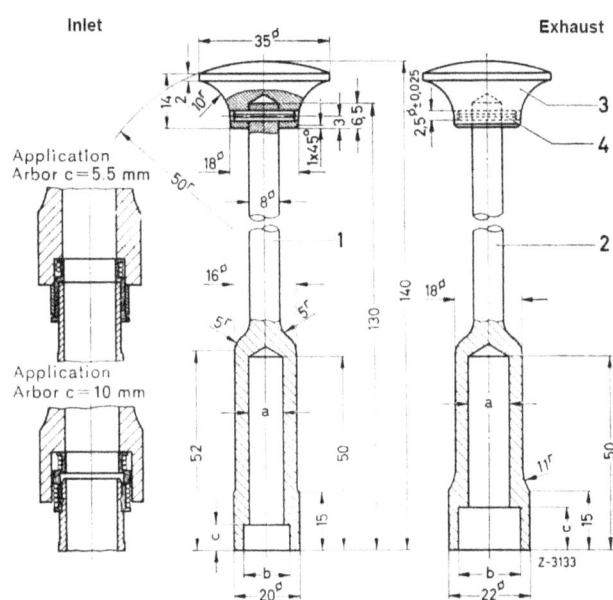

FIG 11 Tools to be made up for fitting new valve seals

Dimension	Inlet	1st version	2nd version
a		9.2	9.2
b		13.3	14.7
c		5.5	10

	Exhaust	1st version	2nd version	3rd version
a		10.2	11.2	11.2
b		14.2	14.2	16.5
c		5.5	5.5	10

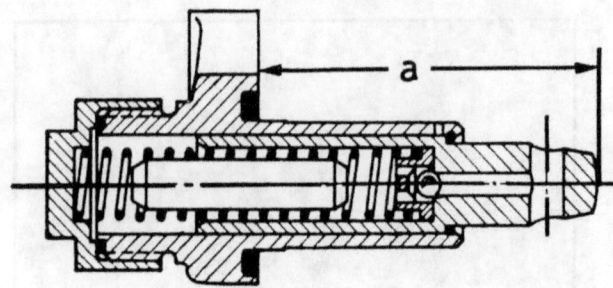

FIG 12 Sectioned view of the timing chain tensioner

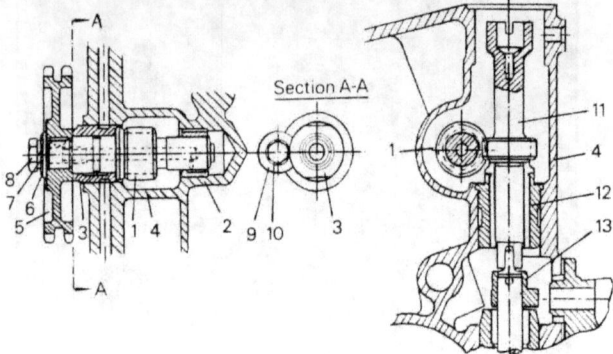

FIG 13 Sectioned views of the distributor and oil pump drive gear

1 Idling gear shaft
2 Rear bearing bushing
3 Front bearing bushing
4 Cylinder block
5 Idling gear
6 Washer
7 Lock washer
8 Hexagon bolt
9 Retaining washer
10 Lock washer
11 Helical gear
12 Bearing with bushing
13 Oil pump drive shaft with cam for fuel pump

Fit the valve to be ground back into the head with a light spring between the valve head and cylinder head. Smear a little grinding paste evenly around the seat. Medium-grade paste should be used at first unless the seats are in such good condition that fine-grade paste can be used immediately.

Use a suction cup tool to press the valve down against the pressure of the light spring and grind with a semi-rotary motion. Frequently allow the valve to rise under the action of the spring and turn it to a new position. Carry on grinding-in until all the pits are just about removed. Clean away the old paste and repeat the process with fine-grade paste until the seats are smooth with a matt-grey finish. **Clean away all traces of grinding paste from the valve, cylinder head and port.**

Valve springs:

The dimensions of the valve springs are given in **Technical Data**. The extension of the springs should be measured with a steel rule while applying the pressure with a modified spring balance. The springs should be rejected and new ones fitted if they are outside the extensions given by more than 10 per cent.

A rough and ready test is to put a new spring end on to the old one and compress the pair between the jaws of a vice. If the old spring is 10 per cent shorter than the new one then the spring is defective and must be renewed.

The valve springs are fitted with their closed coils downwards.

Valve clearances:

The correct position for measuring the clearance is between the back of the cam 6 and the face on the rocker arm 4, as shown in **FIG 9**. The correct clearances are .08 mm (.003 inch) for the inlet valves and .18 mm (.007 inch) for the exhaust valves.

Turn the engine until the base circle of the cam is against the rocker arm and slide the correct thickness feeler gauge into position. Use a torque spanner and adaptor to turn the ballpin 3 upwards until drag is just felt on the feeler gauge as it is moved. If the feeler gauge cannot be inserted then the ballpin must be screwed downwards until the gap is sufficiently large to insert the feeler gauge. Spanners may be used to adjust the clearance but it is most advisable to check the torque required to turn the ballpin 3. If the torque is less than 1.5 mkg (11 lb ft) then the ballpin 3 and its base 1 must be renewed. An adaptor No. 111.589.00.01 is specially made for turning the ballpin in conjunction with a torque spanner.

It may be impossible to reach the correct clearance even with the ballpin screwed fully into its base 1. The clearance can be increased in such cases by fitting a thinner pressure piece 7. The standard pressure piece is 4.5 mm (.177 inch) thick but they are also available in thicknesses of 3.5 and 2.5 mm (.138 and .098 inch).

6 Decarbonizing

Remove the cylinder head from the engine as described in **Section 3**. It is advisable to remove the camshaft, by drawing it out rearwards from its bearings. Do not remove the camshaft bearings, and leave the valves fitted at this stage. Plug oil and waterways with pieces of rag that are sufficiently large not to be pushed through into the castings.

Smear a little grease around the tops of the bores and then turn the engine until one pair of pistons is nearly at TDC. Spring an old piston ring into the bore above the piston so as to protect the carbon around the periphery of the piston. This carbon acts as an additional oil seal and heat shield for the top ring so it should be left in place. Scrape away the carbon from the piston crowns with a sharpened stick of solder or hard wood. **Do not use any abrasives or hard metal tools.** Blow away loose dust and turn the engine until the next pair of pistons are nearly at TDC. When all the pistons have been cleaned use a clean cloth to wipe away the grease and dirt sticking to it from the tops of the bores. A fuel-moistened cloth can be used for the final cleaning but a few drops of oil should be poured around each piston and the engine turned over several times to evenly distribute the oil after such cleaning.

Cast iron cylinder heads may be cleaned with a rotary wire brush mounted in an electric drill. **Light alloy cylinder heads must under no circumstances be cleaned by this method.** Use a sharpened stick of solder or hard wood to scrape away most of the deposits and give the final cleaning using old emerycloth dipped into paraffin (kerosene). After the combustion chambers have been cleaned the valves should be removed for attention as given in the previous section. Clean the ports using a similar method to the combustion chambers but taking great care not to damage the seats in the head or the valve guides.

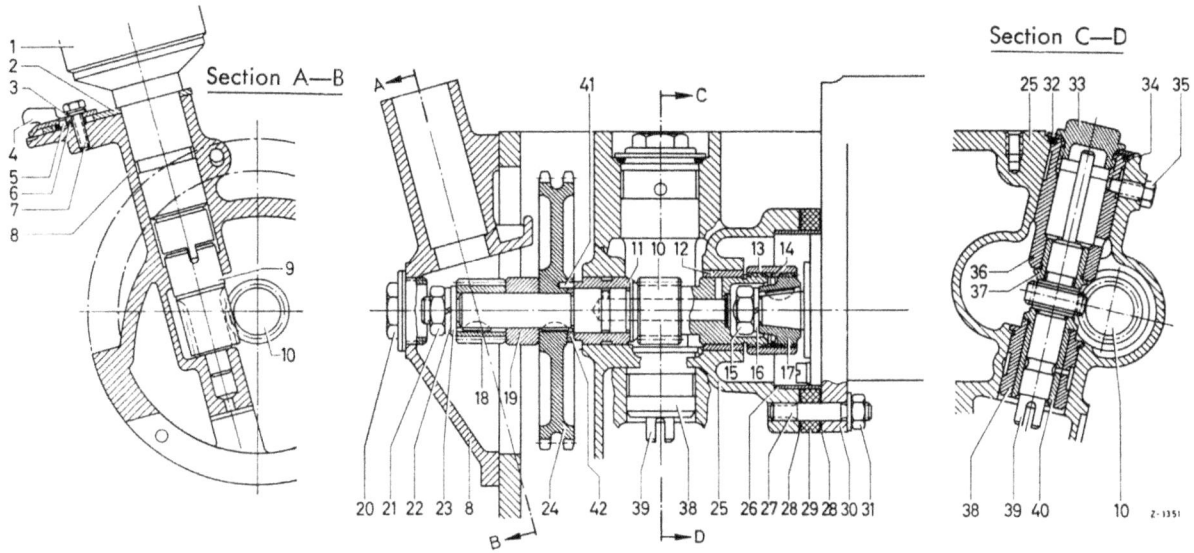

FIG 14 Sectioned view of the distributor and oil pump drive on 230SL models fitted with fuel injection

1 Distributor	11 Bearing bushing front	21 Hexagon nut	32 Cover plate
2 Timing lever	12 Bearing bushing rear	22 Lock washer	33 Screw plug
3 Spring washer	13 Coupling sleeve	23 Shim	34 Rubber ring
4 Hand lever	14 Snap ring	24 Idling gear	35 Hexagon screw
5 Cylindrical pin	15 Hexagon nut	25 Crankcase	36 Pressure piece
6 Eccentric disk	16 Lock washer	26 Bearing sleeve	37 Bearing bushing
7 Hexagon screw	17 Follower	27 Stud bolt	38 Bearing body
8 Distributor bearing	18 Drive sleeve	28 Sealing flange	39 Helical gear
9 Helical gear	19 Spacing collar	29 Insulating flange	40 Bearing bushing
10 Idling gear shaft	20 Screw plug and seal	30 Injection pump	41 Grooved pin
		31 Hexagon nut and washer	42 Stop ring

Reassemble the cylinder head in the reverse order of dismantling. Before fitting the parts clean them thoroughly to remove all traces of abrasive or dirt and lubricate all bearing surfaces with graphited-oil.

7 The valve timing gear and distributor drive

The parts are shown in **FIG 2**. The sprocket 11 and shafts 10 supply the drive to the distributor and oil pump.

Timing chain:

This should be renewed if it is worn. At the same time check the teeth on the sprockets as if they are also worn they will quickly damage a new chain. The normal chain is an endless one and this type should be fitted when the engine is being reassembled after a major stripdown. However, a chain with a jointing link can be fitted in place of the endless type when the engine is still fitted to the car.

1 Remove the valve cover as described in **Section 3** and take off the chain tensioner. Take out the sparking plugs so that the engine rotates easily. As a safety precaution remove all the rocker arms. If the camshaft rotates independently from the crankshaft then there is a danger that an open valve will hit the crown of a piston, causing expensive damage.

2 Turn the engine until No. 1 piston is at TDC and the timing marks on the compensating washer and front camshaft bearing align. Cover the aperture in the engine with cloth to prevent metal dust from falling into the engine and carefully file off two rivets so that a link can be removed.

3 Attach the new chain to the trailing end of the old chain using a jointing link 25 with its open end away from the direction of rotation. Turn the engine in its normal direction of rotation, keeping tension on both ends of the chains. Keep rotating the engine until both ends of the new chain are on the camshaft sprocket. Take off the jointing link 25 and use it to secure the ends of the new chain around the sprocket. The jointing link must be fitted as shown in **FIG 7** with its spring clip to the rear and the open end facing away from the direction of rotation.

4 Check that the timing marks still align with the engine at TDC on No. 1 cylinder. If the timing is incorrect ease the chain a tooth at a time over the camshaft sprocket until the valve timing is correct. Refit the remainder of the parts in the reverse order of removal. The chain tensioner must be fitted empty and filled and bled after it has been fitted.

Sprockets:

Badly worn sprockets will be obvious from the hooked appearance of the teeth and these should be renewed to prevent damaging a new timing chain. When new sprockets have been fitted their alignment should be checked with a depth gauge and special tool No. 187.589.02.23. The special tool provides a datum for using the depth gauge. If the special tool is not available try using a thin steel straightedge and measuring the difference between the sprocket and straightedge with feeler gauges. The misalignment of the sprockets should not exceed 1 mm (.04 inch). If the misalignment is excessive fit a new compensating washer behind the camshaft sprocket to bring it within limits. Compensating washers are available in thicknesses from 2.5 mm (.01 inch) to 3.5 mm (.14 inch) increasing in steps of .25 mm (.001 inch).

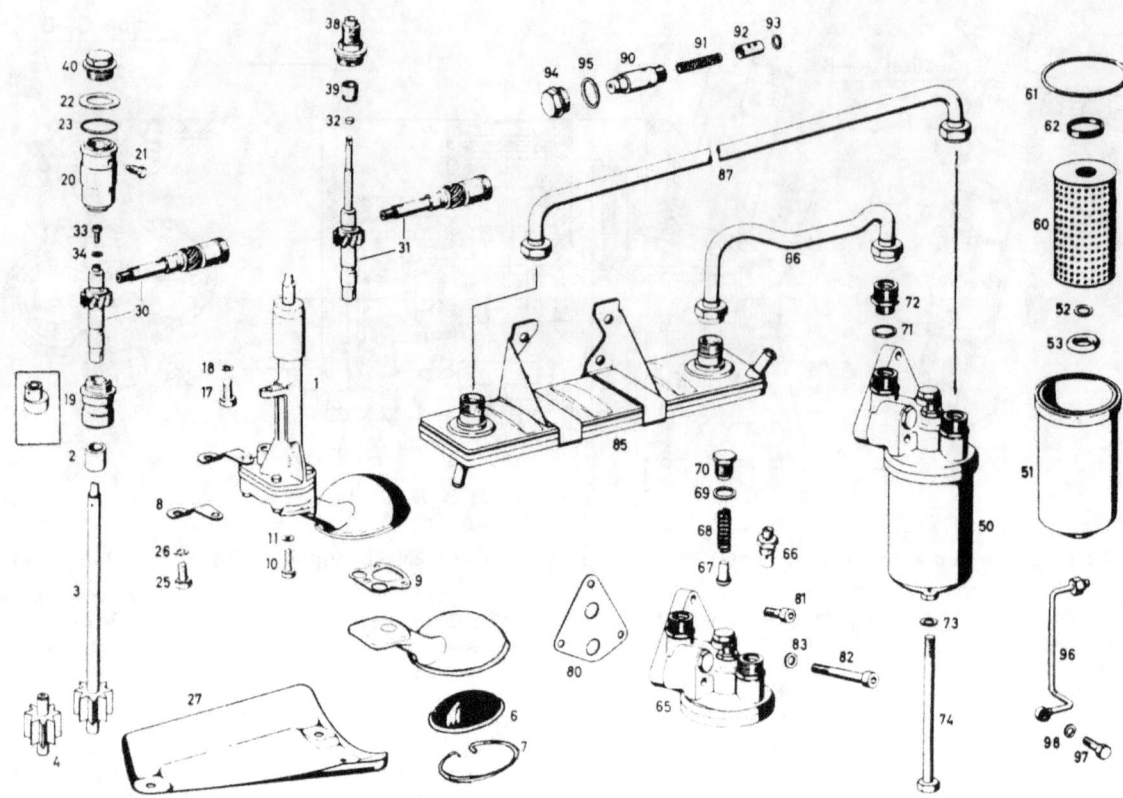

FIG 15 Details of the lubrication system parts

Chain tensioner:

A sectioned view of the tensioner is shown in **FIG 12**. The dimension 'a' should be 51 mm (2 inch) when the unit is free from the car.

Special equipment is required for checking the tensioner and it should be renewed if it is defective. A rough test can be carried out by bleeding the unit when it is immersed in a container of warm oil and then checking that considerable pressure is required to slowly and evenly compress it.

The unit can be dismantled for cleaning or checking of the spring by carefully unscrewing the end cap against the pressure of the spring. The data for the spring is given in **Technical Data**. Reassemble the unit using a new seal under the end cap and refit it to the engine using a new sealing ring. **The unit must be refitted empty and then filled and bled when it is fitted.**

Distributor and oil pump drive:

The sectioned views of the drive are shown in **FIG 13**. The drive for the 230SL model is shown in **FIG 14**.

On later models the drive shafts are nitrided to improve their wearing qualities. The nitrided shafts are of exactly the same dimensions as the earlier shafts and may be fitted in their place, provided that both shafts are renewed. The later shafts are identified by a 1 mm slot turned around them.

The parts can be removed from the engine after taking off the valve cover, chain tensioner, camshaft sprocket distributor and the cover on the front of the engine (see **Section 3**). It is advisable to lay rags into the aperture when the cover is removed to prevent any parts from falling down internally into the engine.

The parts are refitted in the reverse order of removal. When the valve timing marks (on the compensating washer and front camshaft bearing) are aligned at TDC then a mark on the rotor arm will align with a small slot on the top of the distributor case. Before refitting the chain tensioner, but with the camshaft sprocket correctly in place, check if the distributor marks align. If they do not align, slip the timing chain, a link at a time, over the sprocket for the distributor drive until the distributor marks are correctly aligned as well as the valve timing marks.

8 The sump and oil pump

Oil change

Drain the oil from the engine when it is hot after a run. Place a suitable container under the sump and remove the drain plug from it. Leave the oil to drain for as long as possible. Refit the drain plug using a new sealing ring.

Fill the engine to the top mark on the dipstick with fresh oil. Start the engine and let it run for a few minutes and then switch it off again. Check the oil level after five minutes, by which time the level will have settled. Top up as required to bring the level to the top mark on the dipstick. Use clean non-fluffy cloth to wipe the dipstick clean before reinserting it to check the level. Oil changes should be carried out at 5000 kilometre (3000 mile) intervals.

Sump removal:

Only on the earlier models can the sump be removed from the engine with the engine fitted to the car. On later models the sheet-metal part of the sump can be taken off but the casting can only be removed with the engine free from the car.

When the sump is removed from the engine (or the sheet-metal part on later models) check the wire gauze on the inlet to the oil pump. Remove the gauze and wash it in clean fuel if it appears at all dirty or choked. Renew the mesh filter if it is broken or has large holes worn in it.

The procedure for removing the sump on earlier models is as follows:
1. Drain the oil from the engine. While the oil is draining detach the centre tie rod from the relay lever (see **Chapter 10**).
2. Place a jack and block of wood under the transmission casing and use them to raise the rear end of the engine/transmission unit up by about 8 cm (3 inch). Take out the two securing bolts and remove the clutch housing cover.
3. Remove the bolts that secure the sump to the crankcase. Lower the sump and remove it from the car.

Refit the sump in the reverse order of removal. Fill the engine with oil, through the filler on the valve cover, as described for an oil change. Do not overfill the engine as this will lead to high oil consumption as the extra oil is either burnt or leaks out.

Oil pump:

The oil pump can only be removed after the sump has been taken off. The pump is secured to the block by bolts and it is also secured to the second main crankshaft bearing. The details of the pump, as well as the oil filter and oil cooler, are shown in **FIG 15**.

The pump can be dismantled after removing the nuts that secure the parts. If the gears 3 and 4 are worn or damaged they must be renewed as a pair because they are mated together in manufacture. The pump should give long and trouble-free service, as it passes all the oil and is therefore the best lubricated part of the engine. If low oil pressure is caused by a defective oil pump (check all other possible causes first) it is best to fit a new or reconditioned pump.

9 The oil filter and relief valves

The parts are shown in **FIG 15**.

Element renewal:

This should be carried out at every other oil change. In very dirty conditions or if the car is used for short journeys only, especially in cold weather, when the engine never has a chance to heat up fully and evaporate the contaminants, the period between oil changes should be reduced.

If the engine has had major work carried out on it a special finer pore element Part No. 000.184.42.25 should be fitted for the running-in period.
1. Turn the steering to the full right lock so as to have more access room to the filter. Unscrew the central bolt 74 and carefully pull off the case 50 from the filter head. Keep the case upright as it is full of dirty oil.
2. Pour out the old oil from the case and withdraw the old element 60. Throw away the old element as it cannot be cleaned. Wash out the case with clean fuel and use a small sharp tool to prise out the old seal 61, discarding this. Check the seal 62 which remains on the filter head and renew the seal if it is damaged. Similarly check the seal 52 which fits into the casing below the element.

FIG 16 Hold down clamps fitted to the clutch
1 Hold-down clamps   2 Driven plate

FIG 17 The moving parts of the engine

1	Crankshaft	15	Hex bolts	46	Gudgeon pin
12	Flywheel	30	Bearing	49	Bearing shells
13	Ring gear	31	Cover	56	Circlip
14	Dowel pin	32	Fabric seal		

3. Fit a new seal 61 into its groove in the case 51, **making sure that the seal is not twisted and that it is fully in the groove.** Check that the washer 53 and seal 52 are in place in the case, make sure that the seal 73 is still in good condition, and slide a new element 60 into place. Secure the case complete with element back into the filter head.
4. Fill the engine with oil to the top mark on the dipstick. Start the engine and check for oil leaks around the filter immediately. The commonest causes of oil leaks are that either the seal 61 is not correctly in position or the case 51 is slightly tilted and not fully in place.

Relief valves:

The relief valve mounted on the front of the block under the cap nut 94 controls the oil pressure, while another relief valve mounted in the filter head ensures that oil will still reach the engine even if the filter element is blocked. Dirt under the seatings or a weak spring will cause a drop in oil pressure. Remove the valve and clean the parts in fuel. Check the spring against the dimensions given in **Technical Data**.

10 The clutch and flywheel

The full details of the clutch and its servicing are given in **Chapter 5**. This section only deals with removing and replacing the clutch. Before the clutch or flywheel is accessible the gearbox must be removed (see **Chapter 6, Section 2**).

With the gearbox removed proceed as follows:

1 Fit hold-down clamps No. 136.589.23.61 under each of the clutch release levers, as shown in **FIG 16**. These clamps should be left in place until the clutch is refitted, unless the clutch is to be dismantled.
2 Slacken the clutch securing bolts progressively and in a diagonal sequence. When all the bolts are free lift off the clutch assembly and collect the clutch driven plate.
3 The moving parts of the engine are shown in **FIG 17**. Remove the flywheel securing bolts 15 and draw or tap the flywheel 12 rearwards to clear it from the dowel 14. Take care not to allow the flywheel to drop as it comes free.
4 When the flywheel has been removed the bearing for the spigot of the input shaft from the gearbox should be examined. The bearing 30 is a press fit into the end of the crankshaft 1 and is then protected by a cover 31 pressed over it. Renew the bearing if it is damaged or runs roughly. Always renew the bearing on major overhauls.

The parts are refitted in the reverse order of removal. The driven plate is fitted with the side marked 'Kupplungseite' towards the gearbox. The driven plate must be centralized using special mandrel No. 136.589.00.61, or an old input shaft from the gearbox, while tightening the bolts for the clutch. The mandrel is passed through the hub of the driven plate and into the bearing 30, and should only be removed when the clutch securing bolts are fully tightened.

The flywheel:

Check the flywheel for scoring or burn marks on its pressure face. Damage can be removed by precision turning or grinding but as most owners are unlikely to have the facilities necessary the work should be entrusted to a specialist firm. It should be noted that the clutch mounting face must be machined down by an equal amount to preserve the correct distance between the clutch and pressure faces.

If the flywheel is so damaged that the minimum thickness cannot be adhered to then a new flywheel must be fitted. The flywheel is balanced with the crankshaft at manufacture so a new flywheel must be balanced statically to a similar amount. For this reason the agent supplying a new flywheel will require the old one so that the two can be balanced together.

Starter ring gear:

If the teeth of the starter ring 13 are badly worn or broken off then a new ring must be fitted.

1 Drill holes along the root of a tooth to weaken the ring and then use a cold chisel to split it at the weakened point. Take great care not to damage or mark the flywheel itself.
2 Thoroughly clean the periphery of the flywheel with a wire brush. Use emerycloth to remove any high spots. Lay the flywheel, clutch face downwards, onto hard wood blocks.
3 Heat the new ring to a temperature of 200°C, preferably in an oil bath or stove. **Do not overheat the ring or the temper of the metal will be destroyed.**
4 Press the hot ring into place on the flywheel so that the chamfered ends of the teeth are upwards (facing forwards when the flywheel is refitted). Tap the ring fully into place with a soft-metal drift and do not move the flywheel until the ring has cooled completely.

11 The jointing flange

The jointing flange is secured to the rear of the engine by four bolts and the flanges are so machined that they automatically centre the flange when refitting it. The flange can be removed from the engine once the flywheel has been taken off.

When refitting the jointing flange mount a DTI as shown in **FIG 18** and slowly rotate the crankshaft to check the runout of the flange. If the runout exceeds .05 mm (.002 inch) try centralizing the flange by tapping it into place with a soft-faced hammer. If excessive runout cannot be cured by this method then the engine should be taken to an agent who will align the flange by using oversize dowels and counterboring the parts in place.

12 Pistons and connecting rods

The parts are shown in **FIG 17**. The pistons and connecting rods can be removed from the cylinder block after the cylinder head and sump have been removed and the big-ends disconnected. The big-ends of the connecting rods will pass through the cylinder bores so the parts are removed by pushing them out through the top of the bores. On later models the engine must be removed from the car in order to take off the sump casting.

Cylinder bores:

These should be inspected whenever the cylinder head is removed. It is best to measure them when the pistons are out but an indication of the wear can be obtained with the pistons in place. Maximum wear will take place across the thrust axis (which is at right angles to the direction of travel of the car) and approximately 2.5 cm (1 inch) from the top of the bore. A good estimate of the wear can be made by judging the thickness of the unworn ridge around the top of the bore. Ideally the bores should be measured at several points, on and at right angles to the thrust axis, using a suitable gauge. The cylinders must be rebored and oversized pistons fitted if the wear exceeds .12 mm (.005 inch).

New piston rings can be fitted if the wear is not sufficient to warrant reboring but oil consumption is rising. Before fitting new rings only the unworn ridge around the top of the bore should be removed with garage equipment. If this ridge is left in place the new ring will hit the ridge causing the ring to fail prematurely.

Big-ends:

Take off the sump as described in **Section 7**. The connecting rods and bearing caps are marked in order and the numbers indicating the order of both the connecting rods and caps face towards the lefthand side of the engine. If these numbers are not present then the order of the parts must be marked with light punch dots as the positions of the parts must not be interchanged.

1. Remove the nuts that hold the bearing caps in place and lightly tap the connecting rod up the bore so that the bearing cap is freed. Slide the bearing shells 49 out of their recesses and store the parts removed in the correct order for replacement.

2. Clean all the parts thoroughly, including the recesses in the connecting rods and caps as well as the crankpins. Use a micrometer gauge to measure the crankpins at several points. If the crankpins are worn oval or tapered or if they have scores on them then the crankshaft must be removed, the crankpins reground and undersize bearings fitted.

3. Examine the bearing shells 49 and renew them if they are worn, scored or pitted. New bearing shells are fitted as received, apart from cleaning, and they require no machining or boring. **Under no circumstances should the connecting rods or bearing caps be filed in an attempt to take up wear in the bearings or crankpins.** It should be noted that bearing shells are available in two wall thicknesses to ensure that the correct clearance is set.

4. Wipe the bearing shells with a chamois leather and fit them back into place. The shells with oil holes drilled in them fit into the connecting rods. The shells are provided with locating tags which seat into mating recesses. Fit the tag end of the shell into place, hold it there with a finger and spring the other end into place. Lubricate the bearings with clean graphited-oil.

5. Pull the connecting rod down the bore until it fits back onto the crankpin and refit the cap complete with shell. Make sure that the caps are fitted to their original connecting rods and also make sure that all the identical numbers are facing towards the lefthand side of the engine.

6. Tighten the securing nuts to a torque load of 6 mkg (43 lb ft). On 230SL models fitted with bolts Part No. 121.038.03.71 (10 mm external diameter) the correct torque load is 3.75 kgm (28 lb ft). Check that the crankshaft rotates freely when the bearings are secured in place. If the engine has been dismantled it is advisable to prefit each connecting rod to the crankshaft and check that it moves freely before finally reassembling the engine.

Pistons:

Disconnect the big-ends and remove the cylinder head. Press the connecting rods right up the bores until the pistons and connecting rods can be withdrawn from the engine.

Use circlip pliers to remove the snap rings 56 from the pistons. Immerse the piston in very hot or boiling water and the gudgeon pin 46 will be moved out by hand pressure only. Refit the connecting rods to the pistons in the reverse order of removal, after heating the pistons and making sure that the circlips are fully in their grooves. The pistons are marked with an arrow and the word 'Vorn' and these marks must be fitted so that they face the front of the engine.

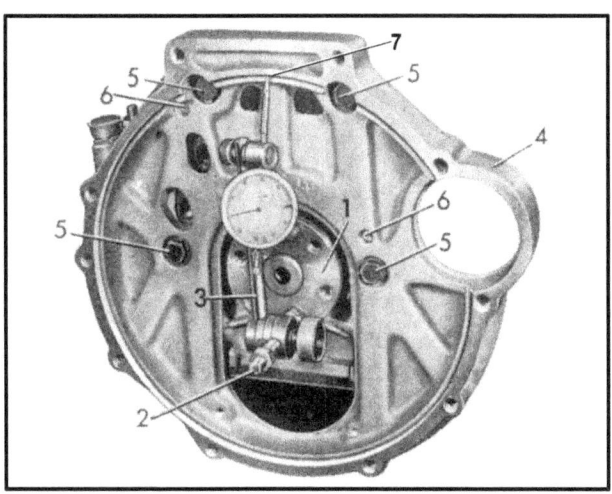

FIG 18 Using a Dial Test Indicator to check the run-out of the jointing flange

1 Crankshaft flange
2 Threaded stud
3 Dial gauge atachment clamped to threaded stud (2)
4 Intermediate flange
5 Fastening bolts
6 Dowel pins
7 Dial gauge check point

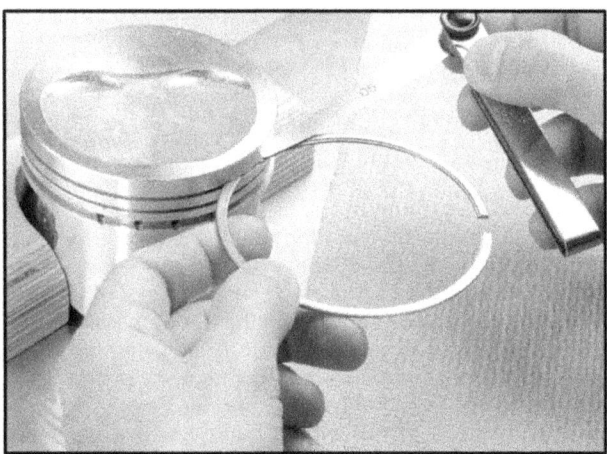

FIG 19 Using a new piston ring to check the groove clearance in the piston

When the pistons are free from the engine their crowns may be cleaned using worn emerycloth dipped in paraffin, provided that all traces of abrasive are washed off with clean fuel before reassembly. The ring grooves should be cleaned out using an old broken piston ring but taking great care to remove only carbon and not metal from the piston. Use a blunt-ended piece of wire to clean out the oil return holes behind the oil control rings.

Fit a new piston ring into the groove in the piston, as shown in **FIG 19**, and use feeler gauges to measure the clearance. If the clearance is excessive a new piston must be fitted otherwise the rings will 'pump' oil into the combustion chamber.

Piston rings:

The best and safest way of removing or replacing piston rings is to use a special expander which grips and opens the ends of the rings so that they can be slid off the pistons. If an expander is not available then use three steel shims, such as discarded feeler gauges. Carefully

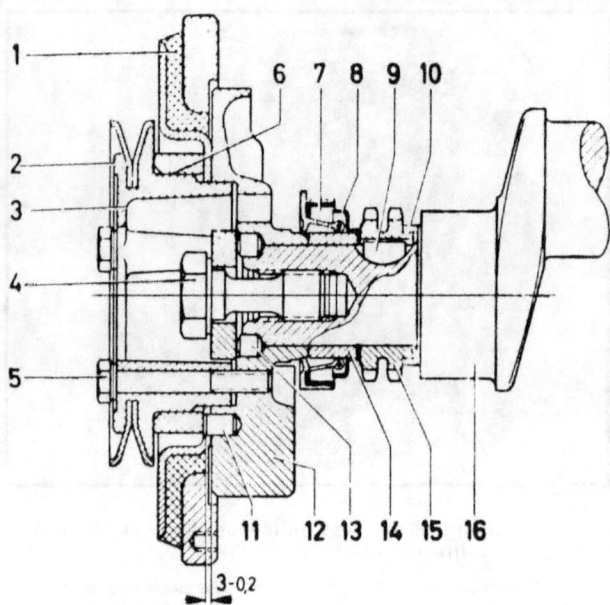

FIG 20 Sectioned view of the crankshaft damper and pulley assembly

1 Vibration damper
2 V-pulley
3 Washer or 3 plate springs
4 Stretch screw
5 Hex bolt
6 Spacer ring
7 Oil seal
8 Oil thrower
9 Woodruff key
10 Compensating ring
11 Dowel pin 8h 8×12 DIN 7
12 Counterweight
13 Dowel pin 8×8 N 37 b
14 Spacer ring
15 Crankshaft sprocket
16 Crankshaft

lift one end of the ring out of its groove and slide a shim under it. Work the shim around the ring pressing the ring onto the land of the piston above it as it comes free. When the complete ring is on the land slide the other other two shims into place under the ring so that they are positioned at equal distances around the piston. Slide the ring up and off the piston, using the shims to protect the piston from damage by the ring. Refit the piston rings in the reverse order of removal. Rings which are stepped or tapered must be fitted with the marking T facing towards the crown of the piston.

Before fitting new rings to the pistons the gap between the ends should be checked. Fit the ring into the top of the bore and use an inverted piston to press it squarely down the bore for about 2.5 cm (1 inch). Measure the gap between the ends with feeler gauges. The gap can be increased by carefully filing the ends of the ring with a smooth file. The gaps and clearances for the piston rings are given in **Technical Data**.

Before refitting the piston and connecting rod to the engine turn the rings until their gaps are spaced equally around the piston and no gap is in line with the gudgeon pin.

Connecting rods:

These are fitted with renewable bushes for the gudgeon pins. If the bushes are worn they can be pressed out and new bushes pressed into place. However, the new bushes require jig reaming to very accurate tolerances and it is advisable to leave the task to an agent. At the same time the connecting rods should be checked for bend or twist using suitable jigs or suitable mandrels, V-blocks and a DTI.

Before refitting the connecting rods clean them thoroughly and blow through the oilways, first with paraffin under pressure and then with compressed air.

Refitting the pistons and connecting rods:

Check that the ring gaps are evenly spaced around the piston. Also check that the piston will be refitted with the arrow pointing forwards and the identification numbers on the connecting rods facing to the left.

Lightly oil the rings and piston. Use a piston ring clamp to compress the rings into the piston grooves. In an emergency a large worm-driven hose clip can be used instead of the proper type of clamp. Lower the connecting rod down the bore and enter the skirt of the piston into the bore, making sure that the parts are fitted facing the correct direction. Gently press the piston down the bore, allowing the clamp to slide off the rings as each one enters the bore. Do not force the piston down and take care that the rings enter the bore as they escape from the clamp. The rings are very brittle and will snap if they catch outside the bore.

When the pistons are refitted, reconnect the big-ends, refit the sump and cylinder head.

13 The crankshaft

The crankshaft cannot be removed from the engine without taking the engine out of the car. However, the front crankshaft seal can be renewed with the crankshaft fitted and the engine in place.

Front oil seal:

A sectioned view of the damper, pulley and oil seal is shown in **FIG 20** and this is the figure that should be referred to. The parts are also shown in **FIG 17**.

A repair scheme can be carried out by an agent if the damper assembly is slightly loose on the crankshaft.

1 Drain the cooling system and remove the radiator (see **Chapter 4**). Remove the fan belt after slackening its tension (see **Chapter 4, Section 4**).
2 Take off the pulley 2 after removing its three securing bolts 5. Use a suitable puller to withdraw the damper 1 from the crankshaft and collect the dowels 13.
3 Carefully, so as not to damage the castings, prise out the old oil seal 7 and withdraw the thrower 8 and spacer ring 14. Use fine emerycloth to remove any sharp edges from the castings and renew the spacer ring 14 if it is damaged or scored.
4 Slide the thrower and spacer back into position. Pack the lips of the new oil seal with high melting point grease and press it back into position so that its flange is firmly against the castings. Take care not to damage the oil seal as it is slid into place along the crankshaft.
5 Refit the damper, aligning the dowel holes and use the stretch bolt and washer to draw the damper back into place. Press the dowels back in and refit the pulley. Refit the fan belt and set the correct tension. Refit the radiator and check for oil and water leaks both before and after starting the engine.

Crankshaft removal:

1 Remove the engine and gearbox from the car. Separate the gearbox from the engine. Take off the hydraulic chain tensioner and remove the camshaft sprocket. Invert the engine onto a suitable stand.

2 Remove the sump, oil pump, clutch and flywheel as well as the damper and pulley assembly. Disconnect all the big-ends and press the connecting rods into the bores so that they are free from the crankpins. Lift the timing chain up off the crankshaft sprocket and use a puller No. 187.589.00.33 to draw the sprocket off the crankshaft.

3 The four main bearing caps are identified for order in the same way as the connecting rod bearing caps. If the marks are not present then make them with light punch marks.

4 Evenly slacken all the eight bolts that secure the bearing caps in place and when they are all loose remove the four bearing caps complete with shell bearings. The second main bearing is fitted with semi-circular thrust washers on either side of it to control the crankshaft end float. Remove the fabric seal 32 **FIG 17** from the rear end of the crankshaft and lift out the crankshaft.

5 The main bearing shells and journals are examined in exactly the same manner as the parts for the big-ends (see previous section). Regrind the crankshaft and fit undersized bearings if the journals are worn or scored. Clean the shells with chamois leather and fit them back into place, making sure that the tags are correctly located and the shells with oil holes are fitted to the crankcase. Lubricate the bearings liberally with clean graphited-oil.

6 Refit the crankshaft with the thrust washers in place but omitting the rear fabric seal. Tighten the securing bolts progressively to a torque load of 8 mkg (58 lb ft) and check that the crankshaft rotates freely. If the crankshaft binds slacken each bearing cap in turn until the stiff one is found. Realign the cap by tapping it lightly with a soft-faced hammer. Lever the crankshaft backwards and forwards with a screwdriver and use either feeler gauges or a DTI to check the end float. If the end float exceeds .040 to .096 mm (.002 to .004 inch) then new or oversized thrust washers must be fitted. It is permissible to lap down the non-bearing sides of the thrust washers in order to increase the end float.

7 Remove the crankshaft again and fit a new fabric seal 32, taking care not to snap the retaining pin. Before fitting the oil seal should be liberally coated with tallow or in an emergency with oil. Press the oil seal into place using a suitable tube to roll down the high spots. Refit the crankshaft as before, tightening the cap bolts progressively. Again check that the crankshaft rotates freely. If the fabric seal is causing it to bind again roll down high spots with a suitable tube.

8 Reassemble the remainder of the engine in the reverse order of dismantling.

14 Reassembling a stripped engine

As the engine is being dismantled the parts should be washed in clean fuel or some similar solvent. Protect bright metal parts with a film of oil to prevent corrosion. Store all the parts carefully so that they are neither damaged or in any danger of being lost. Put small parts into a bag and tie the bag to the main component so that all the parts are readily identifiable.

All the operations have been dealt with in detail in the various sections so that reassembling the engine is mainly a matter of tackling the tasks in the correct order.

Cleanliness is essential. Wash the parts again in clean solvent and either allow them to air dry or wipe them dry with clean non-fluffy cloth. As each part is clean lay it in order onto a bench covered with clean paper. All old gaskets and sealing compound should be removed from the parts. Alloy castings should not be scraped to remove old gaskets but instead soak with carbon tetrachloride to soften the material so that it can easily be removed. Take out sealing plugs and blanks using paraffin under pressure and compressed air to blow through all oil and waterways.

Discard all old gaskets and seals, using new ones on reassembly.

Start by reassembling the cylinder block, replacing all covers and plugs. Fit the crankshaft back into place followed by the pistons and connecting rods. Assemble the timing gear and crankshaft damper and fit the clutch and flywheel into place. Fit the oil pump and the sump can then be fitted and the engine stood upright. Reassemble the cylinder head and fit it back into place. Leave external accessories until last, or even till after the engine has been refitted. Lubricate all bearing surfaces liberally with graphited-oil.

When the engine is back in the car fill up with oil and water. A slight amount of overfilling in the sump will not be harmful at this stage as the filter and oilways are all empty. Leave the sparking plugs out and turn the engine over by hand to check that there is no fouling or any snags. Repeat the test using the starter motor and a well charged battery. Check for leaks. Provided that the engine is satisfactory and turns freely the sparking plugs should be fitted and the engine started. Again check for leaks. When the engine has cooled check all levels and top up as required. Before attempting to start the engine check that the ignition is correctly set and adjusted (see **Chapter 3**).

Use the special fine-pored filter element for the running-in period. Recheck the ignition settings and the cylinder head torque loading after 600 kilometres (500 miles). At the same time change the engine oil and filter element.

15 Fault diagnosis

(a) Engine will not start

1 Defective ignition coil
2 Dirty or incorrectly set ignition points
3 Ignition wires loose or insulation faulty
4 Water or dirt on high-tension leads
5 Faulty capacitor on distributor
6 Battery discharged, corrosion on terminals
7 Faulty or jammed starter
8 Vapour lock in fuel lines (hot weather only)
9 Defective fuel pump
10 Excessive or too little choke
11 Blocked fuel filters
12 Leaking valves
13 Sticking valves
14 Valve timing incorrect (can cause major damage)
15 Ignition timing incorrect
16 High-tension leads connected to the wrong sparking plugs

(b) Engine stalls

1 Check 1, 2, 3, 5, 10, 11, 12, 13 and 16 in (a)
2 Sparking plugs defective or incorrectly gapped
3 Retarded ignition
4 Weak mixture
5 Water in the fuel
6 Fuel tank vent blocked
7 Incorrect valve clearances

(c) Engine idles badly

1 Check 2 and 7 in (b)
2 Air leak at manifold joints
3 Carburetter or fuel injection incorrectly adjusted
4 Worn piston rings
5 Worn valve stems or valve guides
6 Weak exhaust valve springs

(d) Engine misfires

1 Check 1, 2, 3, 4, 5, 9, 11, 12, 13 and 16 in (a) and also check 2, 3, 4 and 7 in (b)
2 Weak or broken valve springs
3 Defective high-tension lead

(e) Engine overheats (see Chapter 4)

(f) Compression low

1 Check 12, 13 and 14 in (a); 4 and 5 in (b) and 2 in (d)
2 Worn piston ring grooves
3 Scored or worn cylinder bores

(g) Engine lacks power

1 Check 2, 11, 12, 13, 14 and 15 in (a); 1, 2, 3 and 6 in (b); 4 and 5 in (c) and also check (e) and (f)
2 Defective cylinder head gasket
3 Fouled or worn out sparking plugs
4 Automatic advance not operating

(h) Burnt valve heads or seats

1 Check 12, 13 and 14 in (a); 4 in (b) and 2 in (d) also check (e)
2 Excessive carbon around valve seat and cylinder head

(j) Sticking valves

1 Check 2 in (d)
2 Bent valve stem
3 Scored valve stem and guide
4 Incorrect valve clearance
5 Gummy deposits on valve stem

(k) Excessive cylinder wear

1 Check 10 in (a) and also check (e)
2 Lack of oil
3 Dirty oil
4 Piston rings gummed up or broken
5 Connecting rods bent or twisted

(l) Excessive oil consumption

1 Check 4 and 5 in (c) and also check (e) and (k)
2 Oil return holes in pistons blocked
3 Oil level too high
4 External oil leaks

(m) Main or big-end bearing failure

1 Check 2, 3 and 5 in (k)
2 Restricted oilways
3 Worn journals or crankpins
4 Loose bearing caps
5 Extremely low oil pressure

(n) Low oil pressure

1 Check 2 and 3 in (k) and 2, 3 and 4 in (m)
2 Choked oil filter
3 Weak relief valve spring or dirt under the seat
4 Faulty gauge or connections

(o) Internal water leakage (see Chapter 4)

(p) Poor water circulation (see Chapter 4)

(q) Corrosion (see Chapter 4)

(r) High fuel consumption (see Chapter 2)

CHAPTER 2 – FUEL SYSTEM

1 Description
2 Routine maintenance

PART 1 CARBURETTER SYSTEMS

3 Maintenance
4 The fuel pump
5 The Zenith carburetters
6 Zenith carburetter tuning
7 The Solex carburetters
8 The hot spot

PART 2 THE FUEL INJECTION SYSTEM (230SL)

9 Fuel filter
10 Fuel pump
11 The injection pump

PART 3 THE ACCELERATOR PEDAL

12 Mechanical transmission
13 Automatic transmission

14 Fault diagnosis

1 Description

The fuel system varies from model to model, the systems for the 230 and 230S being most similar in that they are both fitted with twin carburetters and the fuel is delivered to the carburetters by a mechanically operated fuel pump. The 230SL is fitted with a fuel injection pump and the fuel is injected through an injector for each cylinder. The supply pump for the injection system is electrically driven and mounted just in front of the fuel tank at the rear of the car. The carburetters for 230 models are Solex 38 PDSI, while those for the 230S are Zenith 35/40 INAT. The Zenith carburetters are two-stage where the second stage only starts operating in the upper power range of the engine.

Fuel is stored in a tank at the rear of the car and led to the fuel pump by a system of pipes. **It is essential that the fuel pipes are correctly routed and are not kinked, otherwise the fuel supply to the engine will be restricted.** The level of the fuel in the tank is measured using a float-operated rheostat whose varying resistance alters the reading on the gauge. The tank unit is fitted with bi-metal strips, which light a warning lamp when the fuel falls below a certain level. The bi-metal strips take 4 to 7 minutes to operate and this prevents the warning light from winking on and off if the car is driven with a partially empty tank over rough roads. Fuel is drawn from the tank through a gauze filter surrounding the drain plug, situated under the tank.

There are two systems of ventilating the fuel tank. Normally the filler cap has a breather hole in it and the tank vents through this. If this hole becomes blocked with polish or dirt, the engine will mysteriously fade after the car has been driven for some time and will only start again when the vacuum in the tank has been released or air leaks slowly in. Some models are fitted with a compensating tank in the luggage compartment, as shown in **FIG 1**. Two vent lines connect the tank to the compensating tank and fuel will pass up these lines if the tank is very full, the vapour then passing overboard through a third large-diameter vent line. As soon as a vent line is clear of fuel the fuel will return to the main tank. This system ensures that only vapour is vented and that no fuel is lost through the filler cap. The filler cap is tight-sealed and identified by the stamping 'OHNE LUFTUNG' or 'ohne Entluftning'.

Earlier models were fitted with fuel lines which screw into place on the fuel tank, but later models use short rubber connectors.

FIG 1 The compensating vessel fuel tank vent system

1 Filler neck cover
2 Rubber grommet
3 Fixing clip
4 Fixing clip
5 Rubber grommet
6 Vent line from fuel tank to compensating vessel
7 Vent line from fuel tank to compensating vessel
8 Vent line from compensating vessel into the open
9 Push-in clips with retaining hook
10 Compensation vessel
11 Push-in clips with nose
12 Moltoprene pad
13 Bundy pipe

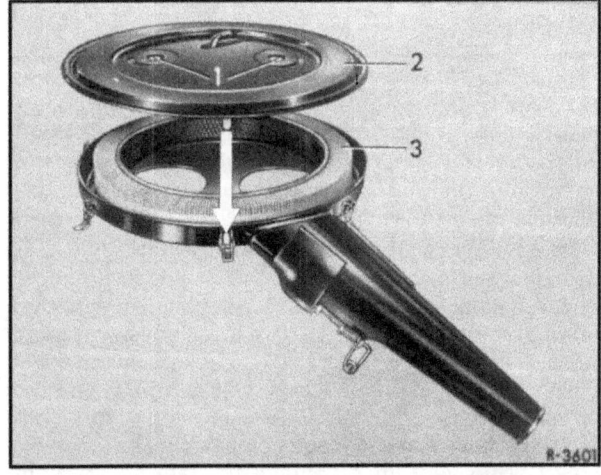

FIG 2 Air cleaner fitted to carburetters
1 Fastening screws 2 Filter top 3 Insert

Only the later type of tank is supplied as a replacement. If a new tank is to be fitted to an old system then the ends of the fuel lines must be sawn off, deburred and the line blown through with compressed air to clean it.

Even the single-stage carburetters fitted to the 230 models are complicated units and if the owner has any doubts concerning his ability to carry out satisfactory adjustments he is strongly advised to take the car to an agent, who will have all the equipment necessary for tuning and checking.

2 Routine maintenance

This section only covers general routine maintenance, and further details for the systems will be given in the first section for each part. Routine maintenance is confined to cleaning the filters and checking the linkages move freely.

Air cleaner:

The standard air cleaner is fitted with a renewable paper element filter. Loose dirt can be removed from this type but after a time the paper will become choked and the element must be renewed. **Paper elements must not be washed in any solvent whatsoever.** For dusty conditions an oil-bath filter can be fitted in place of the standard type.

No exact figures can be given for the distance to be travelled between filter cleanings and in exceptionally dusty conditions it may be necessary to change the oil in the oil-bath filter at daily intervals.

The type of filter fitted to carburetter engines is shown in **FIG 2** and the type fitted to fuel injection models in **FIG 3**. Disconnect the cuff or hose, undo the clips, take off the top and lift out the element. If the element is reasonably clean, tap it all round on a firm surface to dislodge loose dirt and then use an airline to blow from the inside to the outside, finally blowing tangentially across the outside. Refit the element. If it is dirty and cannot be cleaned by this method, discard the old element and fit a new one in its place.

The oil-bath filter is shown in **FIG 4**. Remove the top as before and check the oil. If the oil appears dirty then it should be poured out and the case cleaned out internally. Refill the case, exactly to the mark, with fresh oil and reassemble the unit. If the filter gauze appears dirty it should be removed and washed in clean paraffin (kerosene) or diesel fuel.

Fuel filters:

At regular intervals clean the fuel filters. If they appear excessively dirty or contain water then the drain plug should be removed from the fuel tank and the tank drained. The dirty fuel drained out should not be used except for cleaning purposes. Check the filter in the tank before refitting the drain plug. If the tank is corroded internally then it must be removed for thorough cleaning or renewing.

Icing conditions:

In very cold weather, or in conditions of high humidity and low ambient temperatures, the further cooling caused by the evaporation of the fuel will freeze the moisture in the air as it passes through the carburetter, forming ice in the throat and cutting down performance. Later models are fitted with a valve on the air filter which is counter-balanced by a weight. At low suction the valve stays shut and air is drawn from around the exhaust manifold by a scoop, thus ensuring that it is warmer than ambient. As the suction increases the valve opens and allows cold air to be drawn through when the risk of ice forming is less. The valve should be locked into the cold air position in warm weather when it is pointless to preheat the incoming air charge.

PART 1   CARBURETTER SYSTEMS

3 Maintenance

Routine maintenance is confined to cleaning the fuel line filter and the filter gauze fitted into the fuel pump. The adjustments of the carburetters and linkage should be checked at regular intervals but providing that the engine is running smoothly, full power available and fuel consumption reasonable it is inadvisable to interfere unnecessarily with the carburetters. Dirt in the jets will be the most likely cause of poor running and these should be checked and cleaned before carrying out adjustments.

4 The fuel pump

The fuel pump is mounted on the engine and driven by a cam on the oil pump drive shaft. A diaphragm is pulled inwards by the action of the linkage and the suction draws fuel in through the inlet valve and filter gauze. When the linkage releases the diaphragm it is returned by the pressure of a spring and forces the fuel out through the outlet valve to the carburetter float chambers. The linkage is designed with a 'freewheel' so that when the float chambers are full the fuel pressure holds the diaphragm down and the pump ceases to operate until further fuel is required.

The mounting of the fuel pump is shown in **FIG 5**.

Testing:

Gauges are required to check the pump operation correctly. A simple functional check can be carried out by disconnecting the fuel line to the carburetters and pointing it into a suitable container. Turn the engine over, either by hand or using the starter motor. The engine will be easier to turn if the sparking plugs are taken out. At every second revolution of the engine there should be a good spurt of fuel from the delivery pipe.

Before testing the pump with gauges make sure that the battery is fully charged, otherwise it will not be able to meet the demands made on it. Disconnect the pipe connecting the pump to the fuel tank and fit a vacuum gauge to the fuel pump in its place. Take out the sparking plugs so that the engine will rotate more freely. Operate the starter motor and check that the suction is .3 to .4 kg/sq cm (4.3 to 5.7 lb/sq in) or 230 to 320 mm Hg (9.1 to 12.6 in Hg).

Reconnect the supply pipe to the pump, removing the vacuum gauge, and disconnect the output pipe from the pump. Fit a pressure gauge to the pump, preferably with a T-piece so that the fuel line can be reconnected. Start the engine and let it idle, either on the fuel in the float chambers or with fuel through the T-piece. The delivery pressure at this speed should now read .15 to .20 kg/sq cm (2.1 to 2.8 lb/sq in). High fuel pressure will only be caused by a hardened diaphragm in the pump or by incorrect shimming on the mounting. Low fuel pressure can be caused by several faults in the pump, as well as blocked fuel lines.

Cleaning:

A sectioned view of the fuel pump is shown in **FIG 6**. Unscrew the bolt 12 and remove the cover 10 complete with seal 11. Carefully lift out the strainer (filter gauze) 9 and wash it in clean fuel. Use a small screwdriver to gently scrape out dirt and sediment. Blow out loose dust, sediment and dirt with gentle air pressure. Check that the strainer 9 and seals 11 and 13 are all in good condition, renewing any part that is damaged, and reassemble the parts in the reverse order of dismantling. Make sure that the seals are properly in place otherwise the pump will leak in service.

FIG 3 Air cleaner fitted with fuel injection

1 Air intake silencer lower
2 Air intake silencer upper
5 Air suction tube
6 Air hose
7 Venturi control unit
8 Position markings
9 Hose for engine air-vent line
12 Bracket fixing the air intake silencer to the wheel arch panel
13 Bracket fixing silencer to the cowl

FIG 4 Oil-bath air cleaner

Mounting:

Refer to **FIG 5**. The pump is secured to the crankcase by two nuts. Disconnect both fuel lines, unscrew the nuts and withdraw the pump.

Before refitting the pump turn the engine until the drive cam is at BDC as shown in the figure and measure the dimension (a1). Set the push rod 4 to the start of the delivery stroke and similarly measure dimension (a2). Shims should be fitted to the sealing flange so that the clearance, between the push rod 4 and the drive cam 7, is .4 to .5 mm (.016 to .020 inch) when the pump is in place.

Dismantling:

Remove the fuel pump from the engine and take off the fuel strainer and cover as described for cleaning. Referring to **FIG 6** progressively and diagonally slacken the screws that secure the upper housing 1 to the lower housing 15. Lift off the upper housing.

5 Zenith carburetters

These are effectively two carburetters mounted into one body. Both stages operate into the same inlet manifold and Stage 1 is used for the lower power range of the engine. As engine power increases a vacuum unit operates the throttle butterfly of the second stage to bring it into operation so that it works in conjunction with the first stage. Both carburetters are fitted with an automatically operated choke which closes a strangler valve on Stage 1 The front carburetter is fitted with a scavenge valve that operates at idling speed. The valve opens and allows fuel from the pump to circulate through the valve and then return to the fuel tank through a return pipe. This increased fuel flow, compared to the normal idling requirement, ensures that the fuel does not vaporize in hot weather, causing vapour locks and stalling of the engine. At all running speeds above idle the float chambers are vented into the inlet manifold, but at idling the throttle linkage closes a valve so that the float chambers are vented direct to atmosphere. This prevents the build up of fuel fumes in the manifolds when the engine is stopped. An assembled carburetter is shown in **FIG 7**.

Cleaning:

Take off the air cleaner. The components of the carburetter are shown in **FIG 8**.

1 Disconnect the fuel hose at the carburetter. On the front carburetter also disconnect the fuel return hose. Unscrew the screws that secure the top of the carburetter in place. Slacken the screw 153, as shown in **FIG 9**, and lift off the carburetter cover 139. When refitting the cover, the toggle lever should rest on the circlip 90 when the choke valve 141 is closed.

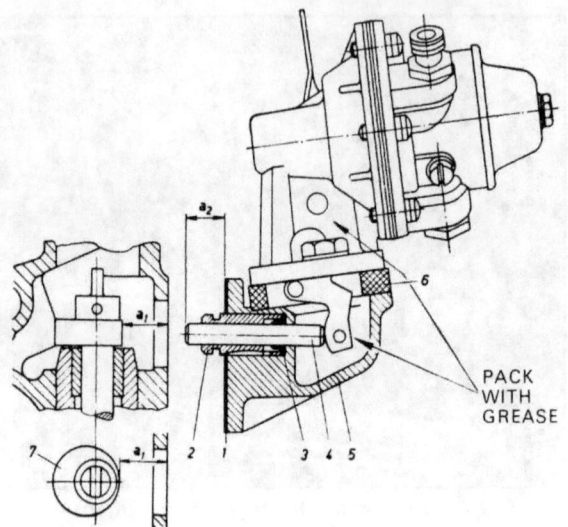

FIG 5 Mechanical fuel pump mounting

1 Sealing flange
2 Bushing
3 Collar
4 Pushrod
5 Intermediate flange
6 Insulating flange
7 Cam on oil pump drive shaft

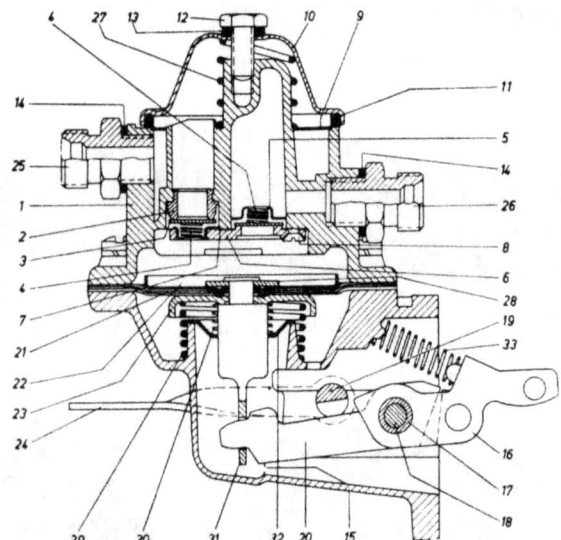

FIG 6 Sectioned view of the mechanical fuel pump

1 Upper housing
2 Valve seat
3 Small valve plate
4 Valve spring
5 Spring retainer
6 Valve plate
7 Gasket
8 C/sunk screw
9 Strainer
10 Cover
11 Sealing ring
12 Hexagon bolt
13 Sealing ring
14 Sealing ring
15 Lower housing
16 Rocker arm
17 Bushing
18 Axle
19 Shaft
20 Link
21 Diaphragm
22 Diaphragm plate
23 Spring support
24 Hand lever
25 Inlet plug
26 Outlet plug
27 Spring
28 Washer
29 Diaphragm spring
30 Spring
31 Link
32 Oil protection plate
33 Pressure spring

The valves can be removed from the upper housing after taking out the screw 8 and the plate 6. Check that the valves are in good condition and **make sure that they are refitted facing the correct directions otherwise the pump will fail to operate**.

If the diaphragm 21 is hardened or split then it should be renewed. Clean out all sediment from the pump before reassembling it in the reverse order of dismantling. The parts in the lower housing 15 can be dismantled but if they are worn it would be better to fit a replacement pump.

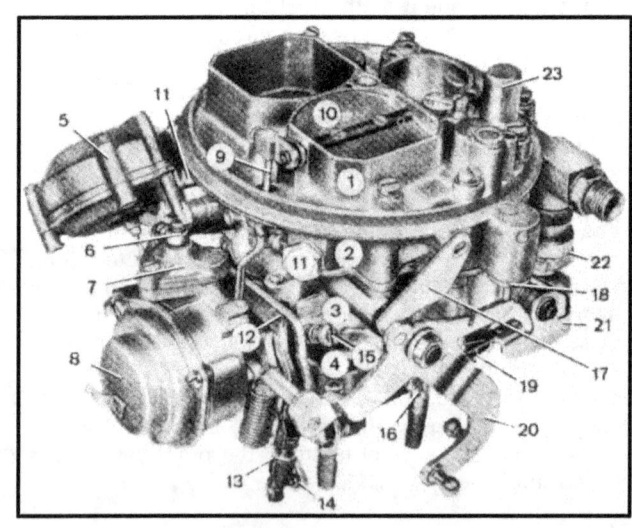

FIG 7 Zenith carburetter

1 Top cover
2 Mounting unit
3 Float chamber
4 Throttle barrel
5 Vacuum chamber
6 Adjustment screw
7 Vacuum diaphragm
8 Choke cover
9 Connecting rod
10 Choke valve
11 Choke tube securing screws
12 Adjustment lever
13 Connecting rod
14 Throttle lever
15 Idle adjust screw
16 Idle mixture screw
17 Accelerator pump lever
18 Float chamber vent valve
19 Float chamber vent valve adjust screw
20 Reversing lever
21 Return valve lever
22 Return valve lever
23 Vacuum diaphragm

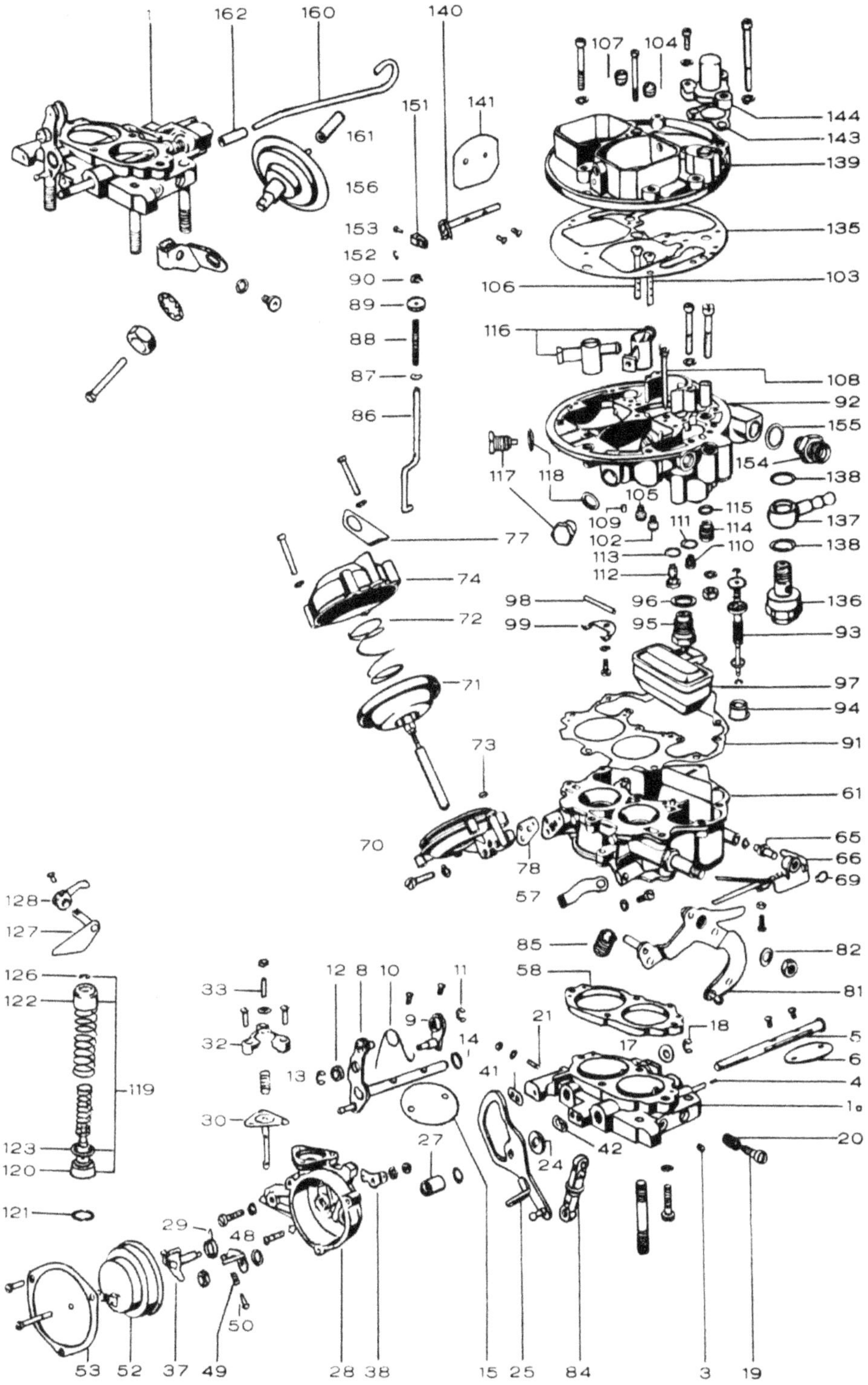

Zenith carburetter

1. Lower mounting
3. Screw plug
4. Screw plug
5. Throttle valve shaft, 1st. stage
6. Throttle valve, 1st. stage
8. Throttle valve shaft, 2nd. stage
9. Hinge lever on throttle control lever
10. Spring
11. Securing clip
12. Roller
13. Securing clip
14. Shaft seal ring
15. Throttle valve, second stage
17. Gasket
18. Stop washer
19. Idling enrichment adj. screw
20. Spring for screw
21. Adjustment screw
24. Washer
25. Throttle lever, 1st. stage
27. Spacer ring
28. Cold starting device body
29. Cam return spring
30. Diaphragm
32. Check valve cover
33. Adjustment screw
36. Securing screw
37. Drive lever
38. Intermediate lever
41/42. Gaskets
48. Pressure lever
49. Pressure lever spring
50. Pressure screw
52. Choke valve cover
53. Collar
57. Bracket
58. Insulating flange
61. Bowl
65. Control pin
66. Operating lever
69. Snap ring
70. Vacuum device body
71. Diaphragm
72. Diaphragm spring
73. Sealing ring
74. Vacuum device cover
77. Cable clamp
78. Seal
81. Control lever
82. Nut
84. Link
85. Return spring
86. Connecting rod
87. Spring stop washer
88. Spring
89. Spring support washer
90. Circlip
91. Gasket
92. Mixture block
93. Ventilation check valve
94. Ventilation valve ring
95. Float needle valve
96. Float needle valve washer
97. Float
98. Float hinge pin
99. Float hinge pin support
102. Fuel jet, first stage
103. Emulsion tube
104. Automatic starter jet, 1st. stage
105. Jet for second stage
107. Automatic starter jet, 2nd. stage
108. Idling jet, first stage
109. Transition jet. second stage
110. Pump suction valve
111. Gasket
112. Pump delivery valve
113. Gasket
114. Enrichment jet
115. Sealing washer
116. Diffuser
117. Spring
118. Sealing washer
119. Pump piston
120. Pump piston
121. Annular spring
122. Guide bush
123. Washer
126. Securing clip
127. Pump lever
128. Inside pump lever
135. Carburetter top gasket
136. Return check valve
137. Banjo connection
138. Sealing washer
139. Carburetter top cover
140. Choke valve shaft
141. Choke valve
143. Full load enrichment device gasket
144. Full load enrichment device
151. Swivel trunnion
152. Securing clip
153. Screw
154. Fuel connection
155. Sealing washer
156. Damper unit
160. Connecting pipe
161. Hose
162. Hose

FIG 8

FIG 9 Disconnecting the choke valve connecting rod

FIG 10 The Zenith main jets
1 Main jets   3 Pump pressure valve
2 Pump intake valve 4 Intermediate jet

FIG 11 The Zenith compensating jets
4 Air compensating jets   5 Choke tubes

2 It is advisable to have several small tins or other means of storage handy, as several of the parts removed from now on will be of very similar appearance and yet they must not be interchanged. Lay the parts in order as they are removed so as to have no difficulty in reassembly.
3 Extract the idling jet 108 and unscrew the jets 104 and 107. Use accurately fitting screwdrivers when removing jets or parts otherwise the slot in the head will quickly become damaged. Lift off the mixture block 92, carefully collecting the gasket 91 and 135.
4 Refer to **FIG 10**. Take out the main jets 1, the pump intake valve 2 and the pump pressure valve 3. Refer to **FIG 11** and take out the air compensating jets 4, choke tubes 5 and the pump piston.
5 Clean all the jets. **Do not poke them through but wash them in clean fuel and then blow through them with compressed air.** Cleaning the jets by poking them through, even with a bristle, will wear the material and alter their flow rates. Clean out the float chamber, gently scraping out sediment if it is caked.
6 Reassemble the carburetter in the reverse order of dismantling. Make sure that the jets are returned to their original positions and not accidentally interchanged.

Further dismantling of the carburetters should only be undertaken for renewing worn or defective parts.

Flooding:

Check that all gaskets and unions are in good order and that it is not a fuel leak that is giving the appearance of flooding. Remove the mixture block and top cover, as for cleaning the carburetter. Invert the mixture block and take out the small screw and lockwasher that secure the support 99. Lift off the support and the float 97 can be removed with its pin 98. Check that the float is undamaged and does not contain any petrol. Renew the float if it is defective. Use a suitable box spanner and unscrew the float needle valve 95, carefully collecting the washer 96 that is fitted under it. Open the valve by pulling the pin outwards and wash the valve in clean fuel. Hold the pin inwards to keep the valve closed and check that the valve does not leak under pressure. If nothing else is available blow through it by mouth to check for leaks. Renew the valve assembly if it does leak.

Reassemble the carburetter in the reverse order. If flooding still persists check the fuel level in the float chamber. Run the engine at idle speed for a few minutes so that the fuel level stabilizes. With reasonable speed remove the top cover and mixture block as before. Use a depth gauge to measure the level of the fuel in the float chamber. The correct level is 21 to 23 mm (.83 to .91 inch). If the level is incorrect alter it by fitting different thickness washers 96 under the float needle valve 95. A thicker washer will lower the fuel level while a thinner one will raise it.

Accelerator pump:

This should start to inject extra fuel when the throttle has been opened 5 degrees and each stroke of the pump should inject .7 to 1.0 cc of fuel. The fuel should be injected so that it misses the pre-atomizer assembly, and hits the bore on the opposite side just by the butterfly throttle valve when it is in its nearly closed position.

The volume of fuel injected can be altered by carefully bending the arm at the point indicated in **FIG 12** and the direction altered slightly by very carefully bending the injection jet. If the pump is defective the plunger can only be renewed as a complete unit.

Automatic choke:

Take off the cover 52 from the automatic choke 28. Push the diaphragm operating rod upwards as far as it will go and at the same time turn the other lever in the opposite direction. The parts are shown in greater detail in **FIG 13**. This operation will close the choke flap 141. Use a suitable diameter drill to check that the gap between the lower edge of the flap and carburetter is 2.4 mm (.094 inch), as shown in **FIG 14**. If the gap is incorrect, fully open the throttle linkage and adjust by turning the adjusting screw 50 as shown in **FIG 15**.

The settings are finally checked with the engine running. Remove the appropriate fuse to prevent the chokes from operating and start the engine without using the accelerator pedal. The engine should then run at its fast-idle speed.

FIG 14   Setting the choke valve using the shank of a 2.4 mm drill

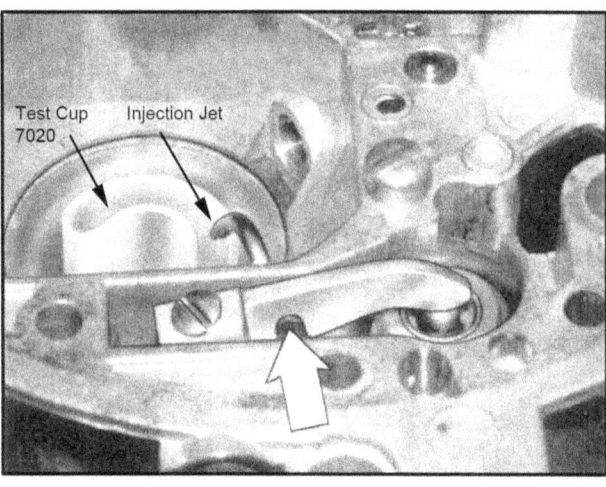

FIG 12   Point of adjustment of the Zenith accelerator pump

FIG 15   Setting the Zenith fast-idle speed

6 Zenith carburetter tuning

The carburetters fitted to the engine and the linkage for operating them are shown in **FIG 16**.

1 Detach the pushrods 9 and 13 and check the system for freedom of movement. Move the reverse levers 7 and check that the throttle butterflies open fully with their full load stops resting against the carburetter body.

2 Disconnect the plastic connecting rods 1. Unscrew the idle adjusting screws 4 on both carburetters until the throttles are fully closed. Screw the adjusting screws 4 back in until the throttles are just on the point of moving and then screw the adjusting screws in one complete further turn. Adjust the lengths of the pushrods 1 to 40 mm (1.6 inch) and refit them.

3 Adjust the length of the pushrod 9 until it can be fitted back into place without moving the linkages and the throttles are still resting against their slow-running adjustment screws. Temporarily attach the pushrod 13 back into place, making sure that the throttles still remain fully closed.

4 Turn the idle mixture adjustment screws 6 fully inwards, without undue force, until they are right in. Back them out 2 turns. The linkage, apart from pushrod 13, is now correctly set and the carburetters are

FIG 13   Zenith automatic choke details

FIG 16 The Zenith carburetters fitted to the engine

1 Connecting rod
2 Throttle valve lever
3 Quadrant lever
4 Idle adjustment screw
5 Pump arm
6 Idle mixture adjustment screw
7 Reversing lever
8 Float chamber vent valve
9 Push rod
10 Adjustment screw
11 Lever
12 Fuel return valve
13 Push rod
14 Relay lever
15 Adjusting nut
16 Roller
17 Quadrant lever

adjusted accurately enough to allow the engine to be started and run until it has reached its normal operating temperature.

5 When the engine is hot and running again disconnect the pushrod 13. Connect a tachometer to the engine. Adjust the speed, using the idle adjustment screws 4 until the engine is running at the correct slow-running speed (750 to 800 rev/min for manual transmission and 850 to 900 for automatic transmissions). Both the idle adjustment screws should be turned in the same direction and by the same amount. If a balance meter is available this should be used to measure the air flow through each carburetter and the idle adjustment screws set so that the air flow is equal at the slow-running speed.

6 Turn the mixture adjusting screws 6 evenly and by the same amounts until the engine is running at its highest idling speed and sounds smooth. Reset the idling speed back to the correct limits, keeping the carburetters balanced. Try a further even adjustment of the mixture adjusting screws to obtain the position of optimum idling and if necessary reset the idling speed yet again. Beyond this point further adjustments will be so small as to be negligible. If difficulty is found in setting the mixture and small adjustments have disproportionate effects, stop the engine and take out the mixture adjusting screws. If their tapered seats have a ring worn into them then renew the screws and again set the mixture correctly.

7 Stop the engine. Use the nut 15 to adjust the lever 14 so that when it is refitted the roller 16 just rests in the limit stop of the quadrant 17 without any tension. Reconnect the pushrod 13. Check the adjustment by starting the engine and the slightest movement of the quadrant should then increase the engine speed from the correct idle.

8 Stop the engine. Check that the reverse lever 7 lifts the pin of the float chamber venting valve 8 by 1.5 to 2.0 mm (.06 to .08 inch) on each carburetter when the linkage is in the idling position. If necessary adjust by very carefully bending the reverse lever 7. With the linkage at idle, turn the adjusting screw 10 on the front carburetter until the fuel return valve 12 is closed. Turn the adjusting screw 10 until the nut of the return valve has moved .3 to .5 mm (.012 to .020 inch) towards valve-open. Secure the adjusting screw by tightening its locknut.

7 The Solex carburetters

These are a single stage carburetter and consequently of much simpler design than the two stage Zenith carburetters. A typical single stage Solex carburetter is shown fitted in **FIG 17**.

Cleaning the carburetter is carried out by removing the top cover and screwing out the jets. The main jet is under a plug at the rear of the carburetter body. Wash the jets in clean fuel and use compressed air to blow through them. **Under no circumstances may the jets be cleaned out by poking wire or bristle through them.** Clean out the float chamber, checking that the float is undamaged. Remove the float to gain access to the needle valve assembly and check that this is clear and does not leak under pressure. Renew the needle valve assembly if it is defective. The float chamber fuel level is correctly set, provided that the float is undamaged and the arm true, when a 1 mm (.039 inch) thick washer is fitted under the needle valve assembly.

The carburetters are tuned and synchronized in a very similar manner to the Zenith carburetters. Manually operated chokes are fitted and these should be adjusted so that after a small movement of the control both cold-start mechanisms start to operate simultaneously. Set both throttles so that they are open by the same amount and then reconnect the linkage so that the throttles are not moved (one turn in of the idle control screws 3 is sufficient for starting). Unscrew the mixture adjusting screws 1½ turns from the fully in positions (taking care

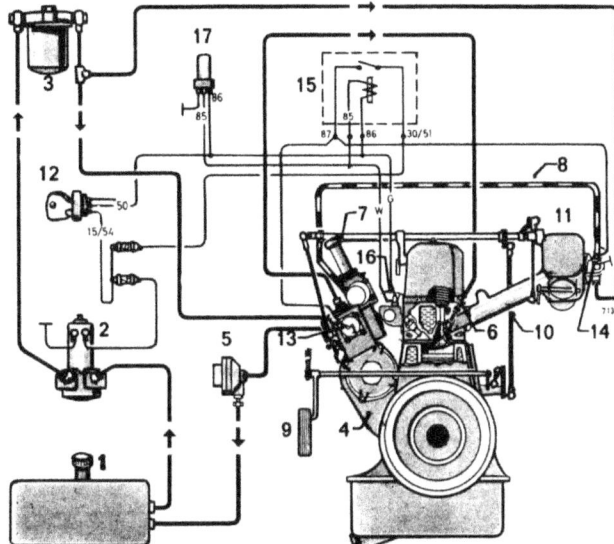

FIG 19 Fuel injection system schematic diagram

Injection system
1 Fuel tank
2 Fuel feed pump
3 Fuel fine filter
4 Injection pump
5 Damper container (return flow)
6 Injection nozzles
7 Cooling water thermostat
8 Additional air line
9 Accelerator pedal
10 Control linkage
11 Mixture controller

Automatic starting aid
12 Starter switch
13 Solenoid for rich mixture on injection pump
14 Electro-magnetic starting valve with atomizer jet
15 Relay
16 Thermo-time switch in cooling water circuit
17 Time switch

not to overtighten onto the tapered seats) and start the engine at these settings. Adjust the idle speed first, preferably using a balance meter to ensure the air flow is equal in both carburetters. Evenly screw both mixture adjusting screws in or out to obtain the fastest possible idle which is consistent with smooth running. Readjust the idling speed and again repeat the mixture and idle adjustments using correspondingly finer adjustments.

The front carburetter may be fitted with a scavenge valve of the type shown in **FIG 18**. This valve increases the fuel flow at idling and therefore cuts down the possibility of vapour locks in hot weather. The valve is set with the throttle butterfly fully closed, not just against the slow-running stop. Slacken the locknut and screw in the adjusting screw 10 until the valve is fully closed. Unscrew the adjusting screw until the valve has moved out by .4 to .6 mm (.016 to .024 inch) and secure the adjusting screw with its locknut. Reset the correct throttle opening (slow-running). If the valve is not correctly adjusted it may limit the fuel flow into the carburetters and thus cut down top-range performance.

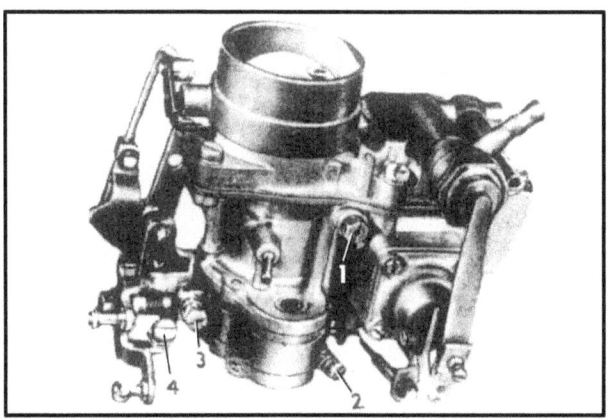

FIG 17 A Solex carburetter

1 Idling fuel nozzle
2 Mixture control screw
3 Idling control screw
4 Starting control screw

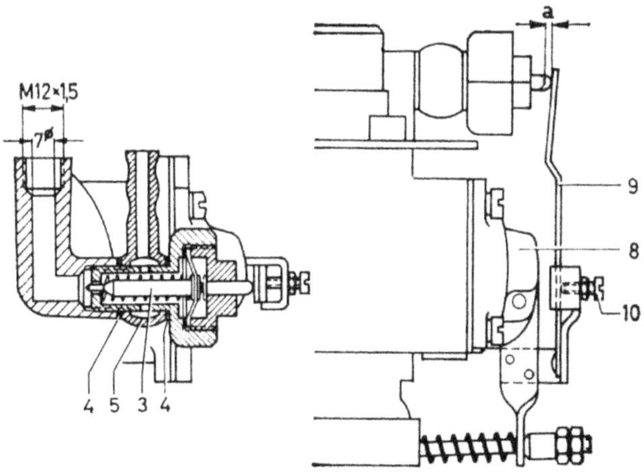

FIG 18 Solex scavenge valve details

3 Valve pin
4 Fibre gasket
5 Ring connector
8 Accelerator pump
9 Spring-loaded pump arm head
10 Adjusting screw   a = .4 to .6 mm

8 Hot spot

When the engine is cold extra fuel is required to overcome the friction of the engine as well as to allow for the wet fuel that is deposited in the inlet manifolds. The amount of fuel deposited is uncontrollable so it can lead to rough running on cold starts. Warming the manifolds evaporates the wet fuel and prevents it being deposited. However heat which warms the manifold when it is cold will only overheat it when the engine is hot, and this will in turn heat the charge entering the engine so that less

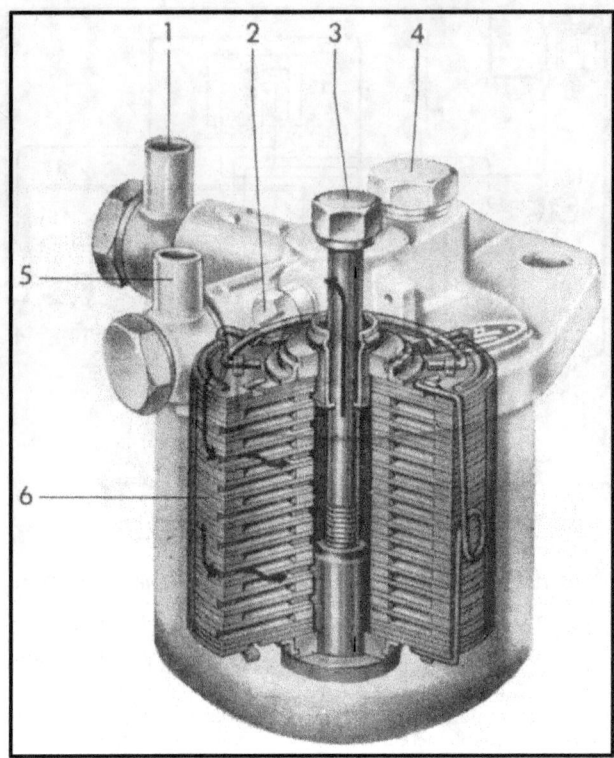

FIG 20   230SL fuel filter

1 Fuel outlet   3 Clamping bolt   5 Fuel inlet
2 Vent screw   4 Filter screw   6 Cellular filter element

9 Fuel filter

Even the minutest specks of dirt that would easily be tolerated by a carburetter can affect the correct functioning of the fuel pump. For this reason a special large fuel filter is fitted which contains a renewable paper element. The element must be renewed at regular intervals to ensure that the fuel to the injection pump is clean. A choked filter, apart from the danger of letting through dirt, will also cut down the fuel supply so the engine may be difficult to start when hot and faltering may occur at high speeds. The details of the fuel filter are shown in **FIG 20**.

10 Fuel pump

The attachments of the fuel pump are shown in **FIG 21** and a ghost view is shown in **FIG 22**.

An electric motor turns the impeller which drives the fuel from the tank to the injection pump. **The motor is sealed and under no circumstances whatsoever should the owner attempt to dismantle or service the motor part of the pump.** Even the renewal of the motor brushes requires the pump to be returned to a Bosch agency.

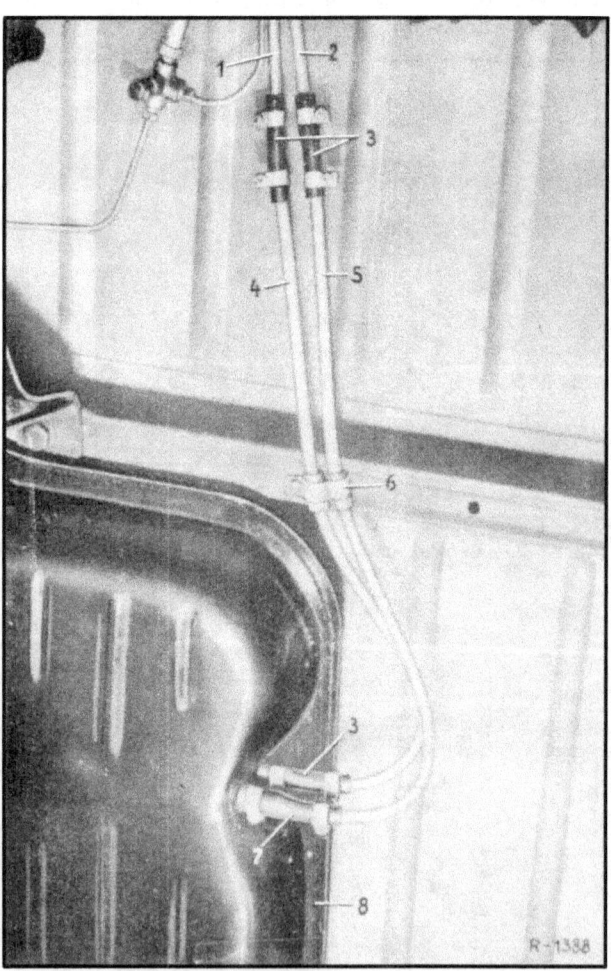

FIG 21   230SL fuel pump attachments

1 Fuel return line   5 Additional fuel intake line
2 Fuel intake line   6 Fixing clip
3 Fuel hose   7 Fuel hose
4 Additional fuel return line   8 Fuel tank

weight of charge can enter (since the charge expands as it gets hotter and the cylinder volume is constant). To overcome this the hot spot is shielded by a valve operated by a bi-metallic spiral. When the engine is cold the valve allows the exhaust gases to play on the hot spot and heat the mixture as it passes. When the engine is hot the bi-metallic spiral closes the valve, which is counterbalanced by a weight, and excess heat is no longer passed to the mixture.

If the bi-metallic spiral burns out a new one must be fitted in its place. Pre-tension the new spiral by a $\frac{1}{2}$ turn when fitting it into place.

After long use the valve may jam and fail to move because of corrosion. Try soaking the valve spindle with Caramba oil, penetrating oil or with crude oil. If this fails to free the valve then a new one should be fitted by an agent. Renewing the valve is beyond the scope of most owners as the valve is welded to the spindle after the new parts have been fitted, and, apart from the lack of equipment, some skill in welding is required to ensure that the correct clearances are kept during and after welding.

PART 2   THE FUEL INJECTION SYSTEM (230SL)

The six-cylinder fuel injection pump fitted to the system is an extremely complex piece of equipment and it is set and adjusted using very accurate special equipment. The work that the owner can carry out without special test equipment is limited and in case of difficulty or poor performance the car should be taken to a Bosch agency. The general schematic layout of the system is shown in **FIG 19**.

Testing:

1 Disconnect the line from the fuel filter to the pump and connect a pressure gauge to the filter outlet. Connect an accurate ammeter in series with the pump and use an accurate voltmeter to check the supply voltage. Switch on the ignition and check that the pump has a minimum voltage supply of 10 volts and that the current consumption lies between 3.1 and 3.5 amps. The delivery pressure should be .4 kg/sq cm (5.7 lb/sq in). If the pressure is low, renew the filter element and repeat the test. If there is a pressure increase then the old filter element was choked. No pressure increase indicates a defect in the pump or a blockage in the fuel lines.

2 Disconnect the return line after having restored the connections broken in the previous test. This flow test should be carried out with a new filter element fitted. Divert the return pipe into a suitably graduated container. Switch on the ignition and check that the pump delivers a minimum of 3.3 litres (5.8 pints) per minute.

3 Make sure that the leak-off pipe is not clogged. When the pump is running watch the end of the leak-off pipe for the formation of fuel droplets. If these form at a fairly rapid rate then the pump sealing is defective and the pump must be renewed. The owner must not attempt to fit a new seal himself.

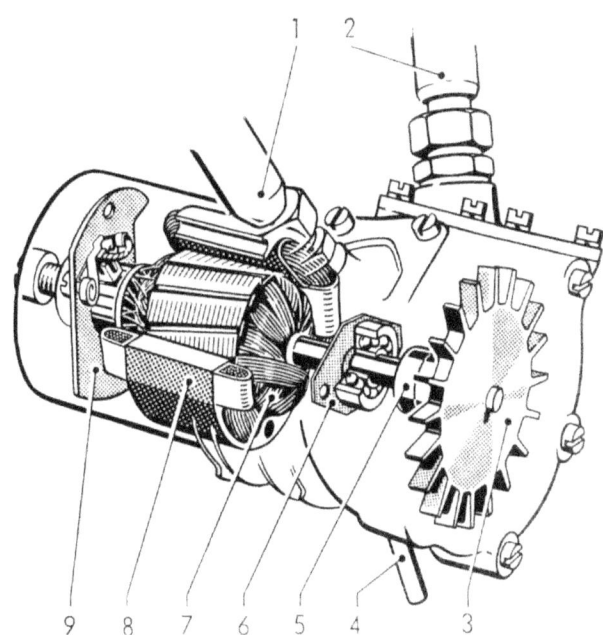

FIG 22 230SL fuel pump

1 Connection delivery side, with check valve
2 Connection suction side
3 Vane
4 Leak-off pipe
5 Slide ring seal
6 Mounting plate
7 Armature
8 Laminated pole
9 Brush holder plate

Servicing:

If the motor part of the pump is defective fit a new or exchange unit to the car.

1 Before removing the pump from the car disconnect the battery or remove the fuse for the pump.

2 When the pump has been removed fit covers to the fuel lines to prevent the entry of dirt. Scribe a light line across the pump coverplate and pump body and then remove the cover by taking out the securing screws. Discard the sealing ring that is fitted into the cover.

3 Use a hook made out of copper wire to withdraw the impeller from the body. Collect the key that secures the impeller to the shaft. Unscrew the check valve that is fitted to the inlet side of the pump and test the valve by blowing and sucking through it by mouth. If the check valve is defective the complete inlet union must be renewed.

4 Clean out the chamber using a hardwood stick and piece of leather. Check for scoring. If there are scores on the pump body between the inlet and outlet ports then the pump is defective and must be renewed. Light wear marks on the coverplate are acceptable but not scores or grooves. If grooves or scores are present on the coverplate they should be lapped off using fine-grade grinding paste spread onto plate glass. Do not use window glass as this is never truly flat.

Reassemble the pump in the reverse order of dismantling, noting the following points:

1 Renew the key that secures the impeller if it is worn. Once the parts are fitted the maximum play should be 18 degrees.

2 Check that the impeller has sharp edges with no score marks on them and refit it so that the inclined sides of the vanes face the pump housing.

3 Discard all the old seals and fit new ones on reassembly.

FIG 23 General view of the fuel injection system

1 Throttle valve lever
2 Full-load stop screw
3 Idle stop screw
4 Control rod
5 Bearing sleeve
6 Control lever
7 Control lever
8 Control rod
9 Adjusting pin bore
10 Control lever
11 Control shaft
12 Bearing bracket
13 Control lever
14 Control rod
15 Adjustment lever
16 Idle stop
17 Full-load stop

11 The injection pump

A general view of the injection system fitted to the car is shown in **FIG 23** and a more detailed view of the injection pump is shown in **FIG 24**.

Maintenance:

At regular intervals check the oil level in the pump using the dipstick. The dipstick is situated at the rear end of the pump just above the idle control knob 18 shown in **FIG 24**. If need be, top up the pump to the correct level.

FIG 24 The fuel injection pump fitted to the engine

1 Control lever
2 Cooling water hose
3 Supplementary air line
4 Injection pipes
5 Cooling water thermostat
6 Cooling water hose
7 Control rod
8 Cold start magnet
9 Full-load stop
10 Adjustment lever
11 Air cleaner
12 Idle stop
13 Fuel line (feed line)
14 Aneroid compensator
15 Fuel line (return line)
16 Hexagon nut
17 Oil line
18 Spring-loaded idle control knob
19 Housing for the thermostat switches
20 Hexagon screw

Operation:

Fuel is injected into the engine ahead of the inlet valve, as shown in **FIG 25**, just as the inlet valve is about to open. The port is heated by the coolant to assist vaporization, which starts to take place in the port and is completed inside the combustion chamber, taking heat from the combustion chamber area. The injectors are sealed units which cannot be repaired and must be renewed if they do not spray in a satisfactory 45 degee cone.

Air for combustion is drawn in through the air cleaner. At idling speeds the butterfly valve is completely closed in the venturi. Running along the top of the intake tubes is a pipe connected to the tubes, seen in cross section in **FIG 25**, and air for idling is drawn through this pipe. At the front end of the idling pipe is a throttle screw which therefore controls the slow-running speed. As the speed increases the throttle butterfly in the venturi is opened and more air is then drawn in through the intake manifold.

An additional cold start mechanism, controlled by thermostats and a cold-start solenoid, injects extra fuel into the manifold for starting from cold. There are two thermostats, one of which measures air temperature and the other the coolant temperature.

The wiring diagram for the cold start mechanism is shown in **FIG 26**.

A schematic layout of the control system is shown in **FIG 27** and the actual parts with the covers removed are shown in **FIG 28** and **FIG 29**. The three dimensional cam, which controls the position of the fuel control rod and therefore the amount of fuel injected at each stroke, can be rotated through 90 degrees with the final position being set from the accelerator position and the load on the engine. The cam can also slide axially under the action of the centrifugal governor so that it takes up a position corresponding to engine speed. The combination of rotation and sliding therefore sets the roller at a height corresponding to all the engine parameters and the fuel injected is therefore correct for these parameters. Excess fuel is injected when the engine is cold.

Removal:

1 Drain the cooling system, keeping the coolant if the inhibitor or antifreeze is still fresh. Remove the battery.
2 Refer to **FIG 24**. Disconnect the water hoses 2 and 6, the supplementary air line 3, the fuel lines 13 and 15 and the oil line 17.
3 Free the control rod 7 from the adjusting lever 10. Disconnect all six injection pipes 4, fitting them with blanks to prevent the ingress of dirt. Disconnect the electrical lead to the cold start solenoid (magnet) 8.
4 Undo the nuts 16 and remove the bracket from the rear of the pump. Draw the pump rearwards and remove it from the car.

If the drive lug is damaged or worn it can be removed and a new one fitted. Hold the lug with special spanner No. 621.589.00.08 and remove the nut shown in **FIG 30**. Take out two of the adjacent screws that secure the flange and use puller No. 621.589.00.33 to remove the drive lug.

The pump is refitted in the reverse order of removal. Before fitting the pump turn the engine until it is exactly at 20 deg. ATDC on the suction stroke of No. 6 (rear cylinder). This is the same as 20 deg. ATDC on the firing stroke of No. 1 (front) cylinder. Turn the pump until the marks shown in **FIG 30** align and refit the pump with these settings.

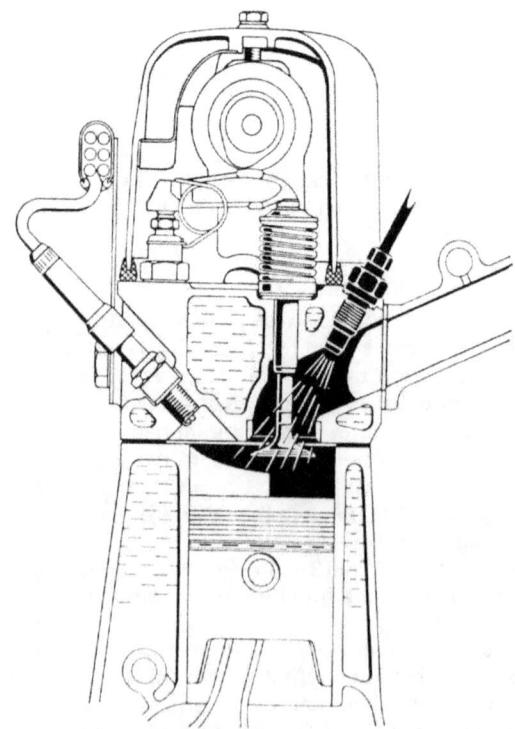

FIG 25 The fuel injection into the engine

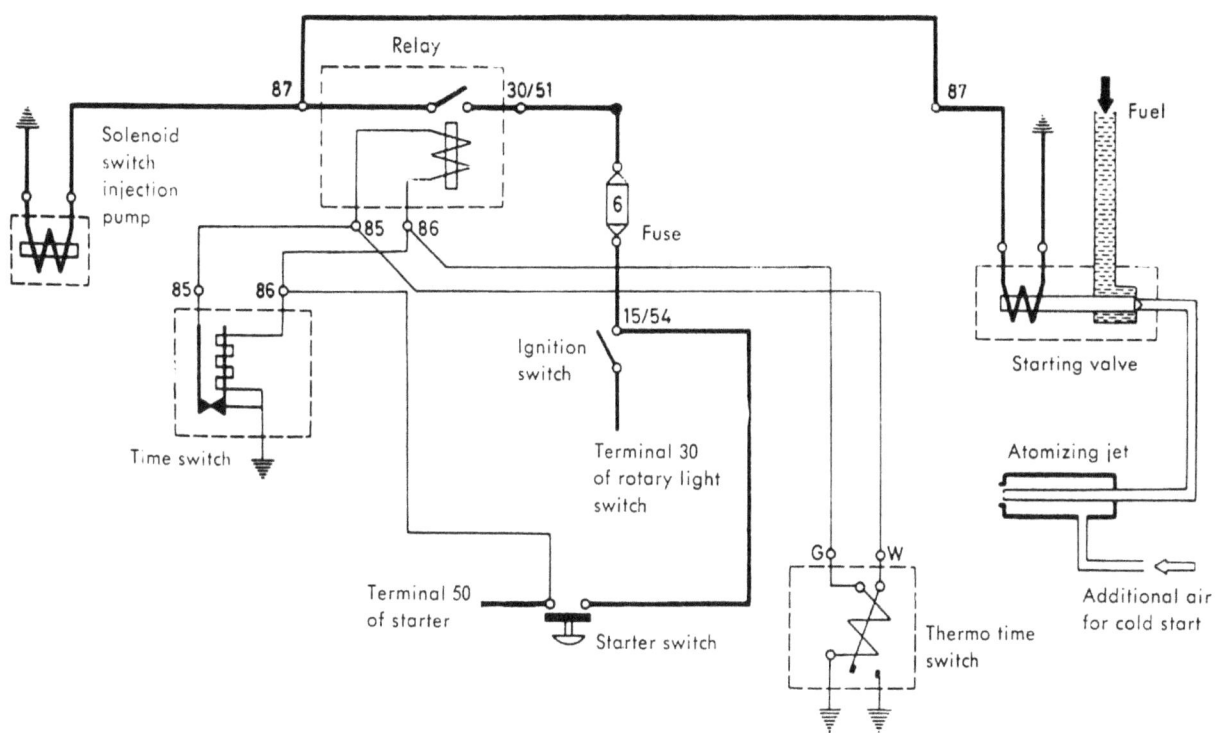

FIG 26 Wiring diagram for the automatic auxiliary cold start mechanism

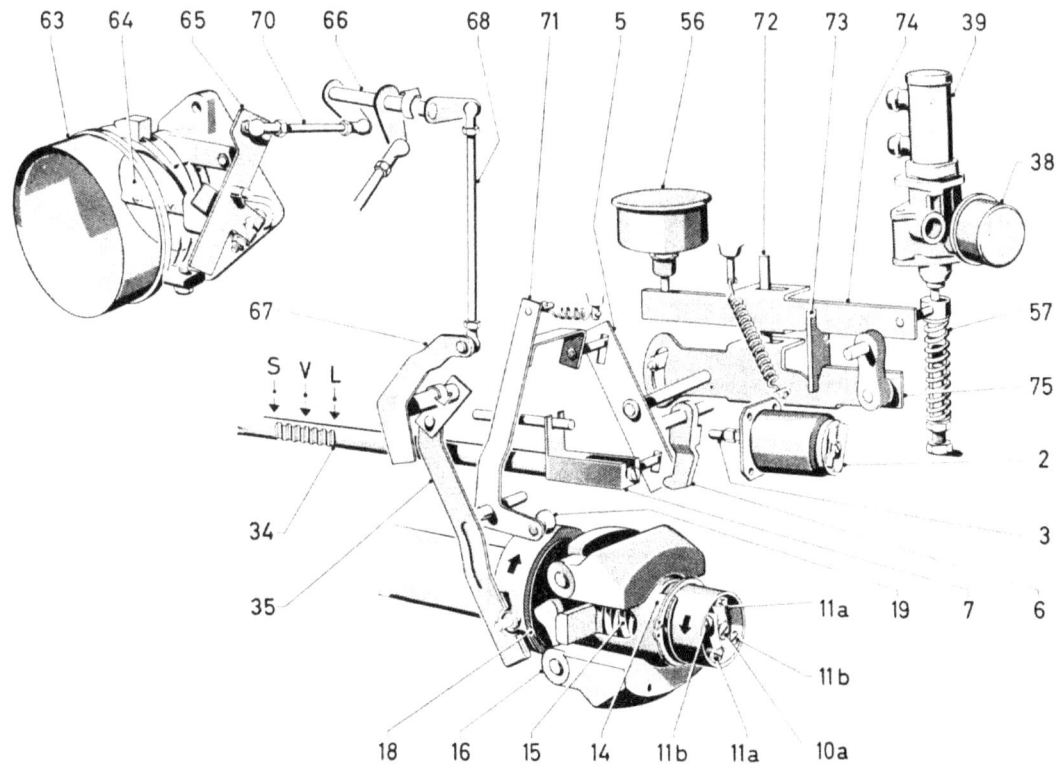

FIG 27 Schematic diagram of the control mechanism for the fuel injector pump

S = Starting position of fuel control rod
V = Full load position
L = Idle position

2 Solenoid switch
3 Actuating rod
5 Reversing lever
6 Starting lever
7 Control rod end

10a Idling speed adjustment screw
11a Partial load adjusting screw (black)
11b Adjusting screw (white, top speed range)
14 Joint
15 Governor springs
16 Flyweight
18 Three-dimensional cam
19 Tracer roller

34 Fuel control rod
35 Adjusting lever
38 Air cleaner
39 Cooling water thermostat
56 Aneroid compensator
57 Guide bolt
63 Venturi control unit
64 Throttle valve
65 Throttle valve lever

66 Control shaft
67 Control lever
68 Control rod
70 Control rod
71 Roller lever
72 Guide bolt
73 Support
74 Rocker
75 Correcting lever

FIG 28 The governor details on the injection pump

1 Starting lever
2 Roller lever
3 Trace roller
4 Three-dimensional cam
5 Governor spring
6 Adjusting screw regulating rod head
7 Idling speed adjusting screw
8 Bottom partial load adjusting screws (black)
9 Top partial load adjusting screws (white)

Adjustments:

Special equipment is essential for nearly every setting operation. The throttle linkage can only be adjusted using special gauges Nos. 127.589.01.23 and 111.589.04.23. The pump and venturi must be set correctly using these gauges otherwise the fuel injected will not be proportional to the amount of air passed by the venturi. The mixture strength should only be adjusted using an exhaust gas analyser. For these reasons the adjustment and setting of the system is best left to a fully equipped agent.

The engine idling speed should be adjusted to 750 to 800 rev/min for manual transmission and 700 to 750 rev/min for automatic transmissions, using the idling throttle adjusting screw.

On models fitted with automatic transmission select a drive gear without operating the accelerator pedal and with the handbrake firmly applied. The idle speed should not drop below 700 rev/min. If the idle speed drops excessively, check the oil pressure switches on the transmission, as well as its lifting magnet, for correct operation. If these operate satisfactorily then the idle speed with drive selected should be altered by varying the length of the control rod for the lifting magnet.

If after adjusting the slow-running speed the engine hunts then the mixture is too rich, while if it shakes and vibrates on its mountings then the mixture is too weak. **Stop the engine.** The idle mixture is adjusted by pressing in the spring-loaded knob 18, shown in **FIG 24**, and turning it a maximum of three notches either side of the basic setting. Turn the knob a notch at a time to the left for weakening the mixture and to the right for enrichment. Start the engine and check the adjustment. The interior parts are rotating with the engine so the engine must be stopped every time an adjustment is made.

Dampers:

Dampers are fitted to the supply and return fuel lines in order to quieten the noise that the fuel makes as it passes through the pipes. A sectioned view of a damper is shown in **FIG 31** and they should both be checked if the fuel flow is noisy.

FIG 29 The control linkage on the injection pump

1 Stilt
2 Correcting lever
3 Guide bolt
4 Centre of gravity of the reversing lever
5 Positive-controlled guide of the correcting lever
6 Rocker

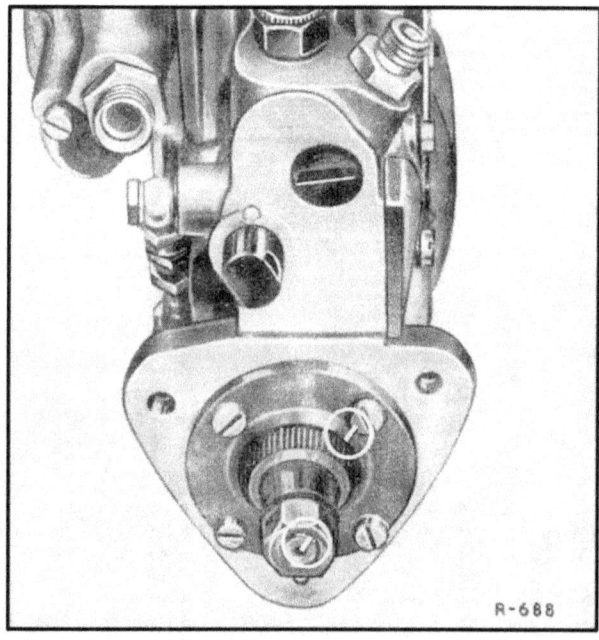

FIG 30 Fuel injection pump timing marks

PART 3 THE ACCELERATOR PEDAL

12 Mechanical transmission

The details of the pedal and linkage are shown in **FIG 32**. Fit a 2 mm (.078 inch) gauge between the pedal and the stop at position 'a' holding down the pedal with a suitable weight. Adjust the length of the pushrod 1, using the turnbuckle 2, until the levers of the carburetter butterfly valves or venturi are against their full-load stops. When the adjustment has been made correctly the stop 9 or 9a should be felt when the pedal is pushed down hard.

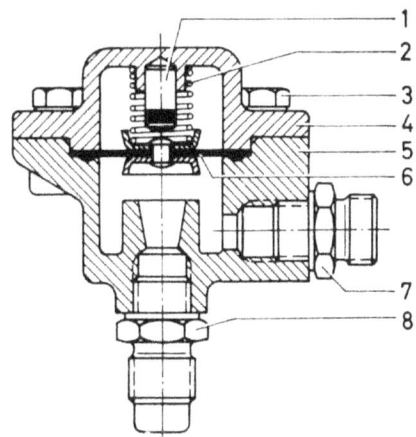

FIG 31   Fuel line damper details

1 Plug
2 Pressure spring
3 Hexagonal bolt and spring washer
4 Cover
5 Housing
6 Diaphragm
7 Threaded union with sealing ring (outlet)
8 Threaded union with sealing ring (inlet)

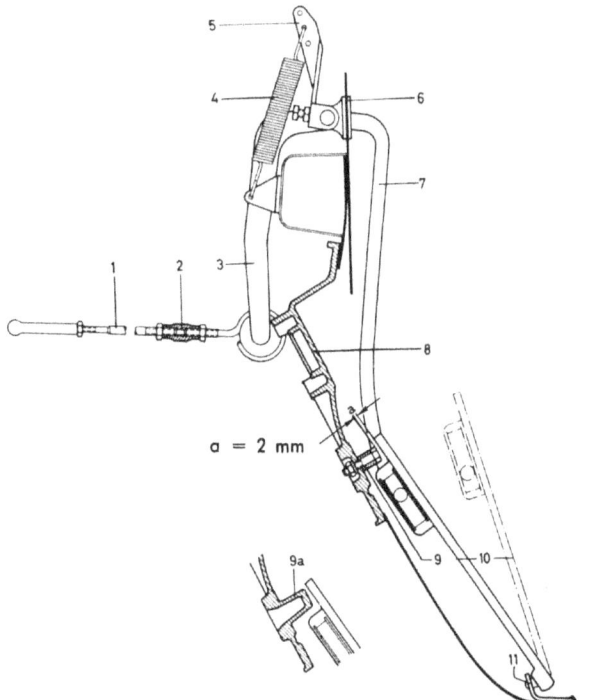

FIG 32   Accelerator pedal and linkage for manually operated transmissions

1 Push rod
2 Turnbuckle
3 Lever on control shaft
4 Return spring
5 Lever for return spring
6 Rubber grommet
7 Adjustment lever
8 Support plate for steering column jacket
9 Stop for foot plate (1st version)
9a Stop for foot plate (2nd version)
10 Foot plate
11 Ball head bracket

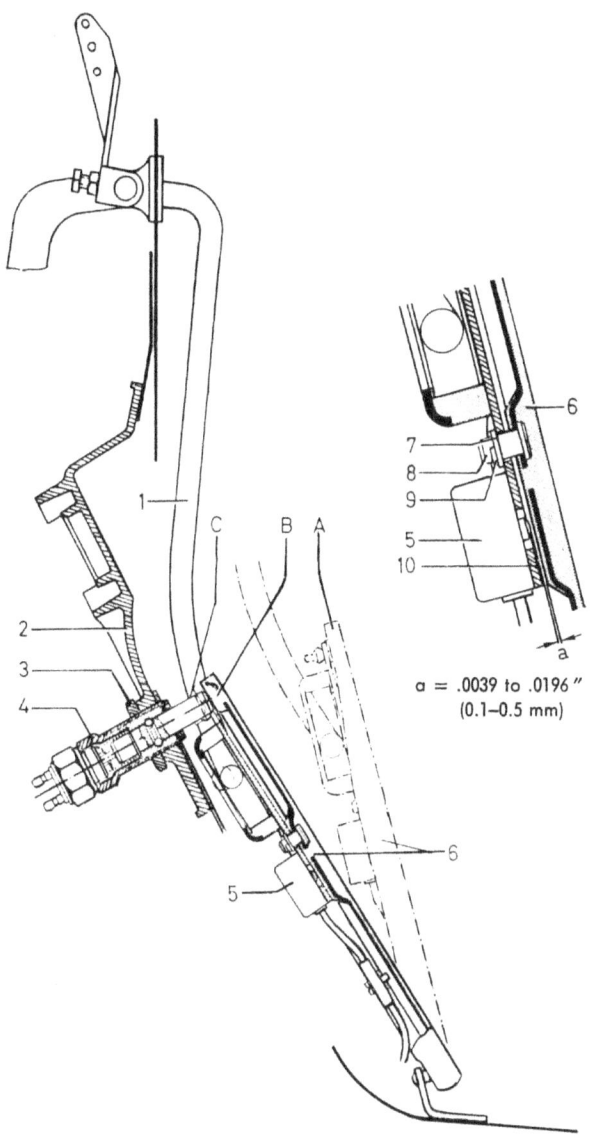

FIG 33   Accelerator pedal, kick-down switch and linkage fitted with automatic transmissions

1 Adjustment lever
2 Coverplate
3 Locknut
4 Kickdown switch
5 Lifting switch-Idle switch
6 Foot plate
7 Compensating washer
8 Bolt
9 Cotterpin
10 Plate
A Idling position
B Full throttle position
C Kickdown position

13 Automatic transmission

The details are shown in **FIG 33**. Press down the pedal until it is just against the kick-down switch in position B. An assistant should check that the butterfly valve lever is 5 mm (.2 inch) from the full-load stop on the venturi. If necessary adjust the position of the kick-down switch to obtain the correct clearance. If moving the switch is not sufficient then adjust the length of the pushrod as well. As a check depress the pedal to the kick-down position C, when the gap between the butterfly valve lever and the full-load stop should be 1 mm (.04 inch) approximately.

14 Fault diagnosis

(a) Engine fails to start (fuel injection system)

1 Current not reaching pump motor
2 Defective fuel pump
3 Badly fouled fuel filter
4 Incorrect starting technique
5 Defective cold start components (some defects in these will also affect starting a hot or warm engine)

(b) Leakage or insufficient fuel delivered

1 Fuel pipes incorrectly routed or kinked
2 Fuel filter choked
3 Defective fuel pump
4 Loose unions
5 Incorrectly adjusted scavenge valve (carburetters only)

(c) Excessive fuel consumption

1 Carburetters or injection pump require adjusting
2 Fuel leakage
3 Sticking controls
4 Defective cold start mechanism
5 Dirty air cleaner
6 Excessive engine temperature
7 Brakes binding
8 Tyres underinflated
9 Idling speed too high
10 Car overloaded
11 Worn carburetters

(d) Idling speed too high

1 Rich fuel mixture
2 Controls sticking
3 Slow-running incorrectly adjusted
4 Worn butterfly valve or spindle

(e) Noisy fuel pump

1 Defective dampers on fuel injection system
2 Loose mountings
3 Air leak into pump
4 Obstruction in fuel line

(f) No fuel delivery

1 Empty fuel tank
2 Float needles in carburetters jammed shut
3 Vent in fuel tank blocked
4 Defective fuel pump
5 Bad air leak on suction side of pump

CHAPTER 3 – IGNITION SYSTEM

1 Description
2 Routine maintenance
3 Ignition faults
4 Removing the distributor
5 Servicing the distributor
6 Setting the ignition timing
7 Sparking plugs
8 Fault diagnosis

1 Description

The distributor is mounted onto the crankcase and is driven at half engine speed by the same shaft that drives the oil pump. The drive is synchronized with the engine so that the contact points open and the rotor arm directs the high-tension voltage to the appropriate sparking plug as the piston is at the firing point and the mixture compressed ready for ignition. The ignition of the mixture takes a certain finite time so the ignition point must be varied according to the engine speed and load on the engine to ensure that full combustion is occuring just after TDC when the maximum pressure rise is required. The distributor is fitted internally with spring-loaded weights which move outwards under centrifugal force. As the engine speeds up, these weights move proportionately outwards and act through a linkage to advance the cam of the distributor in relation to the drive shaft, thus advancing the ignition timing. To cater for the varying loads the distributor is fitted with a vacuum unit connected to the inlet manifold. As the depression in the inlet manifold varies with throttle opening and load, the vacuum unit rotates the baseplate of the contact breakers about the cam, advancing the ignition in proportion to the load and throttle opening.

The distributor is also fitted with a manual control for retarding the ignition so as to cater for lower grades of fuel or variation in engine condition. The manual adjuster is shown in **FIG 1**. Normally the lever 4 is left in the fully advanced position as shown. If a cheap grade of petrol is used the screw 3 should be slackened and the ignition retarded, by moving the lever 4 clockwise, until the engine no longer 'knocks' or 'pinks' under load, and the screw retightened.

All the models covered by this manual are fitted with six-cylinder engines and therefore the distributor cap will have six high-tension plug leads to it (the centre high-tension lead connects to the ignition coil) and the cam on the distributor will have six lobes. The attachment of the distributor to the 230SL models is shown in **FIG 2**.

2 Routine maintenance

The high-tension, ignition coil and distributor cap must be kept free from oil, dirt or moisture at all times. Wipe them clean and dry with soft cloth to ensure that there are no paths for the high-tension voltage to leak away.

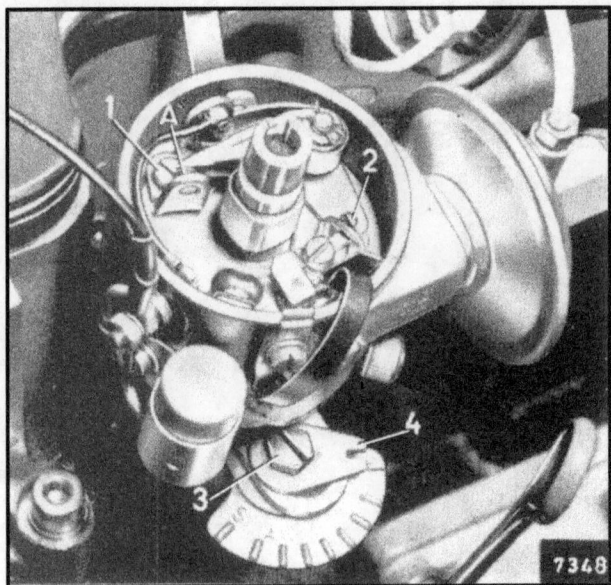

FIG 1 Distributor adjusting points

marked 'Oel' are sufficient and a little grease should be smeared around the cam at the point marked 'Fett'. Occasionally a single drop of oil should be put onto the pivot post for the contacts. **Do not allow oil or grease to come onto the contacts themselves and wipe away all surplus oil and grease from the distributor.** Wipe the rotor arm and distributor cap with soft dry cloth before refitting them.

Cleaning contact breaker points:

After even a short period of use one point will have a 'pip' built up on it while the other point will have a mating pit eroded in it. This is perfectly normal and no action need be taken. Mercedes do not recommend cleaning the points with emerycloth or a file but renewing them when they are so worn that performance is affected. If they are to be reground, and there is sufficient material left, it is advisable to do it using a special jig so that the points are ground flat and meet squarely when reassembled.

Adjusting contact points:

Refer to **FIG 1**, after removing the distributor cap and rotor arm. Turn the engine over by hand until one lobe of the cam is directly under the foot of the moving contact and the points are open at their widest gap. Slacken the securing screw 1 so that the fixed contact can just be moved without it being free. Insert a suitable feeler gauge correctly between the contacts at A. The correct gap for all models is .3 to .4 mm (.012 to .016 inch). Use a screwdriver to turn the adjusting screw 2 until a slight resistance is felt on the feeler gauge as it is moved between the points. Tighten the screw 1 and rotate the engine until the next cam lobe is under the foot of the moving contact. Use the feeler gauge to check that the gap is still correct. Repeat the test on the remaining four lobes. **Because of the pit and crater worn in the points, the gap will not be correct if the feeler gauge is inserted fully between the points.** The feeler gauge should be inserted onto the unpitted area so that it does not bridge the pit and give a false reading.

A more satisfactory method of checking the points gap is to measure the dwell angle using a special meter. The gap must be within the limits given earlier and they should be adjusted so that the dwell angle is $38 \pm ^3_1$ degrees. If, with the correct gap set, the dwell angle is less than 33 degrees then the points must be renewed.

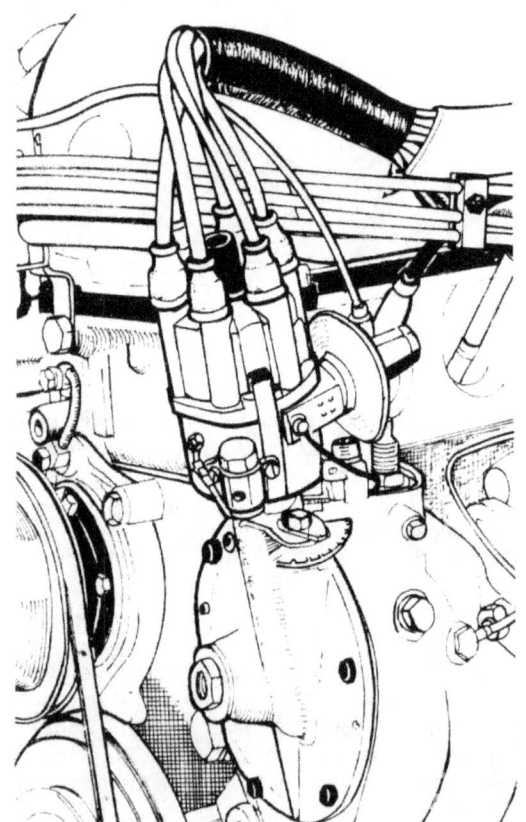

FIG 2 Mounting of the distributor on the 230SL models

The sparking plugs should be cleaned and tested at regular intervals and renewed when they are worn. See **Section 7** for further details.

Distributor lubrication:

The distributor should be lightly lubricated at the points shown in **FIG 3** after the distributor cap and rotor arm have been removed. A few drops of oil at the points

Renewing contact points:

The points must be renewed if they are excessively worn or if their spring is weak. Use a modified spring balance to measure the pressure of the spring.

Take out the two screws that secure the distributor cap holding clips and partially withdraw the contact breaker mechanism. Remove the spring clip from the pivot post and unscrew fully the screw 1 shown in **FIG 1**. Lift out the contact points, carefully noting the positions of all the parts. Fit a new set of points in the reverse order of removal and set the points gap correctly. Check that the moving contact moves freely about the pivot post. If the contact sticks, remove the points and lightly polish the pivot post with fine emerycloth. Lubricate the post with a single drop of oil before refitting the points.

3 Ignition faults

A persistent misfire can be caused by the ignition being faulty. Check that the mixture is at the correct strength (see **Chapter 2**) as incorrect adjustments to the fuel system can also cause misfiring. Check that the points are clean and correctly set.

If the misfire cannot be traced check the sparking plugs and high-tension ignition circuit. Set the engine to idle at a fast speed, either by altering the adjustments or using a clip to open the throttle linkage slightly. Disconnect each high-tension lead in turn from its sparking plug. **It is advisable to use rags or gloves as an insulator when disconnecting the high-tension lead.** If the misfiring becomes more pronounced when a lead is disconnected, then that lead and sparking plug are firing satisfactory. If there is no difference when a lead is disconnected, that sparking plug is not firing. Having identified the non-firing cylinder (or cylinders) stop the engine. Remove the insulating shroud from the end of the high-tension lead and restart the engine. Carefully holding the high-tension lead with rags or a glove place it so that its end is about 5 mm ($\frac{3}{16}$ inch) from a convenient metal part of the engine, but **not near the fuel system**. The spark should be blue, fat and healthy looking.

If the spark is satisfactory then the fault lies in the sparking plug. Remove the plug and either fit a new plug in its place or else clean and test the old one. It should be remembered that even if a plug passes the pressure test the deposits may conduct when they are hot, causing a misfire. It is for this reason that sparking plugs should be renewed at regular intervals.

A weak, irregular spark that is thin and reddish or yellow in colour indicates a fault in the ignition. Check the high-tension lead for perishing or cracking and renew it if it appears defective. Remove the distributor cap and rotor arm from the distributor. Wipe them clean using soft dry cloth, paying especial attention to the crevices between the high-tension lead sockets as well as those between the electrodes in the distributor cap. Examine both the cap and rotor arm for cracks or other damage. Renew any defective parts. Apart from cracks the distributor cap may also suffer from 'tracking' in which case it must be renewed. 'Tracking' will show up as thin black lines between the electrodes or an electrode and a metal part in contact with the cap.

Testing the low-tension circuit:

A quick method of checking that current is passing through the distributor is to remove the distributor cap and flick the points apart with a finger nail. Sparking across the points will show that the distributor is 'live' and quite often a 'crack' will be heard as the ignition coil operates and makes a spark.

A more accurate method is to connect a low-wattage 12-volt test lamp in series between the distributor and the ignition coil, in the low-tension circuit. Turn the engine over slowly by hand and the lamp should light as the points close, going out again as they open. If the lamp stays on continuously then there is a shortcircuit in the distributor. Check for chafing of the insulation on the internal wires, incorrect reassembly or other defects. If the insulation and assembly are correct then disconnect the capacitor and any ignition suppressors fitted to the

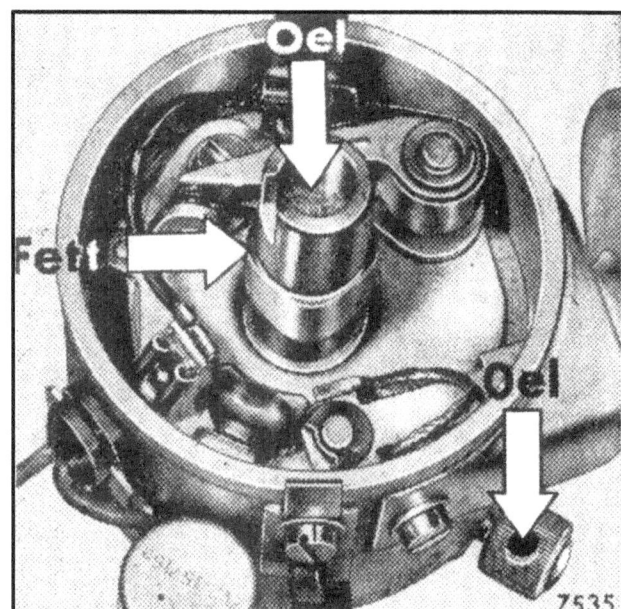

FIG 3 Lubrication points for the distributor

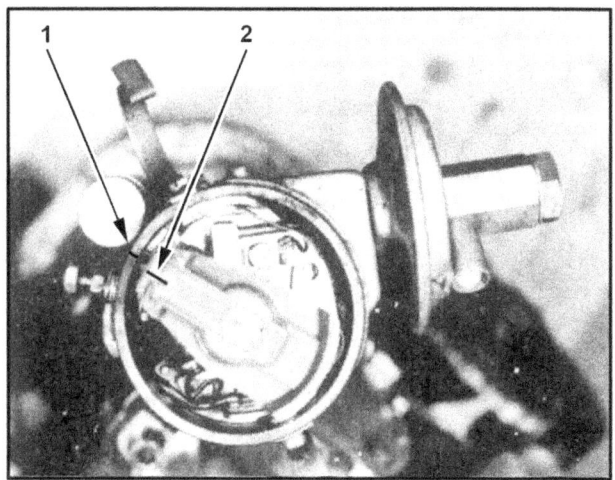

FIG 4 Timing marks aligned in the distributor with No. 1 cylinder at TDC on the firing stroke

distributor as these may be defective and causing a short-circuit. If the lamp does not light at all then the wiring must be traced back until the defect in the supply is found. The ignition circuit is not protected by a fuse.

Capacitor:

These are made up using metal foil wrapped with paper as an insulator. Usually if there is a shortcircuit the current burns away the foil in the area of the defective insulation so that the capacitor is self-healing and short-circuits are rare.

Open circuited capacitors are difficult to detect without special test equipment but they may be suspected if starting is difficult and the contact points are excessively burnt or 'blued'.

Capacitor faults are usually rare so other possible faults should be checked before fitting a new capacitor.

4 Removing the distributor

Free the clips and lift off the distributor cap. The cap can be left in place attached to the high-tension leads. If

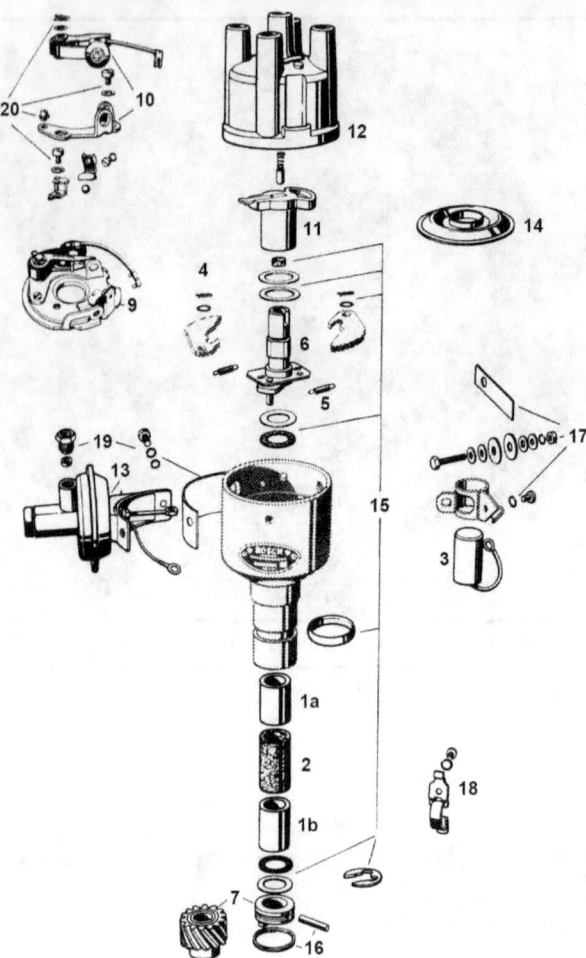

FIG 5 Details of a typical Bosch distributor

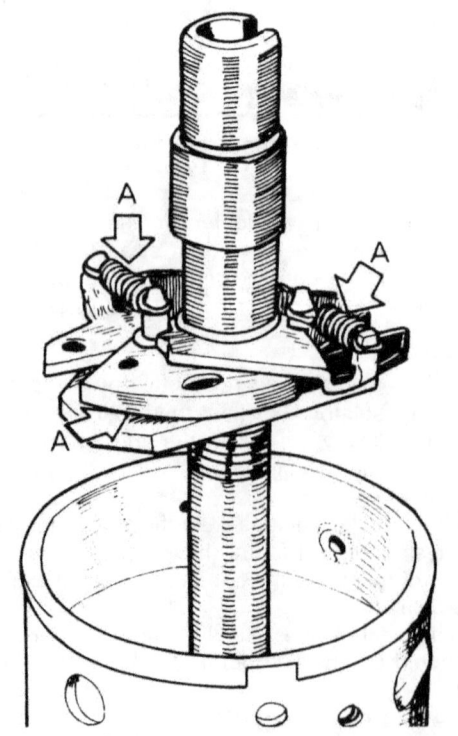

FIG 6 The centrifugal advance mechanism

the high-tension leads are disconnected from the cap, be sure to label them so that they will be correctly reconnected.

Turn the engine until it is at the firing stroke and TDC on No. 1 (front) cylinder. At this point the mark 2 on the rotor arm should align with the mark 1 on the top of the case, as shown in **FIG 4**. If the marks do not align then the drive has been incorrectly reassembled and should be reset as described in **Chapter 1, Section 7**.

Disconnect the small-bore tube from the vacuum unit on the distributor. Disconnect the low-tension lead and the earth lead from the distributor. Take out the securing screw 3 shown in **FIG 1**. The distributor and bearing are held in place by another bolt whose position will depend on the model. In some cases the bolt is in the crankcase while in others it will be an external one of the four additional bolts that secure the cylinder head. When this other bolt has been removed withdraw the distributor from the crankcase.

Refit the distributor in the reverse order of removal. Check that the marks shown in **FIG 4** still align and then accurately set the ignition timing as described in **Section 6**.

5 Servicing the distributor

The details of a typical Bosch distributor are shown in **FIG 5** and the assembled drive shaft and centrifugal advance is shown in **FIG 6**. The figures show a four-cylinder distributor but they are correct generally.

Difficulty may be had in obtaining the correct spares to replace worn parts of the distributor and in the long run it will be found easiest, as well as best, to fit a reconditioned or new distributor in place of one that is worn or defective.

1 Remove the distributor from the engine. Take out the screws which secure the distributor holding clips 18 in place. Take out the screws holding the vacuum unit 13 in place, disconnect the link of the vacuum unit and remove it from the distributor. The contact breaker assembly 9 can now be removed after taking off the rotor arm 11. This should normally be sufficient dismantling for cleaning out the inside of the distributor. The capacitor 3 can be renewed after taking off its clamp. As opposed to most English models the capacitor is mounted on the outside of the distributor.

2 If further dismantling is required, **carefully note the relation of the driving slot in the cam 6 to the offset on the driving dog 7.** Use a suitable pin punch to drive out the pin 16 and pull off the driving dog 7 followed by washer and thrust washer. **Make sure that the lower end of the drive shaft is free from any burrs or damage,** polishing it with emerycloth if required. Push the drive shaft assembly up and out of the casing. If the bushes are worn they can be pressed out and new ones pressed back into place. Great care must be taken to use a well-fitting polished and stepped mandrel for pressing the bush back into place, and once fitted the bush should be run-in with plenty of lubricant on a distributor tester or some other form of rotary drive.

3 The centrifugal advance can be dismantled by disconnecting the small springs 5 and then removing the spring clips. **Great care must be taken not to distort or stretch the springs 5 when removing or replacing them as they control the amount of advance.**

The distributor is reassembled in the reverse order of dismantling, taking great care to ensure that the parts are refitted in the correct relationship. Before reassembly wash all the parts, including felt washers, in clean fuel. Lubricate the bearing surfaces with oil and lightly grease the parts of the centrifugal advance mechanism.

6 Setting the ignition timing

The settings for the static and stroboscopic ignition timing for all models are given in **Technical Data**.

Static timing:

1 Disconnect the low-tension lead between the distributor and the ignition coil and reconnect it with a low-wattage test lamp in series. Take out the sparking plugs so that the engine will turn more easily and also take off the distributor cap so that the points can be observed. Check that the marks on the distributor and rotor arm align when the engine is at TDC on the firing stroke of No. 1 (front) cylinder. The compression stroke before firing is found by covering the sparking plug hole with a thumb and turning the engine until the pressure in the cylinder starts to rise as the engine is turned.

2 Turn the engine, in its normal direction of rotation, until the timing pointer is exactly aligned with the correct timing point on the crankshaft damper. If the point is overshot turn the engine forward a further two revolutions and do not turn it backwards.

3 Slacken the distributor clamp bolt and turn on the ignition. On models fitted with fuel injection it is advisable to remove the fuse so that the electric pump is not left running throughout the adjustments. Rotate the distributor body slightly in either direction until the point is found where the lamp extinguishes. This position is where the contact points have just opened. Tighten the distributor clamp bolt.

4 As a check turn the engine a further two revolutions forwards. As the correct timing is approached turn the engine slowly and stop turning the instant that the test lamp goes out. If the ignition timing is correct then the timing pointer will exactly align with the correct timing mark on the damper. Readjust the timing if required.

5 Remove the test lamps and correctly reconnect the distributor low-tension lead. Refit the sparking plugs and distributor cap.

Stroboscopic timing:

This is the more accurate method as the timing is set with the engine running. Before carrying out the stroboscopic method the static timing must be set with reasonable accuracy to allow the engine to start up and run safely.

1 Connect a stroboscopic light 1 so that it will shine on the pointer 2 and timing marks 3, as shown in **FIG 7**. Also connect an accurate tachometer 4 to the ignition. The instrument shown in the figure is also used for measuring the dwell angle of the points.

2 Mark the edge of the pointer 2 and correct timing mark with thin white lines. Start the engine, taking great care not to allow tools, clothing or hands to touch the moving cooling fan or fan belt, and allow the engine

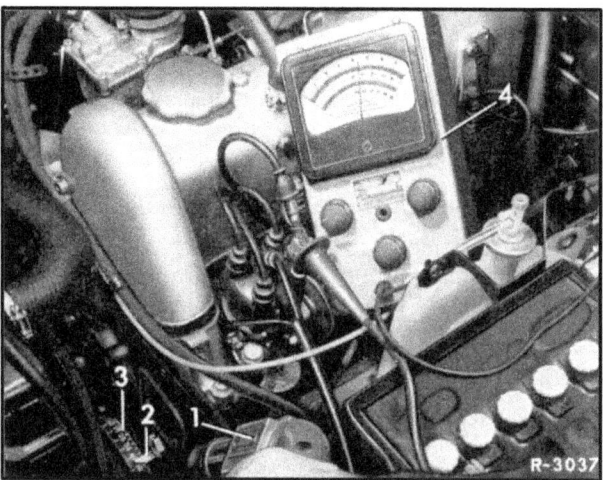

FIG 7 The stroboscopic light and tachometer connected for dynamically setting the ignition timing

to run until it has reached its normal operating temperature.

3 Disconnect the vacuum small-bore pipe from the distributor and set the engine to run at a steady 4500 rev/min. Slacken the distributor clamp bolt and slightly rotate the distributor body in either direction until the edge of the pointer is exactly aligned with the correct timing mark. Tighten the distributor clamp bolt.

4 The stroboscopic light can also be used to check the operation of the centrifugal advance mechanism and vacuum unit. This can be done empirically by slowing and accelerating the engine and checking that the centrifugal advance operates smoothly. Reconnect and disconnect the vacuum pipe to check the operation of the vacuum unit. The various settings are given in **Technical Data** so that exact timing for the various speeds can be accurately checked using the stroboscopic light.

5 Stop the engine and disconnect the tachometer and stroboscopic light.

7 The sparking plugs

Removal:

Slacken the sparking plug by one or two turns using a suitable box spanner. Use an airline or tyre pump to blow away loose dust or dirt from around the plug and then unscrew it fully by hand.

If the sparking plug is stiff or difficult to remove, slacken it as before by a part of a turn. Pour paraffin (kerosene) or penetrating oil around the threads, leaving it to soak overnight. Carefully unscrew the sparking plug. **Great care must be taken not to strip the threads or cross-thread the plug on aluminium alloy cylinder heads.** If the threads are stripped they can be repaired using Heli-Coil inserts.

Refitting:

If the threads in the cylinder head are dirty, clean them out using a well greased tap. Failing a tap, use an old sparking plug with a cross-cut down the threads. Use a wire brush to clean the threads on the sparking plug and then grease them lightly with graphited grease. **Do not** use any other form of grease as it will bake hard and lock the plugs in place. Fit a new sealing ring to the sparking plug if the old one is compressed to less than half its original thickness. Screw the sparking plug fully into place by hand alone and then tighten it using a box spanner or torque wrench.

Examination:

As the sparking plugs are removed they should be stored in the correct order. This is because an examination of the firing ends will give a good guidance as to the conditions inside the combustion chamber.

Reject any sparking plugs that have cracked or damaged insulators as these are certain to misfire. Similarly reject any plugs with badly burnt or eroded electrodes.

A light powdery deposit on the firing end ranging in colour from brown to greyish tan, coupled with some slight wear on the electrodes, indicate that the conditions are normal. White or yellowish deposits which are still powdery are caused by long periods of constant-speed driving or much low-speed city driving. With these types of deposits, cleaning and testing of the sparking plugs is all that is required.

If the deposits are wet and black, they are caused by excess oil entering the combustion chamber. The only cure is an engine overhaul, but fitting a hotter running grade of plug may help to alleviate the problem.

Dry fluffy looking deposits with a black colour are caused by incomplete combustion. This can be caused by excessive idling but it may also be caused by defective ignition or running with too rich a mixture.

Overheated sparking plugs have a white blistered look about the central electrode and if lead-based fuels have been used there may be glints of metal on the central electrode. The electrodes will be excessively burnt away. Some possible causes are poor engine cooling, too weak a mixture, incorrectly set ignition timing, incorrect grade of sparking plug or running at high speeds with the car overloaded.

Cleaning:

It is recommended that the sparking plugs are cleaned at 8000 kilometre (6000 mile) intervals and renewed after 15,000 to 16,000 kilometres (12,000 miles).

Clean the plugs on an abrasive blasting machine and pressure test them after attention to the electrodes. Trim the electrodes using a fine file and then adjust the gap by carefully bending the side electrode. **Never bend the central electrode.** The plug should spark regularly and satisfactorily under a pressure of 5 kg/sq cm (70 lb/sq in).

Clean the external portion of the insulator with a piece of fuel-moistened cloth and keep the insulator free from grease or oil.

8 Fault diagnosis

(a) Engine will not fire

1 Battery discharged
2 Distributor points dirty or out of adjustment
3 Distributor cap wet, dirty, cracked or 'tracking'
4 Carbon brush inside distributor cap broken or jammed up
5 Faulty cable, defective switch or loose connection in low-tension circuit
6 Rotor arm cracked
7 Broken contact breaker spring
8 Contact points stuck open
9 Water on high-tension leads
10 Defective ignition coil
11 Rotor arm omitted on reassembly

(b) Engine misfires

1 Check 2, 3, 5 and 10 in (a)
2 Weak contact spring
3 Defective high-tension lead
4 Sparking plug defective, fouled or incorrectly gapped
5 Sparking plug loose
6 Ignition too far advanced

CHAPTER 4 — COOLING SYSTEM

1 Description
2 Maintenance
3 The radiator
4 The fan belt
5 The thermostat
6 The water pump
7 Frost precautions
8 Fault diagnosis

1 Description

Coolant passes through the internal passages in the crankcase and cylinder head, collecting the excess heat from the engine. The heated coolant then circulates through the radiator where it is cooled, before returning to the engine, by the passage of air over the radiator cooling fins. The circulation of the water is assisted by a centrifugal pump driven by a belt from the engine and the passage of air through the radiator is assisted at low speeds by a cooling fan mounted on the water pump. The coolant also passes through the oil/water cooler so that excess heat is removed from the lubricating oil.

The system is fitted with a wax-filled thermostat valve to ensure a quick warm-up of the engine. When the engine is cold the valve remains closed and the pipe to the top radiator tank is shut off. Instead of passing through the radiator the coolant passes through a bypass hose back to the engine. The coolant also passes through the heater and oil/water cooler. No heat is lost to the cooling air and the engine warms up rapidly. When the thermostat reaches its operating temperature in the coolant the wax melts and the valve starts to open. Coolant then flows through the radiator normally.

The filler cap is fitted with two concentric valves, as shown in **FIG 1**. The outer valve seals against the filler neck and is used for pressurizing the system. The coolant will boil at a slightly higher temperature when it is under pressure and this prevents boiling at localized hot spots in the engine at high operating temperatures. The outer valve opens at a predetermined pressure to release excess coolant or air and keep the internal pressure within limits. When the engine cools the pressure drops and the inner valve opens to allow air to return into the system to prevent a vacuum being formed. The filler cap is secured by a bayonet fitting with a safety device added. The first turn of the cap releases the pressure, while keeping the cap in place, and the remainder of the turn then frees the cap.

The filler cap must not be removed when the coolant temperature is above 90°C (190°F). If the cap is removed above this temperature the sudden release of pressure can cause the coolant to boil and force scalding water over the operator's hand. If the filler cap is defective it must only be replaced with one marked 100, otherwise the system will be set to the incorrect pressure.

The engine contains large amounts of light alloy and therefore it is essential that some form of inhibitor is added to the cooling water. Antifreeze contains its own inhibitors, which last for a year, so antifreeze can be left in all year round and changed at yearly intervals. A list of inhibitors is given in **Technical Data**. These must be added to the cooling water in the proportion of 2.5 to 5 cc per litre (.7 to 1.5 cu inch per gallon) if antifreeze is not used.

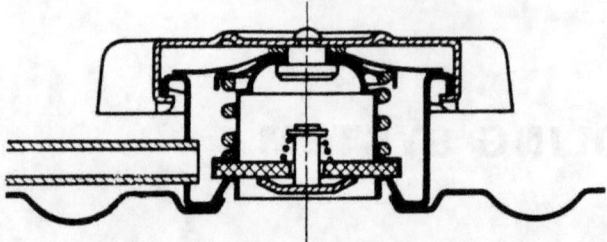

FIG 1 Sectioned view of the filler cap

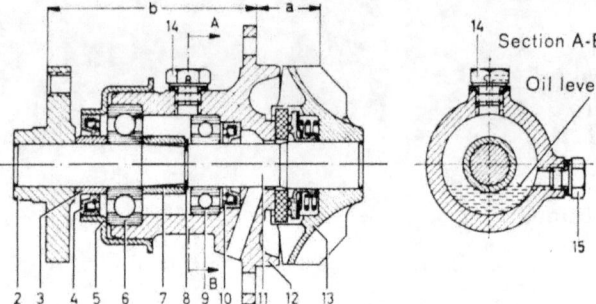

FIG 2 Sectioned view of the water pump

2 Hub
3 Spacer ring
4 Sealing ring
5 Sealing ring retainer
6 Annular grooved bearing
7 Spacer sleeve
8 Snap ring
9 Annular grooved bearing
10 Sealing ring
11 Pump shaft
12 Bearing housing
13 Impeller
14 Filler screw with breather bore
15 Oil level check screw

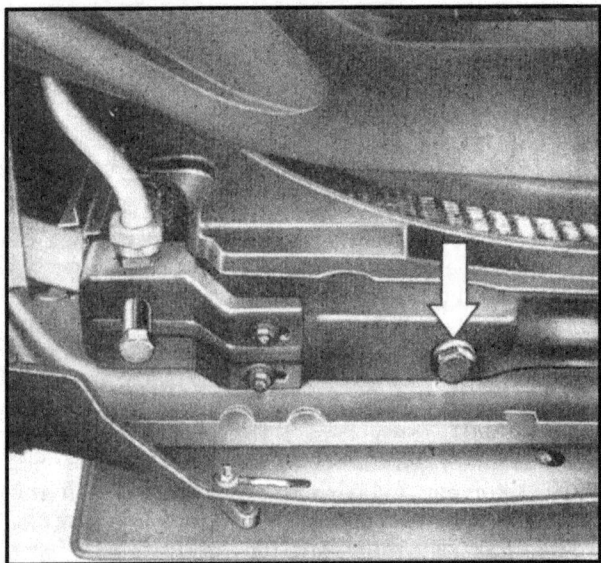

FIG 3 The radiator drain plug, shown on a car fitted with automatic transmission

2 Maintenance

Lubrication:

A sectioned view of the water pump is shown in **FIG 2**. At regular intervals remove the two plugs 14 and 15 from the pump body and top up the pump to the level shown with Hypoid SAE.90 oil. Before refitting the plugs check that the breather in the top plug is clear.

The pump requires 10 cc of oil to fill it from empty and it should be noted that new or reconditioned pumps are supplied empty so they must be filled before being put into service.

Draining:

Set the heater controls to hot and remove the filler cap. Remove the drain plugs from the engine and radiator. **If the antifreeze or inhibitor is still fresh then the coolant should be drained into clean containers so that it can be collected for re-use.** The drain plug for the radiator is shown arrowed in **FIG 3**. The figure shows the radiator fitted to a car with automatic transmission and the oil cooler for this is mounted vertically on the left of the radiator. The position of the engine drain plug is shown in **FIG 4**. Some models may have an alternative position of the engine drain plug as shown in **FIG 5**. When the coolant has drained out disconnect the supply hose to the heater, at the cylinder head, and lower the end of the hose so that the heater drains.

Filling:

On the majority of models the filler cap is fitted directly to the radiator top tank. On the 230SL and some other models a separate header tank is mounted onto the rear bulkhead of the engine compartment as shown in **FIG 6**. The separate header tank may be of slightly different shape on some models but the principles are the same. The tank is connected to the system by the hose 2 and the bleeder hose 5 automatically leads air bubbles up to the header tank.

Make sure that the heater controls are on HOT and the drain plugs fitted. Pour in the inhibitor and then fill the system up to the tag inside the filler neck with soft, clean water. If antifreeze is to be used it is advisable to mix it with part of the water before pouring it into the system. Leave the filler cap off and start the engine. Allow the engine to idle for a few minutes so as to settle the level and disperse any air, then top up to the level of the tag with more clean water.

The tag marks the level of the coolant when the engine is cold but when the engine is hot the level should be approximately 1.5 cm ($\frac{1}{2}$ inch) above the level of the tag. If the engine is hot it should be left running while topping up with cold water. Hot water may be added at any time and in extremely cold climates it is advisable to drain the system, heat the coolant separately and then pour it hot into the engine so that starting will be easier.

Flushing:

It is recommended that the cooling system be flushed out at yearly intervals when the antifreeze is renewed. The system can be flushed by running water through it until it comes out clean from the drain taps. However, it is more effective to degrease and then descale the system.

Drain the system and refill it with a 5 per cent solution of P.3 (Henkel degreasing agent). Use the car normally for a period of 24 hours, making sure that the cooling system reaches its normal operating temperature. At the end of the period drain out the degreasing solution and flush through with clean water. Refill the system with a 5 per cent solution of soda. Leave this descaling solution in the system for a further 24 hours while using the car. Preferably take the car for a long run, as the hotter the system becomes, the more effective will be the descaling. Drain out the solution and flush through with clean water until it comes out clean from the drain holes. Use a hose-pipe to flush through the heater separately, with its hoses disconnected. Refit the drain plugs and refill the system to the correct level with inhibitor or antifreeze and soft clean water.

Hoses:

At regular intervals examine the hoses and check them for softening, hardening or perishing. Renew any hoses that show defects. Check that the hose clips are tight and secure. The hoses must be pushed onto the tube so that they are well over the ridge around the tube and the hose-clip is then fitted to the portion of the hose pushed beyond this circumferential ridge. **The hoses and system should be checked very carefully before adding antifreeze as it is extremely penetrating and will quickly find any small leaks.**

3 The radiator

The hose connections have been varied slightly at different times and a typical layout is shown in **FIG 7**. The radiator fins, and the transmission oil cooler if fitted, should be periodically cleaned by blowing through them in a reverse direction either with an airline or hosepipe. In very bad cases the radiator should be removed from the car and either soaked or scrubbed in a very hot, weak detergent solution.

Removal:

1 Drain the cooling system as described in the previous section. Slacken the hose clips and disconnect the water hoses from the radiator.
2 On cars fitted with automatic transmission, disconnect the hoses at the oil cooler and plug the hoses to prevent dirt from entering. The oil cooler is then removed with the radiator.
3 Remove the mounting bolts and lift the radiator out of the car, collecting the sealing strips.

Refitting:

The radiator is refitted in the reverse order of removal. The interior of the radiator is cleaned by flushing out the cooling system. If the water tubes are choked it may help to invert the radiator and flush through in a reverse direction using a powerful jet from a hosepipe.

The transmission oil cooler should be flushed through with paraffin (kerosene) under pressure and then dried out using an airline.

Note the following points when refitting the radiator:
1 Fit the hoses back into place as the radiator is being lowered into position, as it will be easier than trying to press them on once the radiator is fully attached.
2 Refit the radiator leaving the securing bolts slightly slack. **Check that there is adequate clearance between the front of the cooling fan blades and the rear of the radiator core. Turn the cooling fan and check that there is an even clearance all around between the tips of the blades and the radiator cowl.** When the radiator is correctly positioned fully tighten the securing bolts.
3 Fill the cooling system to the correct level and check for leaks, both when the engine is cold and after it has been run and is hot.

FIG 4 The cylinder block drain plug as fitted to most models

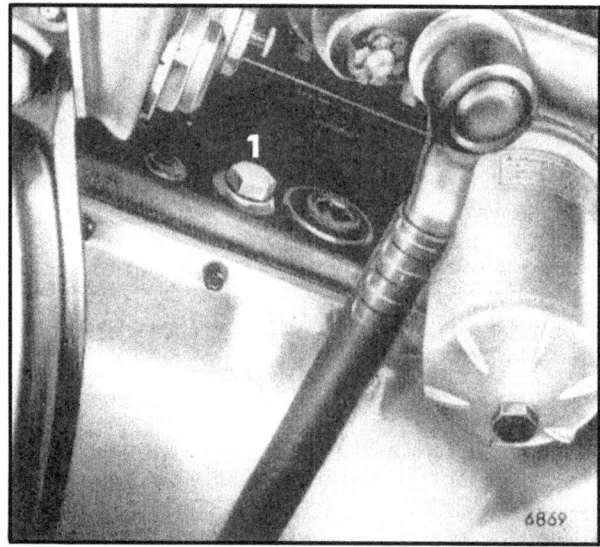

FIG 5 The cylinder block drain plug as fitted to some models

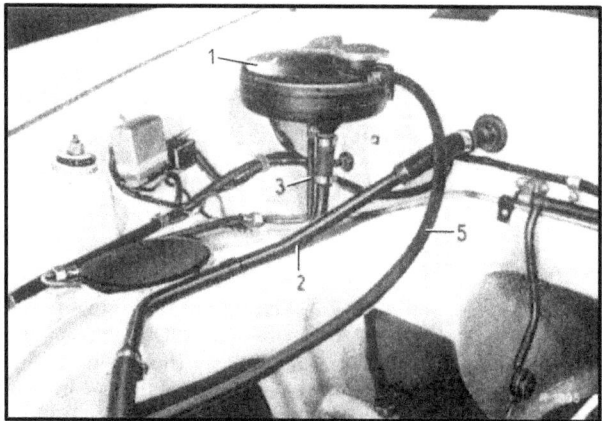

FIG 6 The separate header tank fitted to the 230SL models

1 Cooling water reservoir   3 Bracket
2 Hot water return line   5 Bleeder hose

FIG 7 General arrangement of the water hoses and radiator attachments

1 Top sealing strip 3 Attachment bolts
2 Rubber pad 4 Bottom sealing strip

4 The fan belt

The fan belt drives the water pump (with cooling fan attached to its hub) and the generator (or alternator on later models).

The attachments of the generator are shown in FIG 8 and the attachments of an alternator are shown in FIG 9. The fan belt must be correctly tensioned so that there is a maximum movement of 10 mm ($\frac{1}{2}$ inch) and a minimum of 5 mm ($\frac{1}{4}$ inch) when the belt is pressed by moderate thumb pressure at the centre of a run. If the tension is excessive the alternator or generator bearings will be damaged while the belt being too slack will allow it to slip. If the tension is incorrect, slacken the locknut on the adjusting link and turn the adjusting nut until the tension is correct. Tighten the locknut to secure the adjusting nut.

Removal:

Slacken the locknut for adjusting the belt tension and turn the adjusting nut fully downwards to release the tension of the belt. Ease the fan belt off the driving pulley for the alternator or generator in the direction of normal rotation. If the tension is still such that the belt cannot be fully removed, assist it off the pulley by turning the cooling fan in its normal direction of rotation. Free the belt from the crankshaft pulley and lift it over the fan blades. On cars fitted with the optional power assisted steering, the drive belt for the pump must be removed first. Slacken the bolts that secure the pump and then release the tensioner bolt for the pump. Remove the drive belt in a similar manner as for removing the fan belt.

Refit the belt in the reverse order of removal, assisting it on by turning the cooling fan if need be, and set the correct tension. The tension of the drive belt for the power assisted steering should be adjusted so that it moves 10 to 15 mm (.4 to .6 inch) at the centre of a run using moderate thumb pressure.

5 The thermostat

The operation of the thermostat is shown in FIG 10.

Removal:

1 Drain the cooling system at least far enough so that the level is below the thermostat housing.
2 Remove the four socket-headed bolts that secure the cover in place and ease off the cover 4. Usually the hose is sufficiently flexible to allow the cover to be removed without disconnecting it.
3 Remove the sealing ring 2 and withdraw the thermostat.

The thermostat is refitted in the reverse order of removal, making sure that the thermostat is in place before fitting the sealing ring 2.

Grades:

A thermostat that opens at a higher temperature is available for fitting during the winter. This type of thermostat ensures a quicker warm-up period and hotter water for the heater. **The winter-grade thermostat should not be used in hot weather.**

Testing:

As a rough check feel the top tank of the radiator as the engine warms up. The tank should stay cold and the temperature suddenly rise as the thermostat opens. If the

FIG 8 Water pump attachments and fan belt tensioning points on models fitted with a generator

1 Lock nut 5 Socket screw
2 Clamp nut 6 Narrow Vee-belt
3 Hexagon screw 7 Vee-pulley
4 Tensioning screw

tank heats up gradually then it is likely that the thermostat is defective. For accurate testing the thermostat should be removed from the engine.

Suspend, not lay, the thermostat in a saucepan of water. Heat the water slowly while stirring it with a thermometer and note the temperature at which the valve starts to open. For the standard grade the temperature should be 78 to 79°C. and for the winter grade 87°C. If the valve does not start to open within a few degrees of the correct temperature, or if it sticks in the open position, then the thermostat is defective and must be renewed. A defective thermostat cannot be repaired.

6 The water pump

A sectioned view of the water pump is shown in **FIG 2**. The attachments are shown in **FIG 7**.

Different seals have been fitted to the pump at different times and care must be taken to ensure that only the correct spare parts are used to service the pump.

Removal:

Drain the cooling system. Remove the cooling fan from the front of the pump and then take off the fan belt. The bearing housing assembly can be removed, leaving the pump body attached to the engine, by unscrewing the ring of securing bolts that secure it to the housing and then drawing it out.

If the complete pump is being removed, take out the banjo bolts that secure the copper vent pipe, remove the three securing bolts and lift the pump upwards to clear the crankshaft damper and then out from the car, after disconnecting the hoses.

The pump is refitted in the reverse order of removal, using new sealing rings for the banjo bolts and fitting new gaskets in place of any that have been disturbed.

Servicing:

The pump can be dismantled and new parts fitted but special pullers and a fly press are required for satisfactory

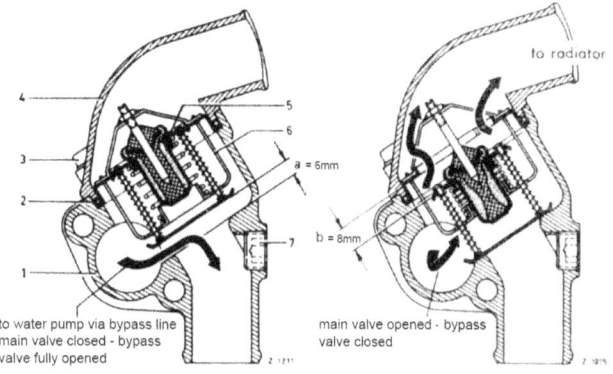

FIG 10   Operation of the thermostat

1 Cooling water thermostat
2 Seal
3 Hexagon socket screw
4 Cover
5 Corrugation[1]
6 Cooling water thermostat element
7 Plug

[1] On later versions the corrugation has been replaced by a check valve on the cooling water thermostat bracket

dismantling and reassembly. If the pump is defective it will have seen long service and rather than try to renew components it will be more satisfactory to fit a new or reconditioned pump in its place. If the pump is dismantled the following points should be noted.

1 Use only the correct type of seals as replacement parts.
2 The impeller should be heated in boiling water before pressing it back onto the shaft as it is an interference fit.
3 The parts must be refitted so that the dimension 'a' is correct at 23 ± .2 mm (.905 ± .008 inch) and the dimension 'b' at 88.9 to 89.0 mm (3.496 to 3.504 inch).
4 When refitting the bearings, the inside of the inner race and the shaft 11 should be degreased and both lightly smeared with Loctite before pressing the bearings back into place. Allow the Loctite to harden for at least 24 hours before filling the pump with 10 cc of Hypoid SAE.90 oil.

If a new or reconditioned pump is fitted to the engine it must be filled with 10 cc of oil before it is put into service, as such pumps are supplied dry.

7 Frost precautions

Antifreeze should always be used in very cold weather. If no antifreeze is used the coolant may freeze in the bottom half of the radiator, as this never becomes really hot in cold weather. Freezing in the radiator will block the system and lead to boiling in the engine and possible damage to the engine.

Preheating the coolant will assist starting in very cold weather, though if the car has been serviced regularly and antifreeze is used in the correct proportions the car should start without special precautions down to a temperature of −25 to −30°C (−13 to −22°F). Preheating can be carried out by draining the cooling system and making the coolant very hot before returning it to the system. There are several recommended makes of electric heater that can be permanently installed into a water hose so that the engine can be kept warm in very cold weather.

The owner's manual gives a full list of the recommended antifreezes but amongst them and generally available are the following:

Gulf Antifreeze and Summer Coolant, Mobil Permazone, Shell Antifreeze (or Antifrost). Veedol Frostfree.

FIG 9   The fan belt tensioning points on models fitted with an alternator

1 Locknut   2 Clamp bolt   3 Adjustment nut

The different models covered by this manual are all fitted with cooling systems of different capacities. The capacity and the amount of antifreeze required are given in the following table. **The quantities are given in litres and the figure in brackets is the amount in Imperial pints.** US measures are labelled as such.

Model and total capacity:	Lowest temperature at which protection is given			
	−10°C (14°F)	−20°C (−4°F)	−30°C (−22°F)	−40°C (−40°F)
230 14 litres, 3.1 Imperial gallons, 3.7 US gallons.	3.2 (6.8)	4.8 (10.2)	6.2 (13.1)	7.3 (15.4)
230S 11.4 litres, 2.5 Imperial gallons, 3.0 US gallons.	2.5 (5.3)	4.25 (9.0)	5.25 (11.0)	5.75 (12.1)
230SL 10.8 litres, 2.4 Imperial gallons, 2.9 US gallons.	2.25 (4)	3.5 (6.25)	4.7 (8.5)	5.5 (9.7)

8 Fault diagnosis

(a) Internal water leakage

1 Loose cylinder head bolts
2 Defective cylinder head gasket
3 Defective oil cooler
4 Cracked cylinder head
5 Cracked cylinder block

(b) Poor circulation

1 Perished or collapsed water hoses
2 Defective thermostat
3 Low coolant level
4 Loose or broken fan belt
5 Engine water passages restricted
6 Radiator water tubes blocked

(c) Corrosion

1 Impurities in the water
2 Lack of inhibitor or antifreeze
3 Inhibitor or antifreeze exhausted
4 Infrequent draining and flushing

(d) Overheating

1 Check (a) and (b)
2 Sludge in the crankcase
3 Incorrect ignition timing
4 Low oil level in the engine sump
5 Tight engine
6 Choked exhaust
7 Binding brakes
8 Slipping clutch
9 Mixture too weak

CHAPTER 5 – THE CLUTCH

1 Description
2 Routine maintenance
3 Servicing hydraulic components
4 The slave cylinder
5 The interior master cylinder
6 The exterior master cylinder
7 Bleeding the clutch hydraulic system
8 The clutch release bearing
9 The clutch
10 Fault diagnosis

1 Description

A sectioned view of the clutch assembly is shown in **FIG 1** and the components of the system, fitted with an interior master cylinder, are shown in **FIG 2**.

The clutch assembly 1 is bolted to the engine flywheel so that it revolves with the engine. The driven plate assembly 14 is splined to the input shaft of the gearbox so that they revolve together. In normal operation the pressure springs 9 act on the pressure plate 11 to thrust it firmly forwards and grip the driven plate 14, by its friction linings 15 and 16, between its front face and the rear face of the engine flywheel. Drive is then transmitted from the engine to the gearbox.

The clutch pedal 3 is pressed, against the action of the return spring 20, and operates the master cylinder 50 through the pushrod 60. Hydraulic pressure is generated in the master cylinder and is transmitted through the flexible hose 84 to the slave cylinder 50. The pushrod 51 of the slave cylinder extends to press the outer end of the release fork 42 rearwards. The release fork pivots about a ball-headed pin in the clutch housing 25 so that its inner end presses the sleeve 40 and release bearing 41 forwards to contact and press in the release levers 3. These levers draw the pressure plate 11 back, against the action of the springs, so that the driven plate is free to revolve independently or even come to a stop with the engine still running. Drive is therefore no longer connected to the gearbox.

On some models an external master cylinder is fitted in the engine compartment instead of inside the car. This type of master cylinder is very similar in construction to the master cylinder fitted to the brakes.

The removal of the clutch from the engine is dealt with in **Chapter 1, Section 10**. It is important to use a centralizing mandrel when refitting the clutch.

2 Routine maintenance

Master cylinder:

At regular intervals check the level of the fluid in the master cylinder reservoir. Irrespective of the position of the master cylinder the reservoir is mounted near the rear bulkhead inside the engine compartment. The reservoir is made of translucent material so that the filler cap does not need to be removed for checking. If the level is low, top up using only an approved hydraulic fluid which meets SAE.70.R3 specification (such as ATE blue). Before removing the filler cap wipe it and the top of the reservoir clean to prevent dirt from falling into the reservoir.

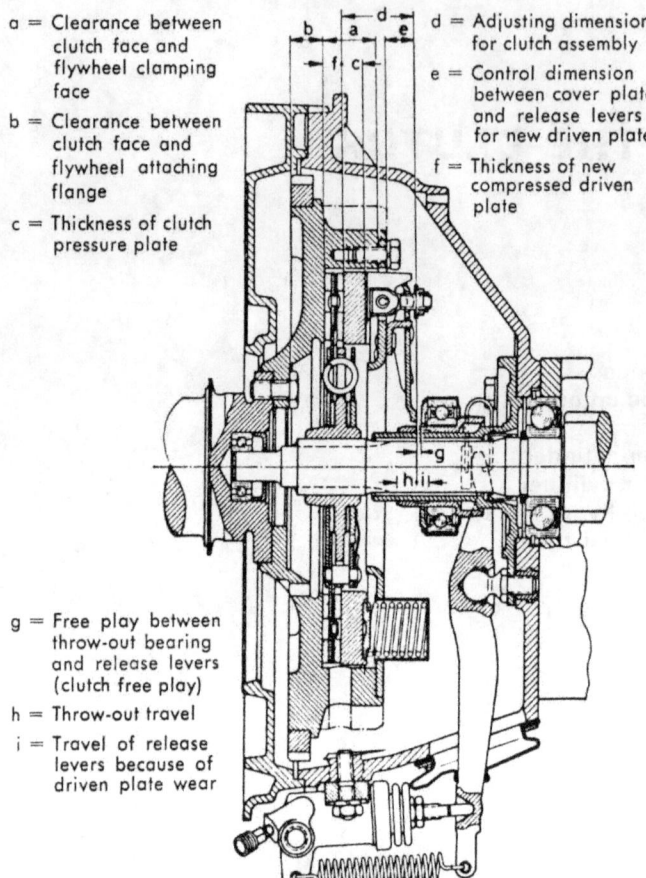

a = Clearance between clutch face and flywheel clamping face
b = Clearance between clutch face and flywheel attaching flange
c = Thickness of clutch pressure plate
d = Adjusting dimension for clutch assembly
e = Control dimension between cover plate and release levers for new driven plate
f = Thickness of new compressed driven plate
g = Free play between throw-out bearing and release levers (clutch free play)
h = Throw-out travel
i = Travel of release levers because of driven plate wear

FIG 1 Sectioned view of the clutch

Constant topping up or a sudden drop in the fluid level indicate a leak in the system. Leaks should be found and rectified as soon as possible otherwise the clutch will drag and eventually fail to release.

Pedal clearance:

The correct pedal clearance is essential for the satisfactory operation of the clutch. If the pedal clearance is not sufficient then the release bearing will always be in contact with the release levers, causing excessive wear, or in bad cases the clutch may never fully engage and slip on engagement.

The adjustment for the internal master cylinder is shown in **FIG 3** and that for the external master cylinder in **FIG 4**. In both cases the adjusting bolts 1 and 31 are eccentric and locked in position by a nut and lockwasher. Slacken the locknut and turn the adjusting bolt until the line scribed on the bolt head, indicating maximum eccentricity, points rearwards on cars fitted with internal master cylinders and in the direction of the pivot pin of the pedals for cars fitted with an external master cylinder. Now adjust the bolt until the clearance 'a' is .2 to .5mm (.008 to .02 inch) in both types. The clearance cannot be measured so it must be set by feel. Tighten the locknut when the adjustment is satisfactory.

Slave cylinder:

At the same time as the pedal clearance is set the slave cylinder should also be adjusted. The method of adjustment is shown in **FIG 5**. The slave cylinder shown is of the later type, secured by nuts instead of bolts, but the principles are the same for the earlier slave cylinder. Disconnect the return spring from the body 1. Move the release lever 2 rearwards until the release bearing can be felt to touch the release levers of the clutch, and then pull the lever back until it is firmly against the pushrod 5. Check the distance S through which it has moved. For correct adjustment the distance S should be 4mm (.16 inch). If the adjustment is not correct, slacken the locknut 3 and, while holding the nut 4 with a spanner, use another spanner to turn the flatted end of the pushrod 5 until the clearance is correct. Tighten the locknut 3 and reconnect the return spring.

3 Servicing hydraulic components

To save repetition for the individual components, general notes on servicing hydraulic components are given in this section. This section applies equally to the braking system (see **Chapter 11**) and to the clutch hydraulics.

It is essential that strict cleanliness is observed when dealing with any parts of the hydraulic system. This includes cleaning the outside of a component before dismantling it, washing the internal parts twice using clean solvent for each wash, covering workbenches with clean paper and even washing the hands before starting reassembly operations.

The method of dismantling each component will be given in the relevant sections.

Seals:

It is advisable to discard all old seals and fit new ones, obtainable in service kits, on reassembly. Take care when ordering new parts as the internal diameters of cylinders vary not only with the different models but also at different periods on the same model.

If the old seals have to be refitted they should be closely examined before reassembly and every possible effort made to fit a new seal in place of a suspect or definitely worn one. Total brake failure may be the consequence of failing to take this precaution. Do not turn a seal inside out to examine it. Check the lips for wear or scoring and check the material for softening, hardening or other form of failure. If the incorrect hydraulic fluid has been used, all the seals in contact with it will soften, swell and then fail. **All the seals in the system must be renewed and the system flushed through with methylated spirits if the incorrect fluid has been accidentally put into the hydraulic reservoir.**

No tools should be used to refit the seals and they should be worked into position using only the fingers. Dip the seal into clean hydraulic fluid and refit it wet. Work the seal around so that it seats fully and squarely into its recess. Make sure that the seal is fitted facing the correct direction, with its lips pointing towards the high-pressure side.

Cleaning:

Only methylated spirits or hydraulic fluid of the correct type (Specification SAE.70.R3) may be allowed to come into contact with the seals. Once the unit has been dismantled the metal parts only may be cleaned in any solvent

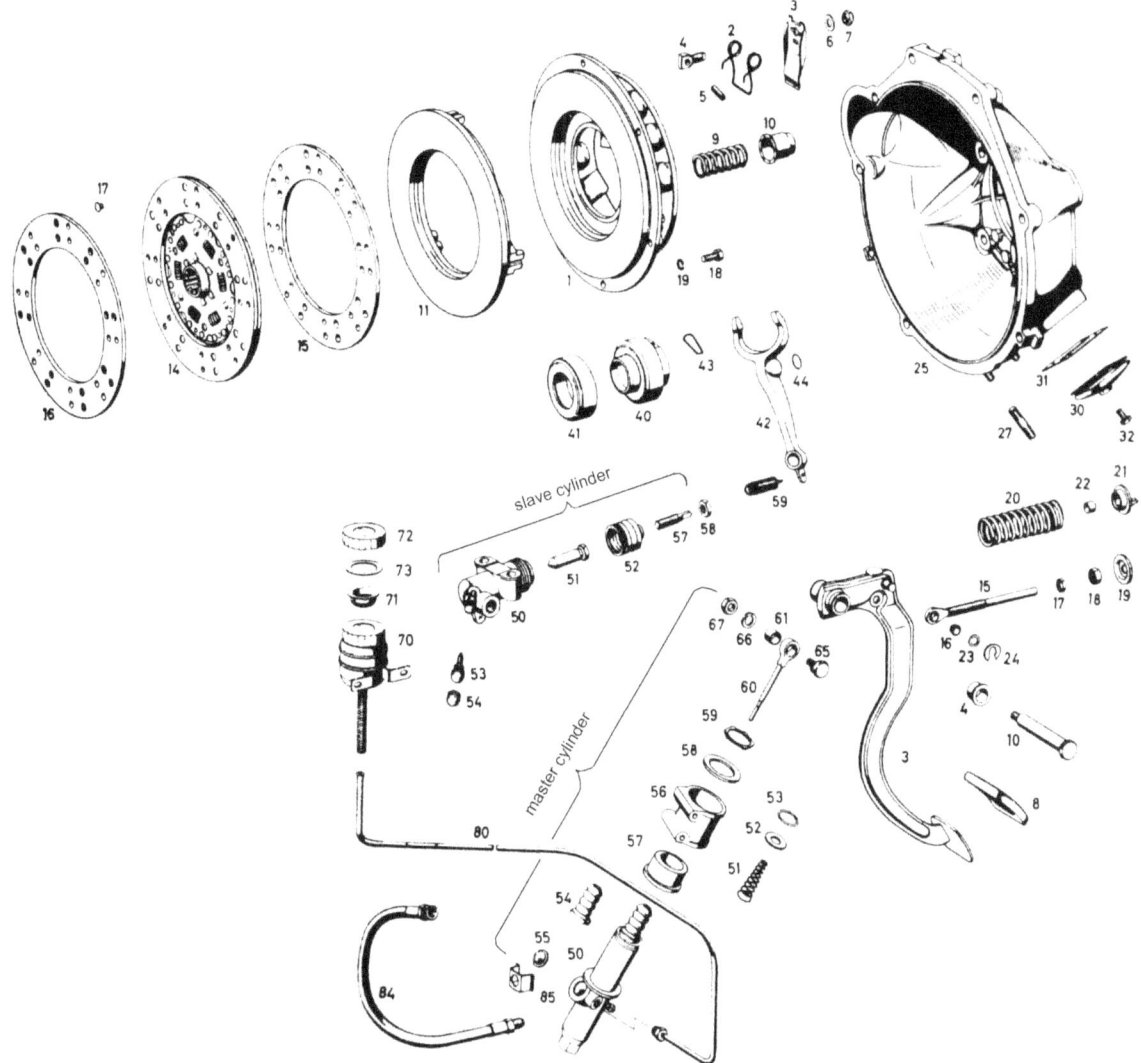

FIG 2 The details of the clutch and its hydraulic release mechanism, fitted with an interior master cylinder

that evaporates rapidly and completely. It is essential that no traces of such solvents are left on the metal parts when the unit is being reassembled. Small bores or passages may be cleaned out by blowing through them with an airline or by very careful poking with a blunt-ended piece of wire. Avoid touching highly-finished parts with the bare hand as the acid on the hand will cause corrosion.

Pipelines can be cleaned by flushing them through with methylated spirits. It is advisable to dismantle the system and renew all seals at intervals of three years. The system should be flushed by pumping at least $\frac{1}{4}$ litre ($\frac{1}{2}$ pint) of methylated spirits through each bleed nipple in the system before it is dismantled.

Examination:

After the parts have been cleaned they should be inspected for wear or defects. Check springs for weakness or corrosion and renew any that are defective. Pay particular attention to the bores of cylinders. These must be smooth with a highly-polished finish. Renew the complete component if the bore shows any signs of wear, scoring or corrosion.

Reassembly:

All internal parts should be dipped into clean hydraulic fluid and refitted while wet. On most components it will be found that the piston complete with seals must be pressed into the bore of the cylinder and it will also be found that the lips of the seals face into the cylinder. Enter the piston carefully, taking care not to tilt it if it is short compared with its diameter and press it in until the seal is just about to enter. Use either the fingers or a very blunt tool to press down the lips of the seal and carefully push the piston into the bore. Make sure that the seal is entered correctly all the way around and that the lips are not bent back or otherwise damaged. Do not rush the operation and withdraw the piston partially if the first attempt is not successful.

4 The slave cylinder

Two mountings and sectioned views of the two main variants of slave cylinder are shown in **FIGS 6** and **7**. If the threads on the clutch housing strip (more likely on the earlier version that is secured by bolts), then Heli-Coil inserts can be fitted to repair the damage.

3 Take off the two securing nuts, bolts on the earlier version, and remove the slave cylinder from the car.

The slave cylinder is refitted in the reverse order of removal, without straining or twisting the flexible portion of the hose. Make sure that the slave cylinder fits flush onto the machined portion of the clutch housing and that at all other points there is a minimum clearance of 1 mm (.04 inch). Insufficient clearance will cause the slave cylinder to bind and the clutch to operate stiffly, and will also lead to early failure of the slave cylinder.

When the slave cylinder has been refitted the reservoir must be refilled and the system bled. Adjust both the pedal and slave cylinder clearances.

Servicing:

The unit is dismantled by removing the protective cap and then using gentle air pressure at the inlet to blow out the internal parts.

Reassemble in the reverse order of dismantling after cleaning, checking and renewing parts.

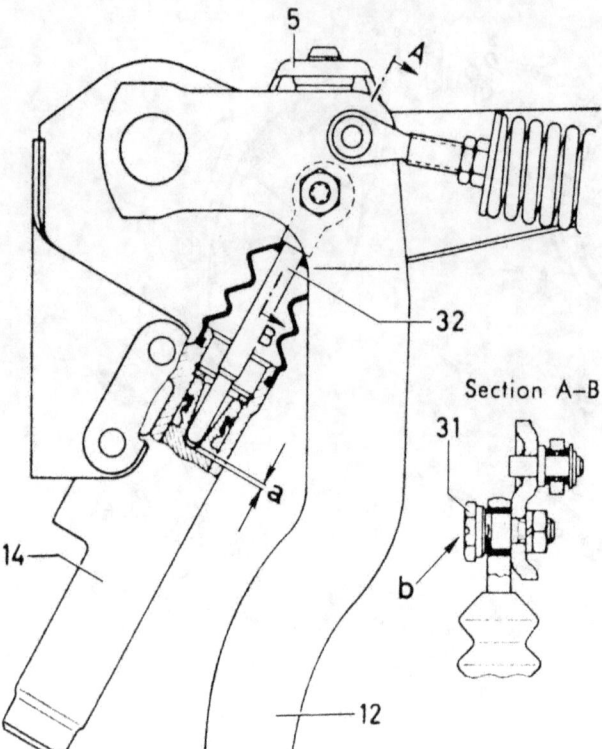

FIG 3 Adjusting the pedal clearance on the interior master cylinder

5 Rubber stop for clutch pedal
12 Clutch pedal
14 Master cylinder
31 Adjusting bolt with hexagon nut and lock washer
32 Piston rod
a = Clearance between piston and piston rod
b = Line marking

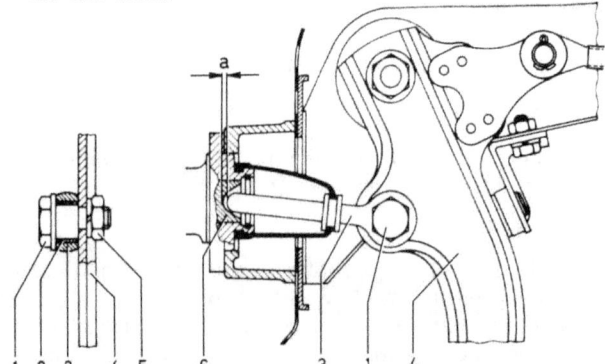

FIG 4 Adjusting the pedal clearance on the exterior master cylinder

1 Adjusting bolt
2 Bushing in piston rod
3 Piston rod
4 Clutch pedal
5 Hexagon nut
6 Piston
a = clearance between piston and piston rod

Removal:

1 Attach a length of plastic or rubber tube to the bleed nipple on the slave cylinder. Put the free end of the tube into a suitable metal or glass container. Slacken the bleed nipple one or two turns and empty the hydraulic system by pumping the clutch pedal.
2 Remove the return spring. Disconnect the union for the flexible hose at the master cylinder end and then unscrew the flexible hose from the slave cylinder, leaving the flexible portion to rotate freely without straining or twisting.

FIG 5 Adjusting the slave cylinder, later type shown

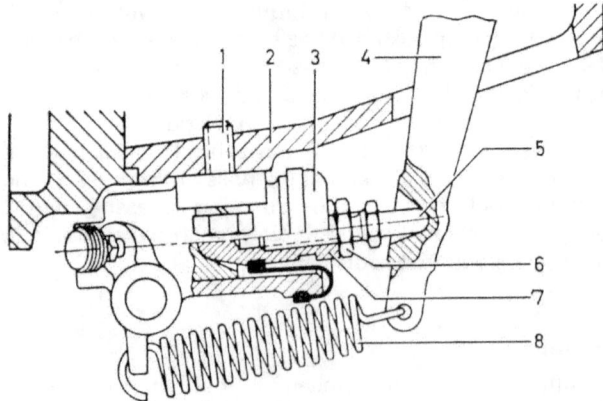

FIG 6 Early slave cylinder

1 Hexagon bolt
2 Clutch housing
3 Protective cap (roll-type cuff)
4 Throw-out fork
5 Push rod (length 49 mm)
6 Hexagon nut
7 Pressure pin (length 38 mm)
8 Return spring (1st Version)

5 The interior master cylinder

The attachments of the unit are shown in **FIG 8** and a sectioned view is shown in **FIG 9**.

Removal:

1 Empty the hydraulic system by pumping the fluid out through the bleed nipple on the slave cylinder.
2 Lay rags in place to catch any drips and disconnect the pipelines 5 and 13 after removing the panel under the cowl. Blank the free ends of the pipes to prevent the ingress of dirt.
3 Undo the nuts 16, remove the bolts and remove the master cylinder 12 from the car.

The master cylinder can be dismantled after taking off the protective rubber cap and removing the snap ring that secures the internal parts in place. Check and reassemble the parts as described in **Section 3**.

The unit is refitted in the reverse order of removal, making sure that the pushrod fits correctly into the piston.

Fill and bleed the system and then adjust the pedal clearance.

6 The exterior master cylinder

A typical unit is shown sectioned in **FIG 10** and its attachments are shown in **FIG 11**. The unit has the reservoir integral with it and most of them are fitted with a bleed screw.

Some earlier models will have a tilt valve, operated by the piston, in place of the bores shown for connecting the cylinder to the reservoir at the end of the stroke. The tilt valve must be removed first before the internal parts are taken out. The internal parts can be taken out after removing the snap ring that secures them in place.

Removal of the unit is done in a straightforward manner by draining the system, disconnecting the pipe 10 and taking off the two securing nuts. Before removing the unit it will be necessary to remove the battery from the car in order to gain access room. Refit the master cylinder in the reverse order of removal followed by filling, bleeding and adjusting the pedal clearance.

7 Bleeding the clutch hydraulic system

This is not routine maintenance and need only be carried out when air has entered the system, either by

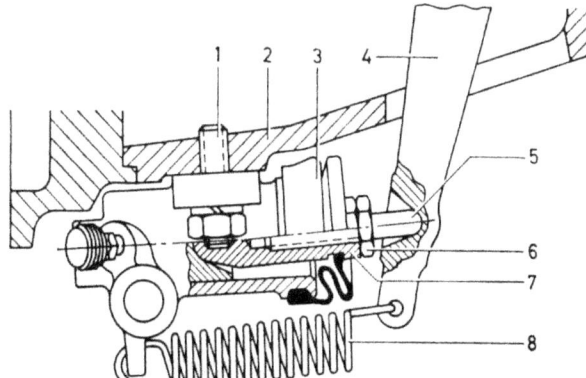

FIG 7 Later slave cylinder

1 Stud bolt
2 Clutch housing
3 Protective cap (bellows-type cuff)
4 Throw-out fork
5 Push rod (length 43 mm)
6 Hexagon nut
7 Pressure pin (length 45 mm or 53 mm)
8 Return spring (2nd version)

FIG 8 The attachments of the interior master cylinder

1 Clutch pedal
2 Brake pedal
3 Cover plate
4 Pipe clip
5 Line to slave cylinder
6 Hexagon screw with washer
7 Steering column jacket
8 Tightening strap
9 Opening for slotted screw
10 Mechanical stop light switch
11 Stop ring for brake pedal
12 Master cylinder
13 Line from reservoir to supply cylinder
14 Piston rod
15 Pressure spring (dead center spring)
16 Hexagon bolt with lock washer and nut
17 Stop screw
18 Pedal lever
19 Plastic plate
20 Hexagon nut
21 Foot plate
22 Bracket with ball heads

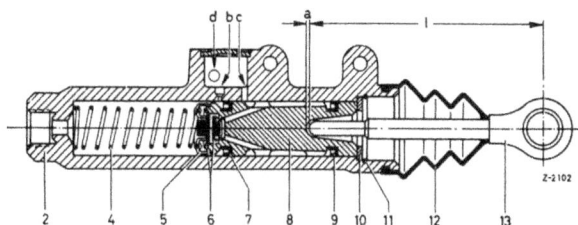

FIG 9 Sectioned view of the interior master cylinder

2 Housing
4 Pressure spring
5 Cap
6 Valve
7 Primary cup
8 Piston
9 Secondary cup
10 Stop washer
11 Snap ring
12 Protective cap
13 Piston rod
a = Clearance between piston and piston rod
b = Compensating port
c = Connecting port
d = Intake port from reservoir
l = Length of piston rod

dismantling or by allowing the level in the reservoir to fall so low that air is drawn into the master cylinder.

If difficulty is experienced in removing all the air the car should be taken to an agent who will bleed the system using pressure equipment.

Before starting to bleed the system fill the reservoir right up with fresh hydraulic fluid (Specification SAE.70.R3 only) and then keep a constant check on the level, topping up regularly as required.

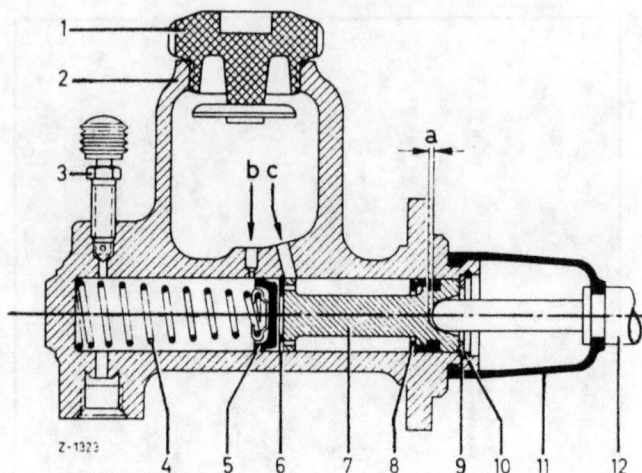

FIG 10 Sectional view of the exterior master cylinder

1 Screw cap	9 Stop washer
2 Fluid reservoir	10 Snap ring
3 Bleed screw	11 Protective cap
4 Pressure spring	12 Piston rod (46 mm long)
5 Primary cup	a = Clearance between
6 Piston cup washer	piston and piston rod
7 Piston	b = Compensating port
8 Secondary cup	c = Connecting port

FIG 11 The attachments of the exterior master cylinder

1 Filler cap	5-9 Brake lines	13 Flash direction signal
2 Filler cap	10 Supply line (pipe)	14 Plug connection
3 Bleed screw	11 Stop light switch	15 Upper beam flash signal
4 Bleed screw	12 Plug connection	16 Plug connection

Do not return fluid that has been bled directly to the reservoir. Preferably discard the old fluid but if it is perfectly clean store it for 24 hours in a sealed clean container to allow all the air bubbles to disperse, before using it again.

On models fitted with external master cylinders bleed through the nipple fitted to the master cylinder first and then bleed through the nipple fitted to the slave cylinder. Internal master cylinders are not fitted with a bleed nipple.

1 Attach a length of plastic or rubber tube to the bleed nipple and dip the free end of the tube into a little clean hydraulic fluid in a clean glass container.

2 Open the bleed nipple one or two turns and have an assistant press the clutch pedal right down to the floor. Close the bleed nipple and then have the assistant release the clutch pedal so that it returns rapidly on its own.

3 Carry on bleeding by this method until the fluid coming out of the tube is perfectly free of any air bubbles. Remove the bleed tube, making sure that the nipple is closed, and top up the reservoir to the correct level.

Any hydraulic fluid spilled onto paintwork should be wiped off immediately as it rapidly softens and removes paint. Dirty hydraulic fluid can be kept as it makes an excellent substitute for penetrating oil. Any such dirty fluid should be clearly labelled so that there is no danger of using it in the hydraulic system.

8 The clutch release bearing

This is fitted inside the clutch housing and in order to gain access to it the gearbox must be removed from the engine (see **Chapter 6, Section 2**).

The bearing is sealed and lubricated for life so it normally requires no attention. It should be examined whenever the gearbox is removed from the engine. **Because the bearing is prelubricated it must be removed from the clutch housing if the housing is washed out with any solvent otherwise the grease will be washed out.** If the bearing runs roughly or appears worn it should be renewed.

The attachments of the bearing are shown in **FIG 12**. Press the spring clips 2 rearwards out of the release lever 4 and then pull them up and out as shown. Slide the release unit off along the input shaft of the gearbox.

The best method of freeing the bearing from its sleeve is to fit a suitable stepped mandrel into the sleeve and then bang the parts firmly down onto a hard surface as shown

FIG 12 The attachments of the clutch release bearing assembly

1 Throw-out unit and bearing	3 Transmission case front cover
2 Spring clip	4 Throw-out fork

in **FIG 13**. Failing this use a suitable puller or as a last resort saw the bearing carefully off the sleeve.

Lubricate the sliding surfaces and annular groove with Kenlube M.621 or some similar grease. The parts are an interference fit so the sleeve should be supercooled (try cooling in a deep-freeze or even in the ice compartment of a refrigerator). Press the new bearing onto the sleeve and refit the parts in the reverse order of removal.

In February 1964 the design of the release unit was completely altered and the version fitted to 230SL models before chassis number 002.500 is shown in **FIG 14**. The later version fitted to all other models covered by this manual is shown in **FIG 15**. The two versions are not interchangeable in any way and an attempt to do so will either ruin the release bearing immediately or else make it impossible to adjust the clutch free play correctly.

9 The clutch

The method of removing and replacing the clutch on the engine flywheel is dealt with in **Chapter 1, Section 10**.

Driven plate condition:

Examine the driven plate for signs of mechanical damage such as loose damper springs, pulled rivets or cracks. Check the hub for worn or cracked splines. Renew the driven plate if it is damaged as above or the friction linings are worn down nearly to the rivet heads.

The friction linings are operating at their maximum efficiency if they have a polished glaze through which the grain of the material is clearly visible. Any oil on the linings will reduce the efficiency of the clutch, causing it to slip, drag or judder depending on the quantity of oil.

Small quantities of oil will leave dark coloured smears on the linings while large quantities will leave a dark glazed deposit. The friction plate may be used again provided that the oil deposits are not so thick as to hide the grain of the friction material. Large amounts of oil will be obvious from the oil-soaked appearance of the linings and the free oil in the clutch housing. In all cases the source of the oil must be found and the leak rectified before refitting the clutch.

Fit the driven plate back onto the input shaft of the gearbox and check that there is no excessive rotational

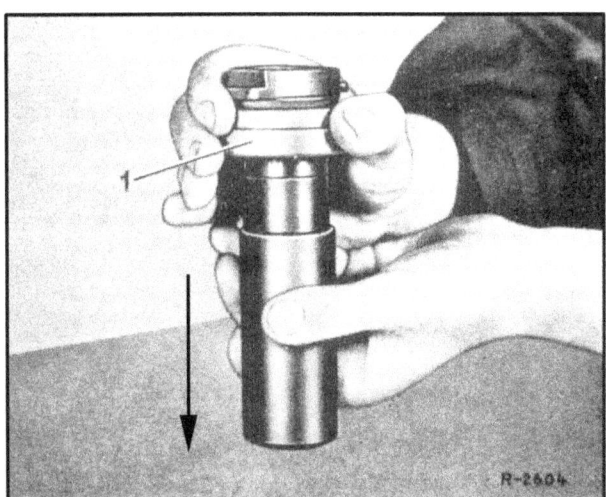

FIG 5:13 Method of removing the release bearing using a suitable stepped mandrel   1 Throw-out bearing

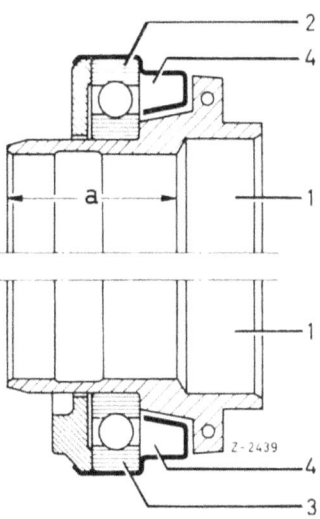

FIG 14 The clutch release bearing assembly fitted to early 230SL models

1 Throw-out unit
2 Throw-out bearing four-cylinder models
3 Throw-out bearing six-cylinder models
4 Circular chamber for grease cake
a = Supporting length of guide sleeve = 31.5 mm

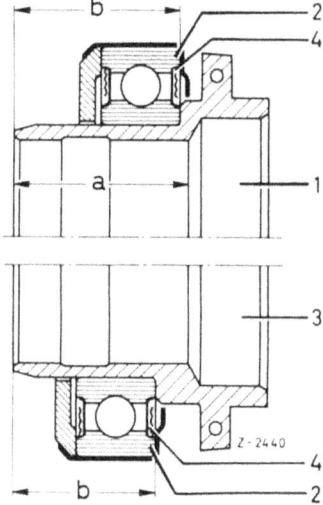

FIG 15 The clutch release bearing assembly fitted to all models except the early 230SL

1 Throw-out unit four-cylinder models
2 Throw-out bearing
3 Throw-out unit six-cylinder models
4 Positive seal
a = Supporting length of guide sleeve = 33.5 mm
b = Length of bearing sleeve for four-cylinder models = 31.5 mm
    for six-cylinder models = 27 mm

play between them, and that the driven plate slides freely on the splines.

Servicing the clutch:

When the clutch has been removed from the engine give it a careful cleaning and thorough examination. The clutch can be dismantled into its component parts but it is not advisable for the owner to do this, as special gauges are required to reassemble the clutch accurately. If the clutch is not assembled accurately one side will grip before the other, causing judder, noisy operation and rapid wear of the release bearing.

Check the cover for cracks, particularly around the mounting holes, and for signs of distortion. The operating face of the pressure plate should be checked for deep burn marks or scores. Light burn marks on the pressure plate are acceptable. Fit a new or reconditioned clutch if the old one is defective or the springs broken.

Before refitting the clutch lubricate pivot points and the splines on the input shaft lightly with Kenlube M.621 or white zinc-base grease.

If the gearbox has been dismantled or an old input shaft is available the input shaft can be used instead of the special mandrel for centralizing the driven plate while refitting the clutch.

10 Fault diagnosis

(a) Drag or spin

1 Oil or grease on the friction linings
2 Incorrectly adjusted pedal clearance
3 Incorrectly adjusted slave cylinder
4 Misalignment between the engine and gearbox
5 Leaking master cylinder, slave cylinder or pipeline
6 Binding of the input shaft spigot bearing in the crankshaft
7 Distorted driven plate
8 Warped or damaged pressure plate
9 Broken driven plate linings
10 Dirt or foreign matter in the clutch
11 Air in the hydraulic system

(b) Fierceness or snatch

1 Check 1, 2, 3, 4 and 5 in (a)
2 Worn friction linings

(c) Slip

1 Check 1, 2 and 3 in (a) and 2 in (b)
2 Weak pressure springs
3 Seized piston in slave cylinder

(d) Judder

1 Check 1, 4, 7, 8 and 9 in (a)
2 Contact area of friction linings not evenly distributed
3 Faulty engine mountings
4 Defective rear suspension or propeller shaft

(e) Rattle

1 Check 2 in (c)
2 Broken spring in driven plate
3 Worn release mechanism
4 Release bearing loose on release lever

(f) Tick or knock

1 Worn spigot bearing in crankshaft
2 Badly worn splines on driven plate hub or gearbox input shaft
3 Worn release bearing
4 Loose flywheel

CHAPTER 6 – GEARBOX

1 Description
2 Removing the gearbox
3 The steering column mounted gearlever
4 The floor mounted gearlever
5 Dismantling the gearbox
6 Reassembling the gearbox
7 Fault diagnosis

1 Description

The standard models are fitted with a fourspeed gearbox. There is synchromesh engagement on all four forward speeds but reverse is engaged by sliding a spur-cut idler wheel into mesh between spur-cut gears on the countershaft and mainshaft assemblies.

The components of the gearbox are shown in **FIG 1**. Selection of the forward speeds is by sliding the outer sleeve 50 or 65 of the synchromesh units 45 and 60, using the selector forks in the top cover. The actual gears themselves are helical cut and are always in mesh but rotate freely on the mainshaft 40. As the operating sleeve of the synchromesh unit is moved towards selection, the appropriate baulk ring 44 or 59 is pressed onto the mating cone of the gear and drive is taken up from the gear to the synchromesh unit and from there to the mainshaft. The mainshaft then starts rotating at its correct speed so that further movement of the operating sleeve can engage it with the smaller teeth on the side of the main gear and make the drive fully positive. This allows the gear to be smoothly selected without jarring as the car is moving, and by having all synchromesh engagement the gearbox can be downshifted into first gear while the car is moving. Reverse gear is selected by sliding the idler 8 into mesh between the gear on the countershaft and the outer sleeve 65 of the first/second synchromesh unit. There is no need for synchromesh engagement as reverse is only selected when the car is stationary.

On the saloon models the gearlever is mounted on the steering column and the parts as well as the top cover are shown in **FIG 2**. The 230SL is fitted with a floor mounted gearlever and the parts of this system are shown in **FIG 3**. The floor mounted gearlever can also be fitted as an optional extra to saloon models.

Lubrication is by oil bath and splash from the revolving gears. Automatic transmission fluid (ATF type A) should be used for lubrication in the manually operated gearbox as well as automatic transmissions. A drain plug 106, with seal 107, is fitted under the gearbox case 1 and a combined level and filler plug 105 is fitted on the right-hand side of the case. This is accessible under a rubber cover in the transmission tunnel.

2 Removing the gearbox

The gearbox can be removed from the car while leaving the engine still fitted. The gearbox is taken out from underneath the car, so the car must be raised on secure ramps or work carried out from a pit. **Do not rely on unsteady supports as these can let the car fall and cause a serious accident.**

1 Disconnect the battery and disconnect the leads to the reverse light switch. Drain the oil from the gearbox.
2 Disconnect the gear selector mechanism. On cars fitted with a steering column gearlever, disconnect the ball joints 144 and 147 of the pushrods 142 and 145 from the ball ends of the levers 120 and 134 of the bearing box assembly (see **FIG 2**). The disconnection points are also shown at 1 and 2 in **FIG 4**. On the models fitted with floor mounted gearlevers remove both nuts 188 and free both pushrods 182 from the top cover of the gearbox. Take out the clamp bolt that secures the fork end 34 to the shift tube 155

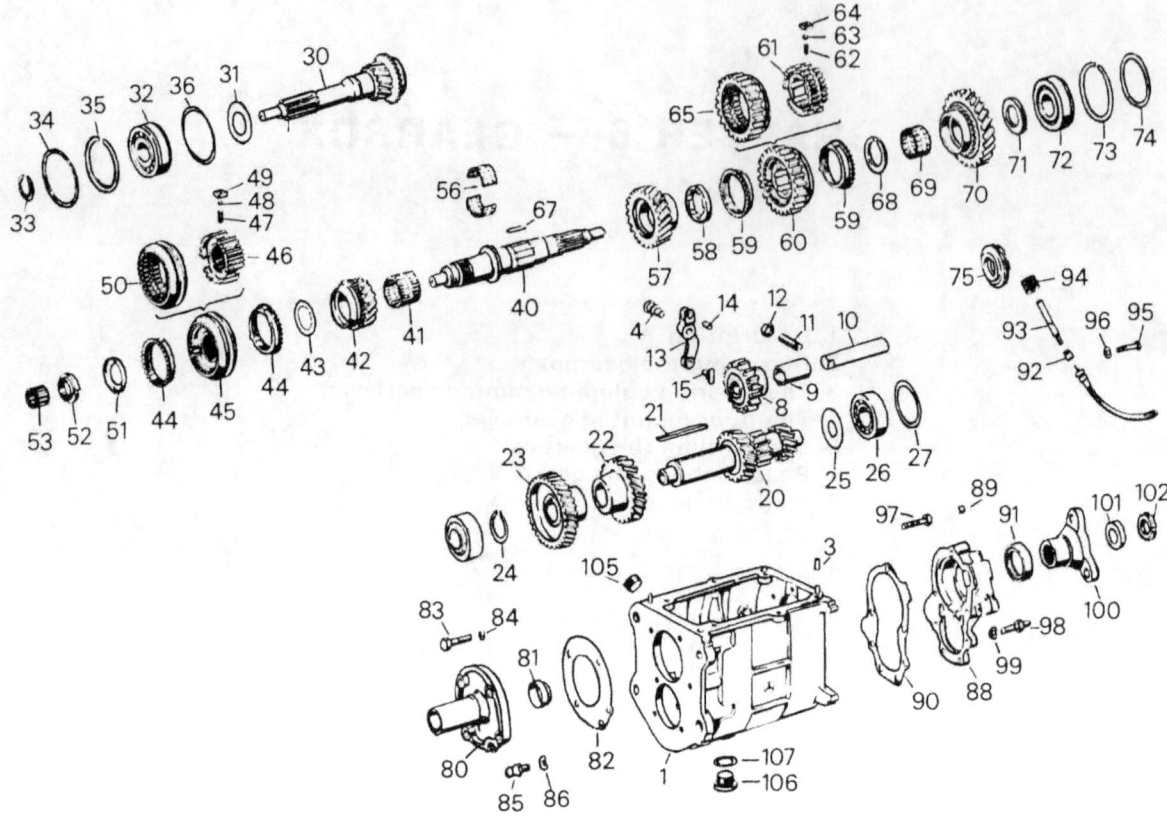

FIG 1 The gearbox components

1 Gearbox case	32 Ballbearing	57 Second-speed gearwheel	82 Gasket
3 Dowel pin	33 Snap ring	58 Lockwasher	83 Coverbolt
4 Pivot pin	34 Spacer ring	59 Baulk ring	84 Washer
8 Reverse idler gear	35 Snap ring	60 Synchronizer unit, first/second	85 Bolt
9 Reverse idler gear bush	36 Shim	61 Synchronizer hub	86 Washer
10 Reverse idler shaft	40 Mainshaft	62 Detent spring	88 Gearbox rear cover
11 Locking stud	41 Needle roller bearing	63 Detent ball	89 Plug
12 Locknut	42 Mainshaft third-speed gear	64 Shoes	90 Gasket
13 Reverse selector lever	43 Serrated (lock) washer	65 Operating sleeve	91 Rear oil seal
15 Engagement shoe	44 Baulk ring	67 Locking key	92 to 95 Speedometer drive parts
20 Countershaft	45 Synchronizer unit third/top	68 Thrust washer	97 Bolts
21 Key	46 Synchronizer hub	69 Needle roller bearing	98 Stud
22 Third-speed gear	47 Detent spring	70 First-speed gear	99 Washer
23 Constant drive gear	48 Detent ball	71 Thrust washer	100 Drive flange
24 Circlip	49 Shoes	72 Mainshaft bearing	101 Lockwasher
25 Thrust washer	50 Operating sleeve	73 Snap ring	102 Grooved nut
26 Ballbearing	51 Lockwasher	74 Shim	105 Oil filler and level plug
27 Shim	52 Grooved nut	75 Speedometer drive gear	106 Oil drain plug
30 Input shaft	53 Needle roller bearing	80 Gearbox front cover	107 Sealing washer
31 Shim	56 Needle roller halves	81 Insert	

and ease the shift tube out. A sectioned view of the floor mounted gearlever is shown in **FIG 11**.

In both cases the shift tubes and pushrods must be held up safely out of the way as the gearbox is being removed or replaced.

3 Working underneath the car, disconnect the propeller shaft (see **Chapter 8, Section 2**). Disconnect the speedometer drive cable from the gearbox and remove the clutch slave cylinder from the clutch housing. Do not disconnect the flexible hose to the clutch slave cylinder but instead take off the mounting nuts (bolts on earlier models) and wire the slave cylinder safely out of the way so that the flexible hose is not strained or twisted.

4 The attachments of the gearbox are shown in **FIG 5**. Use a small jack and block of wood under the rear of the engine to raise the gearbox until the load is just taken off the rear rubber mounting. Undo the nuts that secure the exhaust pipe mounting bracket to the transmission and free the bracket. Scribe lines to mark the position of the support member, as shown at 20 and then remove the support member by undoing the bolts that secure it to the chassis and the nut that secures it to the rubber mounting. On the 230SL the tunnel coverplate must be removed from the chassis by undoing the 16 bolts that secure it. Take off the nuts that secure the mounting assembly to the rear cover of the gearbox and remove the assembly complete with the mounting plate.

5 Remove the two nuts and bolts that secure the starter motor in place. **Slacken both of these evenly otherwise a lug may be broken off the starter**

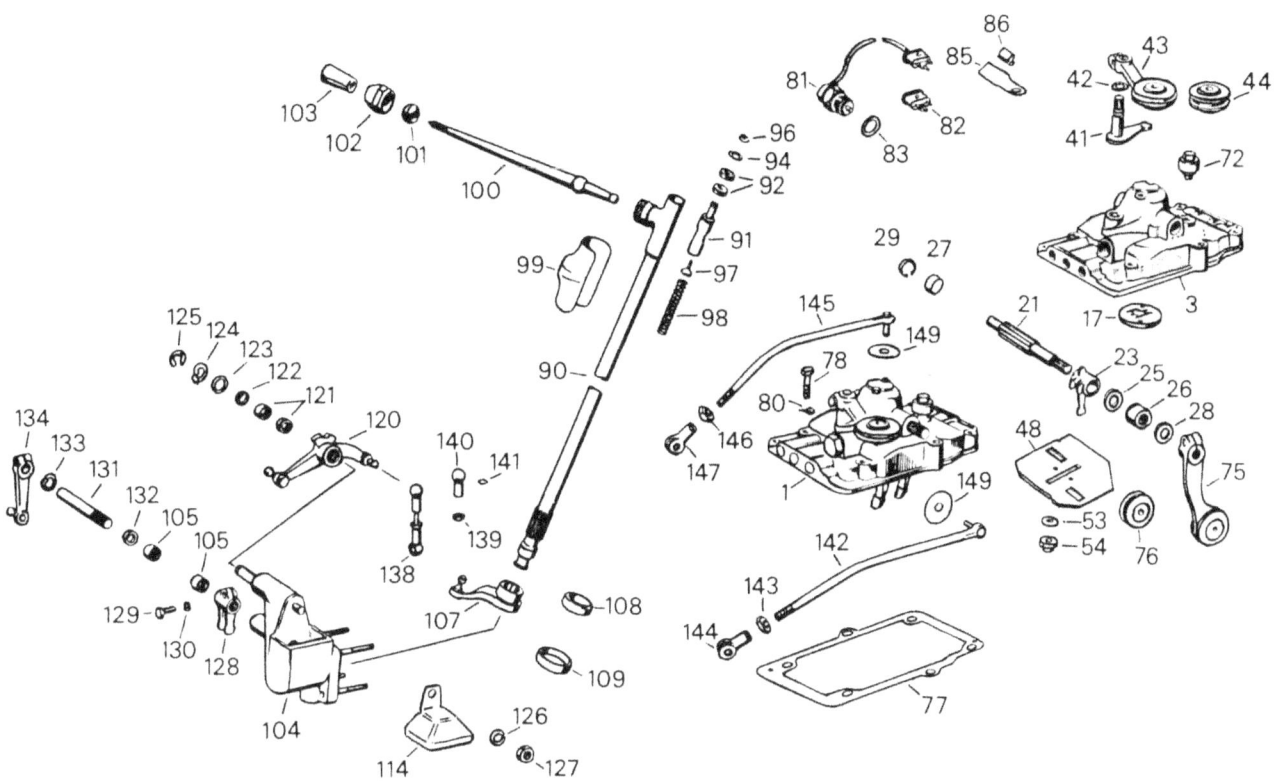

FIG 2 The steering column mounted gearlever parts and gearbox top cover

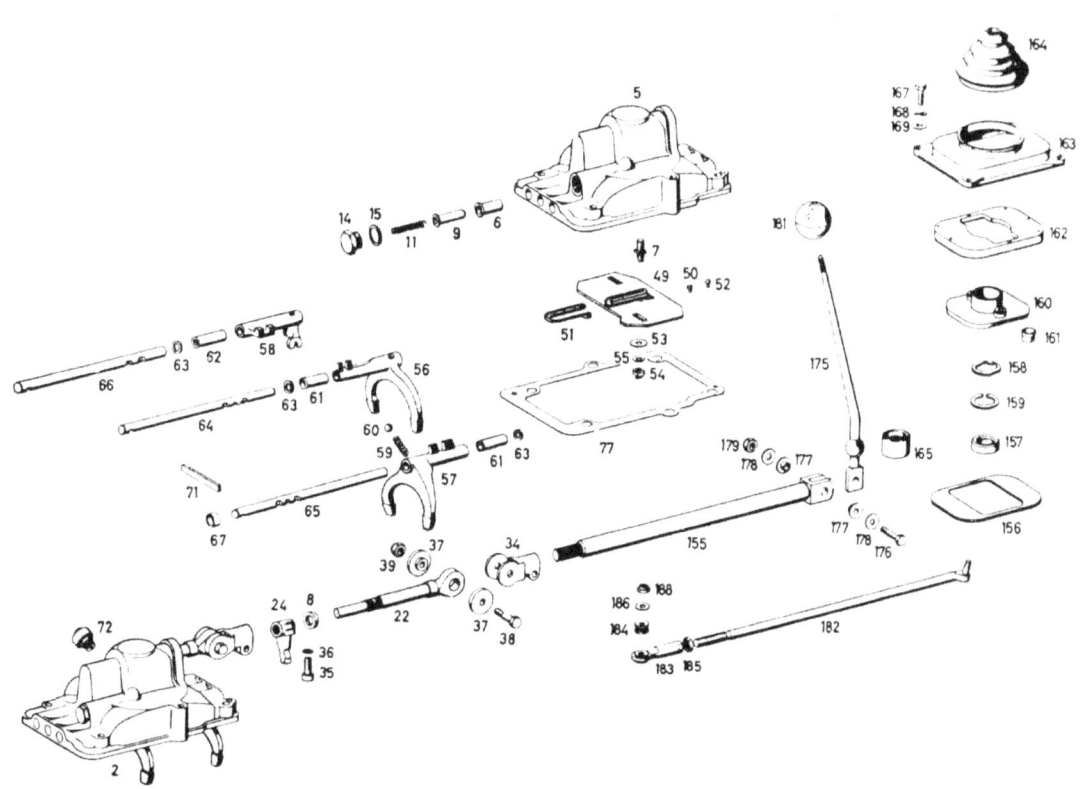

FIG 3 The floor mounted gearlever parts and gearbox top cover

FIG 4 Gearshift bearing assembly fitted to the steering column

1 Selector rod 4 Relay lever 7 Flexible speedometer drive
2 Shift rod 5 Fixing clip 8 Spring-loaded ball connector
3 Cover 6 Selector lever

FIG 5   The gearbox attachments

9 Mounting plate 16 Hexagon nut 21 Hexagon bolts
11 Rubber mounting 18 Hexagon bolts 23 Hexagon bolt
12 Support member 20 Alignment marks 24 Slave cylinder

motor. Remove the bolts that secure the clutch housing to the engine flange. Not all the bolts are readily accessible and it is advisable to have a range of spanners including a socket set with a long flexible drive.

6 Support the weight of the gearbox and withdraw it rearwards until its input shaft is free from the clutch. **Do not allow the weight of the gearbox to hang on the input shaft,** either when removing or replacing the gearbox, otherwise the clutch will be damaged. When the gearbox is free turn it to the right and lower it down out of the car.

When the gearbox has been removed from the engine the following additional points should always be checked:

1 Examine the clutch release bearing and renew it if it is worn or noisy. The release bearing assembly must be removed if the clutch housing is to be washed out with any solvent.
2 Remove the clutch from the flywheel and check the condition of the driven plate and clutch. Fit new parts as required.
3 Rectify any oil leaks that may allow oil to reach the clutch

The gearbox is refitted in the reverse order of removal, noting the following points:

1 Lightly grease the input shaft with white zinc based grease and slide the gearbox back into place, making sure that the shift tubes and pushrods of the selector linkage are not jammed. Do not release the weight of the gearbox until it is firmly in position.
2 When refitting the bolts that secure the clutch housing to the flange, note that the earth cable from the battery attaches to the bolt behind the oil filter and the earth cable for the engine attaches to the top mounting bolt for the starter. Tighten both starter mounting bolts evenly to prevent cracking off a lug from the starter.
3 Refit the rubber support mounting assembly to the rear cover of the gearbox and then attach it to the support member, or tunnel cover on 230SL models. On the 230SL model all the bolts can be tightened immediately but on other models the support 12 should be aligned with the marks 20 made originally and only lightly secured to the chassis, and the bolts 18 fully tightened when the weight of the car is on its own wheels in a level position.
4 Check the adjustment of the rubber mounting. A view of the rear mounting assembly is shown in **FIG 6** and a sectioned view of the rubber mounting for the 230SL is shown in **FIG 7**. The bolt 6 should be turned until the protrusion 'a' is correct at 21 mm (.827 inch) measured with a depth gauge and the nut 19 then fitted while preventing the bolt 6 from turning.
5 When all the parts have been refitted adjust the slave cylinder clearance and fill the gearbox up to the level plug with ATF type A fluid.

3 The steering column mounted gearlever

All the parts have already been shown in **FIG 2**. The details of the later bearing assembly are shown in **FIG 8** and the gearlever attached to the earlier steering column is shown in **FIG 9**. Later versions of the bearing assembly vary little from the earlier versions except that the link is no longer spring-loaded but solid and adjustable, and the drain hole 37a is not fitted to earlier models. The main differences in the later steering column are in the attachment of the steering wheel and not the gearlever.

Stiffness in operation:

1 Check that the steering column is not misaligned. Slacken the bolts securing the coverplate 13 and realign it so as to remove any obstruction. At the same time it is advisable to slacken the nuts that hold the steering column strap to ensure that the column itself is not forced. Retighten all the nuts when the parts are satisfactorily aligned.
2 If the shift lever 31, shown in **FIG 8**, binds in its recess it should be removed and checked. The lever must have freedom of movement in the shift tube and there must also be a slight amount of radial and end play. If necessary, carefully bend the claws of the lever slightly apart or grind them down.
3 If the ball sockets on the pushrods are stiff they should be disconnected and lightly greased before refitting

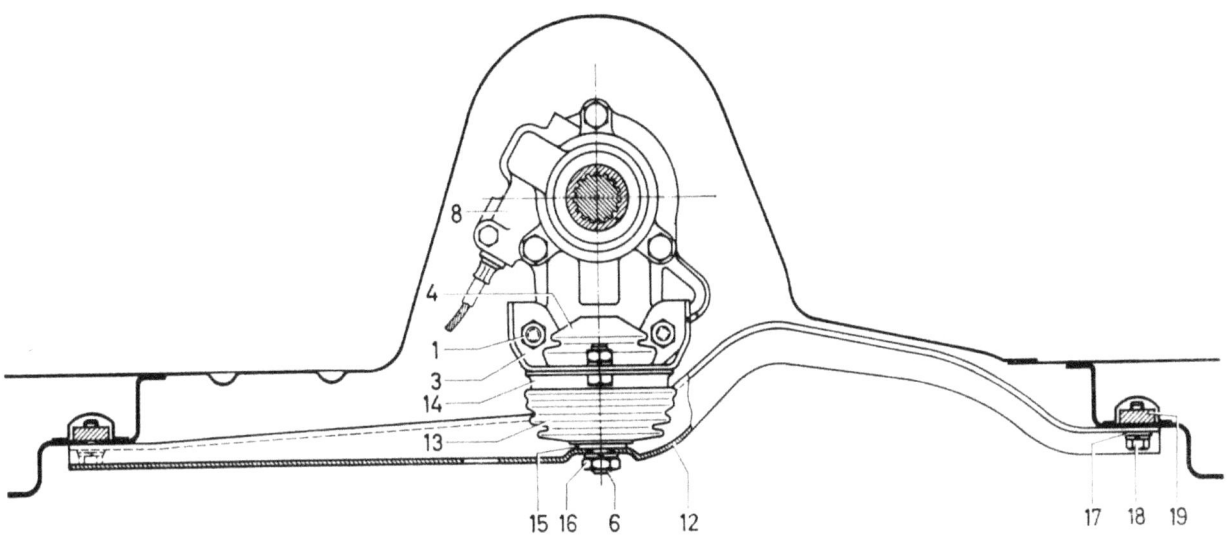

FIG 6 The gearbox rear mounting assembly

1 Hexagon nut	4 Bellows	8 Transmission case rear cover	12 Support
3 Rear engine support	6 Bolt		13 Bellows

14 Rubber mounting	16 Hexagon nut	18 Bolt
15 Sheet-metal cover	17 Washer	19 Nut

them. If this does not cure the stiffness they should be opened slightly using a pair of pliers.
4 If the shift tube is stiff to move its rubber cover should be lubricated with talc. If this fails to cure the fault a modified rubber cover, Part No. 111.268.01.97 should be fitted.
5 Damaged or strained parts should be renewed.

Adjustment:

Check that all the gears engage smoothly and easily. While carrying out a gear selection depress the clutch pedal even though the engine is not running. Check that the reverse gear has a positive resistance against engagement. If reverse gear can be selected without resistance the detent assembly in the gearbox top cover is defective.

Select either second or top gear and check the position of the gearlever as shown at 'a' in **FIG 10**. The dimension 'a' should be 15 mm (.6 inch). The setting of the gearlever can be altered by varying the length of the shift rod but if large alterations are necessary the whole system should be checked for faults, damage or misalignment.

4 The floor mounted gearlever

A sectioned view of the assembly is shown in **FIG 11**. The later version with the forward cranked gearlever and split ball socket was introduced in November 1965. On the later version the cranking of the gearlever means that the gearlever knob is 55 mm (2.16 inch) further forward in all gears.

Removal:

1 Take out the splitpins and remove both castellated nuts 5 from the gearbox top cover. Lift up both pushrods 8 so that their end pieces 7, complete with rubber bushes 6, are freed from the gearbox.
2 Undo the nut and take out the clamp bolt 3 that secures the yoke end 2 to the shift tube 4, and by moving the gearlever draw the shift tube out of the yoke end.
3 Take out all the bolts that secure the cover 14 and partially withdraw the gearlever assembly out from the floor. Remove the splitpins and castellated nuts 20 so

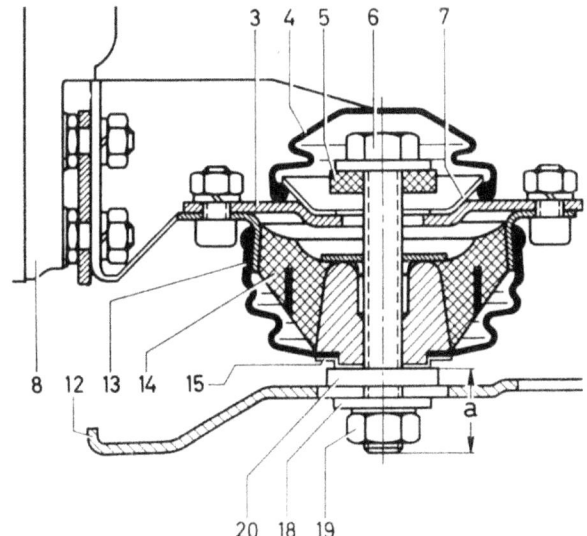

FIG 7 Sectioned view of the rear rubber mounting fitted to the 230SL

1 Hexagon nut	8 Transmission case rear cover
2 Hexagon nut	9 Attachment plate
3 Engine support	10 Collar screw
4 Bellows	11 Hexagon screw
5 Rubber spacer	12 Support
6 Hexagon bolt	
7 Bracket for bellows	

13 Bellows	
14 Rubber mount	
15 Metal cover	
16 Hexagon nut	
17 Spacer ring	
18 Washer	
19 Hexagon nut	
20 Spacer	

that the pushrods 8 can be freed from the assembly, and then remove the assembly from the car.

The parts are refitted in the reverse order of removal. Renew all worn bushes and renew the ball socket assembly if this is worn. The shift shaft 1 on the gearbox should be turned against the reverse gear detent and then pressed in to engage second gear. Move the gearlever 16 into the first/second plane. By moving the gearlever fore and aft only, insert the shift tube 4 into the splines of the yoke end 2 and make sure that it has entered by at least 15 mm (.6 inch) before clamping the parts with the bolt 3.

Once the parts are refitted check the adjustment

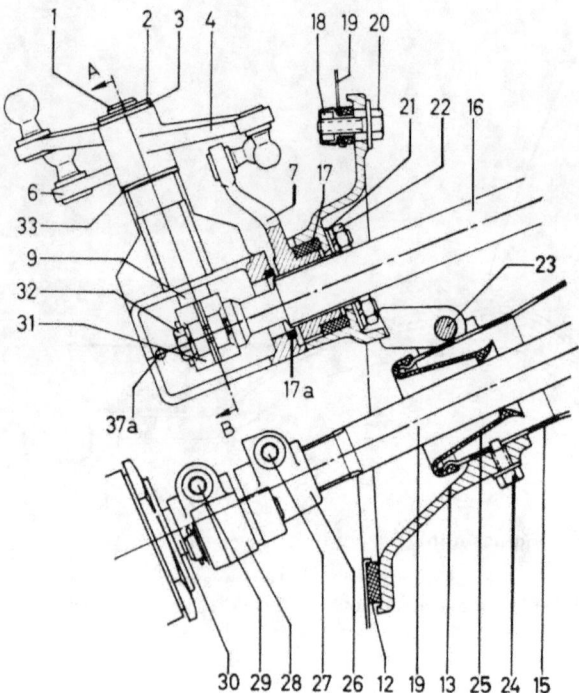

FIG 8 Sectioned view of the gearshift bearing assembly

1 Relay lever shaft
2 Snap ring
3 Washer
4 Relay lever
6 Selector lever
7 Lever on shift tube
9 Selector shaft
12 Rubber gasket
13 Coverplate
15 Steering column jacket
16 Shift tube
17 Vulkollan bush
17a Spacer ring
18 Cage nut
19 Front panel
20 Hexagon screw with washer
21 Washer
22 Hexagon nut with lockwasher
23 Hexagon screw (clamping screw)
24 Stud screw with lockwasher
25 Rubber sleeve
26 Upper flange
27 Hexagon socket screw
28 Lower flange (clamping screw)
29 Hexagon socket screw (clamping screw)
30 Steering worm
31 Selector lever on shift tube
32 Hexagon screw (clamping screw)
33 Spring washer
37a Water outlet bore

Adjusting:

The gearlever will be in the positions shown in **FIG 12** when the parts are correctly adjusted.

Select each gear in turn, while depressing the clutch, and check that it engages smoothly without the gearlever hitting the bearing assembly and that there is resistance to engaging reverse. If the position of the gearlever is incorrect or it hits the bearing then the parts should be adjusted.

1 Slacken both locknuts on the end pieces 7 and remove the castellated nuts 5.
2 Lift the end pieces 7 off the gearbox and by rotating both of them equally adjust the length of the pushrods 8. The pushrods are of the correct length when, with their end pieces refitted to the gearbox, the bearing 12 and their other ends are aligned centrally in the bearing assembly.
3 Refit the castellated nuts 5 and tighten the locknuts on the end pieces 7. Now check the position of the gearlever. Some slight adjustment to the position can be made by slackening the clamp bolt 3 and sliding the shift tube 4 in or out of the yoke end 2, making sure that the minimum penetration is 15 mm (.6 inch).

5 Dismantling the gearbox

The components of the gearbox are shown in **FIG 1** and the components of the different top covers are shown in **FIGS 2** and **3**.

Remove the gearbox from the car, as described in **Section 2**. Loosely refit the drain and filler plugs so that the unit can be washed down externally before starting dismantling. **The clutch release bearing must be removed before the interior of the clutch housing is cleaned.**

1 Remove the bolts that secure the top cover assembly in place. Carefully lever off the top cover, using a screwdriver in the notch provided for that purpose.
2 Free the clutch release lever from its special ball-headed bolt 85 and remove the lever with the dust excluder. Remove the securing bolts that hold the clutch housing and gearbox cover, and remove the parts carefully, collecting the shims that are fitted under them. **The shims must not be intermixed and the sets should be tied together and labelled. This applies to all sets of shims in the gearbox.**
3 At this point a special clamp No. 136.589.38.61 should be fitted to the first/second synchromesh unit 60 so as to keep the parts together. The clamp is shown fitted in **FIG 13**.
4 Free the lockwasher 101 from its groove in the nut 102 and remove the nut. Select both top and reverse gears simultaneously to lock the gearbox while undoing the nut 102. Pull off the drive flange 100.

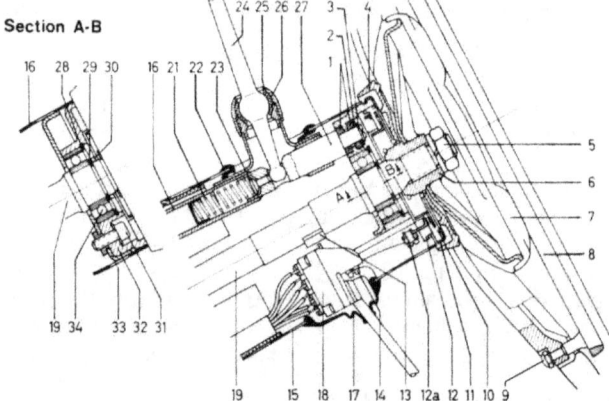

FIG 9 Sectioned view of the gearlever attachment to the steering column

1 Vulkollan ring
2 Washer
3 Snap ring
4 Horn ring, lower part
5 Steering wheel retaining nut with lockwasher
6 Steering wheel
7 Motif
8 Horn ring, upper part
9 Cap nut
10 Annular spring for contact ring
11 Retainer
12 Horn contact ring
12a Screw for cable connection
13 Cancelling cam for flasher switch
14 Screw for attaching flasher switch to steering column
15 Steering column
16 Shift tube
17 Flasher switch rubber cover
18 Flasher switch
19 Steering tube
20 Pressure spring
21 Pressure spring
22 Shift tube rubber cover
23 Spring seat pin
24 Gearlever
25 Ball socket for shift lever
26 Cap
27 Shift tube guide pin
28 Grooved bearing snap ring
29 Steering tube snap ring
30 Pressure spring
31 Socket screw with lockwasher
32 Mounting plate
33 Steering column jacket base
34 Grooved bearing for steering tube

5 Take out the bolts 97 and studs 98 that secure the rear cover 88 in place and withdraw the cover assembly. Pull the speedometer drive gear 75 off the mainshaft 40. The parts of the rear cover can be removed from it after taking out the bolt 95 and using a suitable drift to press out the parts 92, 93 and 94 of the speedometer drive. If the oil seal 91 is worn or damaged it should be prised out and a new one pressed back into the cover.

6 Remove the snap ring 33 that secures the front bearing 32. Also remove the snap rings 35 and 73 from the annular grooves in the bearings 32 and 72. Use a plastic-headed mallet to drive the mainshaft assembly forwards so that it in turn drives the input shaft assembly forwards. Carry on driving until sufficient of the front bearing 32 has been forced out of the case so that it can be fully levered out, using two screwdrivers as shown in **FIG 13**.

7 Drive the input shaft rearwards until the rear bearing 72 can be removed using a similar method to that used on the front bearing. Fit a suitable length of pipe over the rear end of the mainshaft and secure it with the nut 102 so that it acts as a sleeve to keep the parts on the mainshaft. The special clamp fitted earlier can now be removed.

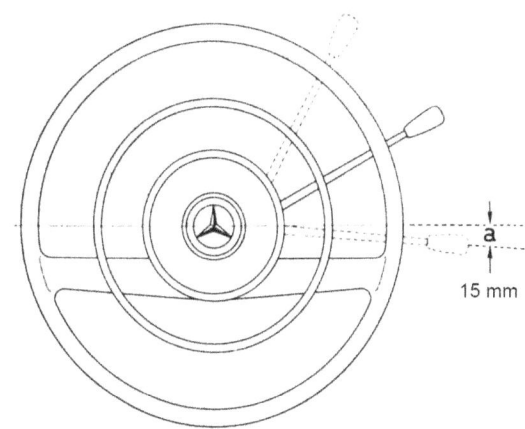

FIG 10 Distance the gearlever knob is below an imaginary horizontal line when the steering column gearshift is adjusted

8 Either hold or tie the mainshaft and input shaft assemblies so that they are held up as far as possible and the gears do not engage with the gears of the countershaft assembly. Drive the countershaft assembly rearwards, using a soft metal drift, until the rear countershaft bearing 26 can be removed. Allow the

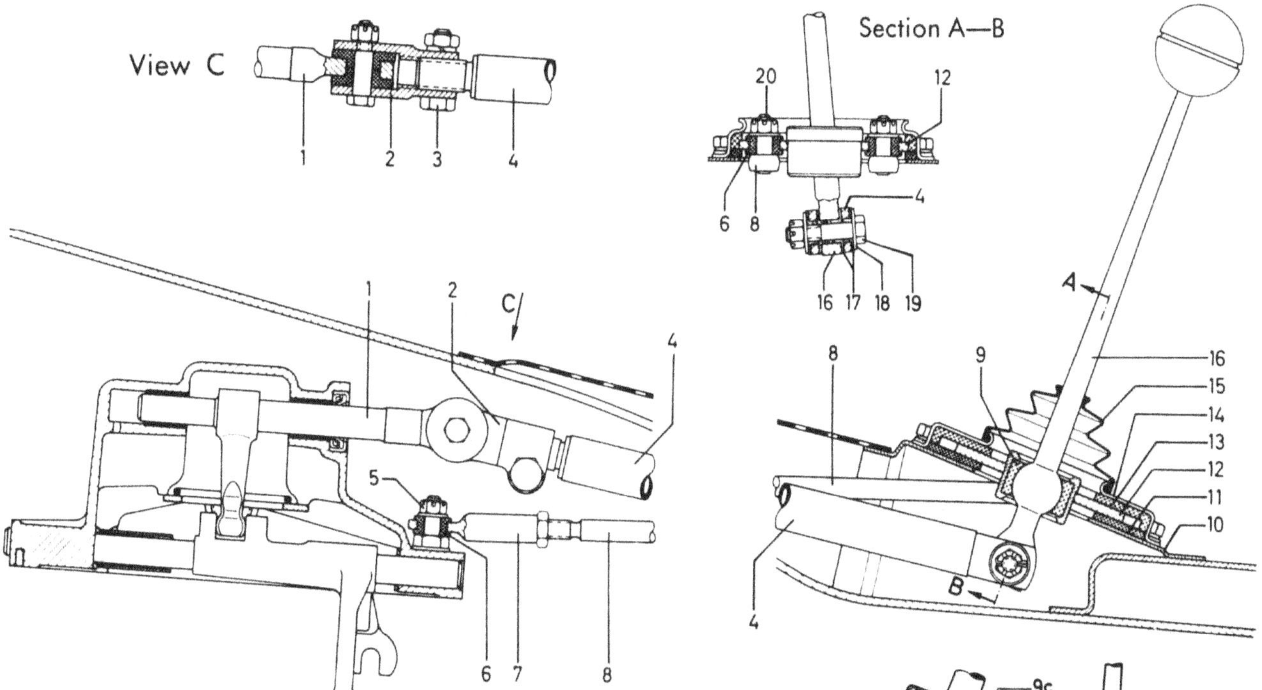

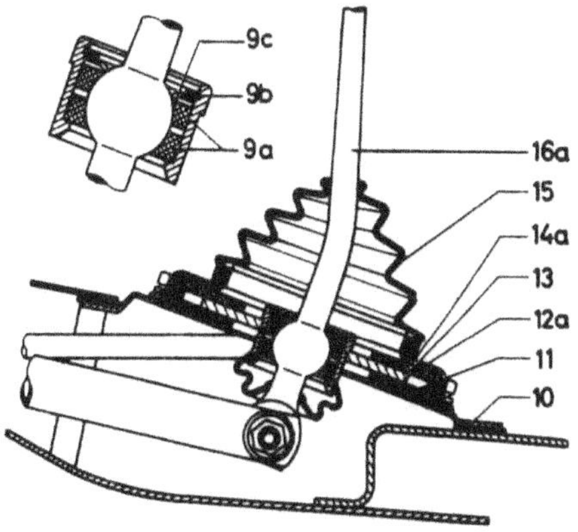

1 Shifting shaft
2 Yoke end
3 Hexagon bolt
4 Shift tube
5 Castellated nut
6 Bushing
7 End piece
8 Pushrod
9 Ball socket (vulkollan)
9a Split ball socket
9b Internal circlip
9c Corrugated washer
10 Transmission tunnel
11 Lower bearing cover
12 Shift lever bearing
12a Shift lever bearing, new version
13 Upper bearing cover
14 Coverplate, early version, sheet metal
14a Coverplate, early version, Vulkollan
15 Cuff
16 Gearlever
17 Bush
18 Washer
19 Hexagon screw
20 Castle nut

FIG 11 Sectioned views of the floor mounted gearshift mechanism

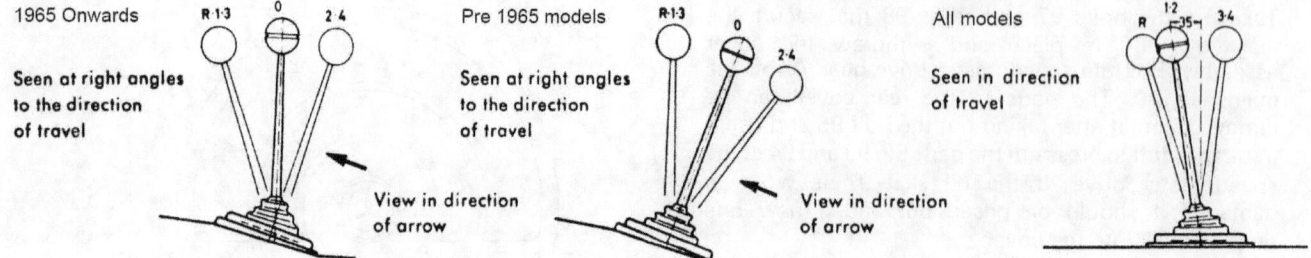

FIG 12 The positions of the gearlever when the floor mounted gearshift mechanism is correctly adjusted

countershaft assembly to fall to the bottom of the casing and remove the front bearing using a suitable extractor.

9 Pull the input shaft 30 out through the front of the case and if required use a suitable puller to remove the bearing 32 from the shaft and extract the needle roller bearing 53. Lift up the front end of the mainshaft assembly and withdraw the assembly out through the top aperture in the case.

10 Lift out the countershaft assembly through the top aperture. If required remove the circlip 24 and use a suitable puller to remove the gears 23 and 22. The key 21 should be carefully tapped out of its slot.

Mainshaft:

Free the lockwasher 51 from its groove in the nut 52 and unscrew the nut. Fit a 'Bulldog' clip over the baulk rings 44 so that they and the synchromesh unit 45 are held together. Mark the front end of the synchromesh unit and withdraw the parts from the front end of the mainshaft 40.

FIG 13 Using two screwdrivers to remove the bearing and also showing the special clamp fitted to the synchromesh unit

Take off the nut 102 and remove the temporary sleeve fitted earlier. Treat the synchromesh unit 60 and baulk rings 59 in a similar manner to the front unit and remove the parts from the rear end of the mainshaft. Remove the key 67 before turning and removing the locking washer 58.

As the parts are removed they should be laid out in order and care taken to note the direction in which the synchromesh units face.

Synchromesh units:

Remove the bulldog clip holding the parts together and take off the baulk rings. **The baulk rings must be fitted to their original positions and not interchanged from one side to the other of the unit.** It is advisable to mark one end of the outer sleeve and hub with a felt-tipped pen so that the parts will be correctly reassembled.

Wrap the synchromesh unit fully in a piece of cloth and press the hub out of the operating sleeve. The cloth will catch all shoes 49 or 64, balls 48 or 63 and springs 47 or 62 as they come free.

Clean all the parts and check them for wear or broken teeth. Renew any weak or damaged springs.

Fit the springs 47 or 62 and shoes 49 or 64 back into the hub 46 or 61, omitting the balls at this stage, and hold the parts in place in the hub using a little grease. Slide the inner hub, so that it faces the correct end as previously noted, back into the operating sleeve 50 or 65. Adjust the position of the hub in the sleeve so that the bores in the hub are just accessible. Press each shoe 49 or 64 into the sleeve so that the bore is exposed and fit a ball 48 or 63 into the bore. Hold the ball in place by pulling the shoe out over it. When all the balls are in place slide the hub back into the sleeve so that the balls click into the annular detent groove inside the sleeve. Fit the baulk rings 44 or 59 back into place on either side of the unit and hold the parts together with a bulldog clip.

6 Reassembling the gearbox

Before reassembling the gearbox clean all the parts and check them for wear or damage. Check all gears for worn or broken teeth. Examine shafts and bushes for wear or chatter marks. Wash the bearings separately in clean fuel and check them for roughness, wear or corrosion. Renew all defective parts.

Mainshaft:

Lightly lubricate the parts with oil as they are being refitted.

1 Mount the mainshaft 40, front end upwards, in the padded jaws of a vice. Refit the needle roller bearing 41 and slide on the third-speed gear 42 with its cone

facing upwards. Fit the serrated washer 43 followed by the synchromesh assembly 45 and its baulk rings 44. Secure the parts in place using the nut 52.

2 Check that the third-speed gear 42 rotates freely and use feeler gauges to measure its end float which is correct at .10 to .18 mm (.004 to .007 inch). If the end float is incorrect selectively fit a new serrated washer 43 to bring the end float within limits. Serrated washers are available in thicknesses from 7.9 to 8.1 mm. When the end float is correct, fit a new lockwasher 51 and tighten the nut 52 to a torque load of 20 mkg (145 lb ft). Lock the nut by drifting the lockwasher into a groove.

3 Remove the assembly from the vice and remount it so that the rear end is now vertically upwards.

4 Slide the second-speed gear 57 into place with its cone upwards. Slide the lockwasher 58 down the splines and turn it so that it locks the gear into place. Check that the gear 57 rotates freely and use feeler gauges to measure the end float. Lockwashers 58 are available in increments of .05 mm (.002 inch) and should be selectively fitted until the end float is correct within the limits of .10 to .18 mm (.004 to .007 inch).

5 When the correct lockwasher has been selected remove it and the gear fitted in operation 4. Fit the halves of the needle roller bearing 56 around the mainshaft, slide back the gear 57 and lock it in place with the selected washer 58, making sure that the slot for the key in the washer faces upwards.

6 Fit the key 67 back into place so that it fits into the slot in the lockwasher 58. Slide on the assembled synchromesh unit 60 complete with its baulk rings 59. Fit the thrust washer 68 back into place with its keyway downwards and fitting over the end of the key. Check that there is a clearance of .1 mm (.004 inch) between the end of the key and the bottom of the slot. If there is not sufficient clearance carefully file the end of the key to bring the clearance within limits.

7 Refit the first-speed gear 70 with its cone facing downwards, followed by the thrust washer 71 with its shoulder upwards. Secure the parts in place with the nut 102 and suitable piece of pipe as a sleeve. Check that the gear 70 rotates freely and that it has the correct end float of .10 to .18 mm (.004 to .007 inch). If the end float is incorrect adjust it by selectively fitting the thrust washer 71, which is available in increments of .05 mm (.002 inch).

8 Remove the parts fitted in operation 7 and then fit them again after fitting the needle roller bearing 69. Secure the parts with the nut and sleeve.

Reassembly:

Reassemble the input shaft and countershaft parts in the reverse order of dismantling. The three main assemblies are similarly refitted by reversing the order of removal. If the old thrust washer 25 for the countershaft assembly is worn or damaged a new one should be fitted in its place. The bearings 32 and 72 are refitted with their annular grooves outwards and are driven in until the snap rings 35 and 73 firmly contact the side of the case.

1 Use a depth gauge to measure the protrusion of the front bearing from the front of the casing, as shown in **FIG 14**. Similarly measure the depth of the recess in the clutch housing as shown in **FIG 15**. Make up

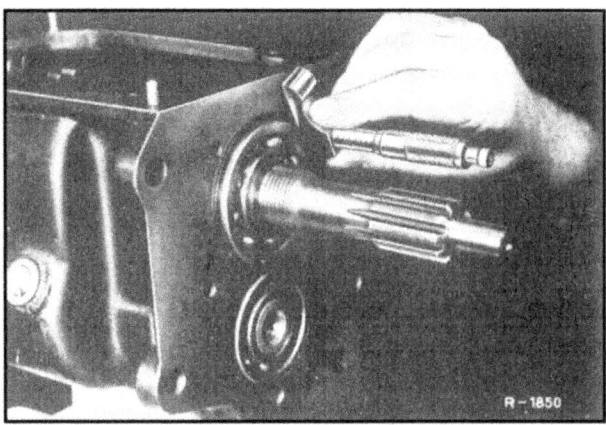

FIG 14 Measuring the bearing protrusion in the gearbox

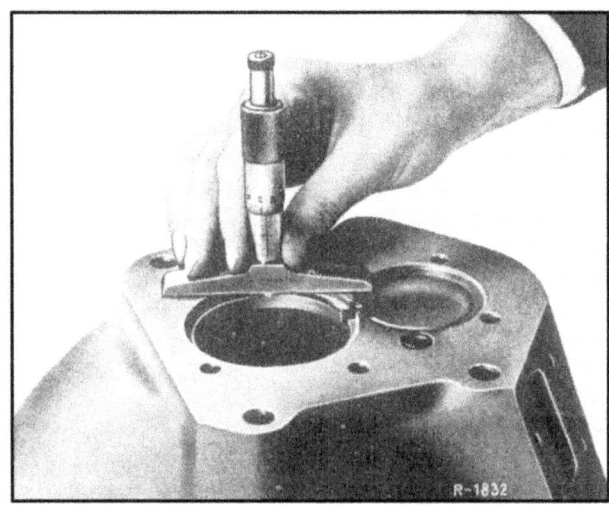

FIG 15 Measuring the depth of the recess in the housing

a shim pack so that the clearance between the snap ring 35 and the end of the recess is .00 to .05 mm (.000 to .002 inch) when the cover is refitted. Refit the clutch housing with the shims in place.

2 Repeat operation 1 on the rear bearing 72 and snap ring 73 so that a shim pack is made up which will give a clearance of .00 to .05 mm (.000 to .002 inch) when the rear cover 88 is fitted, making allowances for the thickness of the gasket 90. Do not yet refit the rear cover.

3 Drive the countershaft assembly, using a soft-faced hammer on the rear bearing 26, until the front bearing is in firm contact with the clutch housing. Make up a shim pack so that the clearance between the rear bearing 26 and the recess in the rear cover 88 will be .15 to .20 mm (.006 to .008 inch) when the cover is in place, making due allowance for the thickness of the gasket 90.

4 Reassemble the speedometer drive parts into the rear cover. Remove the nut and temporary sleeve from the mainshaft and press back on the speedometer drive gear 75. Refit the rear cover assembly using a new gasket and with the made-up shim packs correctly in place.

5 Refit the drive flange 100 and a new lockwasher 101. Tighten the nut 102 to a torque load of 20 mkg and lock it by staking the lockwasher into a groove of the nut.
6 Set the outer sleeves of the synchromesh units to their neutral position and refit the top cover assembly, making sure that the selector forks engage correctly with the outer sleeves and the selector for the reverse idler.

7 Fault diagnosis

(a) Jumping out of gear

1 Gearshift mechanism incorrectly adjusted
2 Broken spring behind detent bar in top cover
3 Excessively worn locating groove in striker rod
4 Worn coupling dogs
5 Screw securing selector fork to striking rod loose

(b) Noisy gearbox

1 Insufficient or incorrect oil
2 Excessive end float on countershaft assembly
3 Worn or damaged bearings
4 Worn or damaged gear teeth

(c) Difficulty in engaging gear

1 Check 1 in (a)
2 Stiff gearchange linkage
3 Incorrect clutch adjustments
4 Worn synchromesh assemblies

(d) Oil leaks

1 Defective gaskets
2 Worn or damaged oil seals
3 Damaged cover or casing faces

CHAPTER 7 — AUTOMATIC TRANSMISSION

1 Description
2 Operation
3 Maintenance
4 Adjusting the linkages
5 Removing and replacing the transmission
6 Fault diagnosis

1 Description

An automatic DB transmission unit can be fitted to the car in place of the standard manually operated gearbox and mechanical clutch assembly.

A fluid flywheel takes the place of the mechanical clutch. The operation of the fluid flywheel is completely automatic so the need for the clutch pedal is dispensed with. The operation of the gearbox is totally different from that of the standard gearbox and uses epicyclic drives instead of meshed gears, the selection of the gears being carried out by the use of brake bands and clutches instead of sliding the synchromesh units into mesh. Control of the brake bands and clutches is carried out by a complicated hydraulic system, using oil which is pressurized by internal pumps.

The unit is fitted with an oil cooler mounted vertically on the lefthand side of the coolant radiator. Metal pipes and flexible hoses connect the automatic transmission to the oil cooler. The removal of the oil cooler, with the radiator, is dealt with in **Chapter 4, Section 3**.

The unit is a very complex piece of mechanism and should only be stripped or repaired by experts. The owner should not be tempted to carry out more work than has been dealt with in this chapter, and if the unit suffers from faults which the owner cannot deal with the car should be taken to a garage or agent specializing in automatic transmissions. Few small local garages have the skill, experience or equipment to deal with automatic transmissions.

Fluid flywheel:

A sectioned view of the fluid flywheel is shown in **FIG 1**. It should be noted that the unit is sealed on manufacture and it cannot be dismantled in service so a defective fluid flywheel must be renewed.

The primary rotor 3 is connected to the engine flywheel so that it rotates with the engine and at engine speed. The secondary rotor 4 is connected to the input shaft of the epicyclic gearbox so that the gearbox is driven when the secondary rotor turns.

The unit is filled with oil and there is a constant flow of this in at 'a' from the gearbox. The oil is returned to the gearbox in the direction 'b' through the ball valve 2.

As the primary rotor turns, it drags the oil around by its vanes and the vanes of the secondary rotor turn this oil drag back into torque to turn the secondary rotor. There is a speed difference between the two rotors in all conditions, though it is only minor when full drive is being transmitted, and the centrifugal force acts to set up a rotational oil flow as shown by the arrows in the figure.

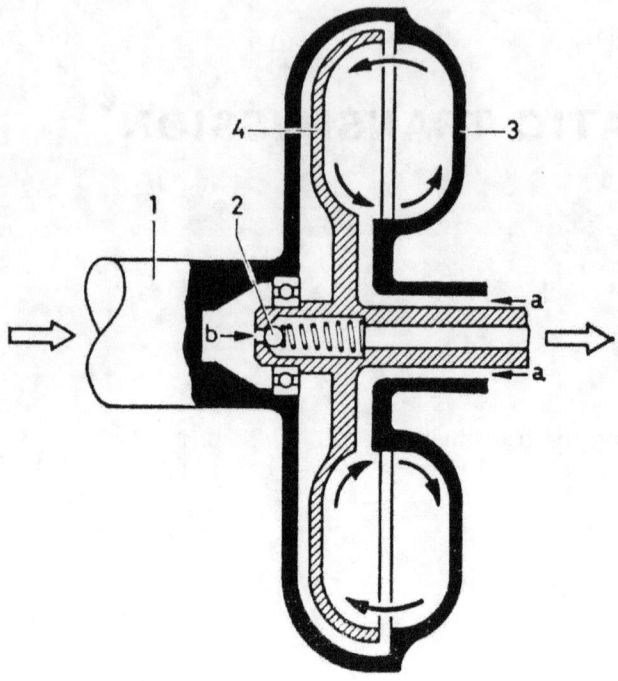

FIG 1 Schematic sectioned view of the fluid flywheel

1 Crankshaft
2 Ball valve
3 Primary rotor with drive shaft
4 Secondary rotor
a Oil feed
b Oil return

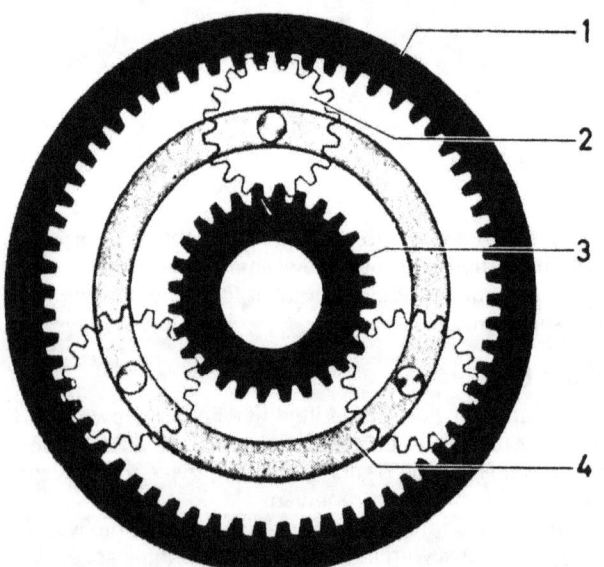

FIG 2 An epicylic gear train

1 Outer gear
2 Planet gear
3 Sun gear
4 Planet gear carrier

The actual flow path of the oil will follow the path of an imaginary coil spring wound round between the rotors and it is this flow which transmits the torque to the secondary rotor. From standstill the secondary rotor will be rapidly accelerated up to nearly the same speed as the primary rotor. In steady driving conditions the secondary rotor will be turning at 98 per cent of the speed of the primary rotor. The 2 per cent losses are due to friction and they are wasted as heat. The greater the percentage of slip the greater will be the losses and the more heat will be produced. The gearbox changes automatically to compensate for the changes in road speed so in normal driving conditions the slip will always be kept within tolerable limits. The only time that the engine should be run at high speed while the drive is selected and the car held stationary is for testing purposes, and even then the period of test should be kept very short to prevent the oil from overheating.

Epicyclic gearbox:

The gearbox gives four forward speeds and one reverse. On saloon models a selector is fitted to the steering column while on the 230SL and as an optional extra on saloons the selector is mounted on the floor. An indicator is fitted to the instruments. The selector is used for selecting forward or reverse drive as well as neutral. It is fitted with extra positions for overriding the gearbox and a separate position for parking. Also fitted is a kick-down switch which comes into operation when the throttle pedal is pressed down beyond the full throttle point. The kick-down switch downshifts the gearbox to the next lower gear provided that the road speed is within limits.

An epicyclic gear train is shown in **FIG 2**. The ratio of the output to input can be altered, or reversed in direction, by driving one component, holding the second and taking the drive from the third. For instance if the drive is put in at the sun gear 3 and the outer gear 1 is held stationary then a slower speed but higher torque drive can be taken from the planet carrier 4. As another example, if the drive is still put in at the sun gear 3 but this time the planet carrier 4 is held stationary, then a slower but reversed drive can be taken from the outer gear 1.

Using a combination of two such epicyclic gear trains and suitable controls and interconnections the gearbox produces its four forward gears and one reverse. A schematic section of the gearbox is shown in **FIG 3**.

Control and lubrication:

The various clutches and brake bands are selected or released by oil pressure controlled from a very complex valve system. The valve system is actuated by oil pressure whose step values are set by a rotating centrifugal governor assembly. Variation in the actual road speed of the change is brought about by a vacuum unit which ensures that upshifts are delayed at large throttle openings.

On the 230SL models extra components are fitted to ensure that the engine idling speed does not drop when drive is selected. The system actually increases the idling speed by opening the throttle linkage slightly but, because of the increased drag from the transmission, the extra power is absorbed and the engine continues to run at the same speed. Two oil pressure switches 3 and 4 are fitted to the automatic transmission, as shown in **FIG 4**, and these control the lifting magnet fitted to the throttle linkage. The lifting magnet is shown fitted in **FIG 5**. Set the correct idling speed of 700 to 750 rev/min with P or N selected and then select a drive gear. If the engine speed now drops below 700 rev/min then there is either a fault or adjustment is required. If the circuit, pressure switches and lifting magnet are all satisfactory, the idling speed with drive selected should be adjusted to a minimum of 700 rev/min by altering the length of the control rod 4.

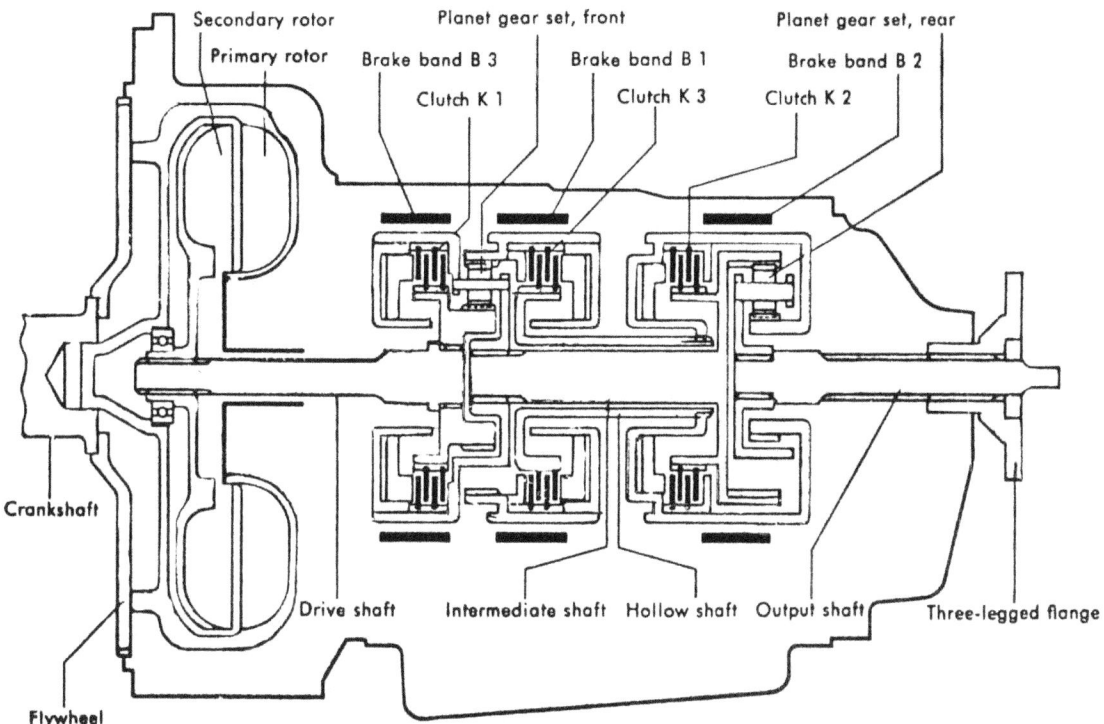

FIG 3 Schematic sectioned view of the transmission

Check that the idling speed is correct both in reverse and forward drives.
Three oil pumps are fitted to the automatic transmission.
The primary pump is fitted into the front housing cover and driven from the input shaft so that the pump always operates when the engine is running, except when the transmission is stalled in gear. The primary pump supplies all the needs of the gearbox up to a road speed of 19 mile/hr. The other two pumps are mounted in front of the rear cover and are driven from the output shaft of the gearbox so that they revolve at a speed proportional to that of the rear wheels. A view with the rear cover removed is shown in **FIG 6**. The secondary pump 3 takes over from the primary pump beyond road speeds of 19 mile/hr. The regulating pump 4 and the governor rotate at a speed proportional to the speed of the rear wheels and therefore proportional to the road speed of the car. The regulating pump and governor between them produce the stepped oil pressures which actuate the valve system for gear selecting.

Also shown in **FIG 6** is the parking lock 7. When the selector is moved to the P position an internal linkage moves the lock into engagement with the parking gear on the output shaft so that the gearbox is locked and the rear wheels cannot rotate.

The selection valve parts are extremely complicated, with special castings that appear like mazes. **Under no circumstances should the owner attempt to dismantle or service these parts.**

Road test:

The owner is not the best person to carry out a road test unless he has had recent experience of driving similar models fitted with automatic transmissions known to be in good order. It is advisable to have the test carried out by a competent mechanic who is experienced in automatic transmissions. The road test consists of checking that the upshifts and downshifts take place at the correct speeds and at the different throttle openings. Details of these are given in **Technical Data**. At the same time the safety devices should be checked, such as starter lock switch, parking lock and the hydraulic safety interlock that prevents selection of reverse or park at speed.

2 Operation

This section gives details of the various selections and their uses as well as other methods of using the transmission.

FIG 4 The oil pressure switches fitted on the 230SL

1 Baffle plate
2 Fixing screws
3 Oil pressure switch, forward
4 Oil pressure switch, reverse

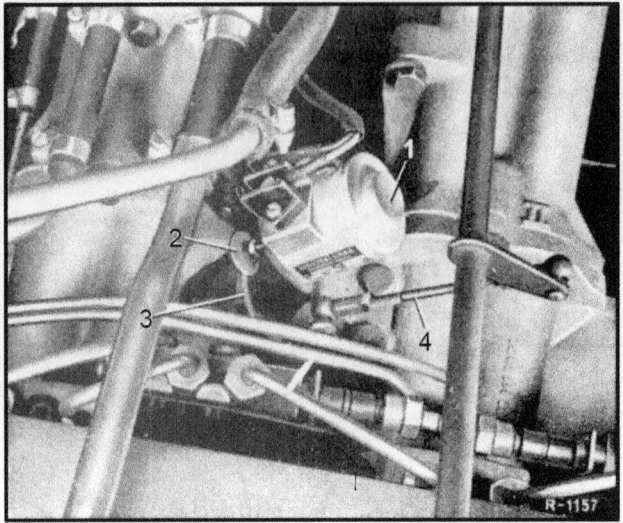

FIG 5 The lifting magnet fitted on the 230SL

1 Lifting magnet   3 Relay lever
2 Shoulder nut   4 Control rod

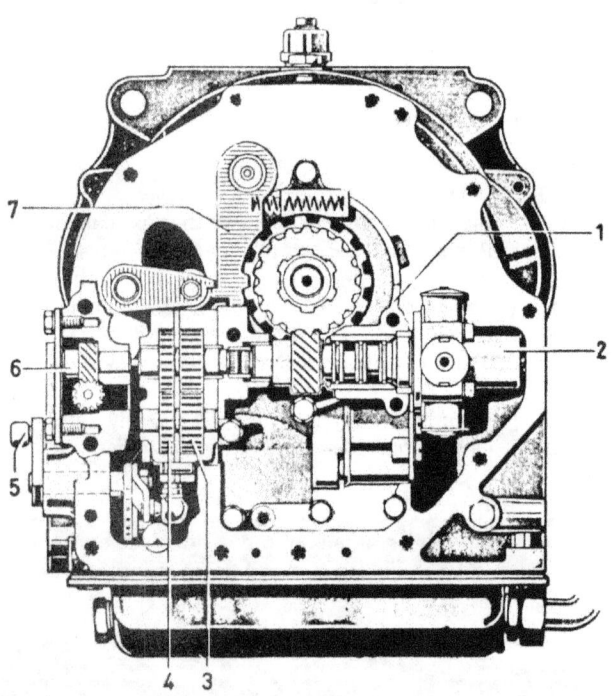

FIG 6 View of the gearbox with the rear cover removed

1 Bearing cap   4 Regulating pump   7 Parking lock
2 Centrifugal governor   5 Selector lever
3 Secondary pump   6 Speedometer drive

Position P:

This is used to lock the transmission when the car is parked. Though it will, and should, hold the car stationary on hills, the handbrake should also be applied. The starter lock switch allows the engine to be started in this selection.

P should not normally be selected when the car is moving, for obvious reasons, but a safety device is fitted to prevent the lock from engaging if P is inadvertently selected when the car is moving forwards faster than 10 kilometre/hr (6 mile/hr).

Position R:

This is equivalent to the reverse on a normal gearbox and should be used as such. The safety device that prevents the parking lock from operating also prevents the reverse being selected when the car is moving forwards faster than 10 kilometre/hr.

Position O:

This is equivalent to the neutral position on a normal gearbox and should always be selected when the car is stationary for long periods. If this position is selected when the car is moving the car should carry on rolling freely with no interconnection between the engine and rear wheels. The position should not be selected above a road speed of 50 kilometre/hr.

This selection and P are the only selections in which it should be possible to operate the starter motor.

On some cars this position will be marked N instead of O but the operation is exactly the same in both cases.

Position 4:

This is the position selected for normal driving. The gears will be selected as required by the road conditions, speed and position of the throttle. The car will start off in second gear unless the throttle pedal is pressed right down to the kick-down position in which case it will start off in first gear. The kick-down will also operate when the car is moving to downshift a gear for rapid acceleration.

Position 3:

This is exactly the same as position 4 except that the gearbox will not upshift into fourth gear. It should be used for driving up and down normal hills. Engine braking will be available when the car is going downhill. **Care must be taken not to overspeed the engine in this selection.** The road speed should not be allowed to rise above the speed indicated by three lines on the speedometer and the engine speed should not be allowed to go above 6000 rev/min for 230 and 230S models or 6500 rev/min for the 230SL models.

FIG 7 The dipstick and filler tube, also showing the separate coolant header tank fitted to some models

Position 2:

This should be selected for mountain passes, very steep hills or towing a trailer on steep hills. The car will start off in first gear with reduced throttle. Third and top gears are isolated so the gearbox will not upshift to them. **For this reason great care must be taken not to overspeed the engine or drive faster than the speed indicated by two lines on the speedometer.**

This selection should also be made when driving for long periods at very slow speeds or driving off from a cold start.

Starting:

An interlock switch is fitted to prevent the starter from operating in any but O and P selections. This is a safety precaution to prevent the car from moving off inadvertently.

The car may be tow- or roll-started if the battery is flat. Use a long tow rope to prevent ramming the towing car when the engine starts and remember that a higher pedal pressure will be required on the brakes until the engine is running. Leave the car in position O (or N) until a speed of 19 mile/hr is reached. Switch on the ignition and select either position 3 or 4 coupled with some throttle opening.

Towing:

The car may be towed for reasonable distances without taking any special precautions other than keeping the speed range between 12 and 31 mile/hr, provided that the transmission is correctly filled with oil and it is also in good condition.

If the distance is long, the speed range cannot be kept, or the transmission is defective, then the propeller shaft should be disconnected at the rear axle and safely supported out of the way.

Note that a higher pedal pressure will be required on the brakes as the vacuum servo reservoir will quickly fill with air.

Parking:

When parking or manoeuvring in confined spaces it is advisable to set a reasonable engine speed with the right

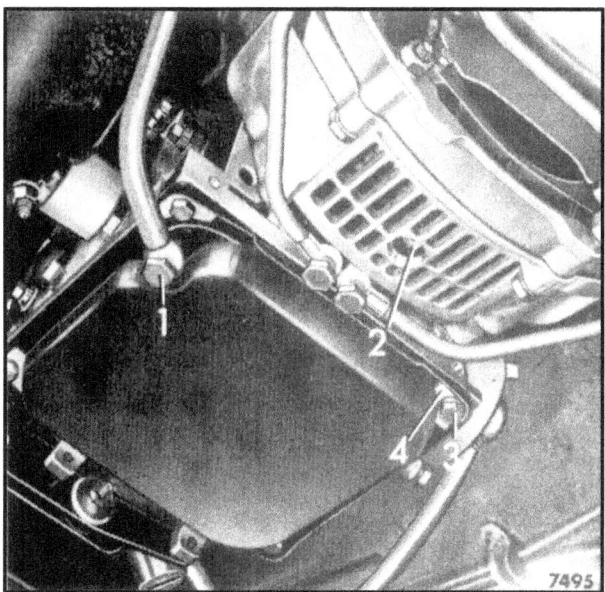

FIG 9 Different type of sump attachment

FIG 10 Circular type of oil filter

foot on the throttle and control the speed of the car with the left foot on the brake. The action is not difficult as it is similar to slipping the clutch on a manual gearbox.

Rocking:

If the car is stuck in soft mud or snow a rocking action will often release it. Set a fast-idle speed using the throttle pedal and move the selector lever backwards and forwards between a forward selection and R. Preferably synchronize the movement of the selector with the movement of the car as it reaches the end of its travel.

3 Maintenance

Check the oil level at regular intervals and before a long run. **The level should be checked with the car standing on level ground, the engine running and the transmission at its normal operating temperature.** Wipe the top of the dipstick and filler tube,

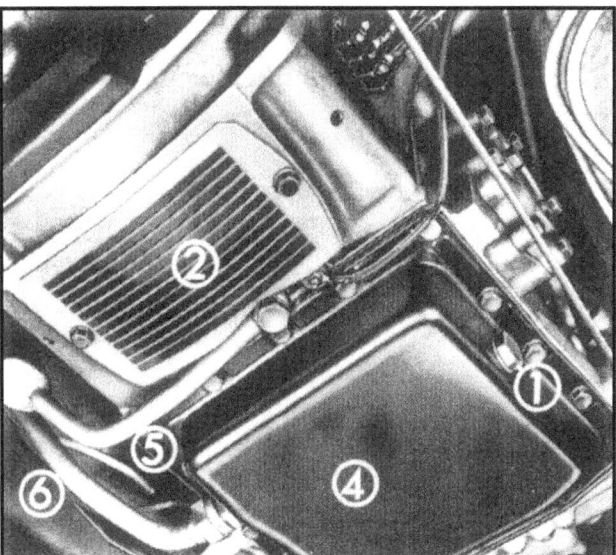

FIG 8 Sump drain plug and stone guard

FIG 11 Square type of oil filter

shown in **FIG 7**, and withdraw the dipstick. Wipe the dipstick clean with a piece of leather or non-fluffy cloth, insert it back into the filler tube and immediately withdraw it once it has reached its full depth. Check the level on the dipstick. The difference between the marks on the dipstick corresponds to .5 litre (1 pint). Top up to the correct level with ATF type A fluid. **Do not overfill the unit as this is nearly as harmful as running with too low a level of fluid.** If the unit is accidentally overfilled drain or syphon out the surplus fluid.

Draining:

The old fluid should be drained out and discarded at 20,000 kilometre intervals and the unit refilled with fresh oil. There are two slightly differing versions of the automatic transmission fitted and they are shown in **FIG 8** and **FIG 9** with their sumps fitted. On the version shown in **FIG 8**, take off the stone guard 2 and turn the engine until the fluid flywheel drain plug (item 3 in **FIG 10**) is accessible. Set the selector to P. Remove the drain plug 1 from the side of the sump and take out the drain plug from the fluid flywheel. When the unit is empty refit both drain plugs, using a new sealing ring under the plug 1. On the version shown in **FIG 9** the fluid flywheel drain plug 2 is accessible through the aperture in the stone guard, but the sump is not fitted with a drain plug. Undo the banjo union 1 from the filler tube, support the sump and remove the four bolts 3 and corner pieces 4. Lower the sump carefully as it will be full of dirty oil, and then tip the oil into a convenient container. Refit the sump and drain plug making sure that the gasket for the sump is in place and in good condition.

Filling:

When the unit is being refilled it will require approximately 1 litre less than the quantity of fluid that it requires

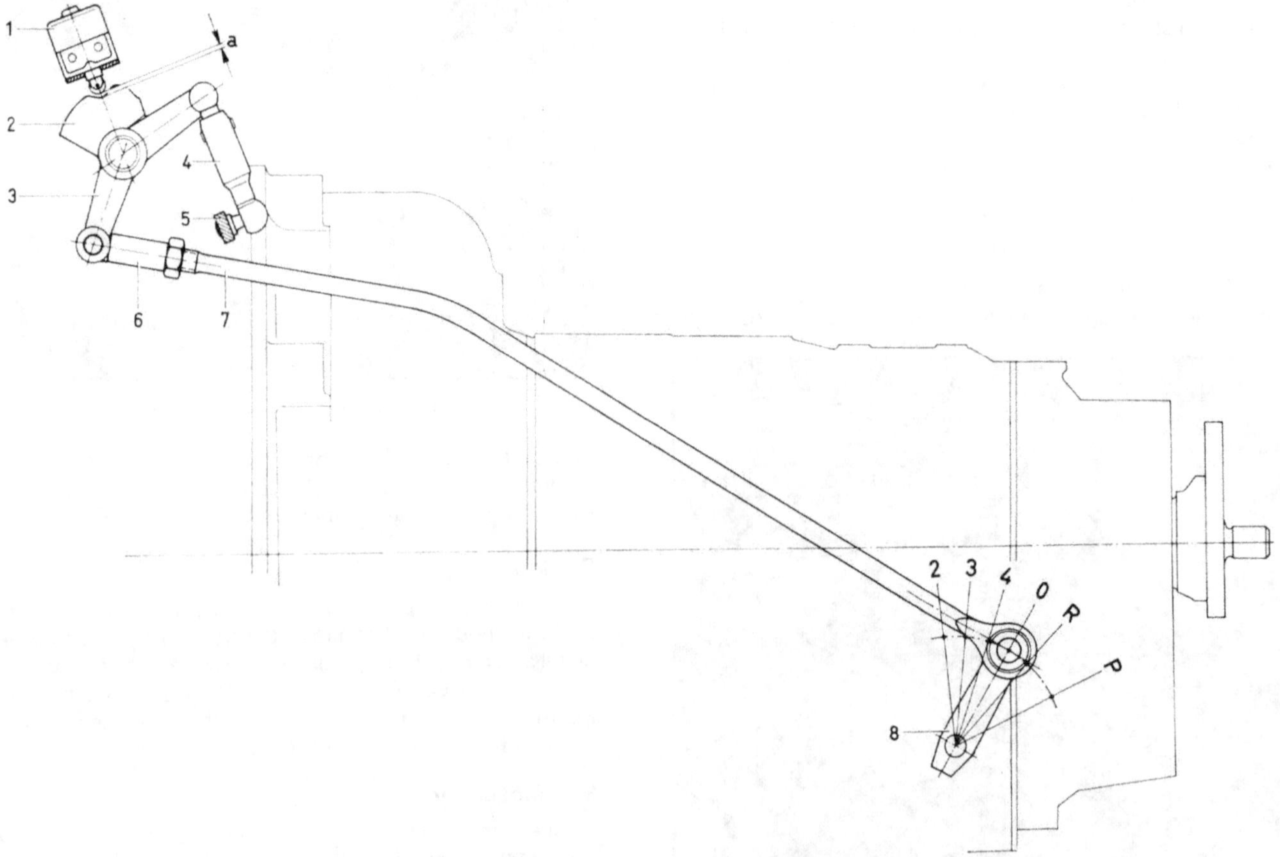

FIG 12 The linkage for the steering column mounted selector

1 Starter lock switch 3 Intermediate lever 5 Shift lever 7 Shift rod
2 Cam disk 4 Resilient intermediate piece 6 Ball socket 8 Range selector lever

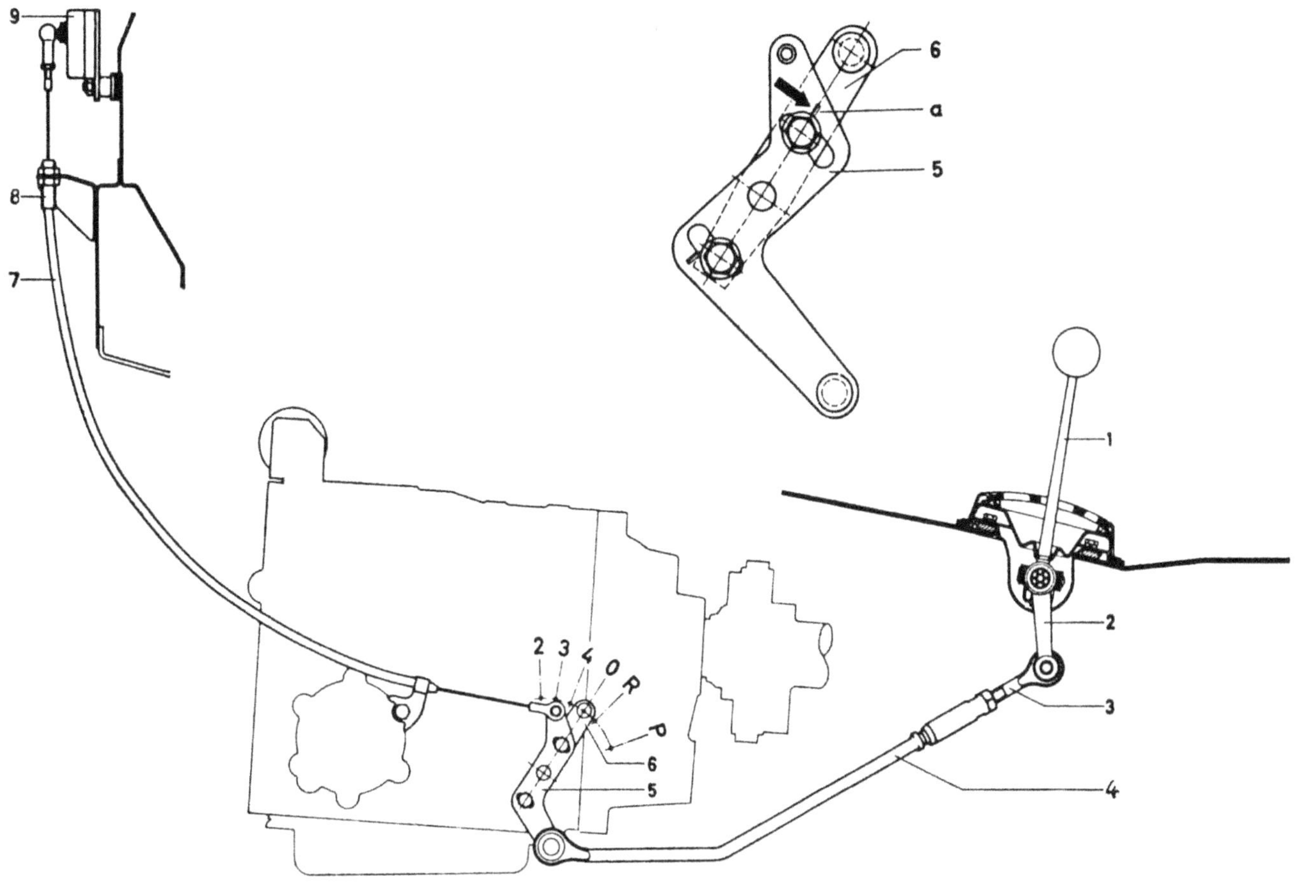

FIG 13 Linkage for the floor mounted selector

1 Selector lever
2 Selector lever bottom section
3 Adjusting lug
4 Shift rod
5 Additional lever
6 Range selector lever
7 Cable pulls
8 Adjusting stop
9 Starter lock and reverse light switch
10 Adjusting mark

from dry. The total dry capacity of the 230 model is 4.5 litres and that of the 230S and 230SL is 4.75 litres.

Fill the unit through the filler tube until the level is at the bottom mark on the dipstick. **It should be noted that this bottom mark is also the full mark if the level is checked with the engine running and the transmission not warmed up but at ambient temperature.** Start the engine and allow it to idle in P selection. Top up the level to the bottom mark on the dipstick as fluid is drawn into the fluid flywheel. Check that the fluid level is at the upper mark on the dipstick after the transmission has reached its normal operating temperature of 80°C (176°F).

Oil filter:

This should be checked and renewed at regular intervals. The two different types of mounting are shown in **FIG 10** and **FIG 11**. Drain the unit and remove the sump to gain access to the filter. The round type of filter is secured in place by the central bolt 8.

Cleanliness:

It is important that cleanliness is observed most carefully in any operation involving the automatic transmission. Even a speck of dirt or fluff in the wrong place will seriously interfere with the operation of the unit.

The outside of the unit and the stone guard underneath it should also be cleaned at regular intervals, particularly if the car is driven over muddy roads. Even though the unit is fitted with an oil cooler, quite a lot of surplus heat is lost through the case of the unit and by air through the stone guard. Mud or dirt will provide insulation and possibly cause the unit to overheat, especially in areas of high ambient temperatures.

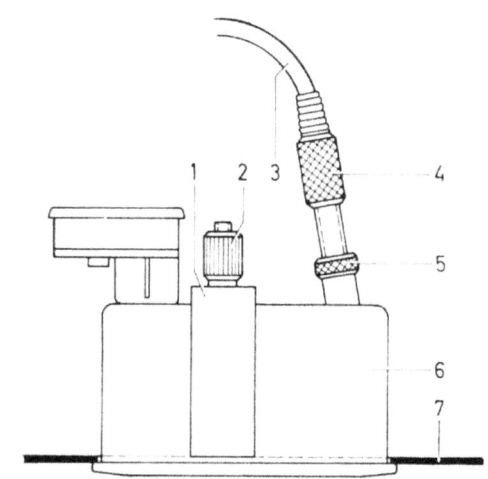

FIG 14 Adjustment point for the selector indicator

1 Clamp
2 Clamp nut
3 Bowden cable
4 Knurled nut
5 Locknut
6 Housing
7 Instrument panel

85

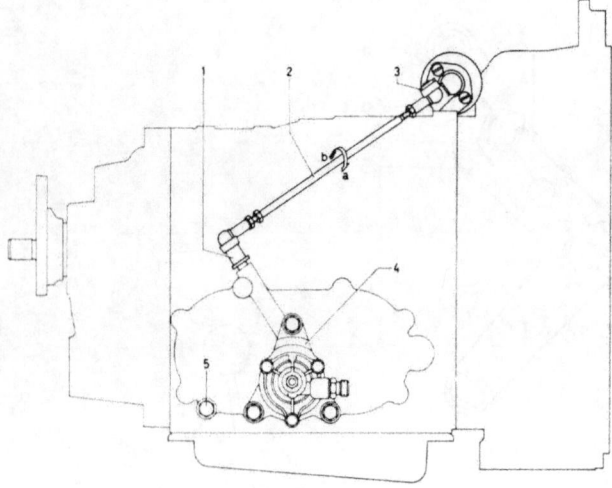

FIG 15 The kick-down linkage

1 Operating shaft
2 Linkage
3 Angle lever
4 Modulating pressure control
5 Measuring connection for modulating pressure

FIG 16 Left side view of the automatic transmission

Key to Figs 16 and 17
1 Clutch housing
2 Return line from oil cooler
3 Hollow screw C 6 DIN 7623
  Sealing ring
  A 12 x 16 DIN 7603 Al 99 F 8
  (2 each per hollow screw)
4 Holding clip
5 Oil pressure switch
  Sealing ring
  A 12 x 16 DIN 7603 Al 99 F 8
6 Oil pressure line
7 Hollow screw 112 990 02 63
  Sealing ring
  A 8 x 12 DIN 7603 Al 99 F 8
  (2 each per hollow screw)
8 Connecting cable
  (oil pressure switch)
9 Feed line to oil cooler
10 Cable adapter
  with cover plate
11 Cable set
  (double-acting solenoid)
12 Double-acting solenoid

Adjustments:

The shift and kick-down linkages should be checked at the same time as the oil is changed. These adjustments are given in the following section.

The brake bands should not be adjusted by the owner as partial dismantling of the unit and special tools are required.

If the unit operates erratically or incorrectly the car should be taken to a suitable agent who will have all the equipment necessary for checking and adjusting the various pressures that the unit requires for its correct operation.

4 Adjusting the linkages

The linkages must only be adjusted when the car is standing level on its own wheels and at its normal operating weight. The only satisfactory method of gaining convenient access is to work from a pit or raise the car on a garage hoist.

Steering column mounted selector:

The details of the linkage are shown in **FIG 12**. Free the ball socket 6 from the intermediate lever 3. Set the selector lever in the car to O (or N) and also set the range lever 8 on the gearbox to O. Slacken the locknut and turn the ball socket 6 on the shift rod 7 until the ball socket fits back onto the ball of the intermediate lever 3 without forcing or moving the selections at all. Secure the ball socket and wire lock it after tightening its locknut.

The starter lock switch 1 must have a clearance 'a' of $1 \pm .3$ mm ($.04 \pm .012$ inch) when the selector is in positions O or P. Slacken the screws which secure the switch. The mounting holes are slotted so that the switch can be moved laterally but not vertically. The switch is not visible from above and about the only method of seeing it is to use a mirror and inspection light from behind. Move the switch until the gap is correct and tighten the securing screws. Check the adjustment by attempting to start the engine in all selections. If the adjustment is correct the starter will only operate in O and P selections.

Floor mounted selector:

The details of the linkage are shown in **FIG 13**. Disconnect the shift rod 4 from the additional lever 5 and the bottom section of the selector lever 2. Slacken the

FIG 17 Right side view of the automatic transmission

FIG 18 Special adaptor for the jack

1 Support plate   2 Base plate   3 Compression springs

bolts and adjust the additional lever 5 so that its centre line aligns with that of the range lever 6 on the 230SL or as shown in the insert on other models and then retighten the bolts. Set the range lever 6 to the O position and similarly set the selector lever 1. Reconnect the shift rod 4 to the additional lever 5 and adjust its length until it fits back onto 2 without moving the settings.

Adjust the length of the cable 7, using the adjusting stop 8, until the starter will only operate at O or P and the reverse lights operate only at R.

Indicator:

The adjustment point for the selector indicator is shown in **FIG 14**. Adjust the length of the cable 3, using the knurled nut 4 and locknut 5 until the indicator corresponds to the position of the selector lever.

Kick-down:

The adjustment of the kick-down switch is dealt with in **Chapter 2, Section 13**. The operating solenoid and its linkage are shown in **FIG 15**. The parts can be seen and adjusted through the aperture in the transmission tunnel. Switch on the ignition but do not start the engine. The linkage should move rearwards with the throttle closed. Lightly depress the accelerator pedal and check that the linkage moves to the central position. Fully depress the accelerator pedal and check that the linkage moves forwards. If the linkage fails to move there is either a fault in the electrical supply, the operating shaft 1 is jammed, or the modulating pressure control is itself jammed.

5 Removing and replacing the transmission

The unit can be removed and refitted in the car without removing the engine. External views of the unit are shown in **FIGS 16** and **17**.

When removing or refitting the unit on its own it is most advisable to use attachment BE.11.857, as shown in **FIG 18**. This attachment keeps the unit level on the jack and yet allows a small amount of movement for aligning.

1 Raise the car to a convenient and safe height for working. Disconnect the battery and drain the fluid out of the automatic transmission.
2 Remove the guard plate from over the modulating transmitter and disconnect the under pressure line from the transmitter. Disconnect the filler tube from the sump. Disconnect and blank the two lines to the oil cooler.
3 Disconnect all electrical leads from the unit, labelling each one as it is freed.
4 Disconnect the speedometer drive cable. Disconnect the handbrake cable at the lever and pull the cable out of its ducts (see **Chapter 11**). Disconnect the shift rods from the unit and lay them carefully out of the way. On the 230SL disconnect the cable to the starter lock switch.
5 The attachments of the unit are shown in **FIG 19**. Free the bracket 1 for the exhaust pipe mounting. Support the power unit with a small jack and block of wood under the sump of the transmission and insert a suitable piece of wood between the engine sump and the front axle support member, as shown in **FIG 20**. Take off the rear support 3 and rubber mounting 2.

FIG 19 Rear attachments of the transmission
1 Front exhaust bracket 2 Rubber mounting 3 Rear engine support

FIG 20 Supporting the engine and transmission

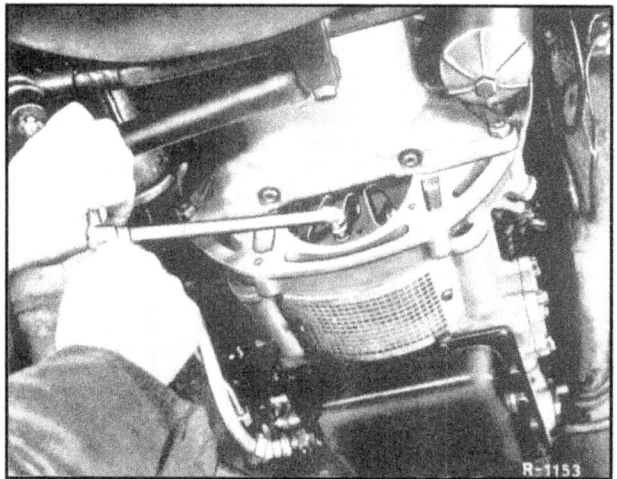

FIG 21 Removing the bolts for the fluid flywheel

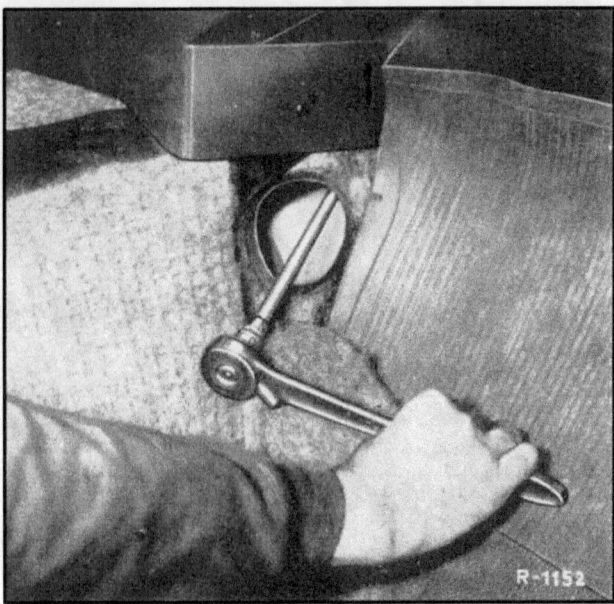

FIG 22 Removing the upper starter motor securing bolt

housing to the engine flange plate. The righthand side bolt is accessible from inside the car but the lefthand side bolt can only be removed from underneath using a long flexible drive and a socket spanner.

9 Support the transmission on a trolley jack and special adaptor. Remove the lower bolts securing the fluid flywheel housing to the engine flange. Check that all connections are disconnected. Push the transmission rearwards until the bearing pin on the torque converter is free from the engine, and lower the unit down and out of the car.

The automatic transmission is refitted in the reverse order of removal. Check all adjustments and refill the unit with ATF type A.

Fluid flywheel:

When the transmission has been taken out of the car the fluid flywheel can be removed from the transmission. Stand the unit vertically with the fluid flywheel uppermost. Screw two M.8 bolts into diagonally opposite securing holes and lift the fluid flywheel out using these two bolts, as shown in **FIG 23**.

The fluid flywheel is replaced in the reverse order of removal. Before lowering it back into place make sure that the fingers on the hollow drive shaft, shown as 1 in **FIG 24**, are aligned with the engagement of the pump gear. **Take great care not to damage the lips of the primary oil seal when lowering the flywheel into place.**

When the fluid flywheel is correctly fitted it will make a grating sound if it is turned because the cooling fins touch the housing. Once the transmission is refitted the fluid flywheel will be supported and its fins will no longer contact the housing.

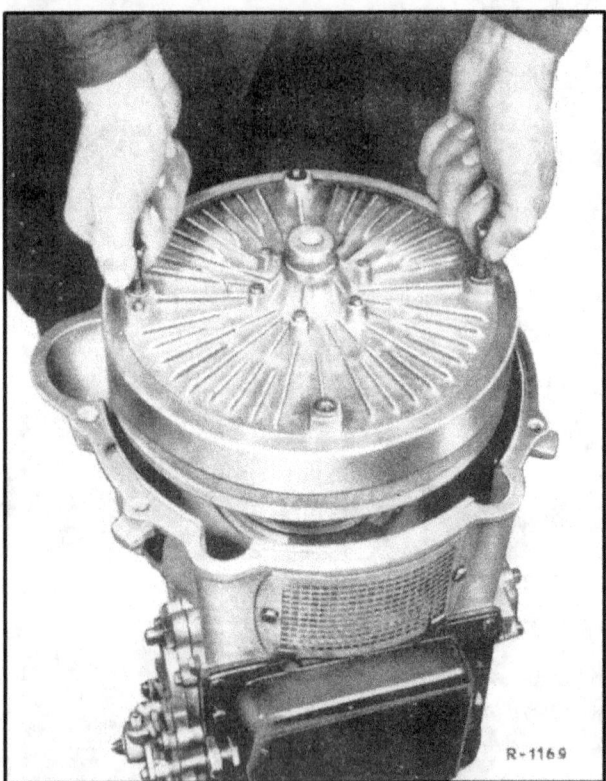

FIG 23 Removing the fluid flywheel

6 Remove the jack and block of wood from under the transmission, allowing the block of wood under the engine sump to take the weight. Disconnect the propeller shaft (see **Chapter 8, Section 2**).

7 Remove the covers from the transmission case and take out all the bolts that secure the fluid flywheel to the engine flywheel, as shown in **FIG 21**.

8 Take out the two bolts securing the starter motor. The bottom bolt is accessible from under the car and the upper bolt should be removed as shown in **FIG 22**. Remove the upper bolts securing the fluid flywheel

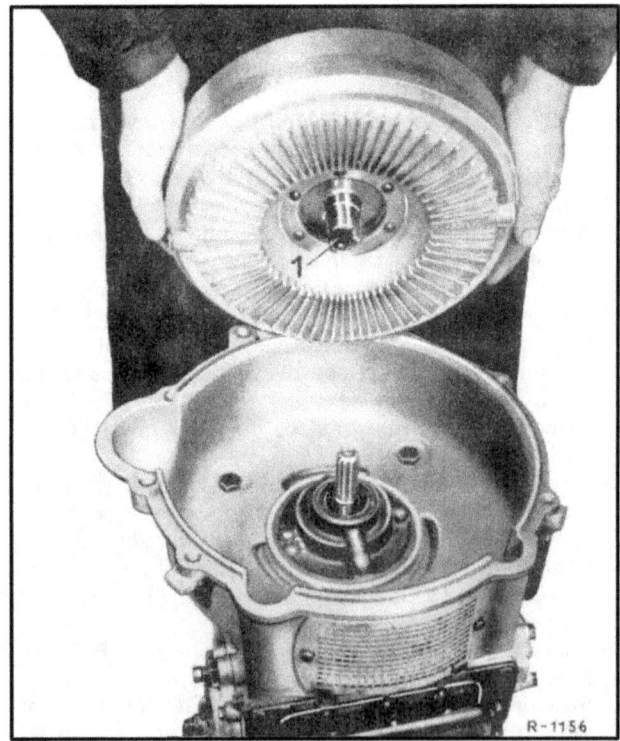

FIG 24 Aligning the fluid flywheel before refitting it

1 Hollow shaft

6 Fault diagnosis

Only a limited list of faults is given in this section as they are the ones that can be cured by the owner. Other faults or causes require the car to be taken to a specialist agent for diagnosis and rectification.

(a) Overheating

1 Stone guard on housing blocked
2 Transmission covered with road dirt
3 Oil cooler blocked
4 Oil cooler fins choked with dirt or insects
5 Incorrect fluid level (either too high or too low)

(b) Engine will not start or starts in gear

1 Linkage incorrectly adjusted
2 Starter lock switch defective or incorrectly adjusted

(c) Noisy operation

1 Low oil level
2 Oil filter dirty or choked

CHAPTER 8 – PROPELLER SHAFT, REAR AXLE AND REAR SUSPENSION

1 Description
2 Removing the propeller shaft
3 Servicing the propeller shaft
4 The rear suspension
5 The drive shafts and hub bearings
6 The rear axle
7 Removing and replacing the rear axle
8 Suspension geometry
9 Modifications
10 Fault diagnosis

1 Description

A typical rear suspension and axle are shown in **FIG 1**. Rubber mountings are used throughout to insulate the body from the suspension. The rear axle is a single-jointed swing axle fitted with a low-positioned pivot. A vertical strut, rubber mounted to the chassis, supports the pivot point. The rear axle is laterally located by a horizontal strut while two torque arms (radius arms) take the torque of the rear axle as well as locating it in the fore and aft plane. The load from the rear axle is taken by two coil springs acting between the torque arms and the chassis. The motion of the rear suspension is controlled by two telescopic dampers. A compensating spring is fitted between the two axle tubes. A hydropneumatic compensating unit may be fitted as an optional extra in place of the steel compensating spring.

The springs are made in a variety of rates and lengths and a selection of dampers is also available. The mounting pads for the rear springs have alternate positions and this, combined with different thicknesses of rubber mountings, allows the suspension to be adjusted for camber or springs of different length. The owner can therefore have a very wide selection of springs and dampers so the suspension can be best suited to the use of the car and the type of area in which it is to be used. Normally if a spring fails or weakens it should be renewed using an identical new spring, but if the use of the car changes permanently, such as from city driving to areas of very poor roads, then consult a local agent to find out the best suspension combination that will suit the new use.

The propeller shaft has been redesigned over the years so that there are three main variations in the type of propeller shaft that can be fitted. The three main variants are shown in **FIG 2** and the figure is self-explanatory. It should be noted that all the propeller shafts are fitted with an intermediate bearing which is attached to the chassis.

2 Removing the propeller shaft

1 The attachment of the propeller shaft to the rear axle is shown in **FIG 3**. The propeller shaft can be turned to a convenient position for working if one rear wheel is jacked up just clear of the ground, and the shaft can then be held in position by applying the handbrake or selecting a gear. Free the lockplates 2 and remove the nuts 3. Pull out the cheese-headed bolts 1 to free the rear end of the propeller shaft.

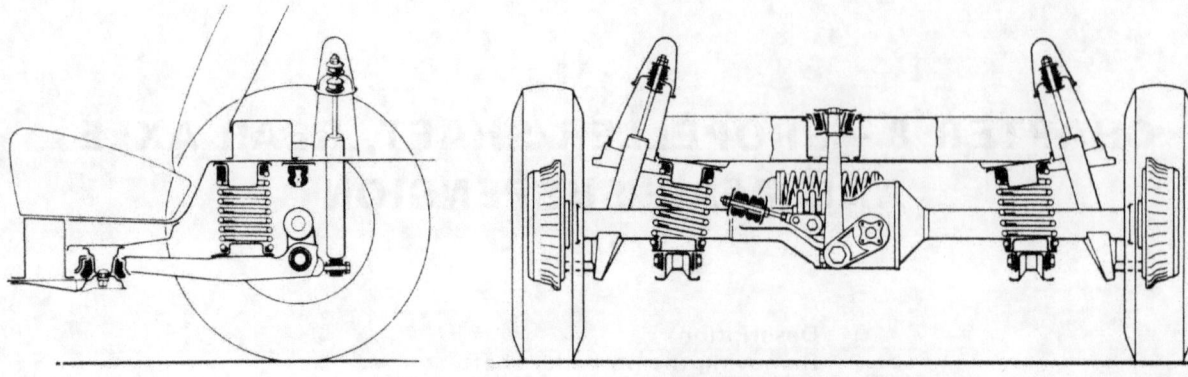

FIG 1 The rear axle and rear suspension

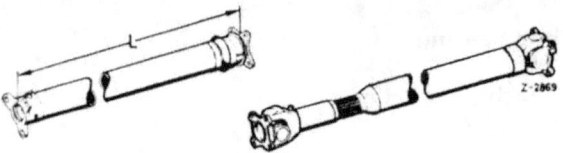

Propeller shaft with slip coupling

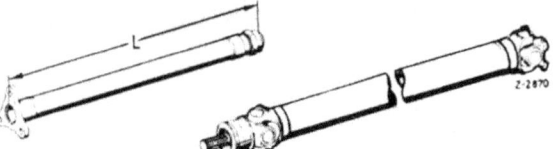

Two-part propeller shaft with clamp nut

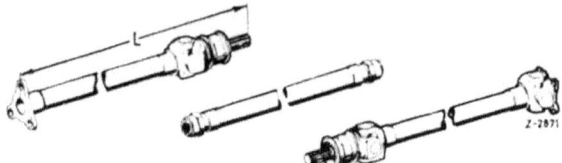

Three-part propeller shaft with clamp nut

FIG 2 Different types of propeller shaft

FIG 4 Attachments of the propeller shaft to the transmission

1 Fitted screws for propeller shaft at the shaft plate
2 Fitted screws for shaft plate at the transmission
3 Shaft plate
4 Front propeller shaft
5 Hexagon clamping bolt
6 Speedometer drive shaft

FIG 3 Attachment of propeller shaft to the rear axle

1 Cheese head screws
2 Locking plates
3 Hexagon nuts
4 Oil drain plug

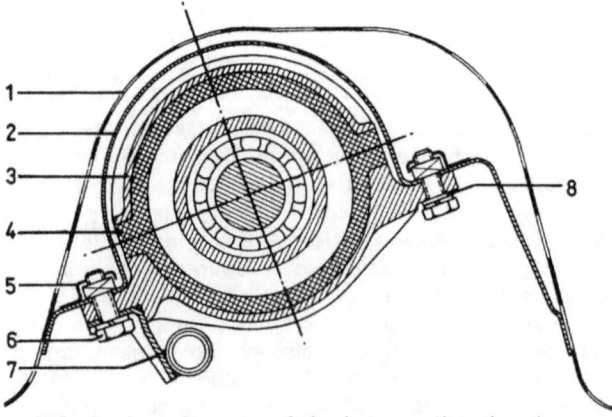

FIG 5 Attachments of the intermediate bearing

1 Chassis base panel
2 Propeller shaft housing
3 Bearing bracket
4 Rubber mounting
5 Cage nut
6 Hexagon bolt with lockwasher
7 Cable bracket
8 Washer

2 Support the power unit with a jack and block of wood under the transmission. Remove the rear support member and rubber mounting assembly from the rear of the transmission. The details of this operation for manual gearboxes are given in **Chapter 6, Section 2** and for automatic transmissions in **Chapter 7, Section 5**.

3 The attachment of the propeller shaft to the gearbox is shown in **FIG 4**. Unscrew the nuts and remove the bolts securing the propeller shaft. On the later propeller shafts fitted with clamp nuts, slacken the clamp nut so that the shaft will slide. Press the shaft rearwards to free it from the front coupling, noting that the shaft plate will remain on the transmission.

4 A sectioned view of the intermediate bearing is shown in **FIG 5**. Scribe lines across the bearing mounting and chassis so that the bearing can be fitted back into its original position. Remove the bolts 6 that secure the bearing bracket 3 to the chassis.

5 Push the propeller shaft slightly forwards so that it clears the rear axle. Lower the rear end and draw the propeller shaft out rearwards from the car, supporting it as it slides.

6 A sectioned view of the front attachment is shown in **FIG 6**. Remove the shaft plate 11 and the rubber sealing ring 3 from the transmission.

The propeller shaft is refitted in the reverse order of removal, noting the following points:

1 Before refitting the propeller shaft it is advisable to use a DTI (Dial Test Indicator) to check that the runout on the drive flanges of the transmission and rear axle is not excessive. If the runout is excessive, try removing the drive flange and turning it to a different position so that the runout is minimized.

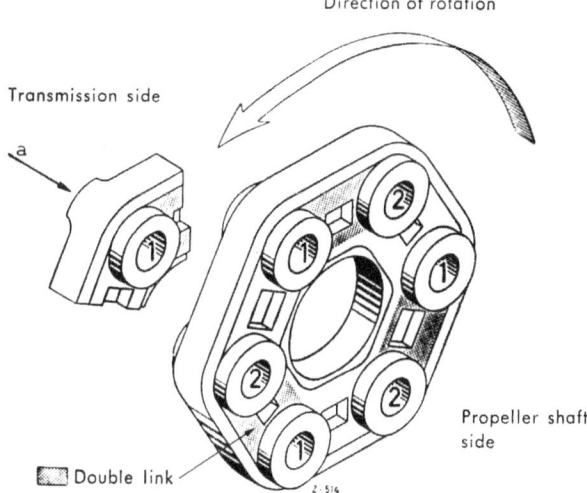

FIG 7 Correct refitting of the shaft plate

1 Connect to three-way flange of the transmission
2 Connect to three-way flange of the propeller shaft

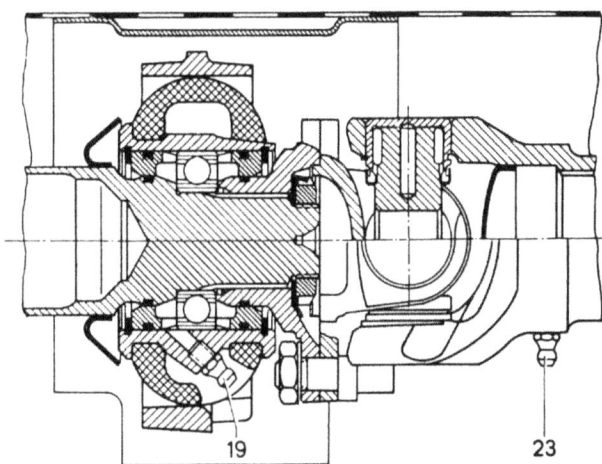

FIG 8 Lubricating the earlier intermediate bearing (See FIG 9 for details of this sectioned view)

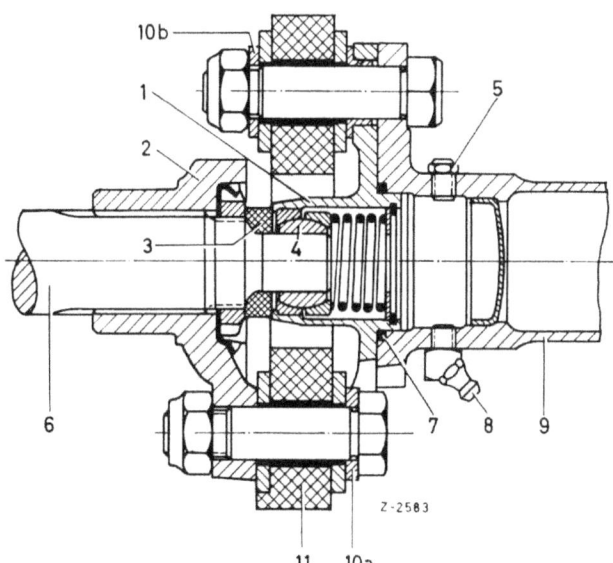

FIG 6 Sectioned view of the propeller shaft front attachment

1 Center cross
2 Three-way flange on the transmission mainshaft
3 Rubber sealing ring
4 Locating ball
5 Relief valve
6 Transmission mainshaft
7 Rubber sealing ring
8 Piston rim grease fitting
9 Front propeller shaft
10a 10b Washer
11 Shaft plate

2 Refit the rubber sealing ring onto the spigot of the transmission shaft. The shaft plate must then be correctly fitted as shown in **FIG 7** so that the double links are under tension in normal rotation. The first bore of each double link is fitted with a small nose 'a' which must face towards the transmission.

3 When self-locking nuts are fitted they should be checked before reassembly. If the nut can be run down the threads of its bolt without the use of a spanner then the nut is worn and a new nut must be fitted in its place.

4 Tighten the front and rear connections before tightening the bolts that secure the intermediate bearing. Make sure that the intermediate bearing is correctly aligned with the marks made previously.

5 On the later models where the shaft is fitted with clamp nuts leave these clamp nuts slack until the car has been lowered back onto the ground and is resting on its wheels. Roll the car backwards and forwards several times to settle the suspensions and set the length of the propeller shaft. If an intermediate shaft

3 Servicing the propeller shaft

At regular intervals grease the propeller shaft through the grease nipples provided. Later models are fitted with intermediate bearings where the bearing is sealed for life and does not require lubrication. The earlier intermediate bearing is shown in **FIG 8** and the two grease nipples of this type can be seen. The later type of maintenance-free bearing can be fitted in place of the earlier type that requires regular lubrication.

If the propeller shaft is defective or worn it is best to fit a new propeller shaft. However the intermediate bearings and universal joint can be serviced and new parts fitted.

The early intermediate bearing is shown sectioned in **FIG 9**, the later maintenance-free bearing in **FIG 10** and the very latest bearing with clamp nut in **FIG 11**.

Dismantling:

1 Pull the centre cross 1 out of the front attachment (see **FIG 6**), complete with the locating ball 4 and its spring. Remove the rubber sealing ring 7.
2 On the earlier types of bearing (without clamp nut) free the locking plates by tapping up the ears 21 and unscrew the nuts 20. Mark the two halves of the flanges, so that they will be reconnected in the same relative positions, and separate the two halves of the propeller shaft.
3 On the later type of bearing fitted with a clamp nut, slacken the clamp nut and pull the halves of the shaft apart.
4 Pull the bearing bracket and rubber mount forward off the intermediate bearing.
5 Pull the slip coupling, shown in **FIG 12**, apart after carefully finding the alignment marks 'a'.

Reassemble the propeller shaft in the reverse order of dismantling, **ensuring that the alignment marks are correctly set.** Renew any parts that are worn or damaged and fit new seals if the old ones are worn. Lubricate the

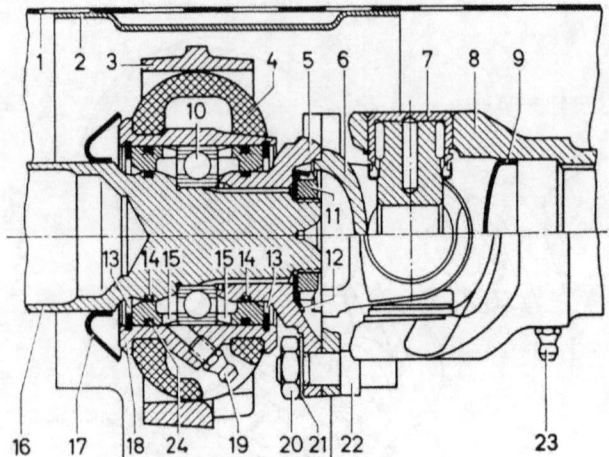

FIG 9 Sectioned view of the early intermediate bearing

1 Chassis base panel
2 Propeller shaft housing
3 Bearing housing
4 Rubber mounting
5 Joint flange front propeller shaft
6 Joint flange rear propeller shaft
7 Universal joint needle bearing
8 Rear propeller shaft slip coupling
9 Cover
10 Annular grooved bearing
11 Grooved nut
12 Locking plate
13 Snap ring
14 Compression ring
15 Spacer ring
16 Front propeller shaft
17 Boot
18 Bearing housing
19 Grease fitting
20 Hexagon nut
21 Locking plate
22 Cheese head screw
23 Grease fitting
24 Rubber sealing ring

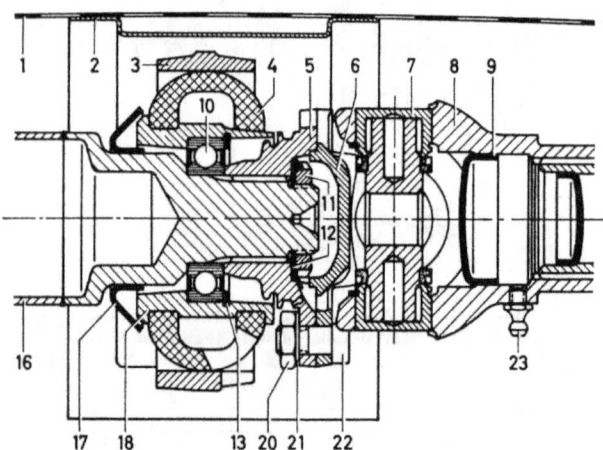

FIG 10 Sectioned view of the later maintenance free intermediate bearing

1 Chassis base panel
2 Propeller shaft housing
3 Bearing bracket
4 Rubber mounting
5 Joint flange front prop shaft
6 Joint flange rear prop shaft
7 Universal joint needle bearing
8 Rear propeller shaft yoke
9 Cover
10 Annular grooved bearing
11 Grooved nut
12 Locking plate
13 Snap ring
16 Front propeller shaft
17 Protective cap
18 Housing
20 Hexagonal nut
21 Locking plate
22 Cheese-head screw
23 Grease nipple

is fitted make sure that it is not touching either of the intermediate bearings and that it is equidistant from both. After rolling the car tighten all the clamp nuts to a torque load of 20 mkg.

6 Grease the propeller shaft through its lubrication points. The grease points for the different types are shown in the various sectioned views of the parts.

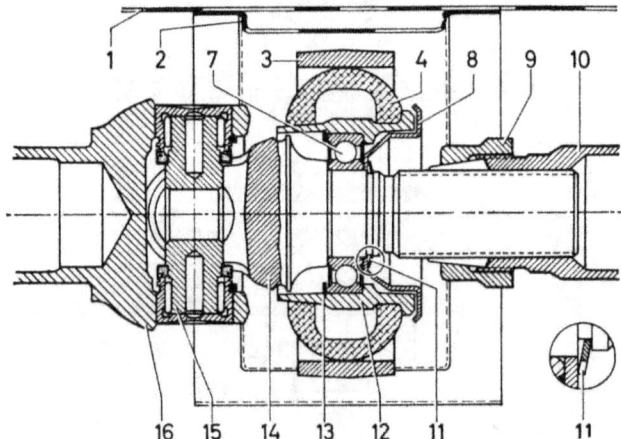

FIG 11 Sectioned view of the intermediate bearing fitted with clamp nuts

1 Chassis base panel
2 Propeller shaft housing
3 Bearing bracket
4 Rubber mounting
7 Grooved ballbearing
8 Protective cap
9 Clamp nut
10 Intermediate shaft or front propeller shaft
11 Snap ring
12 Bearing housing
13 Snap ring
14 Yoke
15 Universal joint spider with needle bearing bushings
16 Front or rear propeller shaft

splines of the slip joint with molybdenum disulphide paste. If the early type of bearing is completely defective it should be discarded and the later type of maintenance-free bearing, complete with bearing housing and joint flange, should be fitted in its place.

When assembling the earlier type of bearing make sure that the bearing bracket 3 and rubber mounting 4 are refitted so that their recesses align with the grease nipple.

Early intermediate bearing:

This is shown sectioned in **FIG 9**. Before servicing the bearing dismantle the propeller shaft.

1 Hold a special spanner No. 111.589.02.07.00 in a vice and mount the front propeller shaft flange using suitable nuts and bolts so that the shaft hangs vertically downwards. Free the locking plate 12 and use a special pin spanner No. 111.589.03.07.00 to remove the grooved nut 11. Mark the relative position of the flange 5 and remove the flange.

2 Use a suitable puller to withdraw the housing 18 complete with the spacer rings 15 and ballbearing 10. Remove the compression rings 14 from the shaft and the flange 5. Take out the two snap rings 13 and press the spacer rings 15 and ballbearing 10 out of the housing. Remove the two rubber sealing rings from the spacer rings 15.

3 Check all the parts for wear or damage after washing the metal parts in clean fuel. Wash the ballbearing 10 separately in clean fuel and renew the bearing if it runs roughly or is worn.

4 Fit the front snap ring 13 back into place and press the front spacer ring 15 into place after fitting a new seal 24 to the spacer. The spacer ring must be pressed right in to contact the snap ring and its recesses should face the bearing with one recess aligning with the grease nipple. Pack the bearing 10 with grease and press it back into place followed by the other spacer ring 15 with a new seal 24 fitted to it. Again the recesses of the spacer should face the bearing. Secure the parts in place with the remaining snap ring 13.

5 Fit new compression rings 14 to the shaft and flange and carefully press the housing assembly back onto the shaft so that the grease nipple will face rearwards on the car. Refit the rubber mounting 4, using a new one if the old one is cracked, perished or grease contaminated. Refit the bearing housing 3 after checking it for cracks or damage.

6 Refit the nut 11 with a new lockplate 12 using the same special tools as for dismantling. Reassemble the remainder of the propeller shaft and lightly lubricate before refitting it.

Maintenance-free intermediate bearing:

A sectioned view of this later bearing is shown in **FIG 10**. The same special tools are required for dismantling and reassembling this type of bearing as for the earlier one. After the flange 5 has been removed the housing and bearing assembly can be removed with a suitable puller. Remove the snap ring 13 and drive out the bearing. **The bearing is sealed for life and must not be washed in solvents.** If the bearing runs roughly or noisily fit a new sealed prelubricated bearing in its place. Examine the remainder of the parts as for the earlier bearing and reassemble the parts in the reverse order of dismantling.

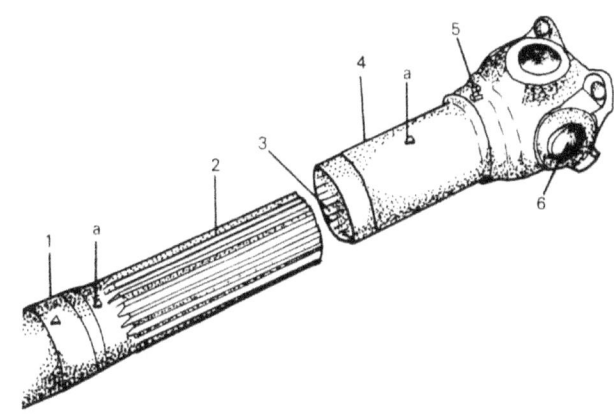

FIG 12 Details of the slip coupling

1 Rear propeller shaft
2 Splineways
3 Felt sealing ring
4 Slip coupling
5 Grease fitting for splineways
6 Universal joint
a Alignment marks for slip coupling

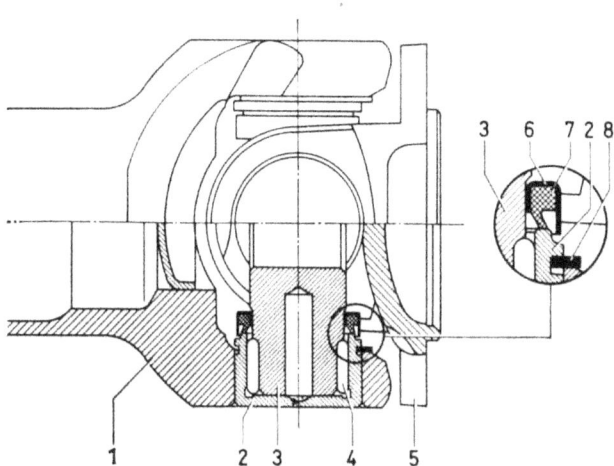

FIG 13 Sectioned view of a universal joint

1 Yoke
2 Needle bearing cup
3 Universal joint spider
4 Needle
5 Joint flange
6 Sealing ring retainer
7 Sealing ring
8 Snap ring

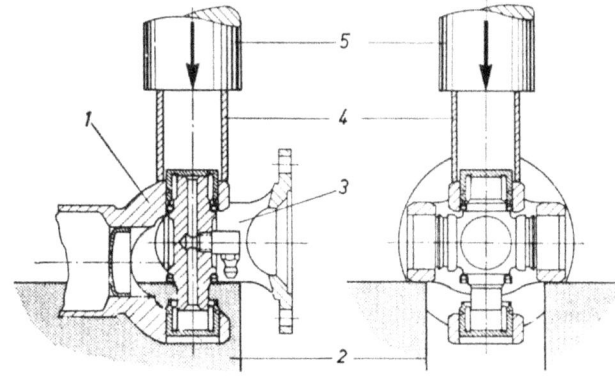

FIG 14 Removing the bearings from a universal joint

1 Yoke
2 Support
3 Joint flange
4 Sleeve
5 Arbor press

FIG 15 General view of the rear suspension and axle looking forwards

1 Rear shock-absorber	4 Brake line	7 Rear brake cable	10 Main muffler
2 Rubber buffer for axle tube	5 Brake hose	8 Torque arm	11 Rear exhaust pipe
3 Rear spring	6 Distributor fitting	9 Brake line (connection to left brake hose)	12 Intermediate muffler
			13 Compensating spring

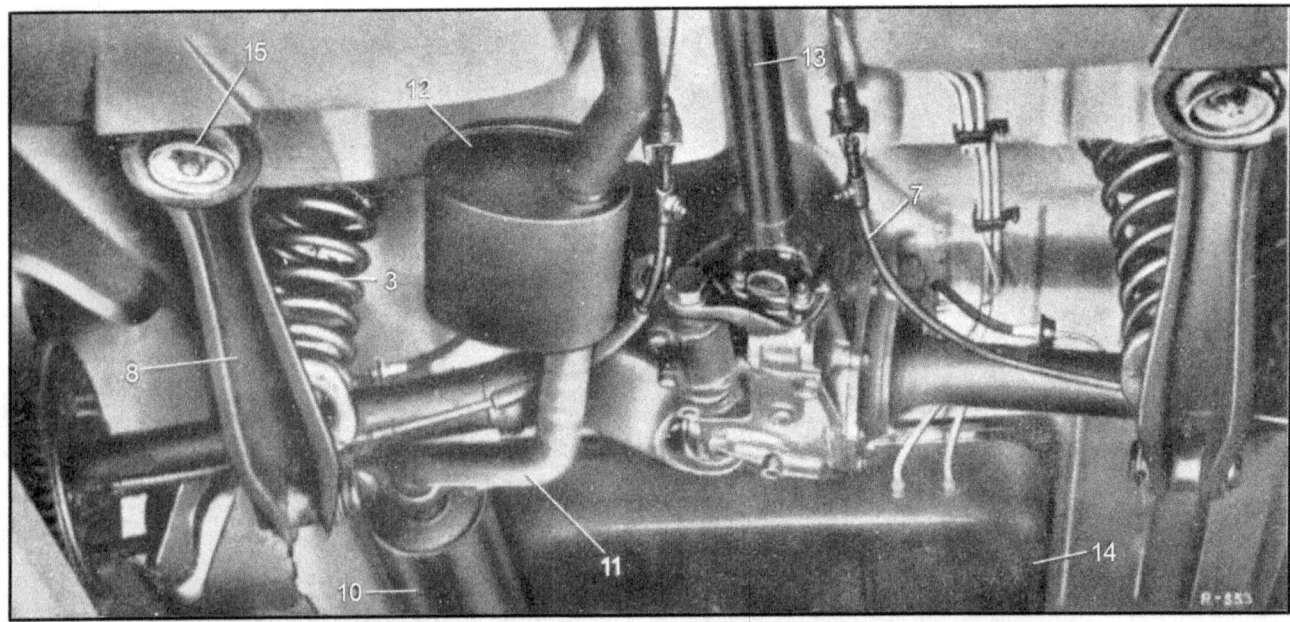

FIG 16 General view of the rear suspension and axle looking rearwards

3 Rear spring	10 Main muffler	13 Rear propeller shaft
7 Rear brake cable	11 Rear exhaust pipe	14 Fuel tank
8 Torque arm	12 Intermediate muffler	15 Front torque arm mounting

Intermediate bearing with clamp nut:

A sectioned view is shown in **FIG 11**. The front or intermediate shaft 10 can be pulled off after slackening the clamp nut 9. Remove the bearing bracket 3, rubber mounting 4, snap ring 11 and protective cap 8. The housing complete with the bearing 7 and snap ring 13 can then be removed from the shaft using a puller. Remove the snap ring 13 and press the bearing 7 out of the housing.

The parts are reassembled in the reverse order of dismantling, taking care to use the correct prelubricated and sealed bearing.

Universal joint:

A sectioned view of the universal joint is shown in **FIG 13**. If a universal joint is to be repaired then it is essential that all the parts supplied in service kit No. 111.410.00.31 are used and parts are not renewed individually. The snap rings are obtainable in thicknesses from 1.45 to 1.7 mm (.057 to .067 inch) in increments of .05 mm (.002 inch). The snap rings should be selectively fitted (opposite snap rings being of the same thickness) so that the joint can be moved by hand without it jerking or there being excessive play.

Dismantle the propeller shaft and proceed as follows:

1 Remove all four snap rings 8 from the universal joint. If the snap rings are difficult to free clean the area of dust, dirt and enamel and also tap in the bearing bushings 2 lightly so as to relieve the pressure on the snap rings.
2 Support the arms of the yoke as shown in **FIG 14** and use a suitable piece of tube to press the yoke down as far as it will go. If a press is not available the jaws of a vice can be used instead. Remove the bearing assembly now exposed. Turn the joint over and remove the opposite bearing in a similar manner.
3 Manoeuvre the yoke off the spider trunnions and then remove the remaining pair of bearings in a similar manner to the first pair.
4 Check the bores in the yoke arms and see that the bearing cups are a light drive fit through them. **If the bores in the yokes are worn the shaft must be renewed.** Check that the seal 7 and their retainers 6 are securely in place. If the seals are damaged remove the old ones and fit new ones in their place. Lightly smear the face of the retainer 6 with jointing compound and use a well fitting hollow drift to press the parts firmly onto the spider.
5 Some universal joints are sealed and packed with grease for life. The new spiders are supplied packed with the correct amount of grease and **on no account should any of this grease be wiped off or wasted.** Any losses must be replaced using nothing but the correct lubricant, which is Mobil-Grease MP.
6 Fit the needles 4 back into the bearing cup 2 using a little grease or vaseline to hold them in place. **The correct number of needles precisely fills the cup and it is essential that the correct number of needles is fitted.**
7 Support a yoke arm and press an assembled bearing half way down the bore of the yoke. Insert a trunnion of the spider into the bearing, **taking great care not to displace any needle rollers.** Press the bearing assembly fully home and secure it with a snap ring 8.
8 Turn the yoke over and press the opposite bearing assembly fully into place and secure it with the snap ring. **Again great care must be taken not to displace the needle rollers.** If a needle is displaced it will snap immediately pressure is applied to it.
9 Refit the remaining pair of bearings in a similar manner. Lightly tap the yoke arms with a soft-faced hammer to settle the bearings and check that the joint articulates freely without excessive play or jerky movements. If the movement is not free, the snap rings must be selectively fitted until the movement is correct.

4 The rear suspension

A general view of the suspension and rear axle looking forwards is shown in **FIG 15** and a similar view looking rearwards is shown in **FIG 16**. The compensating spring 13, or optional hydropneumatic compensator unit, will be dealt with in this section.

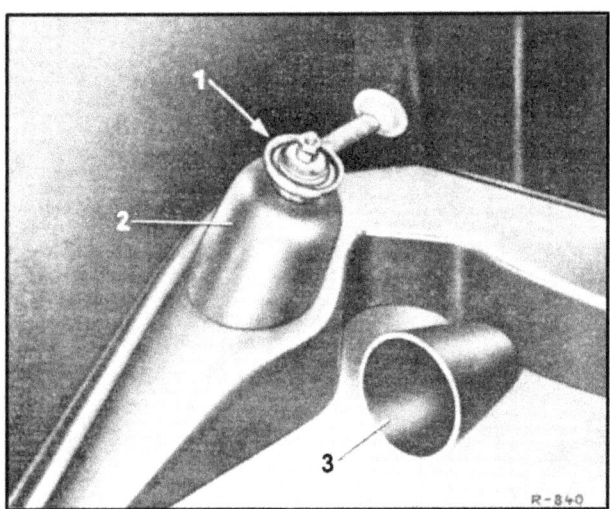

FIG 17 The upper attachment position of the damper

1 Upper shock-absorber attachment point
2 Dome on chassis base panel
3 Rubber protective cap

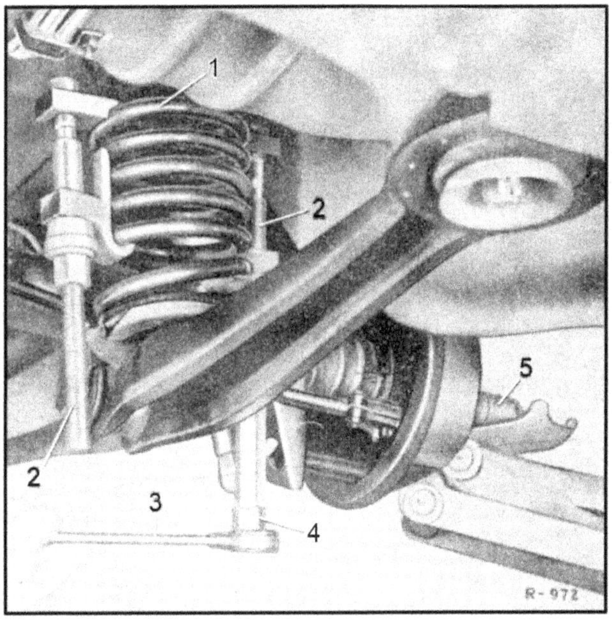

FIG 18 Removing a road spring

1 Rear spring
2 Spring Tensioner 111 589 04 31
3 Ratchet ½" square
4 Hexagon Special Socket 24 mm 111 589 01 09
5 Flange 111 589 01 63

Dampers:

All the different makes of damper fitted are telescopic and as far as the owner is concerned they are sealed units. Bilstein dampers are gas-filled and cannot be dismantled under any circumstances. F & S or Stabilius dampers can be dismantled using special equipment which even a local agent may not have.

The damper mountings vary slightly in detail between the different makes though the instructions for one make apply equally to the others. The main difference is in the shape and direction of the rubber mountings and washers on the upper attachment. **Provided that the parts are refitted as removed no difficulty will be experienced.**

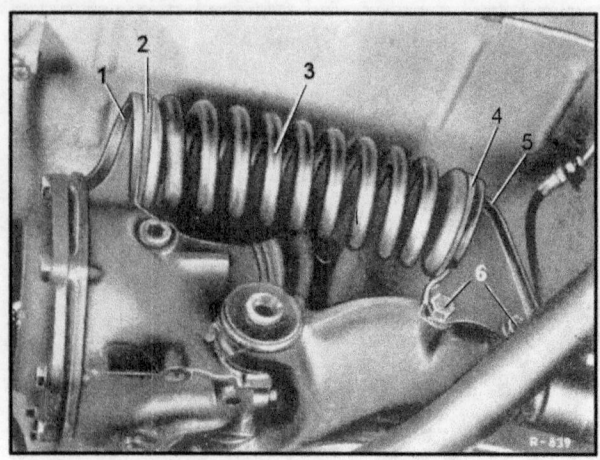

FIG 19 The compensator spring attachments

1 Rear axle bracket 3 Spring 5 Righthand bracket
2 Rubber ring left 4 Rubber ring right 6 Bracket attachment bolts

Damper removal:

Jack up the rear of the car with a jack under the torque arm so that the weight of the suspension is taken on the jack. Remove the road wheel and if possible work from a pit as this will make the task easier. From inside the luggage compartment remove the protective cap 3, shown in **FIG 17**. Take off the locknut and the nut underneath it. Lift off the metal cupwasher and rubber mounting, noting the position and direction of these two for reassembly.

Working underneath the car remove the nut (bolt on later versions) that secures the damper to the pivot pin. Take off the lockwasher and cupwasher and pull the damper off the pivot bolt. Withdraw the damper downwards from the car and remove the remaining rubber mounting and cupwasher from the top end of the damper.

Damper testing:

Special equipment is required for testing the damper but if it fails the following test it is unserviceable and must be renewed. Even if it passes the test it does not mean that it is fully serviceable.

Mount the damper vertically in the padded jaws of a vice. Examine it for signs of physical damage such as a bent ram, dented body or oil leaks. Clean the shaft as this can cause noisy operation when the damper is operated slowly. Operate the damper by hand with partial strokes about the centre point and gradually increase the length of the strokes until they reach the full stroke of the damper. The resistance should be uniform and if it varies or there are pockets of no resistance the damper is defective. Similarly the damper is defective if the resistance is so high that it cannot be moved slowly by hand. The damper is defective if it makes odd noises, especially if the Bilstein dampers whistle or click.

Check that the internal diameter of the lower damper eye does not exceed 30.2mm (1.189 inch). If this diameter is exceeded the rubber mounting will not seat satisfactorily so the damper must be renewed.

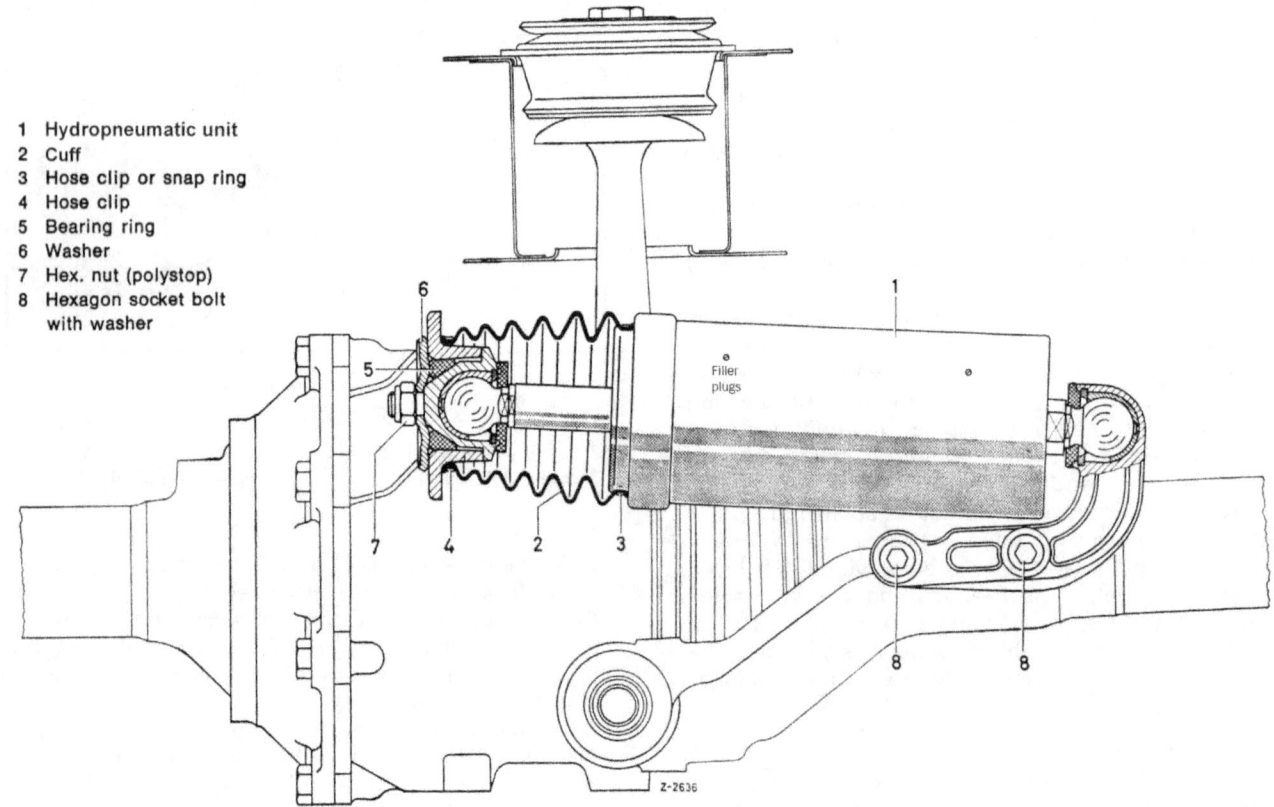

1 Hydropneumatic unit
2 Cuff
3 Hose clip or snap ring
4 Hose clip
5 Bearing ring
6 Washer
7 Hex. nut (polystop)
8 Hexagon socket bolt with washer

FIG 20 Hydropneumatic compensator attachments

Damper refitting:

The damper is refitted in the reverse order of removal, noting the following points:

1. Check all the rubber mountings and renew them if they are cracked, distorted or perished. Ensure that only the correct rubber mountings are used as replacement parts.
2. On earlier models the bore in the chassis for the upper mounting was 15.5 + .5mm and on later models the bore was increased to 16.5 + .5mm (.650 + .020 inch). If a new damper is to be fitted to an old model the bore should be opened up to the correct diameter using a high-speed drill.
3. Check that the fitted depth of the lower damper mounting is 40 —.5mm (1.57 —.02 inch). If the distance is excessive fit washers of 16mm (.63 inch) internal diameter and 23mm (.9 inch) external diameter to bring the compressed depth of the rubber mounting within the correct limits. Do not use washers of different diameters from the ones given as these will stress the mounting unduly.
4. When refitting the upper mounting the nuts should be screwed down so that the lower nut contacts the end of the thread, or the spacer tube fitted on earlier models.

Road spring removal:

1. Jack up the rear of the car and remove the appropriate road wheel. Take the weight of the suspension either with a jack under the torque arm or else using a jack and adaptor as shown in **FIG 18**.
2. Fit a spring tensioner No. 111.589.04.31 on either side of the spring and tighten the spring tensioners as much as possible.
3. Lower the jack supporting the suspension and remove the road spring, held clamped by the tensioners, complete with its upper and lower mounting rubbers. The damper acts as a limit stop so that the jack supporting the suspension can be removed if the damper is still fitted. If the damper has been removed the jack must be left in place so as to support the suspension.
4. Compress the spring in a strong vice and remove the tensioners.

The spring is refitted in the reverse order of removal. Lubricate the rubber mountings with talc and secure them to the spring with small pieces of masking tape.

If the lower spring pan is removed from the torque arm it must be refitted using the original securing holes. The other securing holes are for altering the camber of the rear wheels or, in conjunction with different mounting rubbers, for compensating for the different lengths of the various springs.

The compensating spring:

Different lengths of compensating spring are available and they are adjusted to suit the car by the selective fitting of the rubber mountings 2 and 4, shown in **FIG 19**. In certain cases the camber of the rear wheels can also be adjusted by fitting a different compensating spring and rubber mounting rings.

Jack up the rear of the car until all the load is taken off the two axle tubes. Fit a tensioner 111.589.00.31 between as many of the coils of the spring as possible. Screw up

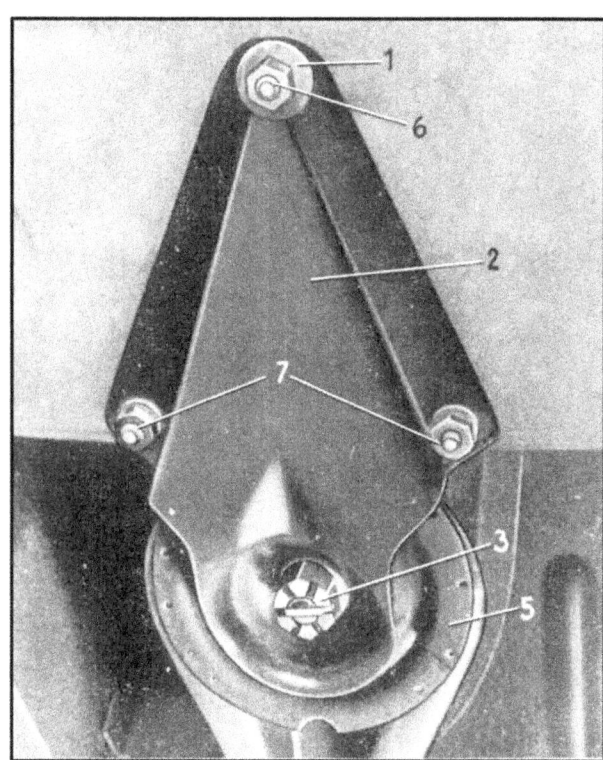

FIG 21 Front attachment of the torque arm

1. Washer
2. Cover plate
3. Shouldered castle nut
5. Torque arm
6. Welded-in hexagon bolt with nut
7. Hexagon bolts with nuts

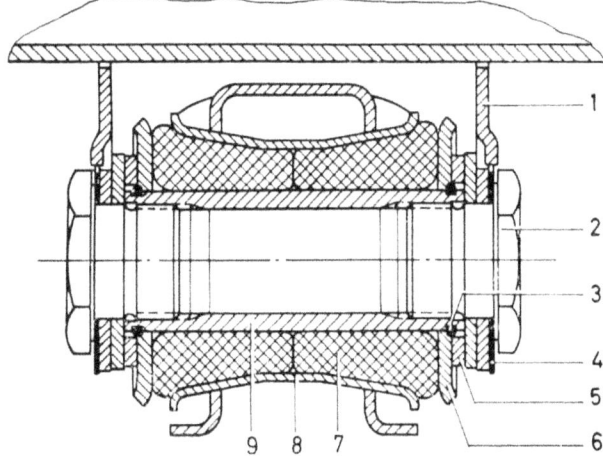

FIG 22 Attachment of the torque arm to the rear axle

1. Mounting support at axle tube
2. Hexagon bolt
3. Snap ring
4. Locking plate
5. Spacer ring
6. Tension disk
7. Rubber mounting
8. Torque arm
9. Pivot pin

the tensioner until the pressure is removed from the bracket 5. Remove the bolts 6 that secure the bracket 5 and remove the bracket, and spring 3 held by the tensioner as well as the two rubber mounting rings 2 and 4.

When refitting the spring attach the bracket 5 by the inner bolt 6 only. Hold the spring, with the mounting rubbers attached to it and compressed by the tensioner, and pivot the bracket 5 onto it so that the other bolt 6 can be fitted. Tighten the bolts 6, remove the tensioner and lower the car back to the ground.

FIG 23 Removing the mounting rubber from the torque arm

Assembly fixture 111.589.09.61.00

1a Baseplate with pilot bush	6 Tension disk
1c Arbor	7 Rubber mounting
3 Snap ring	8 Torque arm

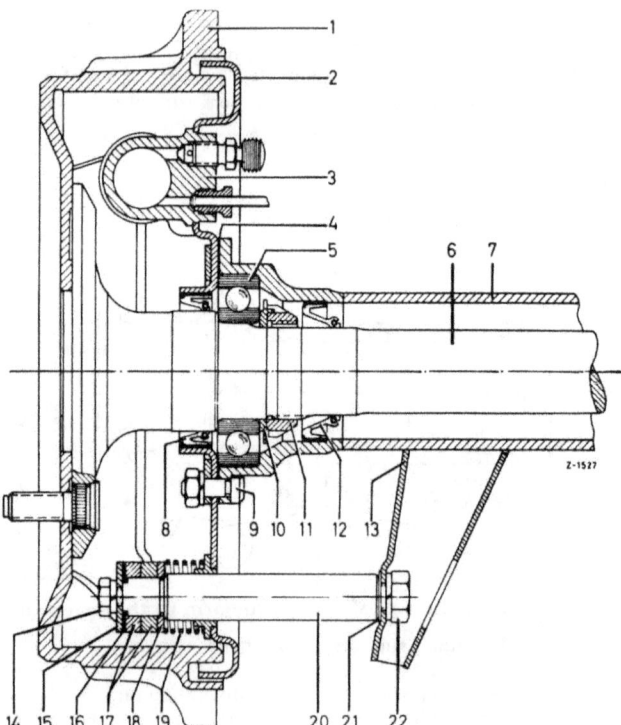

FIG 24 Sectioned view of the rear hub assembly

1 Brake drum	9 Fitted bolt	16 Brass washer
2 Brake anchor plate	10 Locking plate	17 Brake shoe
3 Wheel cylinder	11 Grooved nut	18 Washer
4 Gasket	12 Inner seal	19 Pressure spring
5 Annular grooved bearing	13 Bracket	20 Anchor pin
6 Rear axle shaft	14 Hexagon bolt	21 Washer
7 Axle tube	with lock washer	22 Hexagon bolt
8 Outer seal	15 Washer	with lock washer

Hydropneumatic compensating spring:

This is an optional extra that can be fitted in place of the steel compensating spring. As the wheels move up and down over the road surface the two halves of the axle pivot, and the motion pumps up the hydropneumatic unit so as to set the level of the rear of the car, irrespective of the load that is being carried. The unit requires no maintenance or servicing unless it becomes defective. When adjusting the headlights with a hydropneumatic unit fitted, the car should be loaded at the front seat with 70 kg (150 lb) and the rear of the car rocked strongly 20 to 30 times so as to settle the rear height.

1 To remove the unit it may be necessary to free the lower attachments of both dampers. Raise the rear of the car on jacks and stands until the axle tubes have no load on them.
2 Free the clamps 3 and 4 that secure the cuff 2, shown in **FIG 20**, so that the cuff can be pulled back.
3 Take out the two socket-headed bolts 8, unscrew the nut 7 and lift the unit out of the car. Remove the bearing ring 5.

Refit the unit in the reverse order of removal. The unit must be fitted so that the two filler plugs face the rear of the car.

Torque arm:

The attachment of the front end of the torque arm to the chassis is shown in **FIG 21** and a sectioned view of the attachment to the rear axle is shown in **FIG 22**. On earlier models a cupwasher was fitted in place of the cover plate 2 and on later models the castellated nut 3 is changed for a self-locking nut on the front end attachment.

1 Remove the road spring. Refer to **FIG 21** and remove the cover plate 2, carefully collecting any shims that are fitted under it. Pull the torque arm off its step mounting and if necessary press out the rubber mounting.
2 Take out both bolts 2 from the pivot on the axle (see **FIG 22**) and pull the torque arm, together with spacer rings 5, out of the support bracket 1.
3 If the rubbers in the attachment to the axle require renewal then the rubbers must be compressed so that the snap ring 3 can be removed. The best method is to use an arbor press and the fixture No. 111.589.09.61.00 as shown in **FIG 23**.

The torque arms are reassembled and refitted in the reverse order of removal. **Label the arms as they are removed because they are handed and must not be interchanged.** The rubber ring for the front attachment is marked UNTEN on one face and this face must be fitted downwards. It will assist in refitting the front mounting if the tapered arbor No. 120.589.07.61 is screwed onto the bolt that secures the front mounting as the arbor will guide the mounting and rubber into place. The shims under the coverplate should be adjusted so that they pack the space without moving or straining the coverplate 2.

5 The drive shafts and hub bearings

A sectioned view of a rear hub assembly is shown in **FIG 24**. Before starting to remove the hub assembly take off the brake parts, brake drum, brake shoes, handbrake cable and pulley, and disconnect the hydraulic line from the brake. Further details of the brakes are given in **Chapter 11**. On models fitted with an anchor pin 20, take out the bolt 22 and washer 21.

1 Remove the nuts that screw onto the special bolts 9 which secure the backplate assembly. Use extractor No. 111.589.12.33.00 to draw the hub and drive shaft out of the axle tube, as shown in **FIG 25**. The earlier impact type of extractor should not be used as it could damage the parts.
2 Free the locking plate 10. Secure the drive flange of the shaft using fixture No. 136.589.05.31.00 mounted in a vice and undo the nut 11 using wrench No. 136.589.09.07.00. Use a puller to remove the bearing 5 from the shaft.
3 Prise out the old oil seals 8 and 12 taking great care not to damage the backplate or axle tube bores.

Examination:

Wash all the metal parts in clean fuel or any suitable degreasing agent. The bearing 5 should be washed separately so that it does not collect any dirt from the other parts. Lubricate the bearing with thin engine oil and check it for roughness or noise as it is rotated. Renew the bearing if it is defective or shows signs of wear or corrosion.

Ideally the drive shaft should be rotated between centres and a DTI used to check that it is running truly. The flange may be lightly skimmed down in a lathe to restore accuracy.

A portion of the flange has a screw thread cut on it, as shown in **FIG 26**. The threads are very shallow and can be recut using a strip of 180 grade emerycloth and rubber backing strip stretched across a wooden handle, as shown in **FIG 27**. The threads of the lefthand side drive shaft must be cut righthanded and the righthand side cut lefthanded.

If new drive shafts are fitted check that they are of the correct type. The earlier shafts have a single annular bead around them near the splines, while the later type have two annular beads. The two types of drive shaft are not interchangeable.

Reassembly:

1 Coat the outer surface of the oil seal 8 with jointing compound and press it back into the backplate. Similarly refit the oil seal 12 back into the axle tube.

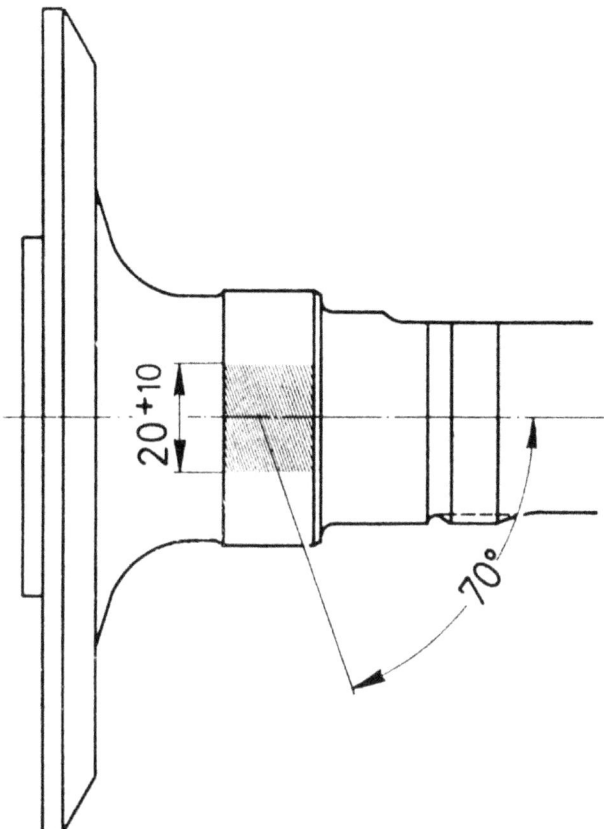

FIG 26 Lefthand side drive shaft with righthand thread pattern

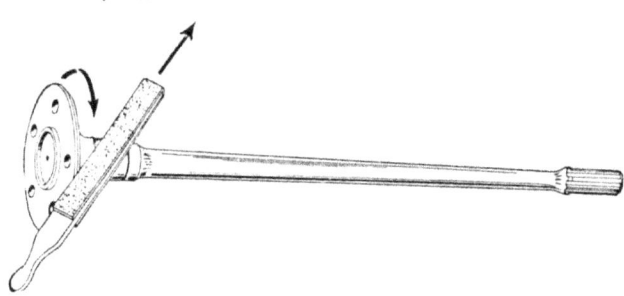

FIG 27 Cutting a lefthand thread on a righthand side drive shaft

New oil seals should be used and they are both fitted so that their lips face towards the differential.

2 Coat the area where the oil seal fits onto the drive shaft with Molykote paste and carefully press the backplate back into position. Pack the bearing 5 with anti-friction grease and press it back into position on the drive shaft. Fit a new locking plate 10 and secure the parts with the nut 11. Peen the lockplate into the nut to lock the nut.
3 Lightly apply jointing compound to both sides of a new gasket 4 and lay it back into position on the backplate. Pack the space surrounding the bearing and between the two oil seals with grease and press the drive shaft assembly back into place. **Take great care not to damage the lips of the oil seal 12 when passing the drive shaft through it.** The same special tool that was used for removing the hub assembly can be used for pressing the assembly back into position. While pressing the parts back it will help

FIG 25 Withdrawing the rear hub assembly

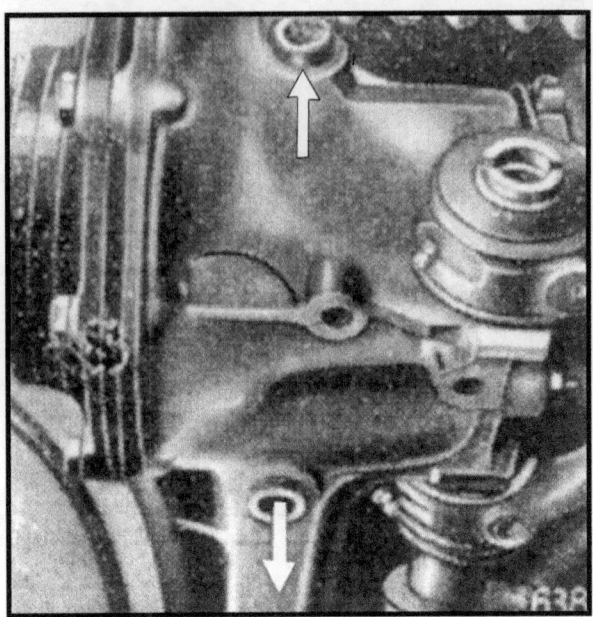

FIG 28 The rear axle drain and filler plugs

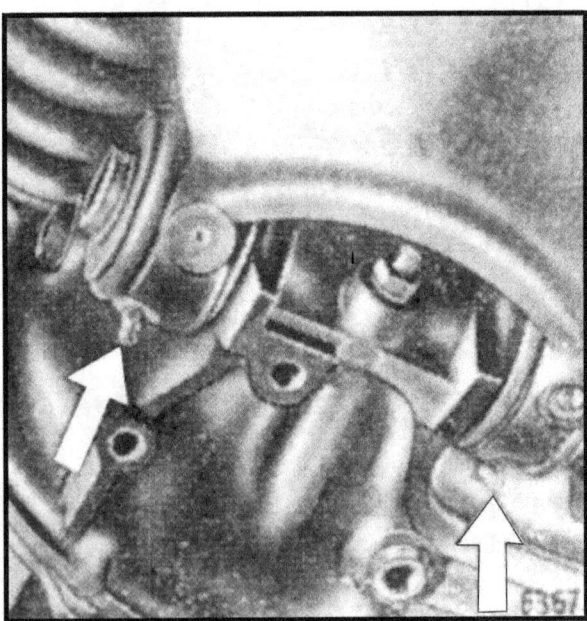

FIG 29 Rear axle pivot point lubrication

essential that the correct tolerances, clearances and pre-loads are set on assembly otherwise the axle will not operate satisfactorily and may fail in service.

There are however various tasks that the owner can carry out without dismantling the axle assembly.

Lubrication:

At regular intervals check the oil level in the rear axle. The level should come to the bottom of the combined filler and level plug. The drain and filler plugs are shown arrowed in **FIG 28**. Use an oil gun to top up the level and allow any surplus to drain out before refitting the filler plug. **Do not overfill the rear axle.** Though there are several recommended brands of oil for the rear axle it should always be topped up with the same brand as it already contains, to prevent any additives affecting each other adversely. If the brand is unknown the oil should be drained out and the unit refilled.

At longer periods the old oil should be drained from the axle and fresh oil used to fill it. Drain the axle while it is hot after a long run. **Do not flush out the axle with any solvents before refilling it as some solvent will remain to dilute the fresh oil.**

The grease nipples for the pivot are shown in **FIG 29**.

Cross-strut:

The cross-strut, shown in **FIG 30**, locates the rear axle laterally. If the rubber mountings are worn or the cups distorted they should be renewed otherwise the riding and handling qualities of the car may be affected.

If the axle is being taken out then only the front link 9 needs to be removed and the attachment at the chassis need not be slackened or freed.

1 Take off the nut 1 after loosening its locknut. Take out the bolts 8 and 10 so that the front link 9 can be removed. Push the cross-strut 5 and rear link 7 rearwards so that they are freed from the rear axle. Withdraw the link from the chassis mounting and collect the cups 2 and rubber buffers 3.

FIG 30 The rear axle lateral support strut

1 Hexagon nut and lock nut	6 Hexagon nut (lock nut)	11 Bolt for connecting pin of the rear axle suspension
2 Cup	7 Rear link	12 Support for rear axle suspension
3 Rubber buffer	8 Hex bolt and spring washer	13 Clamping bolts
4 Retainer on chassis base panel	9 Front link	
5 Cross strut	10 Hex bolt and spring washer	

if the bearing is held in alignment using the guide No. 111.589.08.63.00 to hold it in place just before it enters the axle tube.

4 Reassemble the remainder of the parts in the reverse order of removal. When all the parts are fitted bleed and adjust the hydraulic brakes and also adjust the handbrake (see **Chapter 11**). Check the oil level in the rear axle and top up if required.

6 The rear axle

The rear axle and its attachments are shown in **FIG 15** and **FIG 16**. The compensating spring has been dealt with in **Section 4**.

The rear axle should not be dismantled by the average owner. Skill, experience and special tools are all essential for reassembling the axle correctly and it is

2 Renew the rubber buffers if they are worn, perished or damaged. Similarly renew the cups 2 if they are distorted.

3 Refit the parts in the reverse order of removal. If there is any doubt as to the accurate location of the rear axle the setting should be checked at a garage using special gauges.

Drive pinion seal:

This seal can be renewed if it leaks without removing the axle from the car.

1 Drain the oil out from the axle. Disconnect the rear end of the propeller shaft from the rear axle drive flange.

2 A sectioned view of the pinion is shown in **FIG 31**. Free the locking plate 2 from its groove in the joint flange 3. Use light punch marks to identify the relationship of the flange to the pinion shaft. Prevent the drive flange from rotating, preferably with special spanner No. 111.589.02.07.00, and use the special adaptor No. 111.589.00.07.00 to undo the nut 1. Remove the drive flange.

3 Examine the contact surface of the drive flange and renew the flange if the surface is damaged or scored. The surface has a portion of screw thread cut into it at an angle of 70 degrees.

4 Prise out the old oil seal 5 from the cover 7 and press a new oil seal into place after coating its outside surface with jointing compound.

5 Refit the parts in the reverse order of removal and fill the rear axle to the correct level with oil.

Axle cuff:

A seamless rubber cuff is fitted between the two axle tubes to keep grease and oil in as well as dirt out. The cuff must be renewed if it is damaged or split. A new cuff, of the split type, can be fitted without removing or dismantling the rear axle.

1 Remove the compensating spring (see **Section 4**). Thoroughly clean the axle around the cuff to prevent any dirt from entering when the cuff is removed. Take off the two clips that secure the cuff and remove it by splitting it with a sharp knife.

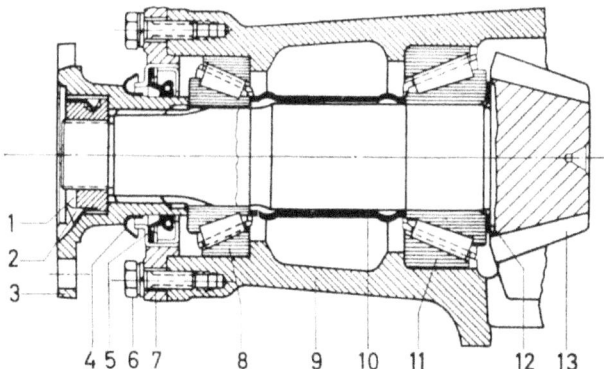

FIG 31   Sectioned view of the rear axle drive pinion

1 Grooved nut
2 Locking plate
3 Joint flange
4 Protective washer
5 Seal
6 Hexagon bolt
7 Cover
8 Front annular taper roller bearing
9 Rear axle housing
10 Spacer sleeve
11 Rear annular taper roller bearing
12 Compensating washer
13 Drive pinion

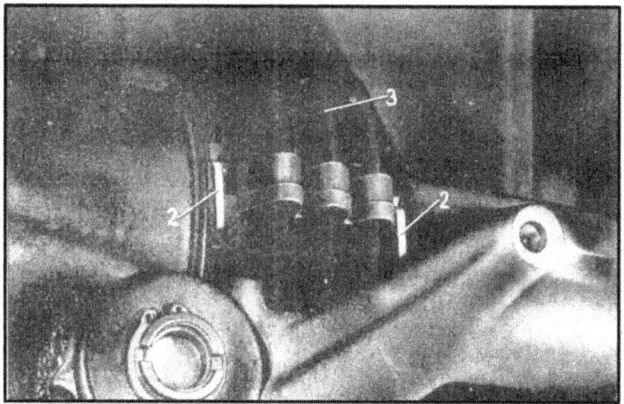

FIG 32   Fitting the split cuff to the rear axle
2 Auxiliary clip   3 Split rear axle cuff

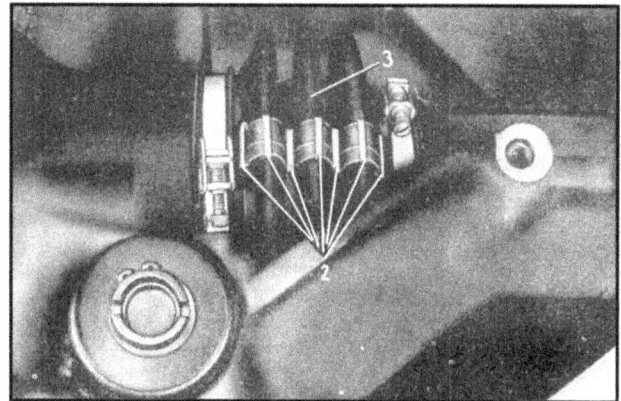

FIG 33   The split cuff fitted to the rear axle
2 Clips   3 Split rear axle cuff

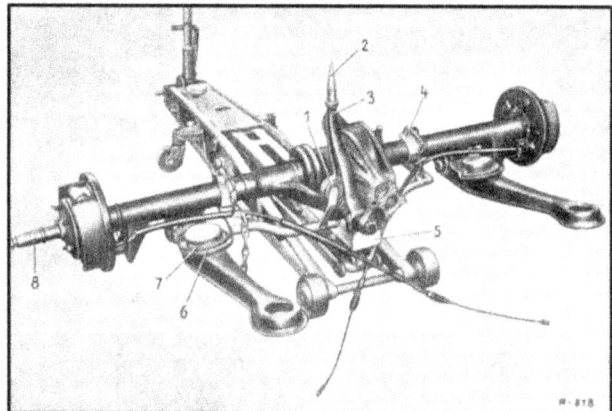

FIG 34   The rear axle ready for refitting

1 Cross strut rubber mounting
2 Conical Installing Arbor 111 589 07 61
3 Rear axle suspension support
4 Support Bracket 111 589 07 61
5 Jack Fixture 111 589 05 61
6 Lower rubber mounting for rear spring
7 Lower spring plate at the torque arm
8 Flange 111 589 01 63 for lifting the axle tubes

2 Auxiliary clips 2 are used to hold the cuff together when it is fitted. Special pliers No. 111.589.06.37.00 must be used to bend the legs of the auxiliary clips and to secure them in place, as shown in **FIG 32**.

3 Bend the legs of the clips inwards to an angle of 45 degrees and fit a clip at either end of the cuff to hold it in place, and then secure it with the original clips.

103

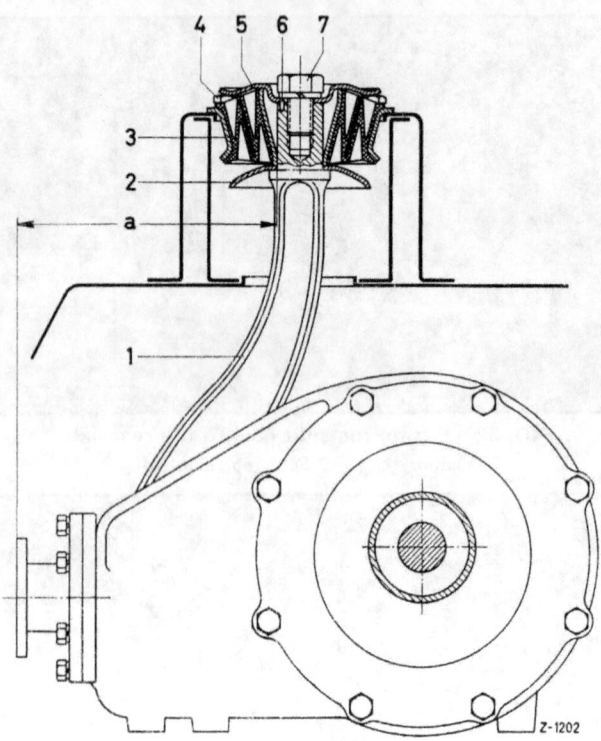

FIG 35 The vertical support attachments

- a 158 ± 1 mm (5.22 ± 0.04 inch)
- 1 Rear axle suspension support
- 2 Lower tension disc
- 3 Rubber mounting
- 4 Bolts for attaching mount to chassis
- 5 Upper tension disc
- 6 Notched cylindrical dowel pin
- 7 Hex. bolt with washer

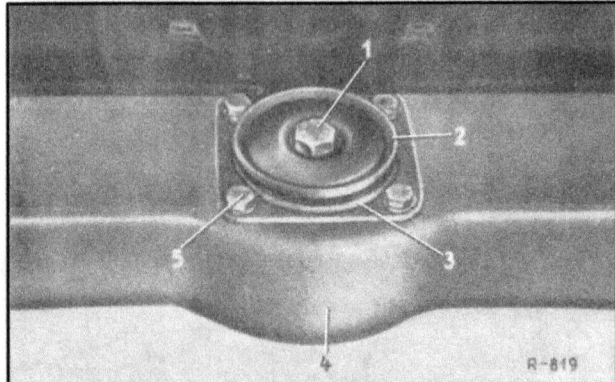

FIG 36 Setting the vertical support arm in relation to the rear axle

- 1 Hexagon bolt
- 2 Upper tension disk
- 3 Rubber mounting
- 4 Cross member on chassis base panel
- 5 Hexagon screw for fastening the rubber mounting to the cross member

exhaust system to the front pipes. Free the rubber rings that secure the main silencer to its chassis brackets by carefully prising them off with a screwdriver. Remove the rear part of the exhaust system, including the silencers.

2 Remove the rear road wheels. Take off the brake drums and disconnect the handbrake cables and hydraulic pipelines (see **Chapter 11**).

3 Remove the road springs, compensating spring and dampers (see **Section 4**).

4 Take out the front link from the locating cross-strut and push the strut rearwards to free it from the rear axle (see **Section 5**).

5 Disconnect the rear end of the propeller shaft from the drive flange on the rear axle (see **Section 2**).

6 Raise the axle tubes until they are both horizontal and clamp them in this position with the fixture No. 111.589.07.61, as shown in **FIG 34**. **It is essential that the axle tubes are supported in this way whenever the rear axle is free, otherwise they will droop too far and cause internal damage to the rear axle.**

7 Support the axle from underneath on a trolley jack. From inside the luggage compartment take out the bolt 7, lockwasher and upper tension disc 5 shown in **FIG 35**. Lower the jack with the axle on it and draw the axle out from under the car.

Refitting:

The rear axle is refitted in the reverse order of removal. The use of the installation cone 2 shown in **FIG 34** will simplify aligning the vertical strut into its mounting hole.

Before refitting the rear axle check the dimension 'a' shown in **FIG 35**, using a steel straightedge and large depth gauge. The dimension should be 158 ± 1mm (6.220 ± .039 inch). If the dimension is incorrect slacken the two clamp bolts and move the strut until the dimension is correct. Failure to observe this precaution will mean that the rubber mountings are fitted under stress so that

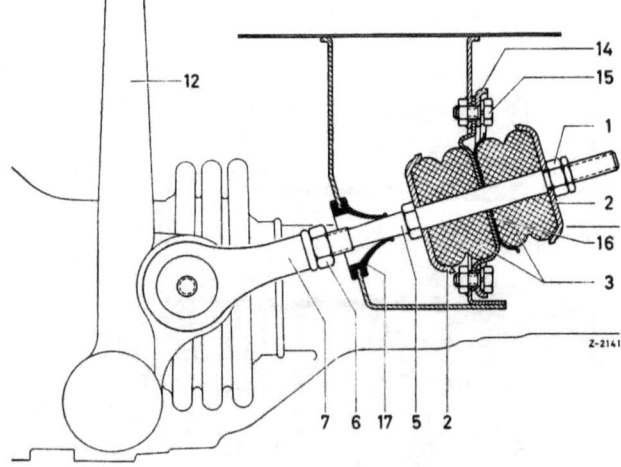

FIG 37 The rear axle lateral support on the 230SL

- 1 Hex. nut with lock nut
- 2 Cup
- 3 Rubber buffer
- 5 Cross strut
- 6 Hex. nut (lock nut)
- 7 Link
- 12 Rear axle suspension carrier
- 14 Retainer for rubber buffers
- 15 Hex. bolt
- 16 Intermediate cup
- 17 Sleeve

4 Seven additional auxiliary clips are then fitted into the cuff at the positions shown in **FIG 33** so as to hold the cuff together.

5 Check the oil level in the rear axle. Refit the compensating spring and lower the car back to the ground.

7 Removing and replacing the rear axle

Views of the rear axle in place are shown in **FIGS 15** and **16**. The rear axle, correctly supported, and ready for refitting is shown in **FIG 34**.

1 Jack up the rear of the car and place it safely onto stands. Undo the clip that secures the rear part of the

they will fail prematurely as well as making rumbling or droning noises when the car is moving.

Check all rubber mountings and renew any that are defective. When the axle has been refitted check the oil level. Fill, bleed and adjust the brakes (see **Chapter 11**).

8 Suspension geometry

Special gauges are essential for checking the location and geometry of the rear axle. The owner should not attempt to adjust the geometry himself but should have the work carried out by a suitable agent who will have all the correct gauges.

Worn or damaged suspension rubbers will affect the handling and geometry and it is within the owner's power to renew all of these.

9 Modifications

The cross-strut fitted to locate the rear axle laterally on the 230SL differs slightly from the earlier version shown. A sectioned view of the strut is shown in **FIG 37**. Basically the strut is the same but in order to remove the inner buffer 3 the retainer 14 must be removed, after taking out the five bolts 15.

The handbrake cable passes through a clip which serves as a lockwasher, as shown in **FIG 38**.

10 Fault diagnosis

(a) Noisy suspension or rear axle

1 Lack of oil or incorrect oil in rear axle
2 Defective dampers
3 Defective damper mounting rubbers
4 Dirt on damper shafts (groaning at low speeds over rough roads)
5 Defective axle mounting rubbers
6 Worn propeller shaft universal joints (clonk on taking up drive)
7 Support arm incorrectly set (rumbling or droning)
8 Defective differential unit
9 Worn bearings

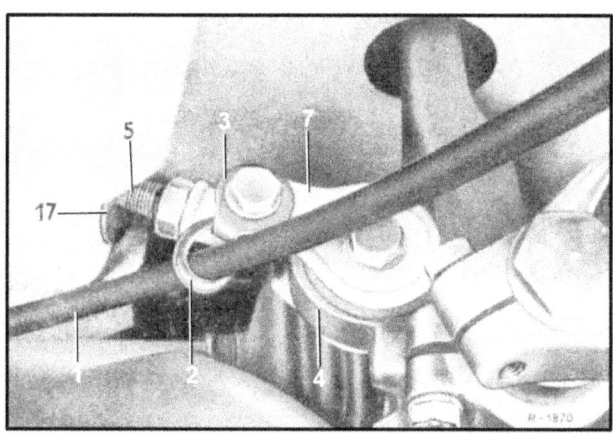

FIG 38 The handbrake cable guide fitted to the lateral support on the 230SL

1 Rear brake cable
2 Rubber eyelet
3 Fixing clip
4 Rear suspension support with rubber mounting
5 Cross strut
7 Link
17 Sleeve for lateral support

(b) Vibration

1 Check 5, 6 and 7 in (a)
2 Propeller shaft out of balance or incorrectly reassembled

(c) Oil leaks

1 Defective hub seals
2 Defective pinion oil seal
3 Defective cuff
4 Defective seals on universal joint spiders
5 Blocked breather on axle casing
6 High oil level in rear axle

(d) 'Settling'

1 Check 5 in (a)
2 Weak or broken road spring
3 Weak or broken compensating spring (or leaking hydropneumatic unit)

CHAPTER 9 - FRONT HUBS AND SUSPENSION

1 Description
2 Routine maintenance
3 The front hubs
4 The front dampers
5 The front road springs
6 The anti-roll bar and flat spring assembly
7 The lateral strut
8 The kingpin assembly
9 The wishbones (control arms)
10 Removing the front suspension assembly
11 Front suspension geometry
12 Fault diagnosis

1 Description

A general view of the front suspension assembly is shown in **FIG 1**. The crossmember is attached to the chassis by rubber mountings and it also carries the front pair of rubber mountings for the engine. The independent front suspension assemblies are mounted onto the crossmember and they consist of unequal length wishbones with a steering knuckle pivoting and swivelling between their outer ends. The inboard ends of the wishbones pivot about bushes and pivot pins attached to the crossmember so that the suspension is free to pivot vertically. The load and movement of each suspension is taken by a coil spring acting between the lower wishbone and crossmember, the movement being controlled by a telescopic damper acting between the lower wishbone and the chassis. The crossmember is located in the fore and aft plane by a flat spring at each end, between it and the chassis. A view of the parts described so far is shown in **FIG 2**. The crossmember is located in the sideways plane by a horizontal cross-strut.

An anti-roll bar interconnects the two independent suspensions. On corners this transfers some of the load from the outer wheel to the inner wheel and thus improves road holding as well as cutting down body roll.

2 Routine maintenance

1 At regular intervals grease all the swivel points on the suspension. The individual grease points are shown arrowed in **FIGS 3** to **FIGS 6**. At the same time the steering idler arm should also be lubricated and this is arrowed in **FIG 7**.
2 At longer intervals repack the hub bearings with grease. The cap can be removed and repacked but it is better to remove the wheel hub, clean out all the old grease and refit the hub correctly packed with fresh grease.

3 The front hubs

A sectioned view of the front hub assembly is shown in **FIG 8**. The oil seal acts directly onto the stub axle and in case of damage or scoring to the sealing face the stub axle can be ground or turned down at this point to remove the damage. The minimum diameter to which the sealing face can be ground down is 44.4 mm (1.748 inch). A shallow return thread is cut into the sealing face on manufacture but this return thread does not need to be recut after grinding down to remove scores or damage.

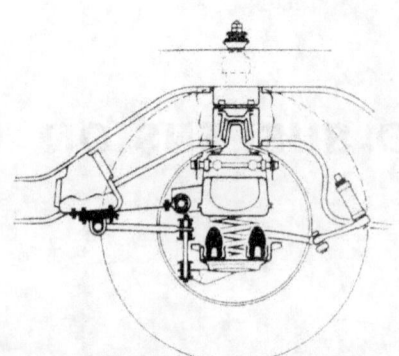 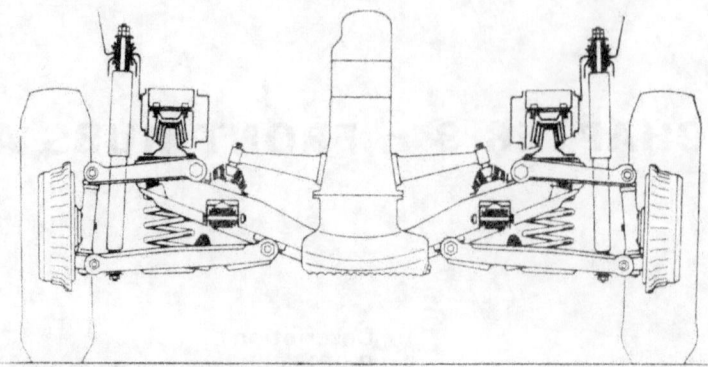

FIG 1 General view of the front suspension

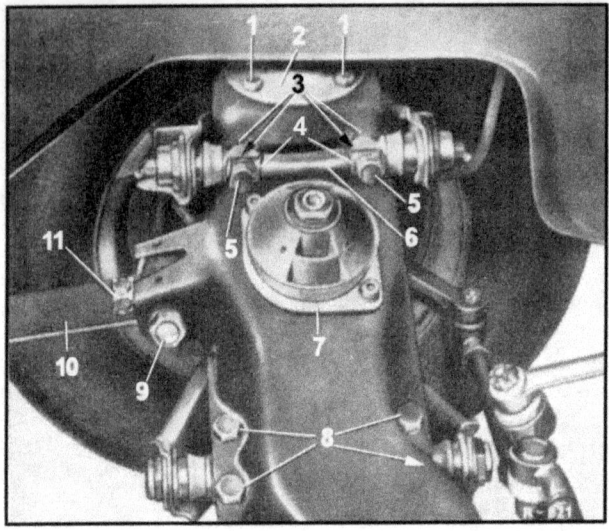

FIG 2 Suspension from above, with engine removed

1 Hex bolt fastening the rubber mount to the front crossmember
2 Rubber mount
3 Shims
4 Locking plate
5 Hex bolt (M 12×1.5×40)
6 Upper control arm pivot pin
7 Rubber mounting of front engine suspension
8 Hex bolt (M 12×1.5×38)
9 Pin fastening the flat spring to the front axle support
10 Flat spring supporting the front axle support
11 Hex bolt (clamping bolt) for the flat spring rubber mount

FIG 4 Front lubrication point on upper wishbone

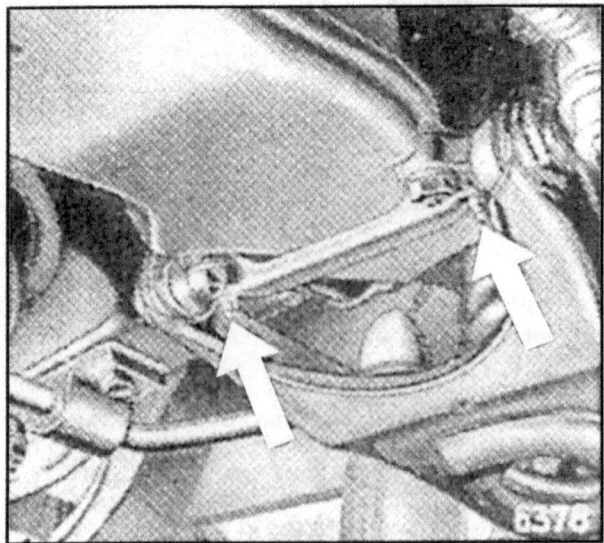

FIG 3 Lubrication points on lower wishbone

FIG 5 Steering knuckle assembly lubrication points

Checking:

A DTI (Dial Test Indicator) should always be used to check the end float of the hub bearings. As a rough test the end float is correct if the washer behind the clamping nut can just be turned by finger pressure alone.

Jack up the front of the car until the front road wheels are clear of the ground. Spin each wheel in turn and check that it rotates freely without any grinding noise. Do not confuse noise from the disc brake with that of defective bearings. If the bearings are noisy or grinding they have either run dry or are worn.

Make sure that the road wheel attachments are secure. Grip the wheel at the six and twelve o'clock positions and attempt to rock it in and out. Repeat the test with the

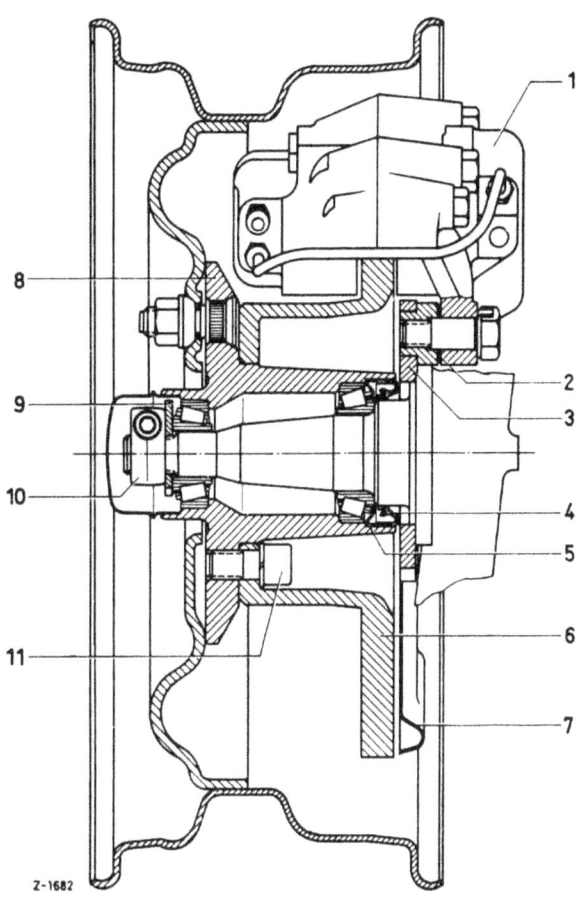

FIG 8   Sectioned view of the hub assembly

1 Brake caliper	7 Cover plate
2 Shim	8 Front wheel hub
3 Bracket for brake caliper	9 Washer
4 Seal	10 Clamping nut
5 Puller ring	11 Hexagon socket screw
6 Brake disk	with lock washer

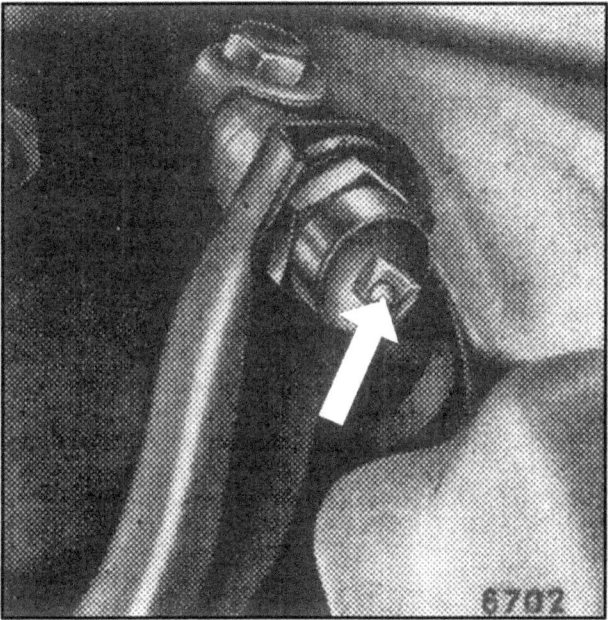

FIG 6   Rear lubrication point on upper wishbone

wheel gripped at the three and nine o'clock positions. If the play exceeds 1 mm (.04 inch) at the wheel rim in the first test then either the bearings or kingpin bushes are defective. If the play is no longer present in the second test then it was caused solely by worn kingpin bushes and these must be renewed otherwise the tyre wear will be excessive. If the play is still present in the second test then it is caused by the wheel bearings.

Do not just tighten the bearings and grease them if they are noisy as, though this may effect a temporary cure, a bearing might be defective and seize at any time. Remove the hub and check the bearings.

Removal:

1 Securely and safely jack up the front wheel and remove the road wheel. Slacken the wheel attachment nuts slightly before jacking up the car. Remove the brake caliper (see **Chapter 11**). Carefully remove the hub cap, preferably using puller No. 180.589.00.33.

2 Refer to **FIG 9**. Slacken the clamp bolt 1a and unscrew the clamp nut 1. Remove the special washer 2. Pull the hub assembly off the stub axle, collecting the inner race of the outer bearing as it comes free.

FIG 7   Lubrication point on the steering idler

109

FIG 9 The hub clamp nut parts

1 Clamp nut
1a Hexagon socket clamp bolt with lock washer
2 Washer
3 Outer annular taper roller bearing

Oil the bearings with very thin engine oil and press the inner races firmly into the outer races while rotating the bearing. Any roughness or defect will show up under this method. Renew both bearings complete if either one of them shows any defect.

Check the stub axle for cracks and examine the seating area for the grease seal to see if it is worn or scored.

Lubrication:

Pack the inner races with anti-friction grease (Texaco or Caltex Marfaco Heavy Duty 2 are both suitable greases) and use the surplus to fill the hub evenly. The quantity of grease required is approximately twice the amount of grease required to fill the hub cap up to its flare rim. Ideally the grease should be weighed and the quantity is then 45 to 50 grammes. **Do not overfill or underfill the hub.** When the hub has been refitted and the end float set the hub cap should be refilled with grease (20 to 25 grammes) and pressed back into place full.

Adjustment:

Reassemble the hub in the reverse order of dismantling and removal. When fitting a new oil seal lightly smear its outside circumference with jointing compound.

Refer to **FIG 9**. While spinning the hub tighten the clamp nut 1 until the hub has a definite resistance to turning. Settle the bearings by giving the stub axle a sharp blow on the end with a soft-faced hammer. Mount a DTI onto the hub so that its stylus rests vertically on the end of the stub axle. Vigorously pull and push on the hub to measure the end float. Slacken the clamp nut 1 a fraction of a turn at a time until the end float is correct at .01 to .02 mm (.0004 to .0008 inch). Before taking each reading spin the hub several times. When the end float is correct tighten the clamp bolt 1a.

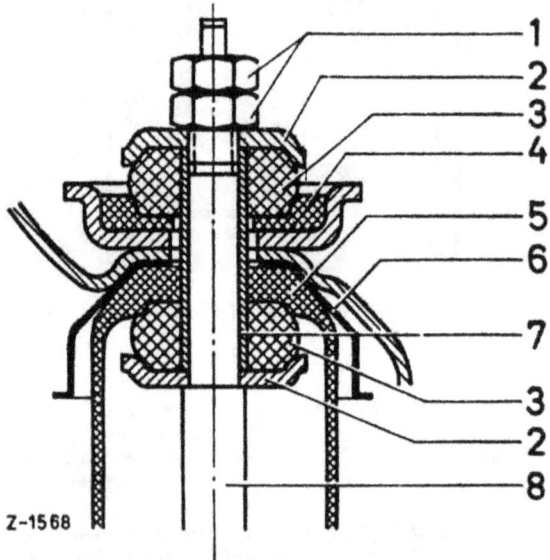

FIG 10 The damper upper attachment

1 Hexagon nuts
2 Cup
3 Upper and lower rubber ring
4 Upper rubber cup
5 Protective rubber sleeve
6 Protective cap at chassis base panel
7 Spacer tube (length 38 mm)
8 Piston rod

Normally the hub should come off with hand pressure but if it is difficult to remove it should be withdrawn using puller No. 136.589.15.33.

3 The inner race of the inner bearing is held into the hub by the oil seal so this must be prised out first if the bearing is to be examined. Normally there is no need to remove the outer races but if they are damaged or worn they should be driven out using a suitable drift.

Cleaning:

Use old rags and newspaper to remove the worst of the old grease. The remainder of the grease can then be washed off with fuel, paraffin (kerosene) or any other suitable solvent. The bearings should be washed separately from the other parts in clean solvent.

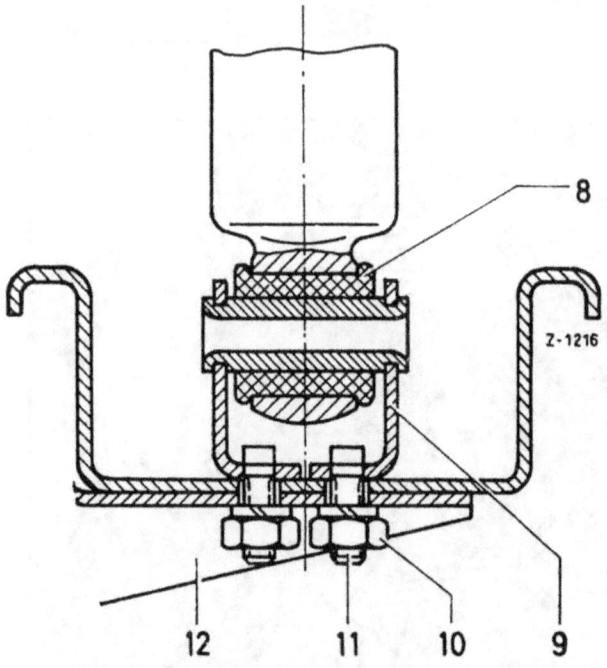

FIG 11 The damper lower attachment

8 Rubber mounting
9 Fixing plate
10 Hexagon nuts with lock washers
11 Threaded pin
12 Lower control arm

110

4 The front dampers

The upper attachment of a typical damper is shown in **FIG 10** and the lower attachment is shown in **FIG 11**. Apart from the lower attachment the front and rear dampers are very similar and most of the instructions for the rear dampers are applicable (see **Chapter 8, Section 4**).

The following additional points should be noted for the front dampers:

1. When removing the dampers it may be necessary to remove the battery and air cleaner in order to gain access to the top mountings.
2. When removing or refitting gas-filled dampers they should be held partially compressed using a tensioning fixture No. 111.589.03.61, as shown in **FIG 12**.

5 The front road springs

A sectioned view of the spring and its attachments is shown in **FIG 13** and the inset shows the stop 15 fitted on 230SL models. The details of the upper attachment, viewed from above, are also shown in **FIG 14**. A general view of the suspension assembly is shown in **FIG 15**.

Removal:

1. Jack up the front of the car and place it securely onto stands. Remove the front road wheel. Free the anti-roll bar (torsion bar) 2 from the lower wishbone (control arm) 14 by removing the link that secures them together (see next section). Remove the damper (see previous section).

FIG 12 Removing a gas-filled damper

1 Front shock-absorber 3 Tensioning Fixture 111 589 03 61
2 Protective sleeve

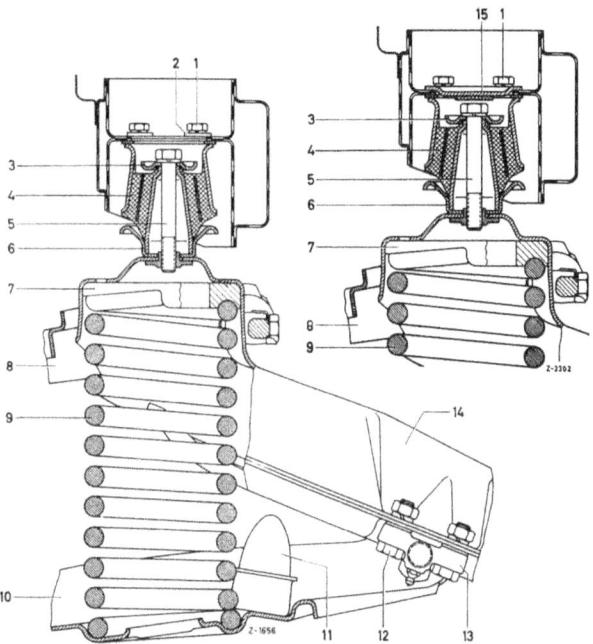

FIG 13 Sectioned view of the spring assembly, inset shows the stop fitted to the 230SL

1 Hex screws with lock washers for fastening the rubber mount
2 Washers
3 Stop plate
4 Rubber mount for front axle support
5 Hex bolt with lock washer for fastening the front axle support to the rubber mount
6 Cup for rubber mounting
7 Rubber mounting
8 Upper control arm
9 Front spring
10 Lower control arm
11 Rubber buffer
12 Hexagon bolts (M 12×1.5×38) with nuts and lock washers
13 Lower control arm pivot pin
14 Front axle support
15 Stop

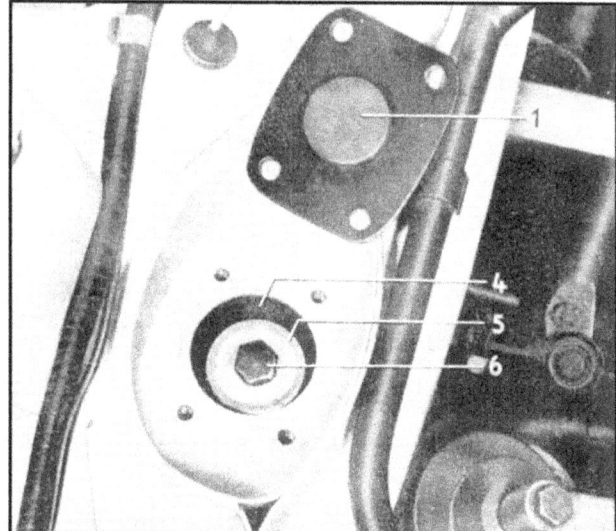

FIG 14 Crossmember mounting attachments

1 Stop 5 Stop plate
4 Rubber mounting 6 Hex bolt with lock washer

2. Remove the inside pair of bolts 20 that secure the inner pivot pin 19 to the crossmember. Refer to **FIG 16** and fit two guide pins No. 120.589.01.31 into the threads in the crossmember, as shown at 5. Support the pivot pin with a jack as shown and remove the remaining two bolts that secure the pivot pin.

FIG 15   General view of the suspension assembly

1 Torsion bar and flat spring mount on chassis base panel
2 Torsion bar
3 Flat spring
4 Damper
5 Upper control arm
6 Flat spring mounting on front axle support
7 Brake hose
8 Steering knuckle
9 Brake caliper
10 Front wheel hub
11 Brake disk
12 Lower damper suspension
13 Tie-rod
14 Lower control arm
15 Torsion bar mounting on lower control arm
16 Front spring
17 Center tie-rod
18 Center brake cable
19 Pivot pin
20 Hex bolt for fastening the lower control arm pivot pin
21 Engine support
22 Hand-brake lever

FIG 16   Removing a road spring
1 Front spring
2 Lower control arm
3 Jack Cradle 111 589 00 63
4 Pivot pin for lower control arm
5 Guides 120 589 01 31

4 Carefully lower the jack so that the pivot pin follows the guide pins. When the pressure on the spring is relieved lift it out together with its mounting rubber.

Springs are available in a wide selection of rates so that the suspension can be matched to the use of the car. Normally a weak or cracked spring should be renewed using one of exactly similar rate and dimensions but if the use of the car alters radically consult a local agent for the best combination of springs and dampers.

Lubricate the mounting rubber with talc and secure it to the spring with a little masking tape. The springs must not be turned over and the difference between the ends is shown in **FIG 17**. Refit the springs in the reverse order of removal. The bolts 12, shown in **FIG 13** may be fitted with their heads upwards on reassembly.

6 The anti-roll bar and flat spring assembly

The bracket that secures the anti-roll bar (torsion bar) to the chassis also secures the front end of the flat spring to the chassis. A sectioned view of the attachments is shown in **FIG 18** and the parts fitted to the car are shown in **FIG 19**.

The eccentric bolts 12 control the castor of the front wheels by varying the position of the flat spring 2 in relation to the chassis. **Before removing the anti-roll bar or flat spring it is essential that lines are scribed across the chassis bracket and flat spring so that the eccentric can be set and the flat spring repositioned as it was before removal or disconnection.**

The bracket 11 for the rubber mounting 10 of the anti-roll bar 9 is freed by taking off the nuts from the bolts 8 and 12. Refit the bracket in the reverse order of removal but turn the eccentric bolt 12 until the previously scribed lines align before fully tightening the nuts.

If the flat spring has been freed from the crossmember of the front axle the front attachment to the chassis should be set and tightened first. Tighten the clamp bolts 7 next and tighten the pivot nut and bolt 6 last of all.

The link connecting the anti-roll bar to the lower wishbone is shown in **FIG 20**. To remove the link take off the nuts 7 and pull out the long through-bolt 4, collecting the cupwashers 2, rubber buffers 3 and spacer tube 5 as they come free. The link is refitted in the reverse order of removal making sure that the dimension 'a' is correct at 23 ± 1 mm ($.906 \pm .040$ inch). The dimension will be very nearly correct if the lower nut 7 is screwed right down to the end of the threads on the bolts 4.

Whenever the anti-roll bar is removed or the parts dismantled check the condition of all rubber mountings removed. Renew any that are damaged, perished or permanently compressed.

7 The lateral strut

This locates the axle assembly sideways, and its attachments are shown in **FIG 21**, while the details of the strut are shown in **FIG 22**. The method of removal

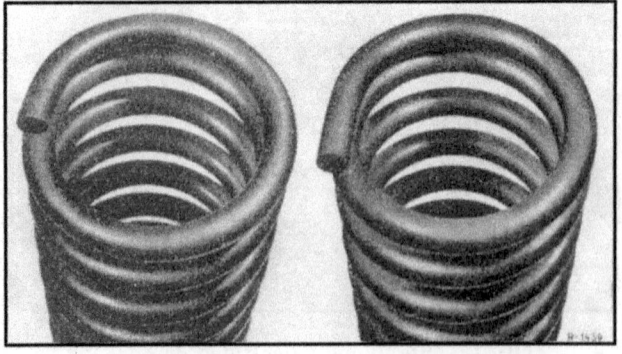

TOP   BOTTOM

FIG 17   Differences between the ends of the road spring

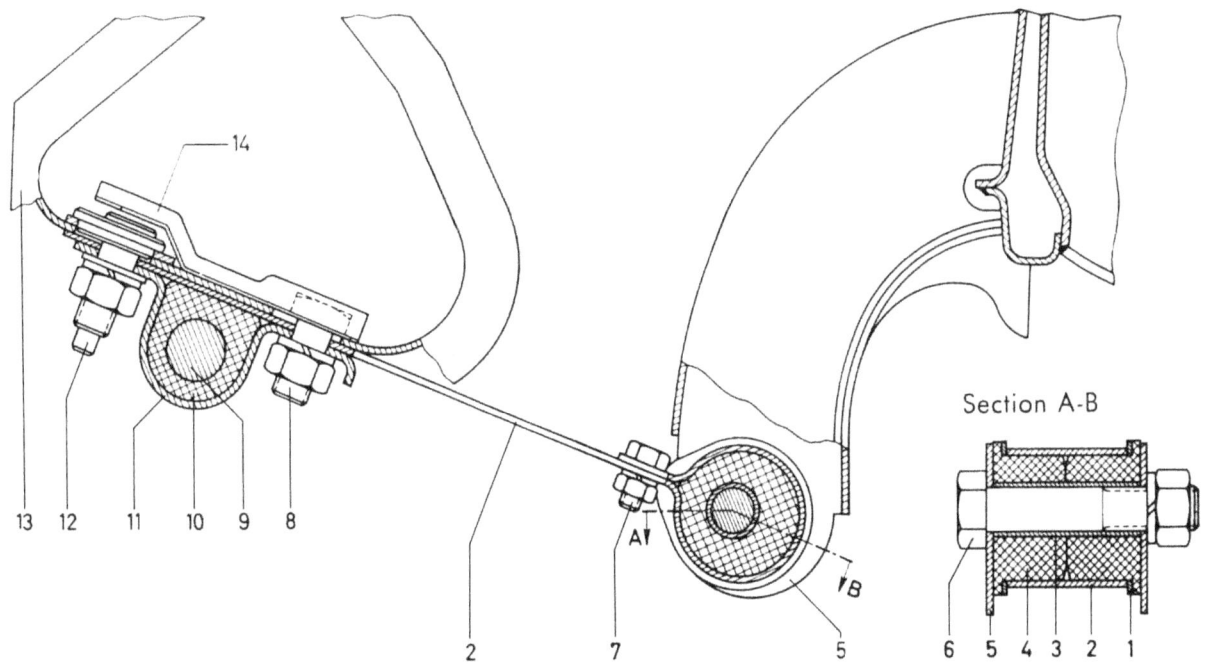

FIG 18 Attachment of the flat spring and anti-roll bar

1 Spacer ring
2 Flat spring
3 Spacer tube
4 Rubber mounting
5 Bearing bracket at front axle support
6 Hex bolt with nut and lock washer
7 Hex bolt (clamping screw) with nut and lock washer
8 Square bolt with nut and lock washer
9 Torsion bar
10 Rubber mounting for torsion bar
11 Bracket for rubber mounting
12 Eccentric with nut and lock washer
13 Bracket on chassis base panel
14 Cage for square bolt and eccentric

is self-evident. Renew the rubber mountings if they are worn or perished.

When refitting the strut leave the clamping bolt 5 loose and refit the strut. Lower the car back to the ground and check that mounting rubbers for the crossmember are not under stress. Tighten the clamp bolt 5 with the car on the ground.

8 The kingpin assembly

A sectioned view of the assembly is shown in **FIG 23**. The eccentric bolt 3 adjusts the camber angle while the threaded pin 2 can be rotated by a special washer to adjust the castor angle of the individual suspensions. If the suspension is dismantled it is most advisable to take the car to a suitably equipped agent for checking the suspension geometry, as this can easily have been altered during reassembly.

Removal:

1 Jack up the front of the car and place it safely onto stands and remove the road wheel. Remove the hub assembly (see **Section 3**). Remove the front damper (see **Section 4**).

2 Raise the lower wishbone and either support it on a jack or hold it up with fixture No. 111.589.09.31, as shown in **FIG 24**. Remove the lockbolt and slacken and remove the eccentric bolt 2 at the top attachment. Take off the castellated nut and remove the threaded pin 3 from the lower attachment. Disconnect the hydraulic pipeline if required and lift the assembly out from the wishbones.

FIG 19 The flat spring and anti-roll bar fitted to the car
(Refer to FIG 18 for key to image numbers)

Dismantling:

The details of the parts are shown in **FIG 25**. Screw out the threaded pin 8. Free the locking plate 2 and unscrew the bottom nut 1. Give the kingpin a sharp blow upwards with a soft-faced hammer to free the tapers and remove the lower steering knuckle 4 with the compensating washer. Withdraw the kingpin from the stub axle support and remove the washers 6. Remove the dust covers.

Reassembly:

Wash all the metal parts in clean fuel and check them for wear or damage. If the kingpin bushes are worn they should be driven out, preferably using drift No. 136.589.09.39.

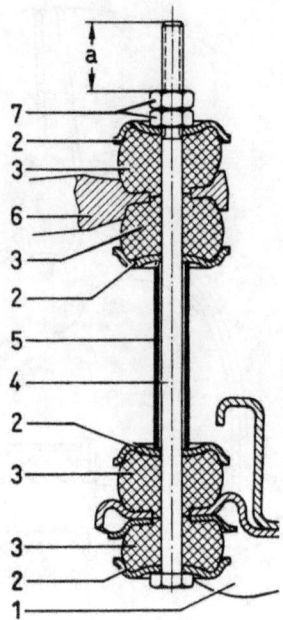

FIG 20 The anti-roll bar link to the lower wishbone

1 Lower control arm
2 Cup washer
3 Rubber buffer
4 Hex bolt
5 Spacer tube
6 Torsion bar
7 Hexagon nuts

Check the stub axle for cracks or signs of wear. Mount it between centres and use a DTI to check that the runout does not exceed .05mm (.002 inch).

1 Refer to **FIG 23**. Press new bushes 8 and 11 into place if the old bushes have been removed. When pressing the bush 8 into place fit an old thrust washer 6 above it so that the dowel pin 17 is not damaged. Line ream both bushes to a diameter of 20.000 to 20.021 mm (.7874 to .7882 inch) preferably using special reamer No. 000.589.03.53.

2 Fit the lower thrust washer 6 into place so that its oil grooves face upwards and it is located by the dowel pin 17. Place the upper thrust washer 5 into place and refit the dust covers 4 and dust sleeve 7.

3 Pass the kingpin through the assembly and make sure that the tapers on it and the lower steering knuckle are perfectly clean and grease free. Fit the compensating washer 12 and press the lower knuckle into place.

4 **Align the two steering knuckles accurately.** The only satisfactory way of doing this accurately is to use the alignment jig No. 120.589.01.61, which uses ground pins passing through the support and lugs. Fit the locking plate 13 and nut 14, tightening the nut to a torque load of 9 mkg. Use feeler gauges to check the end float of the kingpin. On assembly the end float should be adjusted to .05 to .10mm (.002 to .004 inch) by selectively fitting the compensating

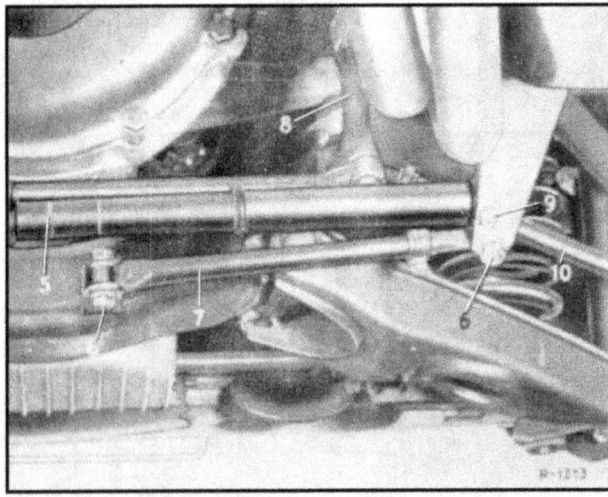

FIG 21 Lateral support strut fitted to the car

5 Steering damper
6 Hexagon bolt with nut and lock washer
7 Front axle lateral support strut
8 Steering relay arm
9 Hexagon bolt with nut and lock washer
10 Right tie-rod

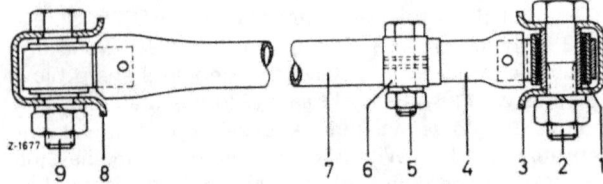

FIG 22 Lateral support strut details

1 Rubber mounting
2 Bolt with nut and lockwasher
3 Mounting hole on chassis base panel
4 Adjustable inside tube
5 Bolt (clamping bolt)
6 Clamp
7 Outside tube
8 Bearing bracket on front axle support
9 Hex bolt

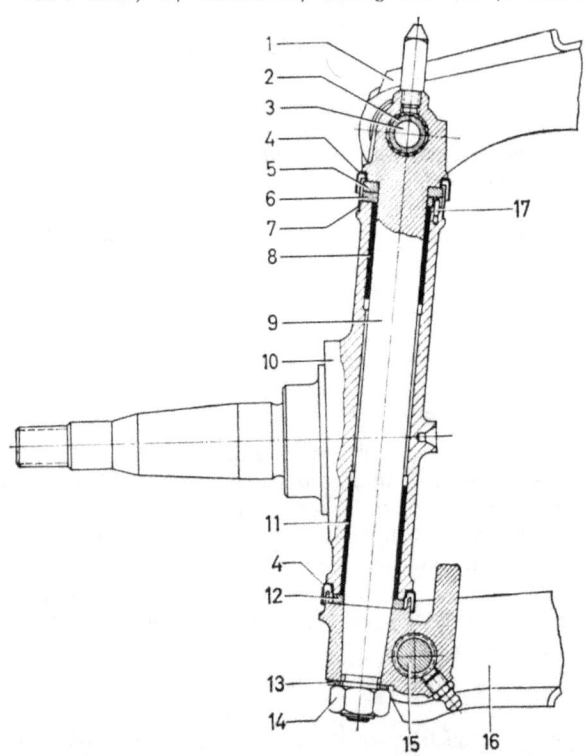

FIG 23 Sectioned view of the kingpin assembly

1 Upper wishbone
2 Threaded pin
3 Eccentric bolt
4 Dust cover
5 Thrust washer upper
6 Thrust washer lower
7 Dust sleeve
8 Upper bearing bush
9 Kingpin
10 Steering knuckle
11 Lower bearing bush
12 Compensating washer
13 Lock washer
14 Hex. nut
15 Steering knuckle support with threaded pin
16 Lower wishbone
17 Dowel pin

washer 12 but in service the end float may wear to .5 mm (.02 inch) before the steering is affected. Renew the thrust washers if they are worn and then find the correct thickness of compensating washer to bring the end float within limits. Lock the nut when the adjustment and alignment is satisfactory.

5 Attach the lower steering knuckle support to the lower wishbones, using new sealing rubbers. The threaded pin is fitted with its head at the rear of the suspension. Tighten the nut to a torque load of 9 mkg and use a new splitpin to lock it.

6 A sectioned view of the upper attachment is shown in **FIG 26**. Screw the threaded pin 7 back into the knuckle so that it protrudes evenly on both sides and the groove is to the front. Refit the steering knuckle to the upper wishbones using the eccentric bolt 1. Use new sealing rings and make sure that the nose of the adjusting washer 4 fits into the groove in the threaded pin.

7 Refit the remainder of the parts in the reverse order of removal. Bleed the brakes before refitting the road wheel.

9 The wishbones (control arms)

The details of the upper wishbone are shown in **FIG 27** and those of the lower wishbone are shown in **FIG 28**. If the suspension has been damaged in an accident or by 'kerbing' the car the wishbones should be removed and checked on special jigs.

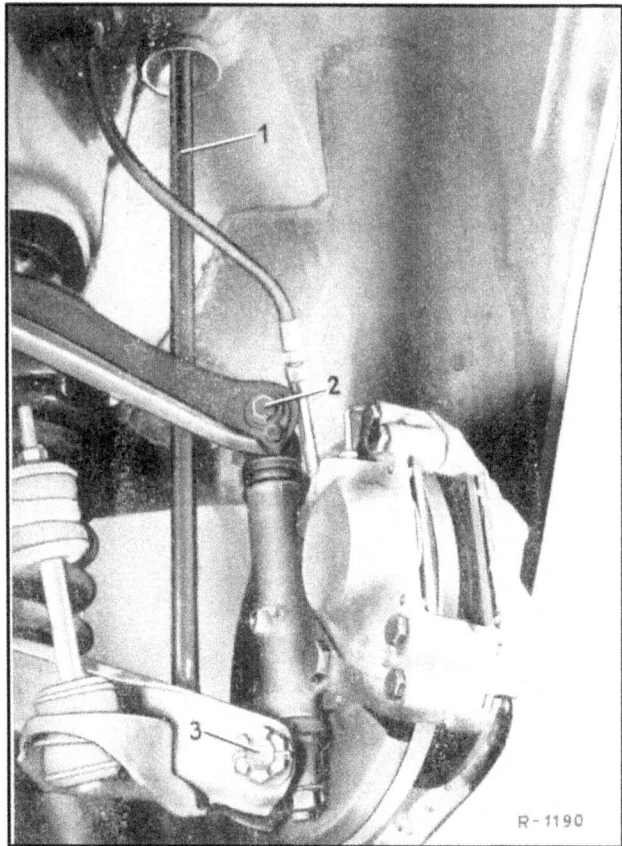

FIG 24 Kingpin assembly attachments

1 Supporting fixture 111.589.09.31
2 Eccentric bolt of upper steering knuckle mounting
3 Threaded pin of lower mounting

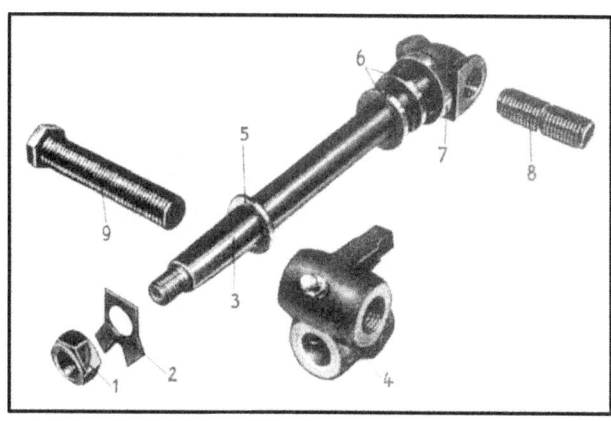

FIG 25 Details of the kingpin

1 Hex. nut
2 Lock washer
3 Kingpin
4 Steering knuckle support
5 Shim
6 Thrust washer
7 Dust cap
8 Threaded pin top
9 Threaded pin bottom

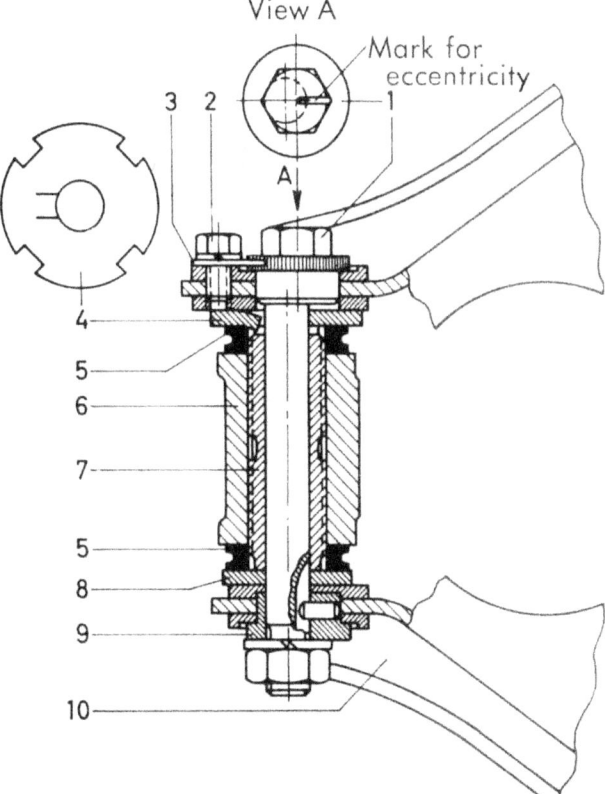

FIG 26 Sectioned view of the upper steering knuckle

1 Eccentric bolt for camber adjustment
2 Bolt with lockwasher
3 Locking plate
4 Adjusting washer for castor adjustment
5 Rubber sealing ring
6 Kingpin
7 Threaded pin
8 Washer
9 Eccentric bushing with dowel pin
10 Upper wishbone

Removal:

1 Jack up the front of the car and remove the kingpin assembly. The wheel hub can be left in place on the assembly. Remove the road spring.

2 Unscrew the threaded bushings 4 that secure the wishbones. Take out the bolts that secure the pivot pins 2 and remove the parts from the crossmember.

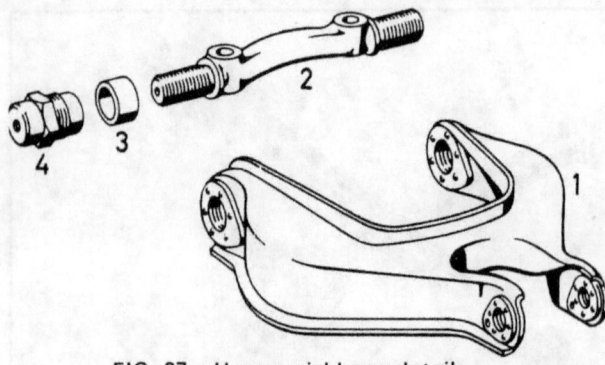

FIG 27 Upper wishbone details

Key to Figs 27 and 28
1 Wishbone
2 Pivot pin
3 Rubber sealing ring
4 Threaded bushing
5 Additional rubber buffer

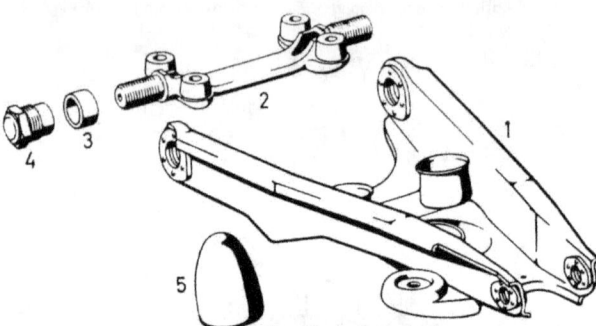

FIG 28 Lower wishbone details

Reassembly:

1 Fit new rubber seals onto the pivot pins 2 and refit the pivot pins to the wishbones.
2 Screw in the threaded bushings 4 and tighten them to a torque load of 18 mkg. Check that the pivots 2 turn freely in the bushings without any binding and set the pivots so that the threads are evenly distributed on each side. A wishbone stamped with the number 31 beside the boss has an M.31 thread and requires a bushing with an annular groove cut below the threaded portion.
3 Attach the pivots to the crossmember and reassemble the remainder of the parts in the reverse order of removal.

10 Removing the front suspension assembly

1 Jack up the front of the car and place it securely on stands. Remove the front road wheels and the following parts; the dampers (see **Section 4**), the road springs (see **Section 5**), the anti-roll bar and flat springs (see **Section 6**) and the lateral strut (see **Section 7**). Loosely reconnect the inboard ends of the lower wishbones.
2 Disconnect the handbrake cables and the flexible hydraulic brake hoses (see **Chapter 11**). Disconnect the tie rods from the steering lever arms (see **Chapter 10**).
3 Remove the air cleaner and battery if this has not already been done. Place the support bracket No. 111.589.03.31 onto the left and right cowls and use the bracket of the fixture to support the engine by the water pump. Wind up the handle on the fixture so that the engine is slightly raised and the load taken off the engine mountings. If the correct special tool is not available a hoist may be used to take the weight of the engine but great care must be taken to see that the car is not moved or the hoist disturbed. A jack and block of wood under the sump should be used as an added safety precaution once the axle is out.
4 Remove the bolts that secure the engine to its mountings. Support the axle from underneath on a trolley jack. It is advisable to use fixture No. 111.589.02.63 on the jack as this has arms to support the wishbones.
5 From inside the engine compartment remove the stop and bolts that secure the crossmember rubber mountings, shown in **FIG 13** and **FIG 14**. Lower the jack and draw the assembly out from underneath the car.

Check all the rubber mountings and renew any that are worn or perished. Refit the suspension assembly in the reverse order of removal. Bleed the brakes and adjust the handbrake.

11 Front suspension geometry:

The castor can be adjusted by resetting the positioning of the flat locating springs or by screwing the threaded pin in the top steering knuckle attachment. The camber is adjusted by turning the eccentric adjusting bolt in the top steering knuckle attachment.

Special gauges and equipment are essential for checking the suspension geometry and the owner should not attempt to alter the settings himself but should take the car to a suitably equipped agent.

12 Fault diagnosis

(a) Wheel wobble

1 Unbalanced front wheels
2 Broken or weak front springs
3 Defective rubber mountings
4 Worn hub bearings
5 Uneven tyre wear
6 Worn suspension linkage
7 Loose wheel attachments

(b) 'Bottoming' of suspension

1 Check 2 in (a)
2 Rebound rubbers worn or missing
3 Defective dampers

(c) Heavy steering

1 Neglected lubrication
2 Incorrect suspension geometry

(e) Excessive tyre wear

1 Check 6 in (a); 3 in (b) and 2 in (c)

(e) Rattles

1 Check 2 and 3 in (a) and 1 in (c)
2 Damper mountings loose or worn
3 Anti-roll bar broken or rubber mountings worn

(f) Excessive rolling

1 Check 2 in (a); 3 in (b) and 3 in (e)

CHAPTER 10 – THE STEERING SYSTEM

1 Description
2 Routine maintenance
3 Ball joints
4 The steering linkage
5 The mechanical steering box
6 Servicing the mechanical steering box
7 The power assisted steering
8 Front wheel alignment
9 The steering wheel
10 Steering column lock
11 The steering column
12 The 230SL steering column
13 Fault diagnosis

1 Description

There are various versions of the steering column but all models use a recirculating ball steering box. A sectioned view of the steering wheel attachment on the earlier steering column is shown in **Chapter 6, FIG 9**. The later steering column is fitted with a shock absorber between the steering wheel and the column and a sectioned view of the steering wheel attachment is shown in **FIG 1**. The 230SL is fitted with a divided tube steering column and a sectioned view of the column is shown in **FIG 2**.

The lower end of the inner steering tube is connected to the worm drive of the steering box by a flexible connector. Rotation of the worm drives the steering arm around in an arc and this steering arm is connected to the steering linkage by a ball joint. The attachments of the steering box are shown in **FIG 3**. The other end of the centre steering tie rod 18 is connected to the arm of an idler so that the linkage moves as a parallelogram when the steering arm rotates in its arc of movement. The outer ends of the centre tie rod are connected to the outer tie rods, which move the steering levers on the suspension units to provide the actual steering movement at the road wheels.

The ignition switch is mounted onto the steering column and is so designed that it can also be used to lock the steering in the straight-ahead position.

A damper is fitted between the centre tie rod and a bracket on the chassis to damp out vibrations or steering wobble. The damper is sealed, telescopic, and must be renewed if it is defective.

Power assisted steering may be fitted as an optional extra. This is powered by a pump driven from the engine and uses automatic transmission fluid type A as its working medium.

2 Routine maintenance

Greasing:

The ball joints in the linkage are all sealed for life and do not require routine greasing. However, some of the very earliest models may be fitted with grease nipples on the ball joint and these should be greased at the same time as the suspension. This early type of ball joint is no longer obtainable and replacement parts are all sealed. The only other part of the steering that requires regular greasing is the idler lever and this has been dealt with in **Chapter 9, Section 2**.

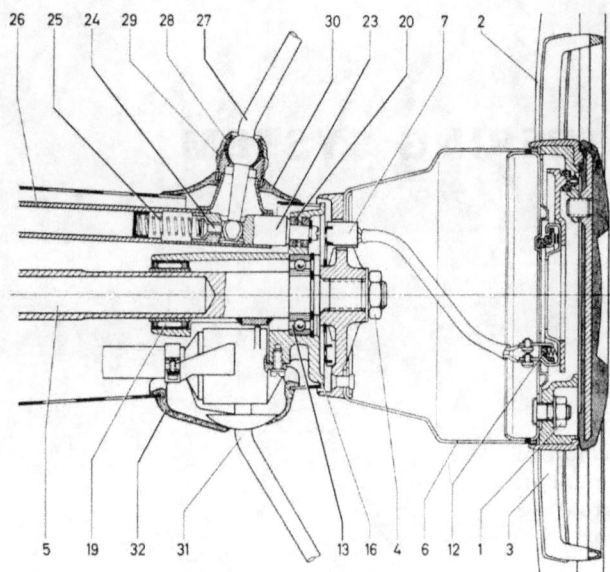

FIG 1 Attachment of the steering wheel to the column fitted with a shock absorber

1	Hex. nut with spring washer	20	Vulkollan ring
2	Steering wheel	23	Guide pin
3	Signal ring (horn ring)	24	Spring seat pin
4	Hex. nut with spring washer	25	Compression spring
5	Steering tube	26	Shift tube
6	Steering column shock absorber	27	Shift lever
7	Slip ring with cable	28	Ball socket
12	Contact ring	29	Cap
13	Annular grooved bearing	30	Rubber cover
16	Mounting plate	31	Combination switch
19	Needle bearing	32	Rubber cover

Oil level:

On lefthand drive models turn the steering to full left lock and on righthand drive models to full right lock. Take out the filler plug, arrowed in **FIG 4,** and use a depth gauge to measure the oil level. The correct oil level is 40 mm (1.6 inch) below the bottom of the threaded bore.

Power steering:

1 Check the level in the reservoir after the car has been used, so that the power steering has reached its normal operating temperature, and with the engine running at idling speed. Undo the butterfly nut and lift off the reservoir top. **Take great care not to allow any dirt to fall into the reservoir.** If the level is low, top up to the mark M shown in **FIG 5** with ATF type A. The mark is approximately 12 mm ($\frac{1}{2}$ inch) below the reservoir top.

2 At 48,000 kilometre (30,000 mile) intervals renew the filter element in the base of the reservoir. The fluid should be syphoned out of the reservoir when changing the filter and to prevent contamination fresh fluid should be used to refill the reservoir.

3 At regular intervals check the drive belt tension. The tension should be such that the belt can be moved 10 to 15 mm (.4 to .6 inch) at the centre of a run using moderate thumb pressure. If the tension is incorrect, slacken the bolts that secure the pump and adjust the

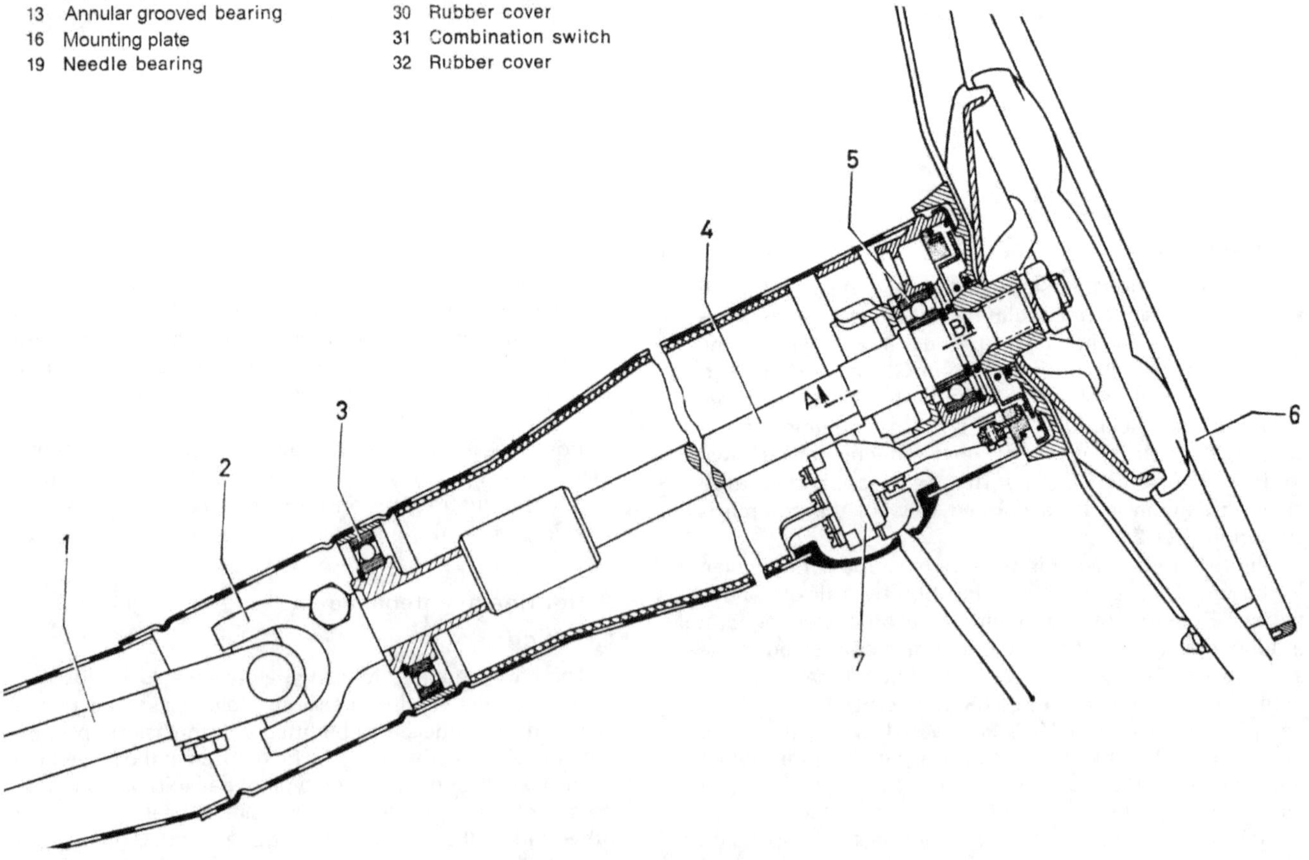

FIG 2 Sectioned view of the 230SL steering column

1	Lower steering tube half	3	Annular grooved bearing	5	Annular grooved bearing
2	Universal joint	4	Upper steering tube half	6	Horn ring
				7	Combination switch

tensioning bolt until the belt tension is correct. Retighten the bolts that secure the pump once the tension is set.

3 Ball joints

These are used to connect the tie rods, allowing them to move and transmit pressure without excessive play. The ball joints are fitted into the tie rods, or threaded tie rod ends, so that they cannot be renewed separately but must be renewed with the tie rod end or complete tie rod.

A worn ball joint will either show up as the linkage is moved, because of the play between the parts, or else it will show as excessive play when the tie rods are levered apart.

A sectioned view of a typical ball joint is shown in **FIG 6**. The ball on the pin 1 rotates freely in the plastic bearings 4, while the taper on the pin fits tightly into a mating taper on the steering lever 15. The two tapers are pulled together and secured with the castellated nut 14.

The ball joint is greased in manufacture and the amount of grease is normally sufficient to last the life of the ball joint. **It is most important that the rubber cuff 2 is always in good condition.** If the cuff is split or damaged grease will leak out and, far worse, dirt will enter causing the joint to wear rapidly. The ball joint cannot be cleaned or flushed out so if dirt has entered the ball joint should be renewed as it will rapidly become

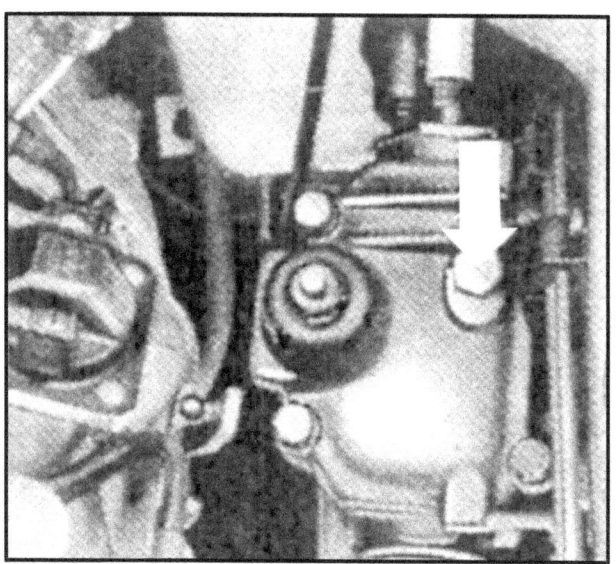

FIG 4 Filler plug for the steering box

FIG 5 Level mark for the power assisted steering

FIG 3 Attachments of the steering box

1 Cover plate	8 Lower clamping hex socket bolt	12 Hexagon locknut
2 Steering column jacket	9 Upper clamping hex socket bolt	13 Steering gear arm
3 Rubber cuff		14 Tie-rod
4 Lower flange of steering coupling	10 Screw plug in steering housing cover	15 Castle nut with splitpin
5 Mounting bolts		16 Ball joint for center tie-rod
6 Upper flange of steering coupling	11 Adjusting screw for pressure block assy of steering shaft	17 Ball joint for tie-rod
7 Steering tube		18 Center tie-rod

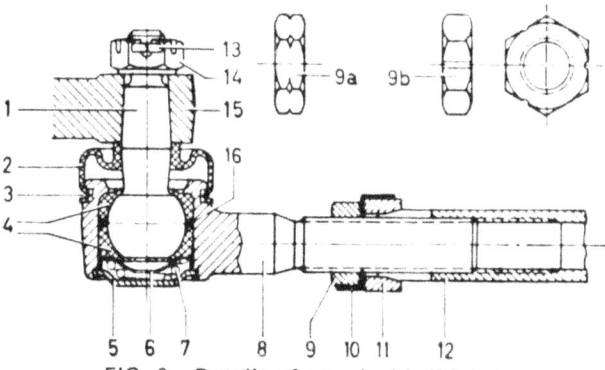

FIG 6 Details of a typical ball joint

1 Ball pin	6 Retainer	11 Clamping ring
2 Rubber cuff	7 Compression spring	12 Tie-rod tube
3 Clamping ring		13 Splitpin
4 Vulkollan bearing bushing	8 Tie-rod	14 Castle nut
	9 Hexagon nut	15 Steering lever
5 Cover	10 Locking plate	16 Spacer ring

FIG 7 The steering linkage details

1 Steering gear arm
2 Left tie-rod
3 Center tie-rod
4 Hex bolt with lockwasher
5 Steering damper
6 Hex bolt with nut and lockwasher
7 Strut for front axle lateral support
8 Steering relay arm
9 Hex bolt with nut and lockwasher
10 Right tie-rod

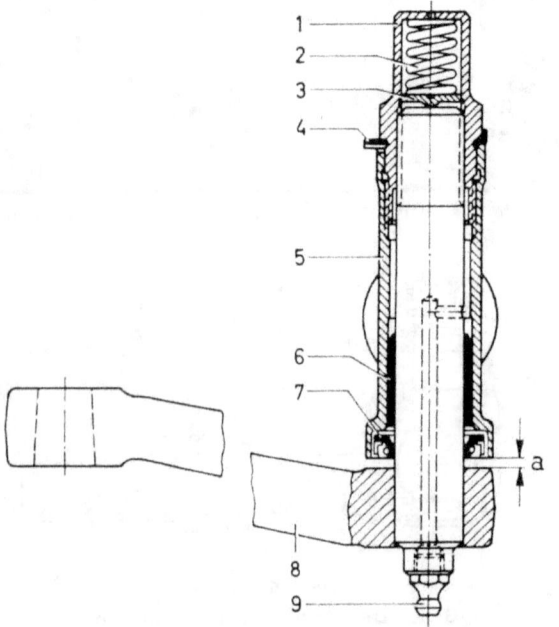

FIG 8 Sectioned view of the relay arm

1 Cover plate
2 Pressure spring
3 Thrust washer
4 Locking plate
5 Trunnion housing
6 Bushing
7 Grease seal
8 Steering relay arm with pin
9 Grease nipple

defective. **Regularly examine all the cuffs and renew them if they are worn or show signs of splitting.** When a new cuff is fitted pack some extra anti-friction grease into the ball joint.

Separating the two tapers of a ball joint often appears extremely difficult even after the castellated securing nut has been removed. **Never hammer on the end of the threaded pin as this will cause internal damage even if the threads are protected by hammering onto a spare nut.** Special extractors are made for freeing the ball joints and these should be used wherever possible. Part of the extractor slides under the tie rod and the bolt is then tightened to press the tapers apart. If an extractor is not available the ball joint can still be separated. Leave the securing nut on the last few threads as this will prevent the parts from flying apart if the taper is suddenly freed. Lay a block of metal against one side of the tapered eye and either pull or lever the tie rods apart. Hammer on the side of the tapered eye opposite to the metal block and the tapers will quickly free.

4 The steering linkage

A general view of the linkage is shown in **FIG 7**.

Steering damper:

The damper is freed by taking out the bolts 4 and 9 that secure it to the brackets on the centre tie rod and chassis. When refitting the damper make sure that the end marked 'Rahmseitte' is fitted nearest to the chassis bracket. Before refitting the damper make sure that its rubber mountings are in good condition and renew them if they are defective or worn.

On cars designated for use in dusty areas there is a rubber sleeve fitted around the damper to prevent the entry of dirt and dust. All replacement dampers are supplied with this rubber sleeve already fitted.

The damper can only be tested at a garage using special test equipment but it should be rejected if it shows signs of physical damage. Check that the length between centres is 330±2 mm (13±.08 inch) when the damper is fully compressed.

If the car has been 'kerbed' or involved in an accident with possible damage to the suspension, check the safety clearances on the damper. Connect the damper at one end only and turn the steering from one full lock to the other. **Check that the steering lock is limited by the stops on the suspension units and not by the internal safety stops in the steering box.** The damper must have a further movement of 5 mm (.2 inch) at either lock to ensure that it is not jamming at full lock.

Relay arm (idler link):

Three versions of the relay arm are fitted, all basically similar. The earliest version is shown sectioned in **FIG 8**. The later versions differ in the design of the seals. The later version is fitted with a modified seal and separate Vulkollan ring above it. This modified seal and ring can be fitted directly in place of the earlier seal. The very latest version has the Vulkollan ring integral with the seal.

1 Free the arm 8 from the tie rod assembly. Remove the grease nipple 9 to prevent it being damaged.
2 Free the locking plate 4 and unscrew the coverplate 1. Remove the spring 2 and thrust washer 3. The relay arm 8 and pin can then be removed from the housing 5. If either the pin or arm are worn or damaged they must both be renewed as they are only supplied as a complete assembly.
3 If the bush 6 is worn extract the seal 7 and drive out the old bush with a suitable drift. Press a new bush into place, with its chamfered edge leading. Ream out

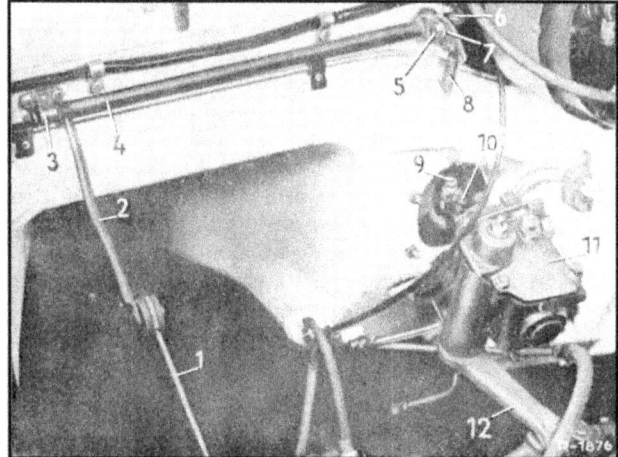

FIG 9 Attachments of the 230SL steering box

1 Regulating rod   5 Hex bolt   9 Clamp bolt
2 Lever   6 Mounting   10 Clamp bolt
3 Mounting   7 Lever   11 Steering box
4 Control shaft   8 Return spring 12 Steering gear arm

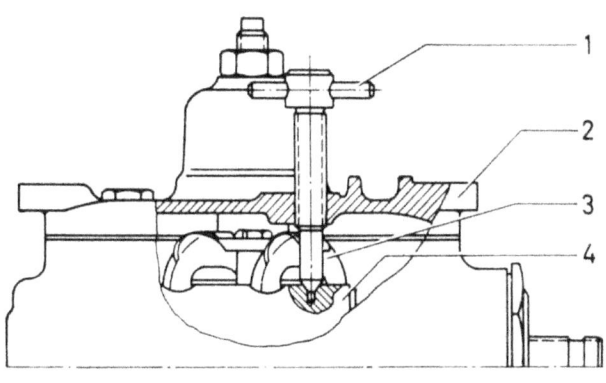

FIG 10 Centralizing the steering box

1 Center Position Check Screw 111 589 00 23
2 Steering housing cover
3 Ball guide tube of the steering nut
4 Steering nut

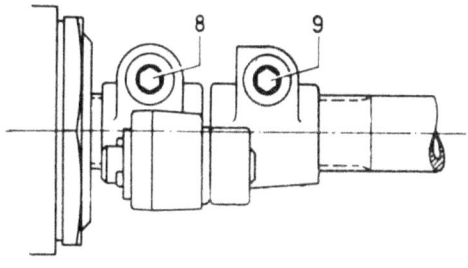

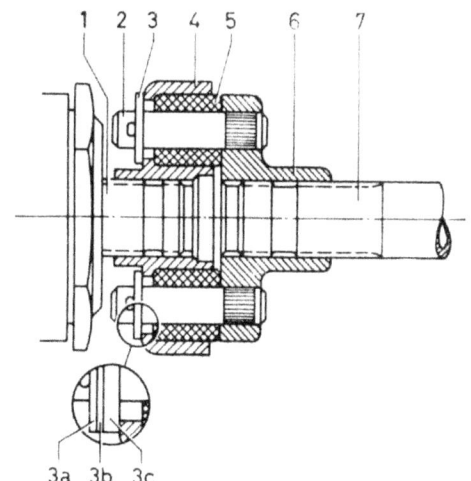

FIG 11 Steering coupling details

1 Steering worm   4 Lower flange
2 Bolt   5 Bushing
3 Washers   6 Upper flange
  3a Steel washer   7 Steering tube
  3b Spring washer   8 Lower clamping bolt
  3c Plastic washer   9 Upper clamping bolt

the new bush to a diameter of 18.006 to 18.024 mm (.7089 to .7096 inch).

4 Use the later type of seal and Vulkollan ring. Fit the Vulkollan ring into place and then press in the new grease seal. Make sure that the seal 7 is fitted so that its lips face outwards, preventing the entry of dirt but allowing surplus grease to escape.
5 Smear the pin with grease and press it back into place through the housing. Refit the thrust washer 3 and spring 2. Screw on the coverplate 1 until the dimension 'a' is correct. The coverplate is fitted with an internal

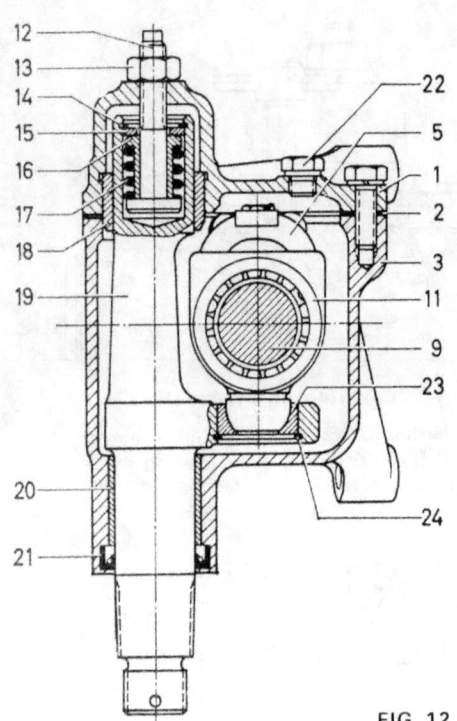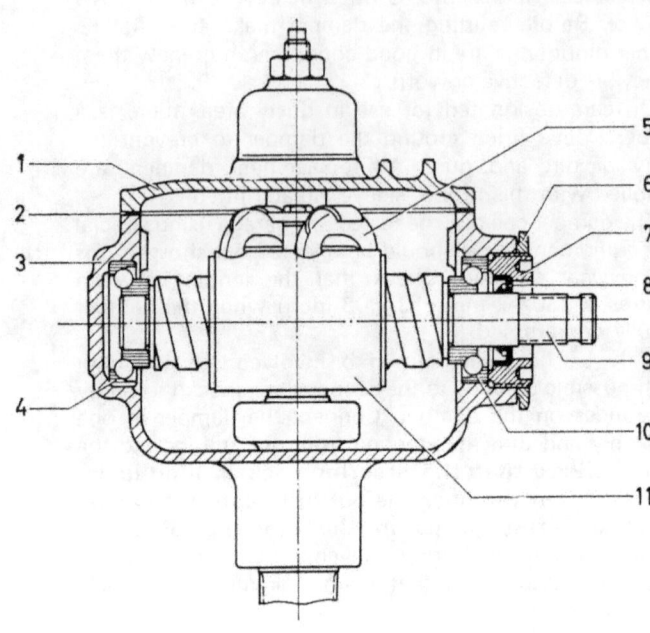

FIG 12 Sectioned views of the steering box

1 Steering housing top cover	7 Adjusting ring
2 Gasket	8 Grease seal
3 Steering housing	9 Steering worm
4 Angular contact bearing	10 Angular contact bearing
5 Ball guide tube	11 Steering nut
6 Hexagon nut	12 Adjusting screw
13 Hexagon nut	19 Steering shaft
14 Snap ring	20 Lower bearing bushing
15 Thrust washer	21 Grease seal
16 Pressure sleeve	22 Screw plug
17 Compression spring	23 Ball cup
18 Upper bearing bushing	24 Snap ring

thread which differs in pitch from the outside thread so that as the coverplate is screwed on the clearance 'a' will decrease. Set the relay arm in the straight ahead position and adjust until the clearance is 2.5 mm (.1 inch). The clearance must not be less than 1 mm (.04 inch) otherwise there is a danger that the arm will bind at full lock. Once the setting is correct lock the coverplate with the locking plate 4.

6 Press the grease nipple 9 back into the pin and lubricate the unit with a grease gun. Reconnect the arm to the tie rods and check the front wheel alignment.

5 The mechanical steering box

The steering should be checked for play. at the steering wheel, while an assistant holds the front wheels to prevent them from moving. If the circumferential play at the steering wheel rim exceeds 25 mm (1 inch) then the play is excessive.

Check through the steering linkage, kingpin bushes and wheel bearings for wear or damage. Renew any defective or worn parts. If after renewing worn parts the steering play is still excessive, the steering box should be removed from the car and adjusted on the bench. **Do not adjust the steering box while it is still fitted to the car.**

Removal:

The attachments of the steering box are shown in **FIG 3**. For information the attachment on the 230SL is shown in **FIG 9** and it can be seen to be basically similar.

1 Remove the castellated nut 15 and its splitpin so that the ball joint 16 can be freed from the steering arm 13.

2 Take out the socket-headed clamp bolt 8 securing the steering coupling lower flange 4 to the drive shaft of the steering box.

3 Take out the three bolts 5 that secure the steering box in place. The heads of the bolts are on the other side of the chassis bracket and are not shown in the figure.

4 Pull the unit slightly downwards to free the steering gear worm drive from the lower flange of the steering coupling and remove the steering box from the car.

The unit is refitted in the reverse order of removal. Set both the steering wheel and steering box in the straight ahead positions before reconnecting them. **FIG 10** shows the most accurate method of centralizing the steering box. Remove the filler plug, and turn the steering box until the hole in the steering nut 4 is aligned with the threaded hole. Screw in the special Centre Position Check Screw No. 111.589.00.23 so that it locks the box as shown at 1 in **FIG 10**. **Do not turn the steering while the box is locked otherwise damage will be caused to the parts. Only the special bolt should be used, as this has the correct end shape for fitting into the steering nut.**

Steering coupling:

This should be checked whenever the steering box is removed. The details of the steering coupling are shown in **FIG 11**. The bolts 8 and 9 correspond to the bolts 8 and 9 shown in **FIG 3**.

1 Either remove the steering box or remove the bolts that secure it and the bolt that secures the lower flange so that the steering box can be slid down to free the coupling.

2 Remove the clamp bolt 9 that secures the upper flange to the steering column inner tube and pull the coupling off the steering column.
3 Remove the splitpins from the two bolts 2, pull off the washers 3 and separate the upper from the lower flange. Remove the two bushes 5 from the lower flange 4.
4 Reassemble the coupling in the reverse order of dismantling. It will be necessary to slightly squeeze the flanges 4 and 6 together in a vice so that the new splitpins can be fitted. On the earliest models the steel washers 3a were not fitted but the coupling should be reassembled with these in place. The part number of the washers is 136.990.95.40. On the earlier couplings the bores for the bushes were fractionally larger and if the bushes are loose, even after selectively fitting the largest diameter bushes, the lower flange 4 should be renewed. Loose bushes will cause a cracking noise as the coupling is turned.

Adjusting steering worm play:

Sectioned views of the steering box are shown in **FIG 12**.

The steering box cannot be adjusted while fitted to the car and it must be removed before adjusting it.

1 Release the pressure of the pressure block by slackening the locknut 13 and turning the adjusting screw 12 inwards.
2 The method of adjustment is shown in **FIG 13**. Hold the adjusting ring 7 with a pin wrench and remove the hexagon nut 6. Lightly smear the threads and jointing face of the nut 6 with a little jointing compound and screw it back into place until it is just slack.
3 Use the pin wrench to turn the adjusting ring until the end float on the worm is correct at .00 to .01 mm (.0000 to .0004 inch) and tighten the nut 6 to secure the adjusting ring. Check that the end float is still correct and that the worm turns quite freely.
4 If when the correct end float is set the worm does not turn freely, then the steering box must be dismantled and checked for internal faults.

Adjusting the pressure block:

1 Remove the locknut 13, smear its threads and jointing face lightly with jointing compound and screw it back loosely into place.
2 Unscrew the adjusting screw 12 until it rests against the spacer sleeve. Remove the filler plug and centralize the unit accurately using the special bolt as shown in **FIG 10**.
3 Turn the adjusting screw 12 in by $\frac{1}{8}$ to $\frac{1}{4}$ turn and lock it with the nut 13. Remove the special centralizing bolt. Turn the steering box through its full range of movement and there should be a slight increase in resistance at the centre point but on no account must the unit bind at any point.
4 As an additional check use a torque spanner to turn the steering arm through its range of movement. A torque reading of 1.75 to 2.25 mkg should not be exceeded at any point.

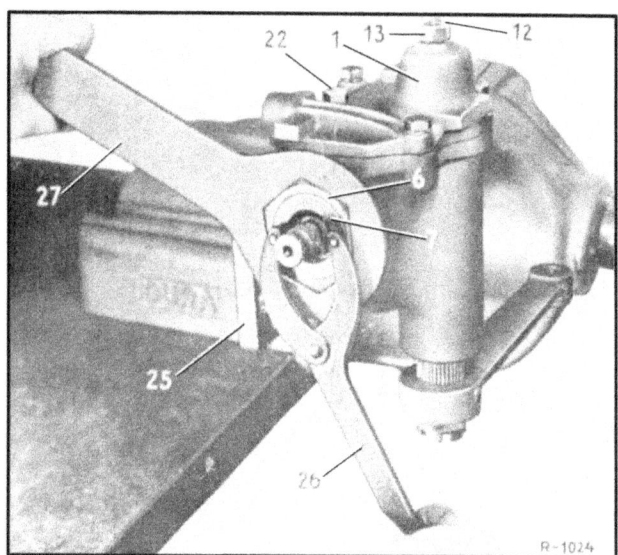

FIG 13 Adjusting the steering worm end float

1 Steering housing cover	12 Adjusting screw	26 Pin Wrench 000 589 00 05
6 Hexagon nut	13 Hex locknut	
7 Adjusting ring	22 Screw plug	27 Special Wrench 180 589 00 01
	25 Assembly plate	

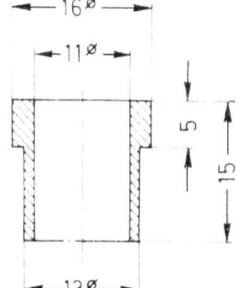

FIG 14 Dimensions for making up pressure block

6 Servicing the mechanical steering box

Remove the unit from the car as described in the previous section. Sectioned views of the unit are shown in **FIG 12**. Before starting to dismantle the unit make up a flat plate of metal with suitable holes drilled in it to secure the steering box to the plate, using nuts and bolts. Hold the plate in a vice to give a secure mounting for working on the steering box.

1 Take out the splitpin and remove the nut that secures the steering arm. Use a suitable puller to withdraw the steering arm from the shaft 19. For ease of reassembly it is advisable to make aligning light punch marks on both the arm and the end of the shaft.
2 Slacken and remove the locknut 13 and screw in the adjusting screw 12 to relieve the pressure. Take out the four securing screws and remove the top cover 1. Invert the unit and pour out the oil from inside it.
3 Slacken the nut 6 and completely unscrew the adjusting ring 7, using the tools shown in **FIG 13**. Press the steering worm 9 out of its mountings and remove it up and out of the housing complete with the steering nut 11. Do not unscrew the steering nut from the worm.
4 Take the ball retainers off the bearings and label the retainers so that they will be refitted to the correct

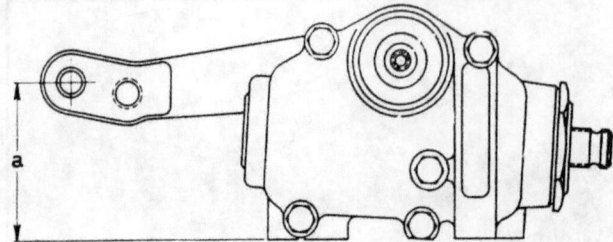

FIG 15 Check dimension for refitting the steering arm

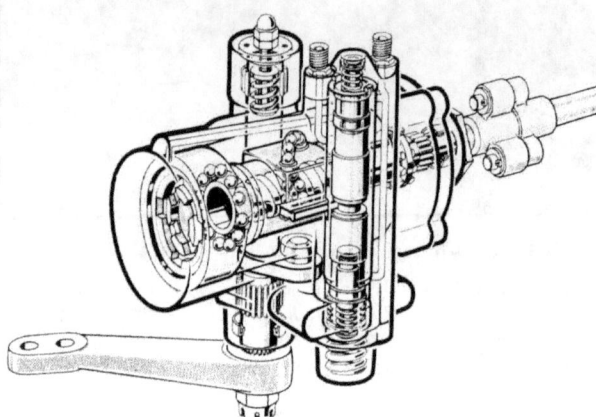

FIG 16 Sectioned view of the power assisted steering box

bearings. Remove the outer races of the bearings 4 and 10 from the housing 3. The outer race of the bearing 10 can be driven out with a suitable drift but the outer race of the bearing 4 must be removed by careful levering with a large screwdriver. Use a suitable puller to remove the inner races from the steering worm. **Keep all the parts of the one bearing separated from the parts of the other bearing.**

5 Make up a pressure block to the dimensions shown in **FIG 14**. Fit the pressure block to the adjusting screw 12 under the locknut 13. Tighten down the locknut so that the pressure block presses against the thrust washer 15 until the snap ring 14 can be removed. Slacken off the locknut and dismantle the parts of the shaft 19.

Examination:

1 Check that the steering worm turns freely in the steering nut. If the worm binds or any part is damaged then the complete assembly of steering nut and worm must be renewed as a whole. If the nut is accidentally unscrewed from the worm feed the balls back into the ball guides. **All the balls are selected and mated on manufacture and if only a single ball is lost then the complete assembly must be renewed.**
2 If the steering shaft 19 is found to be worn or scored it should be renewed. The ball cup can be renewed separately.
3 Check the housing for damage or cracks, paying particular attention to the area around the internal safety stops.
4 If the bushes for the steering shaft are worn or scored they should be pressed or driven out and new bushes pressed back into place. The new bushes should be reamed to an internal diameter of 30.007 to 30.020 mm (1.1814 to 1.1819 inch).
5 Extract any damaged or worn oil seals and fit new ones in their place.

Reassembly:

The steering box is reassembled in the reverse order of dismantling, noting the following points:
1 Pack the bore of the steering shaft 19 with grease before sliding the shaft back into place.
2 Screw out the adjusting screw 12 until the spring 17 is coil bound before fully tightening the nuts that secure the cover 1.
3 Refit the steering arm to the shaft, aligning the marks previously made. Centralize the unit with the special bolt as shown in **FIG 10**. Check that the dimension 'a' shown in **FIG 15** is correct at 76 ± 3 mm ($3.0 \pm .12$ inch).
4 Set the adjustments on the steering box and then refill it with .3 litre (.5 pints) of Hypoid SAE.90 oil. Check for oil leaks before refitting the unit.

7 The power assisted steering

The components are all complicated and if the steering is defective it is most advisable to take the car to an agent for checks and rectification.

A sectioned view of the steering box is given in **FIG 16**. The installation of the pump is shown in **FIG 17** and the installation of the reservoir is shown in **FIG 18**. It is essential that all the hose connections are tight, otherwise fluid will leak out or air be drawn into the system. If the operating fluid has a milky appearance, this is caused by minute air bubbles so the suction side should be checked through for leaks.

FIG 17 The mounting of the pump for the power assisted steering

7 Reservoir
7a Clamp bolt
14b Flange plate
17a Connecting hose
80 High-pressure oil hose
80a Elbow on high-pressure oil pump
82 Support for high-pressure oil pump
85 Narrow V-belt
86 Pulley

A sectioned view of a typical reservoir is shown in **FIG 19**. The design of the reservoir has been changed slightly from time to time but in all cases the basic details are the same.

Testing:

Check that the system operates smoothly from lock to lock. Leave the engine running between 700 to 800 rev/min. Put a piece of masking tape around one of the wheel spokes, to protect the spoke, and on the tape make a mark which is 190 mm ($7\frac{1}{2}$ inch) from the centre of the steering wheel. Hook a spring balance over the spoke at the marked point, keep the spring balance tangential to the steering wheel (right angles to the spoke), and measure the load required to turn the steering wheel. The load should not exceed 3.5 kg (7.7 lb).

If the steering is jerky when used, check that the driving belt tension is correct.

Bleeding:

If the level in the reservoir has fallen so low that air has been drawn into the system or if air has been drawn in through leaking connections then the operation of the steering will be erratic and the pump will run noisily.

The installation of the steering unit is shown in **FIG 20**. Remove the cover from the fluid reservoir. Attach a length of plastic or rubber tube to the bleed nipple 12 on the steering box and dip the free end of the tube into the reservoir. Start the engine and top up to the mark with ATF type A fluid. **Make sure that the tube is always held firmly onto the bleed nipple and that it always points into the reservoir.** If the tube comes free large quantities of fluid will be lost in a short time.

Open the bleed nipple two turns and turn the steering quarter of a turn on either side of the central position. Carry on turning the steering until all the air has been bled out of the steering box. Close the bleed nipple and remove the bleed tube. Top up to the level marked in the reservoir and refit the reservoir cover.

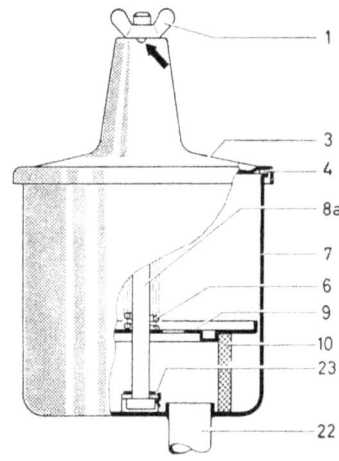

FIG 19 The latest reservoir version for the 230SL

1 Wingnut
3 Cover with damping dome
4 Gasket
6 Pressure spring
7 Reservoir
8a Screw
9 Baffle plate
10 Filter element
22 Connecting pipe
23 Locking device

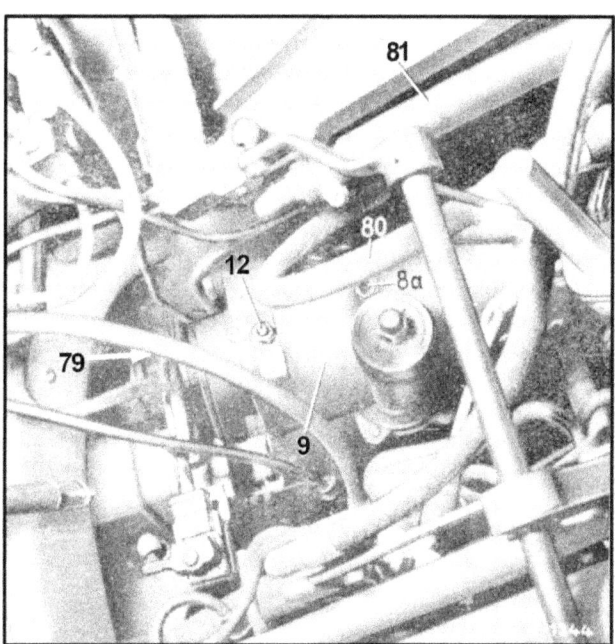

FIG 20 Power assisted steering unit fitted

8a Center position check screw 111 589 02 23 00
9 Steering housing
12 Bleed nipple
79 Hexagon socket screw (clamping screw)
80 High-pressure oil hose
81 Oil-return hose

FIG 18 The mounting of the reservoir for the power assisted steering

1 Wing nut
2 High-pressure oil pump
3 Cover
7 Reservoir
7a Clamp bolt
14b Flange plate
17a Connecting hose
80 High-pressure oil hose
80a Elbow on high-pressure oil pump
81 Oil return hose
82 Support for high-pressure oil pump
83 Hexagon screw with nut, washer, locking plate, and lock washer
84 Clamping screw
85 Narrow V-belt
86 Pulley

8 Front wheel alignment

Track:

This can be checked and set by the owner though a more accurate setting will be made by a garage using special equipment.

The alignment is checked with the car carrying its normal tools, spare wheel and fuel tank full. If the fuel tank is partially empty put weights into the luggage compartment to compensate for the fuel. One gallon of fuel weighs approximately 8 pounds.

The alignment must also be checked with the front wheels locked at the straight-ahead position. Remove the filler cap from the steering box and with the aid of an

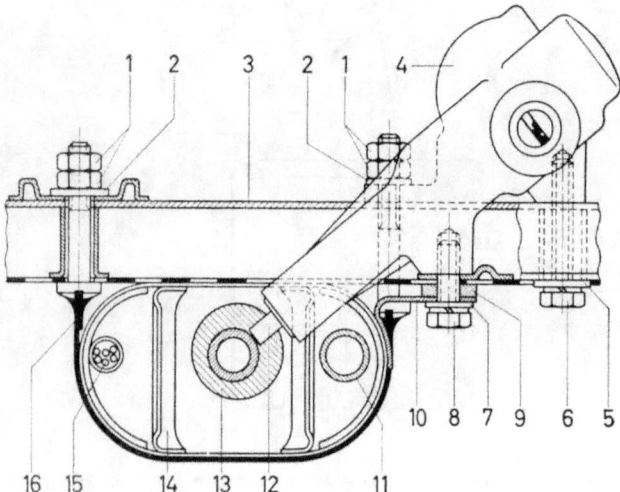

FIG 21 Steering column lock mounting on models except the 230SL

1 Hexagon nuts
2 Washers
3 Crossmember
4 Steering lock
5 Washer
6 Hex bolt with lock washer
7 Washer
8 Hex bolt with lock washer
9 Spacer washer
10 Bracket on steering column jacket for attachment of steering lock
11 Shift tube
12 Lockbolt of steering lock
13 Lock ring on steering tube
14 Steering column jacket
15 Wiring harness for flash signal switch and horns
16 Steering column strap

inspection lamp turn the steering until the special bolt can be fitted as shown in **FIG 10**. **Do not turn the steering once this special bolt is in place or damage will be caused to the parts.**

Drive the car onto a suitable level surface, set the front wheels in the straight-ahead position and push the car forwards for a few yards to settle the bearings and suspensions. When measuring do not push the car backwards to align a mark but instead push it forwards until the wheels have completed a further revolution, if the mark is overshot.

Measure, as accurately as possible, the distance between the wheel rims at wheel centre height and at the front of the wheel rims. Mark the positions measured with chalk and push the car forwards so that the wheels turn exactly half a revolution and the chalk marks are again at wheel centre height but at the rear of the wheels. Again measure the distance between them as accurately as possible.

The difference between the two dimensions represents the alignment of the front wheels. The dimension at the front should be less than the dimension at the rear by 2 ± 1 mm ($.08\pm.04$ inch) for the alignment to be correct.

If the alignment is incorrect adjust both the lefthand and righthand side outer tie rods by equal amounts until the correct alignment is obtained. Once it is correctly set remove the centralizing bolt, check the oil level and refit the filler plug.

Check that the full lock of the steering is limited by the stops on the suspension units and not by the internal safety stops in the steering box.

Driving the car with the front wheels out of alignment will cause uneven tyre wear and leave one edge of the tread with a characteristic feathered appearance.

If there is any difficulty in setting the correct alignment or if the safety stops limit the full lock of the steering, the car should be taken to an agent who will use special gauges to check the lengths of the tie rods in case they have been damaged or bent.

9 The steering wheel

On all models the steering wheel can be removed after taking off the nut that secures it to the steering tube. The splines are parallel so no extractor is needed to pull the steering wheel off. Before attempting to remove the steering wheel pull off the central motif.

Make light punch marks on the steering wheel hub and splines of the steering tube so that the steering wheel can be correctly aligned when it is refitted.

Refit the steering wheel in the reverse order of removal, aligning the previously made marks. On models fitted with a shock absorber at the top of the column, secure the nut and washer to a socket spanner with a little masking tape so that the nut can be started onto the thread. Remove the masking tape before fully tightening the nut.

On models fitted with a shock absorber the steering wheel can be removed, leaving the shock absorber in place. Pull off the motif as before and take off the five nuts that secure the steering wheel to the shock absorber. Partially lift off the steering wheel, disconnect the cable from the contact ring and remove the steering wheel.

10 Steering column lock

The lock on the 230SL models will be dealt with separately in **Section 12**.

The later version of the lock is shown in **FIG 21**. Earlier versions are very similar except they do not have the spacer washer 9 fitted and on some models the lefthand side bolt that secures the strap 16 will be longer as it has to pass through an extra channel section member.

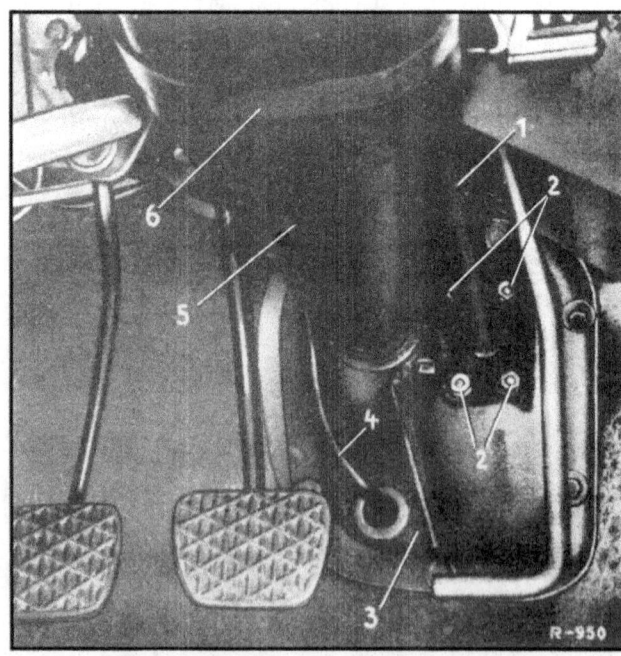

FIG 22 Steering column attachments

1 Shift tube
2 Hexagon nuts for attaching the bearing assembly of the steering wheel shift system
3 Coverplate
4 Cable for reversing light switch
5 Steering column jacket
6 Tightening strap for steering column jacket

Removal:

1 Disconnect the battery. Remove the instrument cluster (see **Chapter 13, Section 8**). Turn the ignition key to position 1 and remove the key from the lock.
2 Remove the nuts 1 from the bolt nearest to the lock that secures the steering column strap 16.
3 Take out the two bolts 6 and 8 that secure the lock, carefully collecting the spacer 9 if it is fitted. Slide the lock out of its cutout in the jacket and remove it downwards. Disconnect the electrical leads, labelling them for ease of reconnection and remove the lock.

Refit the lock in the reverse order of removal and check that it operates correctly. All ignition locks are fitted with three positions as follows:

Position 0:

The ignition is switched off and the steering column locked. The key can be removed from the lock.

Position 1:

The ignition is off but the steering column is free to rotate and the key can be removed from the lock.

Position 2:

The ignition is switched on, the clearance lights (if fitted) automatically switched off and the key is trapped in the lock. Further rotation of the key from this position operates the starter for as long as the key is held against the spring loaded stop. An interlock is fitted so that the key cannot be turned to the start position twice from position 2 and the key must be returned to at least position 1 before the starter can be operated again.

If the switch is checked with the instrument cluster removed, blank the pipe for the oil pressure gauge otherwise the engine will pump oil through the pipe.

FIG 23 230SL steering column attachments

1 Clutch pedal
2 Brake pedal
3 Cover plate
4 Pipe clip
5 Line to extraction cylinder
6 Hex bolt with lockwasher
7 Steering column jacket
8 Tightening strap
9 Opening in steering column jacket for clamping ring
10 Mechanical stoplight switch
11 Stop ring
12 Clutch master cylinder
13 Line from reservoir
14 Piston rod
15 Pressure spring (dead center spring)
16 Hex bolt with lockwasher
17 Stop screw
18 Adjustment lever
19 Plastic plate
20 Hexagon nut
21 Footplate
22 Mounting plate

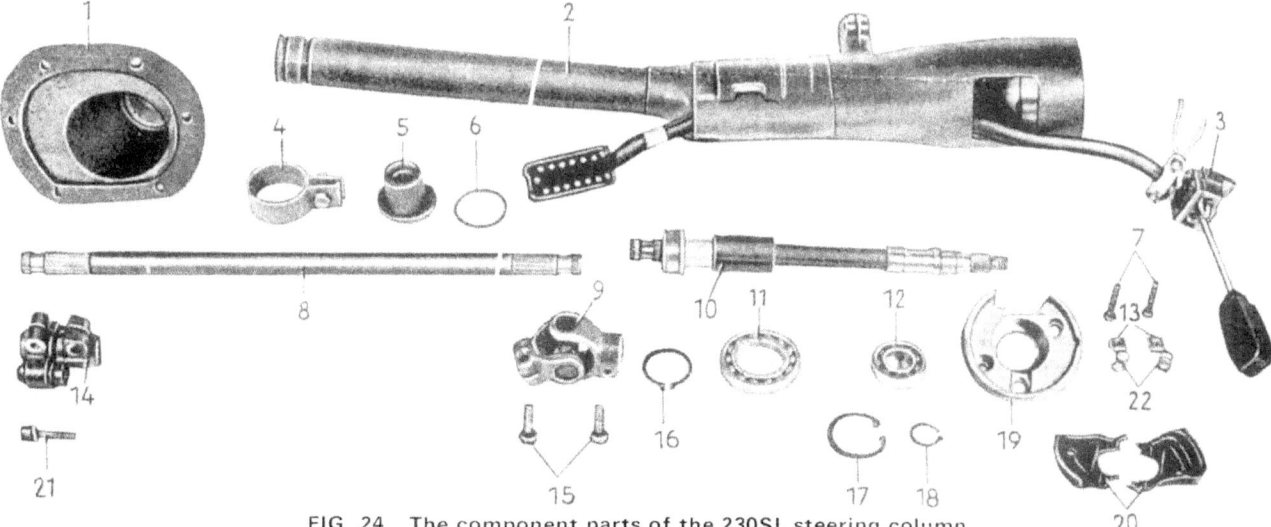

FIG 24 The component parts of the 230SL steering column

1 Coverplate with rubber gasket
2 Steering column jacket
3 Combination switch
4 Pipe clip
5 Rubber sleeve
6 O-ring
7 Hexagon socket screw
8 Lower steering tube half
9 Universal joint
10 Upper steering tube half
11 & 12 Annular grooved bearings
13 Square nut
14 Steering coupling
15 Bolt with lockwasher
16 to 18 Snap rings
19 Mounting plate
20 Locking assembly half
21 Hexagon socket screw
22 Pressure spring

FIG 25 Removing the 230SL steering column

1 Door contact switch
2 Combination switch
3 Contact ring
4 Flexible drive shaft
5 Hexagon nut
6 Washer
7 Escutcheon
8 Steering lock

11 The steering column

The 230SL steering column will be dealt with separately in **Section 12**. The attachment of the steering column is shown in **FIG 22**.

Removal:

1 Disconnect the battery. Remove the steering column lock. Disconnect the shift tubes from the shift levers on the gearchange bearing assembly (see **Chapter 6**).
2 Remove the remaining nuts that secure the steering column strap (see **FIG 21**). Free the multi-pin plug for the steering column wires. Disconnect the cable 4 at the reverse light switch and pull the lead back through the grommet in the coverplate 3.
3 Take out all six bolts that secure the coverplate 3 to the cowl and withdraw the steering column from the car.

Refit the steering column in the reverse order of removal, making sure that it is correctly aligned with the front wheels.

12 The 230SL steering column

A sectioned view of the column is shown in **FIG 2** and its attachments are shown in **FIG 23** while the parts of the dismantled column are shown in **FIG 24**.

Removal (including steering column lock):

Refer to **FIG 23**.

1 Disconnect the battery. Remove the instruments. Set the lock to position 1 and remove the key. Remove the steering wheel.
2 Slacken the clip 4 and remove it from the jacket 7. On cars fitted with normal steering undo the two clamp nuts that secure the coupling to the inner tube and worm drive of the steering box. On cars fitted with power steering the bolts 6 must be removed and the coverplate 3 lifted up to expose the clamp bolts as the power steering unit is longer than the normal one. If the complete steering column is to be removed then these bolts 6 should be removed on all models.
3 Slacken the clamp bolt that secures the lock to the steering column jacket. Remove the nuts that secure the clamping strap, similar in design to the one shown in **FIG 21** except that the lock is not mounted with it. Push the steering column jacket 7 forwards until it no longer engages with the lock. The parts at this stage are shown in **FIG 25**. Turn the lock through 90 degrees so that it hangs downwards and remove it through the bracket, taking care not to damage the escutcheon on the dash.
4 When all the attachments are undone, including the multi-pin plug, lift out the steering column.

The parts are refitted in the reverse order of removal.

13 Fault diagnosis

(a) Wheel wobble

1 Worn hub bearings
2 Defective or worn suspension
3 Unbalanced wheels and tyres
4 Slack or worn steering connections
5 Incorrect suspension and steering geometry
6 Defective steering damper

(b) Wander

1 Check 2, 4 and 5 in (a)
2 Front and rear suspensions not correctly aligned
3 Uneven tyre pressures
4 Uneven tyre wear

(c) Heavy steering

1 Check 5 in (a)
2 Neglected lubrication
3 Steering box maladjusted
4 Very low tyre pressures
5 Steering tube bent or misaligned
6 Defective bearings in steering column

(d) Lost motion

1 Check 1 and 4 in (a) and 3 in (c)
2 Defective steering coupling
3 Loose steering wheel or badly worn attachment splines

(e) Power steering 'grunts' or 'drones'

1 Low oil level

(f) Steering wheel jerks when power steering operated

1 Loose driving belt

CHAPTER 11 – BRAKING SYSTEM

1 Description
2 Maintenance
3 Flexible hoses
4 The disc brakes
5 Servicing a brake caliper
6 Brake linings and brake drums
7 Servicing the rear brakes
8 The master cylinder
9 The brake servo unit
10 Bleeding the brakes
11 The handbrake
12 Fault diagnosis

1 Description

All the models covered by this manual are fitted with Girling disc brakes on the front wheels and Simplex drum brakes on the rear wheels.

All four brakes are hydraulically operated from the foot brake pedal but the handbrake operates only the rear brakes, using a mechanical linkage. The hydraulic system is fitted with a tandem master cylinder which is effectively two separate master cylinders combined in series into the one body. One chamber of the master cylinder feeds the brakes on one axle while the other chamber feeds the other pair of brakes. The hydraulics are so designed that, apart from a common reservoir, the two systems are hydraulically independent and a fluid leakage from one system will still allow the other system to operate at full efficiency, though with a longer pedal travel. Pressure is taken from the master cylinder through metal pipelines and flexible hoses to the individual wheel brakes.

The handbrake on the 230 and 230S models is of the pistol grip type but on the 230SL a handbrake lever is fitted on the transmission tunnel.

The disc brakes consist of a caliper mounted rigidly to the suspension unit and a disc rotating with the wheel hub. Hydraulic pressure presses the pistons of the caliper simultaneously and equally inwards so that the disc is gripped between the friction pads in the caliper. The piston seals are slightly distorted so that when the hydraulic pressure is released the seals draw the pistons back to give a running clearance between the friction pads and disc. Excessive clearance allows the pistons to slide through the seals and this also occurs as the friction pads wear, so that the disc brakes are self-adjusting.

On the drum brake the drum is fitted to and revolves with the wheel hub. Two shoes, with friction linings on their outside faces, are fitted to the brake backplate in such a way that a hydraulic cylinder between their ends will expand them into contact with the drum when hydraulic pressure is fed to the cylinder. The opposite ends of the shoes pivot about a post on the backplate and wear on the linings is taken up by eccentric adjusters which have to be set at regular intervals.

An ATE Type T.51 vacuum-assisted servo is fitted as standard on all the models covered by this manual. The servo reduces the pedal pressure required for a given retardation. It is so designed that if it fails the brakes will operate with full effectiveness except that a higher pedal pressure will be required.

FIG 1   Adjusting the rear drum brakes

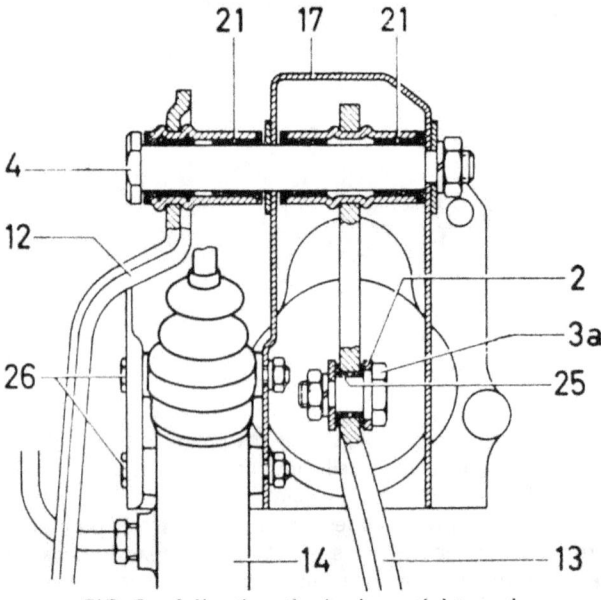

FIG 2   Adjusting the brake pedal travel

 2 Piston rod of power brake
 3a Adjusting screw with hex nut and lockwasher
 4 Pivot pin with hex nut and lockwasher
 12 Clutch pedal
 13 Brake pedal
 14 Supply cylinder
 17 Pedal support
 21 Bushings in the pedals
 25 Brake pedal bushings
 26 Hex bolt with nut and lock washer

The instructions given in Chapter 5, Section 3 should be read before dismantling any hydraulic component as these instructions are relevant to most parts.

2 Maintenance

Fluid level:

Regularly check the fluid level in the master cylinder reservoir. The reservoir is made of translucent plastic so that the filler cap does not need to be removed in order to check the level. The level should fall slowly and steadily over a period of time as the friction pads on the disc brakes wear, and provided that the level does not fall too low this may be ignored. Any sudden sharp drop or increase in the rate of falling should be investigated immediately as it may be the result of a leak. Do not ignore leaks but trace and rectify them immediately as they can cause partial or total brake failure.

Wipe the top of the reservoir and the cap clean before removing the cap, so as to prevent dirt falling into the reservoir. If the level is low top up using only a recommended fluid, such as ATE blue, as the incorrect fluid will cause the seals to swell and fail. Brake fluids are of the correct type if they meet the SAE.70.R3 specification.

Brake adjustments:

The front disc brakes are self-adjusting. The thickness of the friction material should be checked at regular intervals and the pads renewed if the linings are worn to less than 2 mm (.08 inch).

The rear brakes should be adjusted at regular intervals, and certainly when the brake pedal travel becomes excessive. The adjustment points are shown in **FIG 1**. Jack up each rear wheel in turn and check that it rotates freely, allowing for the drag of the rear axle. Turn each adjuster in the direction shown in the figure until a strong resistance is felt and the brake shoes are in firm contact with the drum. The road wheel should now rotate only with heavy pressure. Slacken back each adjuster until the wheel rotates freely again. Lower the car back to the ground.

Pedal movement:

The tandem master cylinder has no free play so there should be no brake pedal clearance. Instead the system is adjusted to give the correct amount of pedal travel. A sectioned view of the adjuster is shown in **FIG 2**.

The method of adjustment on the 230SL is similar except the adjusting bolt is in the engine compartment (see **FIG 28**). Slacken the locknut and turn the adjusting screw 3a until the notch on its head (indicating the direction of maximum eccentricity) is pointing rearwards. Exact positioning of the adjusting screw is then set so that the full travel of the pedal is 152 mm (6 inches).

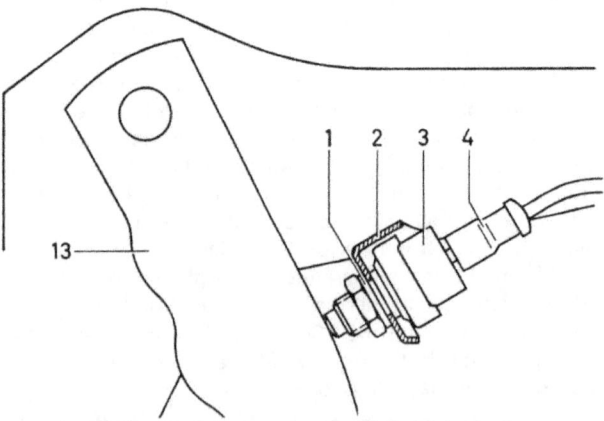

FIG 3   Adjusting the brake light switch

 1 Shim
 2 Bracket for stoplight switch
 3 Stoplight switch
 4 Plug connection
 13 Brake pedal

The mechanical brake light switch, shown in **FIG 3**, should be positioned by varying the thickness of the shims 1 until the brake lights operate when the pedal 13 has been depressed by approximately 20 mm ($\frac{3}{4}$ inch).

Handbrake:

The adjustment point is shown in **FIG 4**. On some earlier models the adjusting wingnut 4 may be on the relay lever as shown at 1 in **FIG 5**. On 230SL the adjustment is made inside the car, on the handbrake lever, by rotating the nut 10 shown in **FIG 6**.

Jack up the rear wheels and check that they rotate freely. Shorten the length of the cable, using the adjusting nut until the correct position of the control is reached. With pistol grip handbrakes there should be three to four more notches available after the control has been pulled out with firm pressure. On the 230SL the adjustment is correct when the brakes start to apply with the lever at the first tooth on the ratchet, and the lever can be pulled up three notches with medium force.

When the brakes have been adjusted it is essential to check that they are not binding. Drive the car for a few miles without using the brakes at all. Select neutral and check that the car coasts freely and comes gradually to a halt. When the car has come to a stop check that all four brakes are cool. Heat in any brake shows that it is binding.

Preventative maintenance:

Regularly check through the system, removing the brake drums from the rear wheels and the dust covers from the front disc brakes. Examine the brake linings and friction pads, fitting new ones when the wear limits are exceeded. Brush out dust and dirt from the brakes. At the same time examine all the pipe runs for damage, corrosion and leaks. Renew defective pipes or hoses and renew the flexible hoses at intervals of five years.

The system should be drained and flushed through with methylated spirits, to clean out the pipelines, at intervals of three years and the complete system should then be dismantled. Fit all new seals and renew any defective components.

FIG 4 Adjusting the later version handbrake

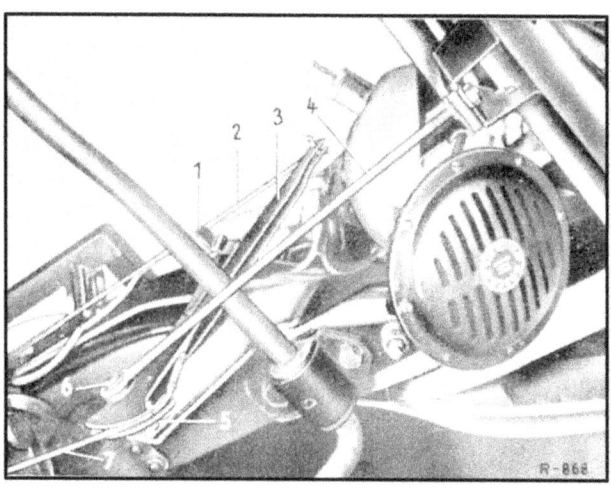

FIG 5 Adjusting the earlier version handbrake

1 Wingnut
2 Front brake cable
3 Brake lever
4 Support rod
5 Splitpin
6 Pivot pin
7 Center brake cable

Use only hydraulic fluids which meet SAE.70.R3 specification. A short list of suitable fluids is given in Technical Data. Use nothing but fresh clean fluid for filling the reservoir.

After long service the discs may become covered with a dark hard deposit. Efficiency can be restored by having a garage clean off this deposit, using special pads in place of the friction pads, and driving the wheel with a dynamic type wheel balancer.

Lubrication:

Regularly grease the pedal pivots and the handbrake cables through the grease fittings on the parts.

3 Flexible hoses

Hoses which show any defects such as softening, perishing or hardening must be renewed immediately. If a hose is blocked and cannot be cleared using compressed air then the hose must be renewed. **Do not attempt to clear blocked hoses by poking wire through them.**

Removal:

When removing or replacing a flexible hose the flexible portion must not be twisted or strained in any way.

Hold the hose with a spanner on its adjacent hexagons and use another spanner to undo the union nut that secures the metal pipeline. Take care, as after long service the union nut may also stick and twist the metal pipe with it. If the hose is secured to the bracket by a locknut remove the locknut while still preventing the hose from rotating. In many cases the hose will be secured to the bracket by a retainer. Remove the retainer to free the hose. The other end of the hose can now be unscrewed, using a spanner on its hexagonal flats, allowing the flexible portion to rotate freely.

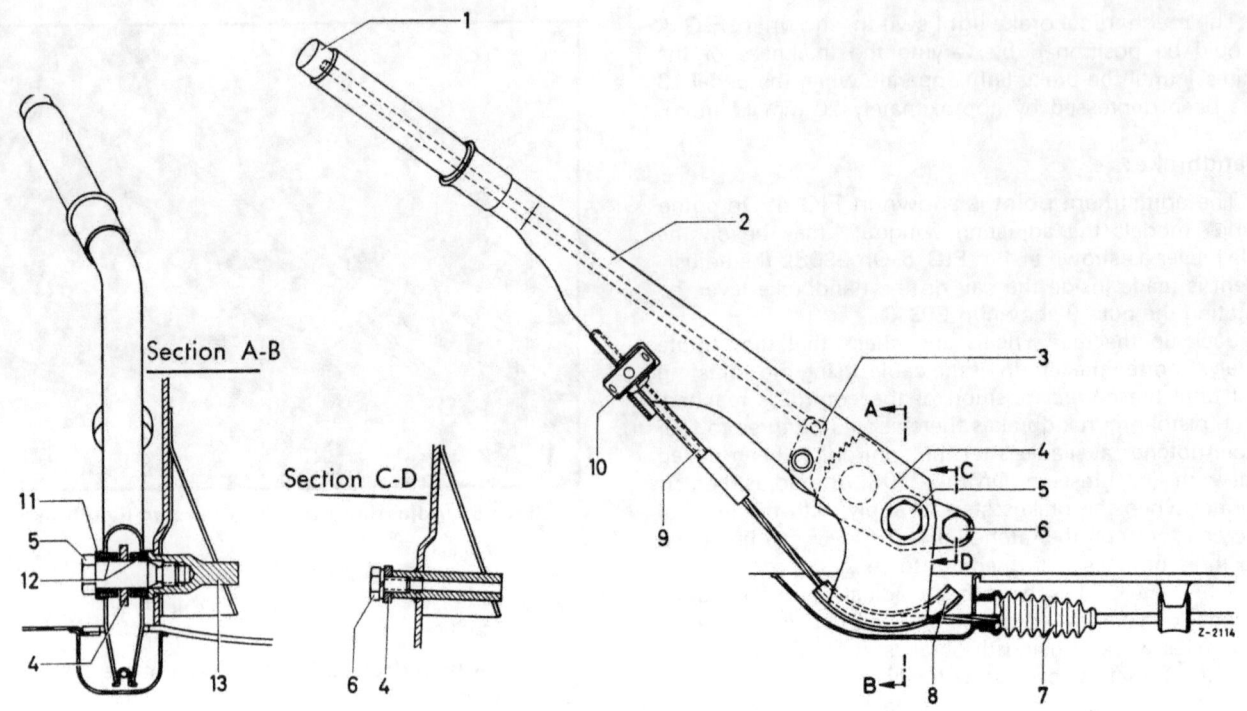

FIG 6 The handbrake lever and adjusting point on the 230SL

1 Push button
2 Handbrake lever
3 Pawl
4 Ratchet
5 Pivot bolt
6 Hex bolt with lock washer
7 Rubber sleeve
8 Brake cable guide
9 Front brake cable
10 Circular four-hole nut
11 Washer
12 Bearing bushing
13 Threaded member for fastening brake lever to chassis base panel

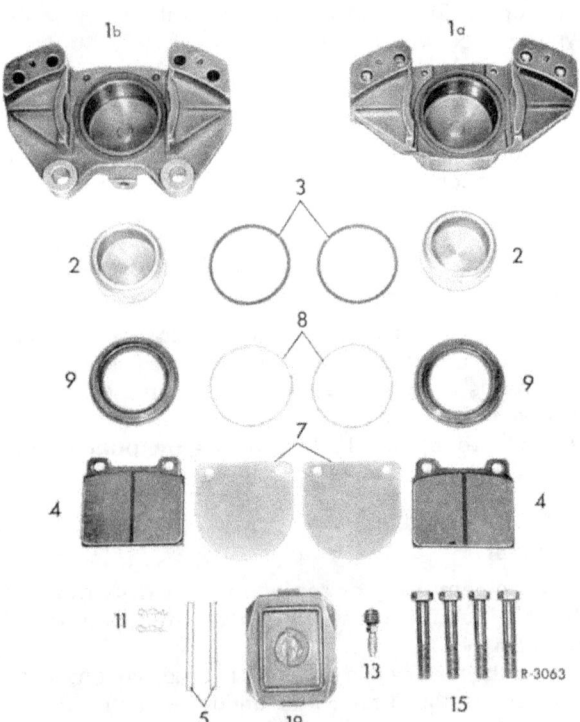

FIG 7 Components of the Girling type 17/2 caliper

1 a Outer brake caliper half
1 b Inner brake caliper half
2 Piston
3 Piston seal
4 Friction pad
5 Retaining pins
7 Heat screening plates
8 Clamping wire
9 Dust cap
11 Locking clip
13 Bleed screw with rubber cap
15 Hexagon screw
18 Cover plate

Refitting:

Refit the hose in the reverse order of removal. When the hose is in place check that it will not foul or chafe onto any adjacent structure. Do not check just at the static position but ensure that the hose is free as the suspension moves through its range.

4 The disc brakes

230 and 230S models are fitted with Girling Type 17/2 disc brakes. A few models will be fitted with Teves brakes instead of the Girling but apart from the design of the pistons Teves and Girling 17/2 brakes are very similar and may be treated in exactly the same manner. The components of a 17/2 brake are shown in **FIG 7**.

The 230SL is fitted with a Girling Type 17/3 disc brake. There are three variations of this brake, the main differences being in the connections of the pipelines and the two later versions being fitted with heat shields behind the pads. The components of the earlier 17/3 disc brake are shown in **FIG 8**. The latest version is very similar except that there is no connecting line 6 and the fluid passes between the cylinders by internal passages.

The halves of the calipers have been shown separated in the figures but this is for the purpose of illustration only. **The owner must not separate the two halves of the caliper and because of the internal seals the caliper must only be washed with methylated spirits or clean hydraulic fluid.**

Renewing friction pads:

Remove the dust cover, if fitted, and check the thickness of the remaining friction lining. New pads must be fitted if the linings are worn down to 2 mm (.08 inch). Do not attempt to bond new linings onto the old pads.

A typical attachment of the friction pads is shown in **FIG 9**. Remove the spring clips 21 and draw out both lockpins 10. Withdraw the friction pads 6 from the caliper using wire or a hooked tool through the eyes on each pad. If heat shields are fitted spring these out, carefully noting the position in which they were fitted.

Use a small stiff brush (a bottle brush is ideal) to clean out any dirt and dust from inside the caliper. Check the dust cap for cracks or damage.

Fit a length of plastic or rubber tube over the bleed nipple of the brake and open the bleed nipple. Aim the

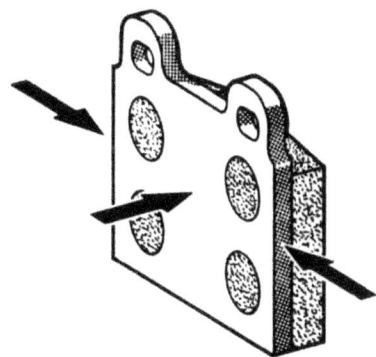

FIG 10 Surfaces on the friction pads that should be lightly lubricated with Molykote paste

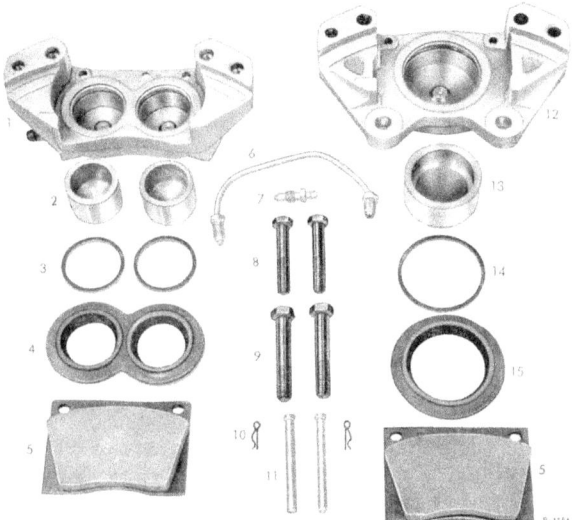

FIG 8 The components of the early Girling type 17/3 brake caliper

1 Outer caliper half   6 Connecting line   11 Retaining pin
2 Piston   7 Bleed screw   12 Inner caliper half
3 Piston seal   8 Hexagon screw   13 Piston
4 Dust cap   9 Hexagon screw   14 Piston seal
5 Friction pad   10 Spring clip   15 Dust cap

FIG 9 Typical method of securing the friction pads, shown on 17/3 type caliper

2 Brake disk   10 Lock pin
6 Friction pad   21 Spring clip
9 Brake caliper   26 Heat screening plate

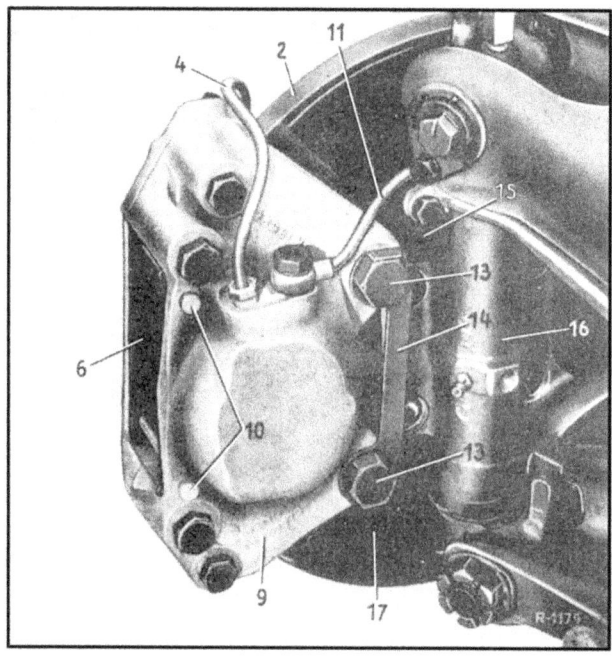

FIG 11 Attachments of the early 17/3 type brake caliper

2 Brake disk   13 Hexagon fitting screw
4 Connecting line   14 Locking plate
6 Friction pad   15 Steering knuckle bracket
9 Brake caliper   16 Steering knuckle
10 Locking pin   17 Cover plate
11 Brake line with connector

free end of the tube into any suitable container. Carefully press or lever each piston back into its cylinder and close the bleed screw when all the pistons are returned. If the bleed nipple is not opened then the other pistons must be clamped while pressing one in, otherwise the hydraulic pressure will force the other out. Opening the bleed nipple also allows surplus fluid to be ejected. If all pistons are pressed back then the fluid level in the reservoir will rise and may even overflow if some is not syphoned off. **Hydraulic fluid rapidly softens and removes paint.**

Refit the heat shields. Lightly lubricate the new friction pads with Molykote Paste U on the surfaces arrowed in **FIG 10** and refit them in the reverse order of removal.

Top up the reservoir to the correct level with fresh hydraulic fluid. Pump the brakes several times before driving the car so as to set the correct clearances. Before using the car normally it is advisable to bed-in the new friction pads otherwise the brake action may be uneven.

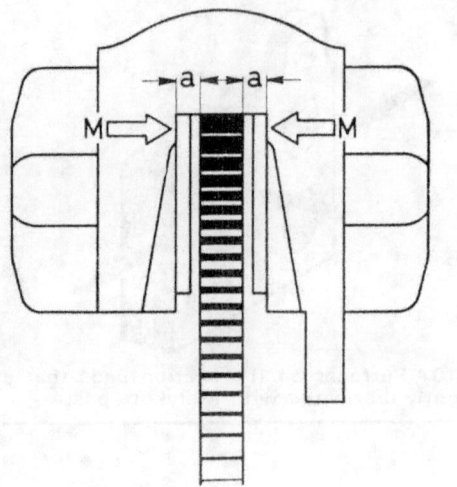

FIG 12 Positions for checking the fitting of the brake caliper

M = Measuring point

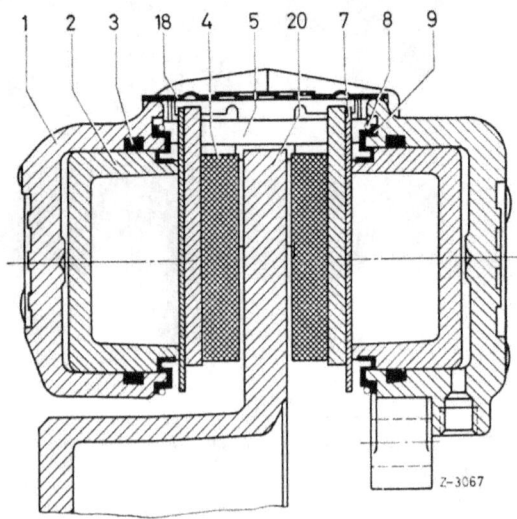

FIG 13 Sectioned view of the 17/2 type caliper

1 Brake caliper
2 Piston
3 Piston seal
4 Friction pad
5 Retaining pin
7 Heat screening plate
8 Clamping wire
9 Dust cap
18 Cover plate
20 Brake disk

copper washers for the union and fit new ones on reassembly.

1 Disconnect the flexible hose to the metal pipeline 11 as instructed in **Section 3**. Take precautions to collect any fluid that drains out to prevent it damaging paintwork, and blank the pipes to prevent the entry of dirt.

2 Free the locking plate 14 and unscrew the bolts 13. On earlier versions of all models the caliper attachment bracket is riveted to the suspension and shims are fitted between the caliper and its bracket. Later versions have the bracket integral with the suspension and no shims are fitted. Carefully collect the shims if they are fitted.

3 Slide the caliper off the disc and remove it from the car.

The caliper is refitted in the reverse order of removal. Make sure that the disc runs parallel to the caliper and use feeler gauges to check the gaps 'a' at M in **FIG 12**. On the earlier versions the gaps can be equalized by selectively fitting the shims between the caliper and its bracket. On the later versions the gaps cannot be altered and if they differ the steering knuckle should be checked for damage or distortion.

Brake disc:

Remove the brake caliper and then take off the hub assembly as instructed in **Chapter 9, Section 3**. Separate the disc from the hub by taking out the socket-headed bolts that secure the two together.

Before refitting the disc to the hub, scrupulously clean the mating surfaces and make sure that there are no specks of dirt on them. Bolt them up tight and correctly refit the hub assembly. Mount the DTI (Dial Test Indicator) so that its stylus rests vertically against the outer operating face of the disc and a short way in from the outer edge. Press the hub firmly inwards to take up its end float and rotate it so that the run out on the disc can be measured. If the run out exceeds .12 mm (.005 inch) remove the parts and fit the disc back to the hub aligning different mounting holes. If rotating the disc relative to the hub does not bring the run out within correct limits the disc must either be reground or a new disc fitted in its place.

After a short period of use concentric scores will appear on the disc. These will not affect performance unless they are deeper than .5 mm (.02 inch) or if there are radial scores. A certain amount of scoring can be removed by specialist grinding but if the scores are very deep or the disc has already been machined to the limit then a new disc must be fitted.

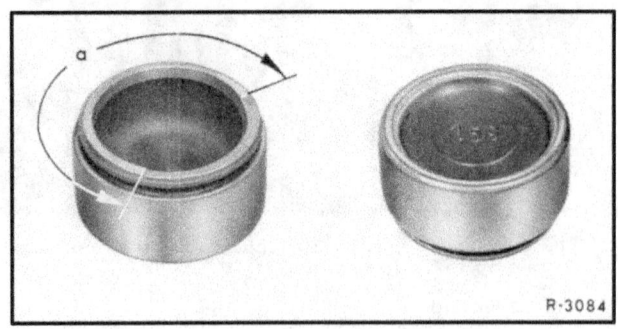

FIG 14 Teves brake pistons

Slow the car from 80 to 40 kilometer/hr (50 to 25 mile/hr) several times in succession and then allow the brakes to cool in the airflow before gently stopping the car. Avoid heavy or prolonged braking for the first hundred miles (160 kilometers).

Removing a brake caliper:

The attachment of the earliest 17/3 brake is shown in **FIG 11**. Different length bolts 13 are used on different versions and the shape of the lockplate 14 also varies as do the positions of the hydraulic connections. If the pipe is connected using banjo bolts then discard the

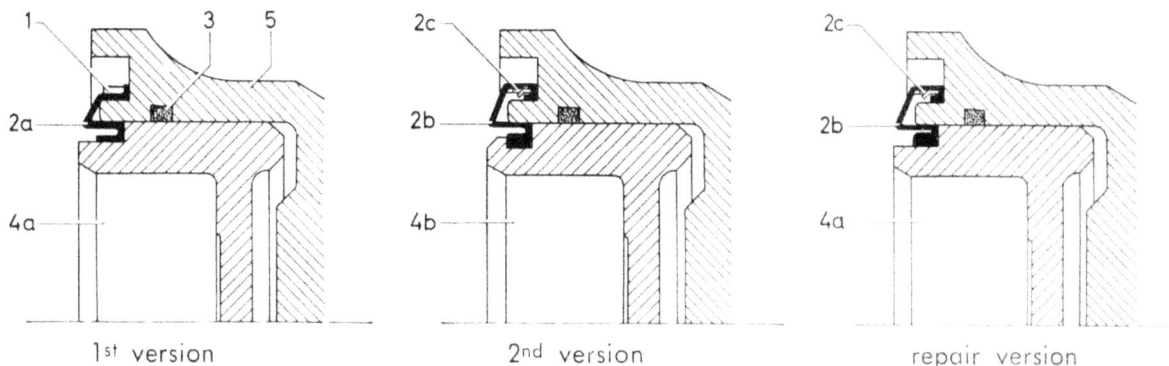

FIG 15 The different types of seals and pistons fitted to the Teves disc brake

1   Split clamp ring
2a Dust cap 1st version
2b Dust cap 2nd version
2c Closed clamp ring
3   Piston seal
4a Piston 1st version
4b Piston 2nd version
5   Brake caliper

5 Servicing a brake caliper

A sectioned view of a typical disc brake is shown in **FIG 13**. The 17/2 brakes are fitted with only one piston per side but the general details are still accurate. On Teves brakes the heat shields are clipped to the pistons and only removed with the pistons. **Under no circumstances may the halves of the caliper be separated on any model of brake.**

Dismantling:

1 Remove the caliper from the car and take out the friction pads, as described in the previous section.
2 Remove the pistons with their dust caps from the caliper. On all models the pistons should be ejected by applying an airline to the inlet and using air at a pressure of .5 kg/sq cm (7 lb/sq in) to blow out the piston. On models fitted with an interconnecting pipe between the cylinders it is easy to blow out each cylinder in turn, though it is advisable to fit a piece of wood in place of the disc so that the pistons are not damaged. On other models the pistons should be clamped so that they do not move while one piston is removed and the orifice of the cylinder should then be sealed with a piece of rubber held in place by a metal plate and suitable clamp to prevent air leakage.
3 If a piston is jammed in place, clamp the others and reconnect the caliper to the brake line. Bleed the brake through its bleed nipple and apply a steadily increasing pressure on the brake pedal until hydraulic pressure forces the piston out. Wrap the caliper in rags to contain any fluid and make sure that the flexible hose is not strained.
4 Remove the dust cap and use a sharp tool to carefully prise out the seal from the cylinder. Take great care not to damage or score the bore of the cylinder.

Cleaning and examination:

Wash all the parts with methylated spirits, hydraulic fluid or hydraulic cleaning fluid. **Do not use any other solvents.** The parts are examined as described in **Chapter 5, Section 3**. Faint dust rings on the pistons or part of the bore outside the seal may be removed by carefully using fine-grade emerycloth or 'Crocus' paper. Scores or corrosion necessitate renewal of the complete assembly.

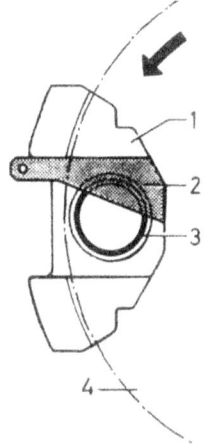

FIG 16 Aligning the Teves piston
1 Brake caliper
2 Piston Gage 001 589 30 21 00
3 Piston
4 Brake disk

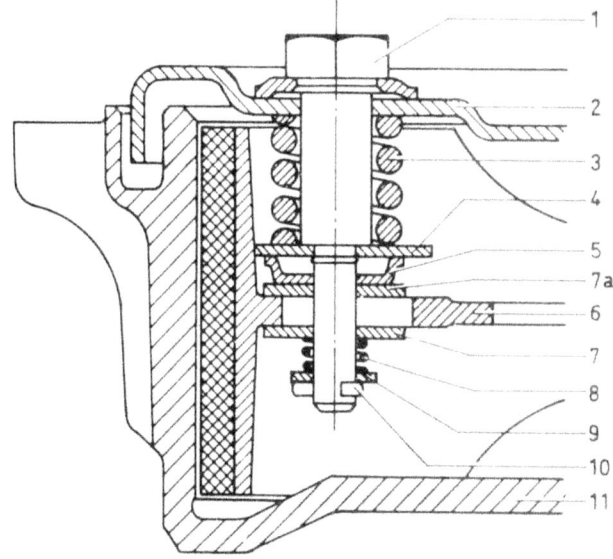

FIG 17 Sectioned view of the brake adjuster

1 Adjustment bolt
2 Brake anchor plate
3 Pressure spring
4 Eccentric plate
5 Cup washer
6 Brake shoe
7 Washer
7a Washer
8 Pressure spring
9 Washer
10 Split pin
11 Brake drum

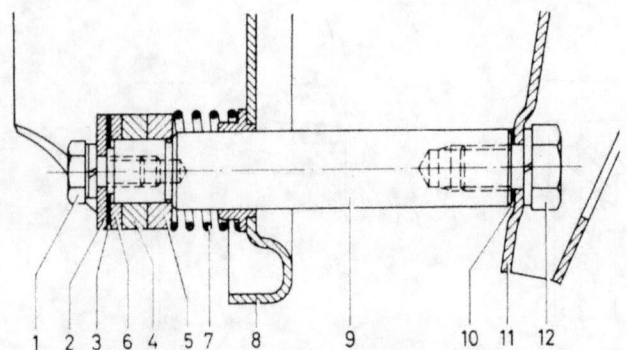

FIG 18 Sectioned view of the brake pivot post assembly

1 Hex bolt
2 Washer
3 Brass washer
4 Outer brake shoe
5 Inner brake shoe
6 Washer
7 Pressure spring
8 Brake anchor plate
9 Anchor pin
10 Shim
11 Bracket
12 Hex bolt

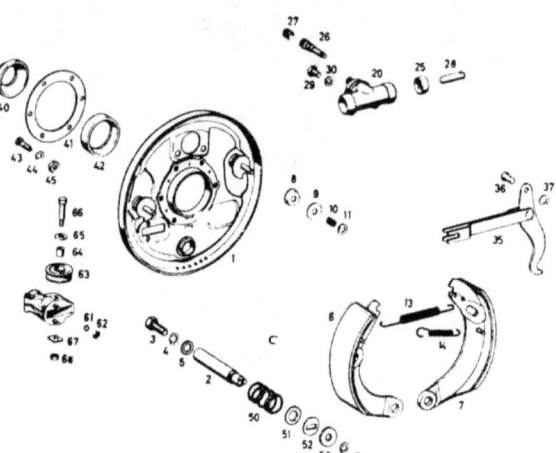

FIG 19 The components of the drum brake

6 Brake linings and brake drums

All the models covered by this manual are fitted with malleable-iron brake shoes which are 65 mm wide. Depending on model the brake drums are either grey cast iron or Alfin. All the Alfin brakes are fitted with cooling fins on the outside as are some of the cast iron drums.

Brake drums:

The drum can be removed after the rear road wheel has been taken off. Slacken back the adjusters so that the brake shoes are clear of the drum. The drum may be pulled off but if it sticks three puller screws No. 191.589.00.35 should be used. Evenly screw the special screws into the threaded holes in the brake drum so that they push the drum off the hub.

Drums which are lightly scored or have burn marks on them can be reconditioned by turning off the damage in a lathe. The dimensions for machining are given in **Technical Data**. The drums must be mounted on an arbor when machining them as a chuck will slightly distort the drum, causing it to be non-circular.

Fit new drums in place of any that are cracked or have such damage that it cannot be machined out.

Brake linings:

These must be renewed if the lining material has worn down to a thickness of 1.5 mm (.06 inch) for bonded shoes or are approaching the rivet heads on riveted shoes. They must also be renewed if the linings are contaminated with oil or grease as there is no satisfactory method of removing all the contaminant. The owner should not attempt to reline the shoes as the result will most likely produce unsatisfactory braking. Fit exchange shoes onto which the linings have been professionally bonded or riveted.

Identification of parts:

The Teves pistons differ from the pistons fitted in Girling brakes. Teves pistons have a matt chromium-plate finish, a dished head and a cutout as shown in **FIG 14**. Girling pistons are flat, bright-chrome finished, with no cutout. **The pistons must not be interchanged between the two makes.**

Teves brakes are fitted with two different types of piston and two different dust seals. The earlier type of dust seal Part No. 000.589.54.88 must be fitted only with the earlier type of piston but the later seal can be used with either type of piston. The differences are shown in **FIG 15**.

When refitting Teves pistons the cutout must be aligned with a gauge as shown in **FIG 16**. A special pair of pliers No. 000.589.36.37.00 is available for turning the piston into position once it is fitted.

Reassembly:

The parts are reassembled, after dipping internal parts into clean hydraulic fluid, in the reverse order of dismantling. Take great care to insert the piston squarely into the bore as it is very easy to tilt the piston and jam it in the bore.

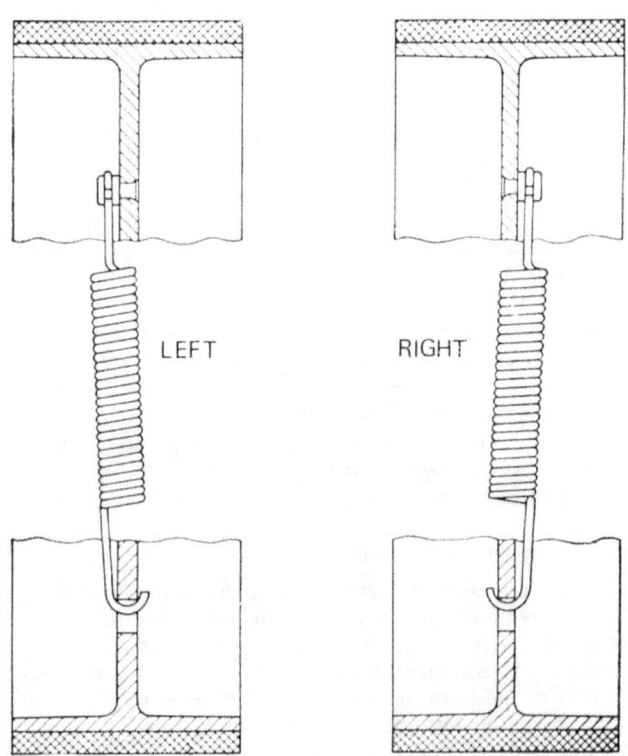

FIG 20 Correct fitting of the return springs

Removing brake shoes:

Securely jack up the rear of the car and remove the road wheel and brake drum.

1. A sectioned view of the brake adjuster is shown in **FIG 17**. The shoe is freed from the adjuster by taking out the splitpin 10 and removing the washers 7 and 9 with the spring 8.
2. The pivot assembly for the shoes is shown in **FIG 18**. Take out the bolt 1 and remove the washers 2 and 3.
3. Free the return springs from the brake shoes. The best method of doing this is to use special pliers No. 000.589.01.37, one leg of which passes through the eye of the return spring while the other padded leg fits against the lining on the shoe. If the special pliers are not available, thread a length of strong cord through the eye of the spring and pull on the cord so that the tension of the spring is overcome and it can be disconnected.
4. The parts of the brake are shown in **FIG 19**. Disconnect the handbrake cable from the handbrake lever assembly 35 and lift out the shoes.

Refit the shoes in the reverse order of removal. Lubricate all pivot points lightly with zinc-based grease or a suitable molybdenum disulphide paste. Before refitting

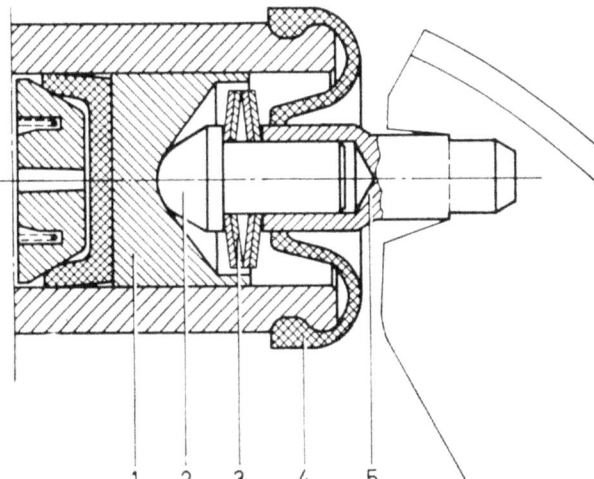

FIG 21 Sectioned view of the rear wheel cylinder with sping-loaded actuating pin

1 Piston   3 Cup spring   5 Guide pin
2 Bolt   4 Rubber boot

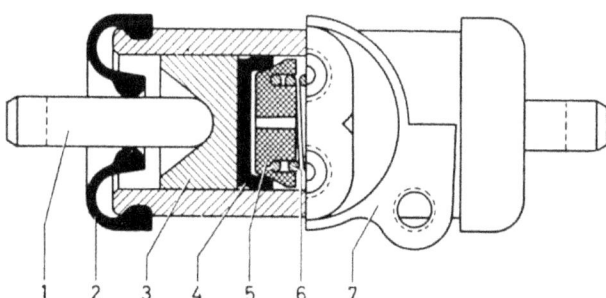

FIG 22 Section view of rear wheel cylinder with solid actuating pin

1 Actuating pin   4 Cup   7 Wheel cylinder
2 Rubber boot   5 Piston cup expander
3 Piston   6 Spring

FIG 23 Master cylinder and brake servo attachments on the 230SL

FIG 24 Master cylinder and brake servo attachments on the 230SL

Key to Fig 23 & 24

1 Power brake T 51/200
2 Reservoir
3 Tandem master cylinder
4 Special check valve
5 Residual pressure valve
7 Bearing bracket
8 Distributor fitting
9 Brake line to rear wheel brake
10 Brake line to distributor fitting
11 Reservoir for supply cylinder
12 Bracket for reservoir
13 Bracket for oil pressure gage line
14 Adjusting screw with hex nut and lock washer
15 Relay lever
18 Piston rod
19 Vacuum hose
21 Check valve

the shoes it is advisable to compress the spring on the pivot post, using special clamp No. 180.589.01.37 as this will make the task easier. The return springs are handed and must be refitted as shown in **FIG 20**. Refit the brake drum and adjust the brakes before refitting the rear wheel.

7 Servicing the rear brakes

The linings and brake drums have already been dealt with in the previous section.

If braking is poor but the linings still have plenty of wear left, reconditioning the faces of the linings will

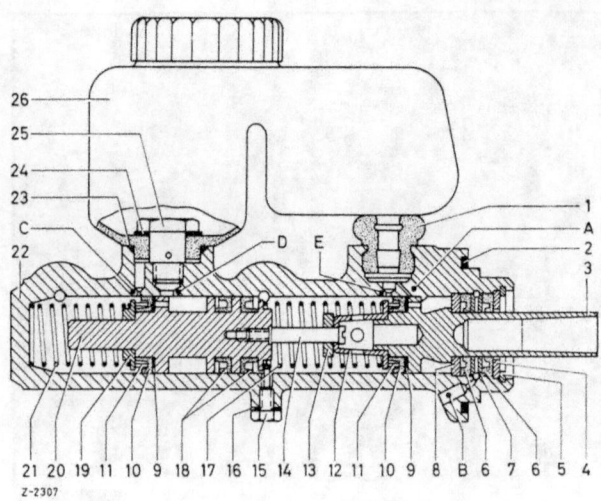

FIG 25 Sectioned view of the earlier master cylinder

1 Plug
2 O-ring
3 Piston (push rod circuit)
4 Piston stop washer
5 Piston stop ring
6 Vacuum seal
7 Spacer ring
8 Support ring
9 Piston cup washer
10 Primary cup
11 Thrust ring
12 Spring retainer
13 Piston stop washer
14 Connecting screw
15 Stop bolt for intermediate piston
16 Sealing ring (copper)
17 Pressure spring
18 Ring cup
19 Spring retainer
20 Intermediate piston (floating circuit)
21 Pressure spring
22 Housing
23 O-ring
24 Spring washer
25 Hollow bolt
26 Reservoir

A Refill port (push rod circuit)
B Leak port
C Compensating port (floating circuit)
D Refill port (floating circuit)
E Compensating port (push rod circuit)

often effect a cure. One method is to have the agent mill the linings with a special tool that fits onto the brake with it in place on the car. A simpler method is to have the operating face of the brake drum sand blasted and use the roughness of the drum to clean off the glazed and burnt surface of the lining. When the drums have been sand blasted and refitted, use the brake gently a few times and then drive normally. The roughness on the drum will rapidly be worn smooth again. The sand blasting method cannot be used when soft linings, such as Johns-Manvile, are fitted, as such linings will become scored instead of ground off.

The brake should be cleaned at regular intervals and any oil or grease should be wiped out with a petrol-moistened cloth. Leaks must be rectified. The rear hubs are dealt with in **Chapter 8, Section 5** and a sectioned view of the hub and brake is also shown there in **FIG 24**. New oil seals should be fitted to the hub if oil is leaking through the old ones. If the brake is contaminated by hydraulic fluid (recognizable by its smell) then the fault lies in the wheel cylinder.

Wheel cylinders:

Two types of wheel cylinder are fitted and they are shown in **FIG 21** and **FIG 22**. The wheel cylinders can be removed after the brake drum has been taken off but with the brake shoes still fitted. Turn the adjusters in the direction shown in **FIG 1** until the brake shoes are as far out as they will go. Remove the bleed nipple and undo the union nut that secures the pipe to the cylinder. Remove the wheel cylinder after taking out the bolts that secure it to the brake backplate. The task will be easier if the brake shoes have been removed.

The internal parts of the wheel cylinder can be removed with gentle air pressure and both types are serviced following the instructions given in **Chapter 5, Section 3**. Bleed and adjust the brakes after the wheel cylinders and brake drums have been refitted.

8 The master cylinder

The basic design of the master cylinder is the same on all models though there have been detail changes.

The attachment of the master cylinder on the 230SL is shown in **FIG 23** and **FIG 24**. The first version is shown; on later models the connections to the master cylinder are reversed in that the front chamber feeds the front brakes and the rear chamber the rear brakes. The attachments on the 230 and 230S are very similar except that a smaller brake servo is fitted.

Removal:

1 Syphon the fluid out of the reservoir 2 and pump the remainder of the fluid through bleed nipples on the front and rear axles. Use a suitable length of tube over the bleed nipple to guide the fluid into a container. Note that both axle systems must be drained as they are hydraulically independent.

2 Disconnect the pipelines 9 and 10 from the master cylinder. Later master cylinders will have two pipes connecting to the front chamber, and the distributor fitting 8 which splits the supply to the front brakes will no longer be fitted, also the pipe 9 will connect to the rear chamber. Blank the pipes to prevent the dirt entering.

3 Take off the two nuts that secure the master cylinder to the servo and lift the master cylinder out of the car. Take great care not to drip any hydraulic fluid onto the paintwork when lifting out the master cylinder.

Refit the master cylinder in the reverse order of removal. Bleed both brake system after refitting the master cylinder.

Operation:

A sectioned view of the earliest master cylinder is shown in **FIG 25**. Later versions differ in the porting and the interconnection between the primary piston 3 and the secondary piston 20. On the second version the screw 14 and stop washer 13 are completely omitted while on the third version they are reversed and screw into the primary piston 3. The operation of all versions is exactly the same.

When the brake pedal is applied the piston 3 is forced down the bore of the cylinder. This pressure is fed to the brakes on one axle and at the same time forces the secondary piston 20 down the bore of the cylinder. Pressure is built up in the front chamber by this action and is fed directly to the brakes on the other axle. When the pedal is released the springs 21 and 17 return the pistons back up the bore, the pressure drops, and the chambers are connected to the reservoir through their small ports. A check valve maintains a slight residual pressure in the lines to the rear brakes but the lines to the disc brakes are allowed to return to nil pressure. The connector, and check valve, to the rear brakes is bonderized while the connector to the disc brakes is cadmium plated.

If a leak develops in either system the secondary piston 20 will move forward until the spring 21 is coilbound, allowing pressure to build up normally in the rear chamber, or the primary piston 3 will move forwards until it contacts the secondary piston so that pressure can be built up in the front chamber. The reservoir is fitted with an internal baffle so that, if one system empties, the other system will still have a supply of fluid.

Dismantling:

Refer to **FIG 25** after removing the master cylinder from the servo unit.

1. Unscrew the hollow bolt 25 and remove it with its washer 24. Ease the reservoir out of the plug 1 and remove the plug 1 and sealing ring 23.
2. Use a suitable drift to press the piston 3 down the bore so that the pressure of the return springs is taken. Unscrew the retaining bolt 15 and discard the copper sealing washer 16, fitting a new washer on reassembly.
3. Still keeping the piston pressed down with a drift remove the stop ring 5. Release the piston and remove the internal parts from the cylinder. If the parts stick tap the open end of the cylinder onto the palm of the hand to dislodge them.
4. Dismantle the internal parts and remove the seals. On the earlier version the thrust ring 11 was loose so that the piston cup washer 9 and primary cup 10 could be removed. On later versions the thrust ring is peened into place.

Reassemble the unit in the reverse order of dismantling, following the instructions given in **Chapter 5, Section 3**. Make sure that all the seals are correctly fitted and take great care when entering them into the bore of the cylinder.

9 The brake servo unit

The attachment of the servo unit on the 230SL model is shown in **FIG 23** and **FIG 24**. The T51/200 unit fitted to the 230SL is fitted with two power pistons and a sectioned view of the unit with the master cylinder fitted is shown in **FIG 26**. The 230 and 230S models are fitted with a T51/100 unit which is of similar design but has only one power piston so consequently it is shorter. A sectioned view of the T51/100 unit is shown in **FIG 27**.

When pressure is applied by the brake pedal the valve mechanism allows a proportionate amount of air to enter through the air filter and act on the rear face of the power piston. The front chamber of the unit remains at vacuum from the inlet manifold so the power piston moves forward to act on the primary piston of the master cylinder and so applies the brakes. In the event of failure a direct mechanical link is established between the brake pedal and master cylinder.

Modifications:

The check valve 21 (see **FIG 24**) can be removed and replaced by a plain adaptor, in which case a check valve is fitted into the hose 19. The elbow with check valve incorporated is coloured white, while the plain elbow is coloured black to avoid accidental interchange of parts. The check valve in the hose must be fitted with its arrow pointing towards the inlet manifold.

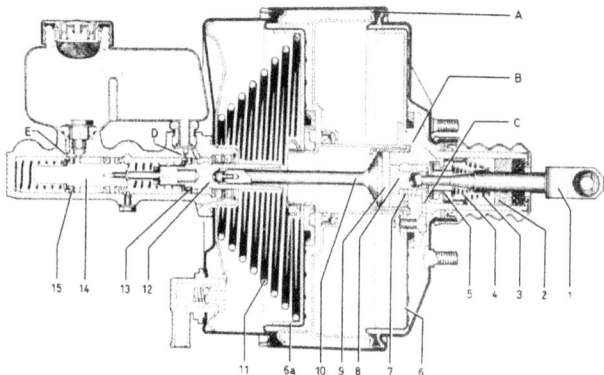

FIG 26 Sectioned view of the ATE T.51/200 servo unit with master cylinder attached

1 Valve operating rod
2 Filter
3 Valve rod return spring
4 Poppet return spring
5 Poppet assembly
6 Rear power piston
6a Front power piston
7 Stop disc
8 Valve plunger
9 Reaction disk
10 Pushrod
11 Pressure spring (piston return spring)
12 Piston (pushrod circuit)
13 Primary cup
14 Intermediate piston (suspended circuit)
15 Primary cup

A Passage to front atmosphere chamber
B Vacuum passage in control housing
C Atmosphere passage in control housing
D Compensating port (pushrod circuit)
E Compensating port (suspended circuit)

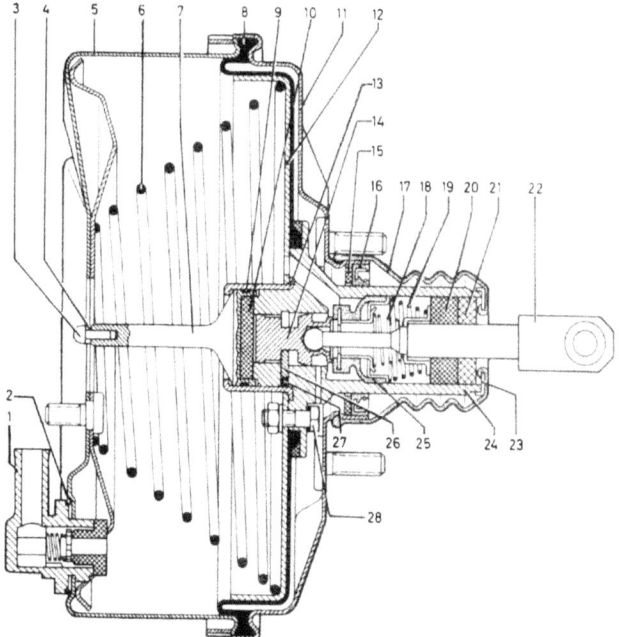

FIG 27 Sectioned view of ATE T.51/100 servo unit

1 Check valve
2 O-ring
3 Pressure button
4 Compensating washer
5 Front vacuum cylinder
6 Pressure spring (piston return)
7 Pushrod
8 Roller-type diaphragm
9 O-ring
10 Reaction disc
11 Rear vacuum cylinder
12 Diaphragm retainer
13 Guide bush
14 Valve plunger
15 Guide ring
16 Sealing ring
17 Boot
18 Poppet return spring
19 Valve rod return spring
20 Filter
21 Silencer
22 Valve operating rod
23 Silencer bracket
24 Control housing
25 Poppet assembly
26 Stop disc
27 Seal
28 Hex screw with washer and nut

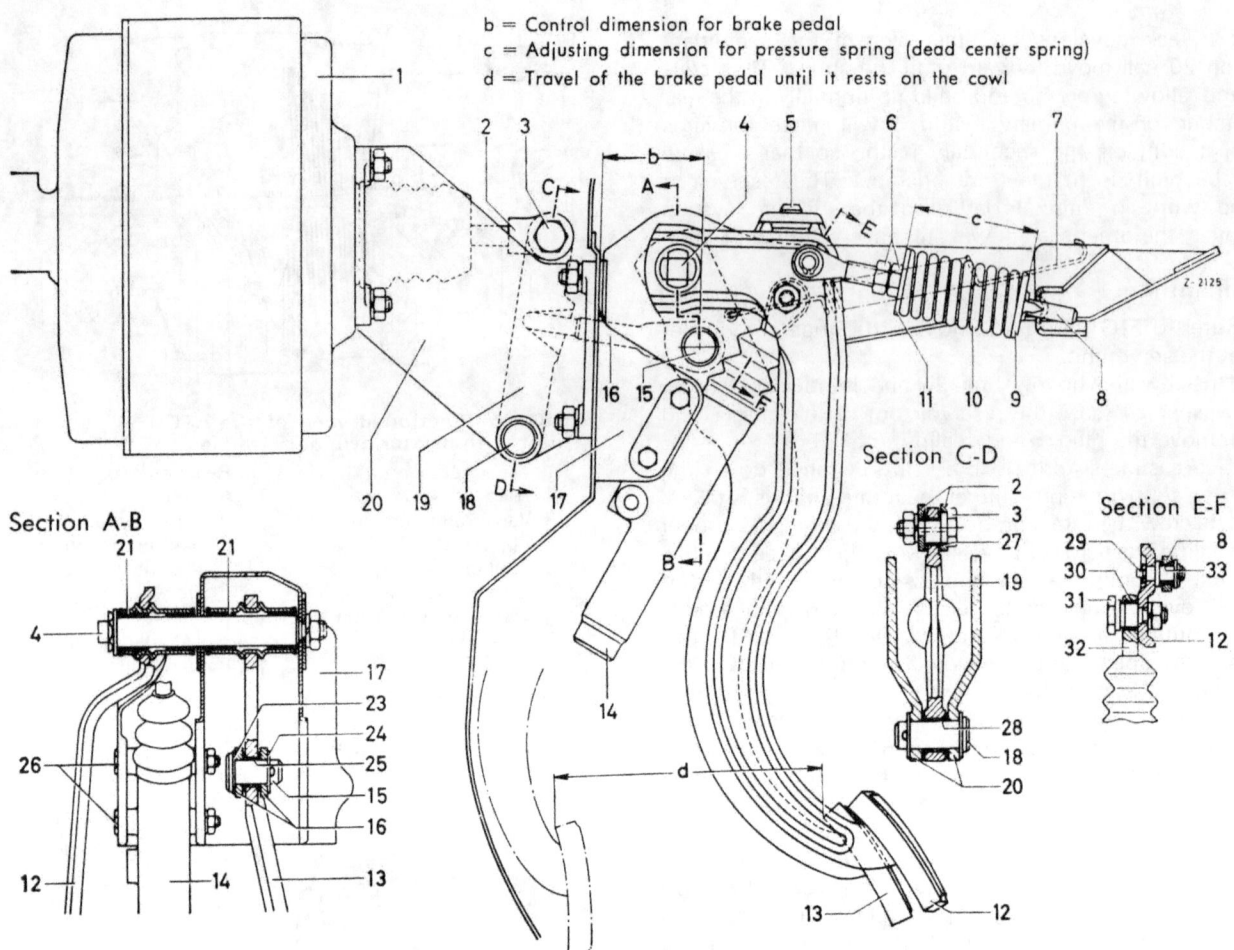

FIG 28 Arrangement of the pedals on the 230SL

1 Power brake T 51/200	11 Spring retainer
2 Piston rod of power brake	12 Clutch pedal
3 Relay lever adjusting screw	13 Brake pedal
4 Pivot pin	14 Clutch master cylinder
5 Rubber stop for clutch pedal	15 Collar bolt
6 Hexagon nut	16 Push rod for intermediate lever
7 Return spring for brake pedal	17 Support for pedals
8 Push rod for pressure spring	18 Collar bolt with washer and cotter pin
9 Spring retainer	19 Intermediate lever
10 Pressure spring (dead center spring)	
20 Bearing bracket	28 Bushing in the intermediate lever for collar bolt
21 Bushing for brake and clutch pedal	
23 Spring washer	29 Pivot pin for push rod
24 Washer	30 Bushing in the piston rod
25 Bushing in the brake pedal for collar bolt	31 Adjusting screw with lock washer and hex nut on the clutch pedal
26 Hex bolt with lockwasher and nut	32 Piston rod
27 Bushing in the intermediate lever for adjusting screw	33 Bushing in the push rod

Some models may be fitted with a plastic fuel separating vessel in the hose 19. This collects fuel droplets in the mixture when the engine is started from cold and prevents them entering the servo unit. If such a vessel is used it must be fitted at the lowest point of the hose and in such a way that it hangs downwards.

Checking:

Start the engine and allow it to build up vacuum in the reservoir by opening the throttle and letting it snap shut. Have an assistant slowly pump the brake pedal while feeling the unit by hand. The pistons should be felt to move as the unit operates and it may also be possible to hear the hiss of air as it enters through the filter.

Removal:

The unit is removed with the master cylinder still attached to it. Drain the hydraulic system and disconnect the brake pipes to the master cylinder, as described in **Section 8**.

A sectioned view of the brake pedal assembly on the 230SL is given in **FIG 28** and a similar view of the other models is given in **FIG 29**.

In all cases remove the adjusting bolt 3 (or 3a) so that the piston rod 2 of the servo is freed. On the 230 and 230S models take off the two nuts in the engine compartment and the third nut inside the car that secure the intermediate flange 36 and remove the servo with the flange attached. On the 230SL take off the nuts that secure the servo to the bearing bracket 20 and remove the unit leaving the bearing bracket in place on the car.

Refit the unit in the reverse order of removal. Fill and bleed both brake systems once the unit is in place.

Maintenance:

Maintenance is confined to renewing the air filter at 100,000 kilometer intervals. The unit must be removed

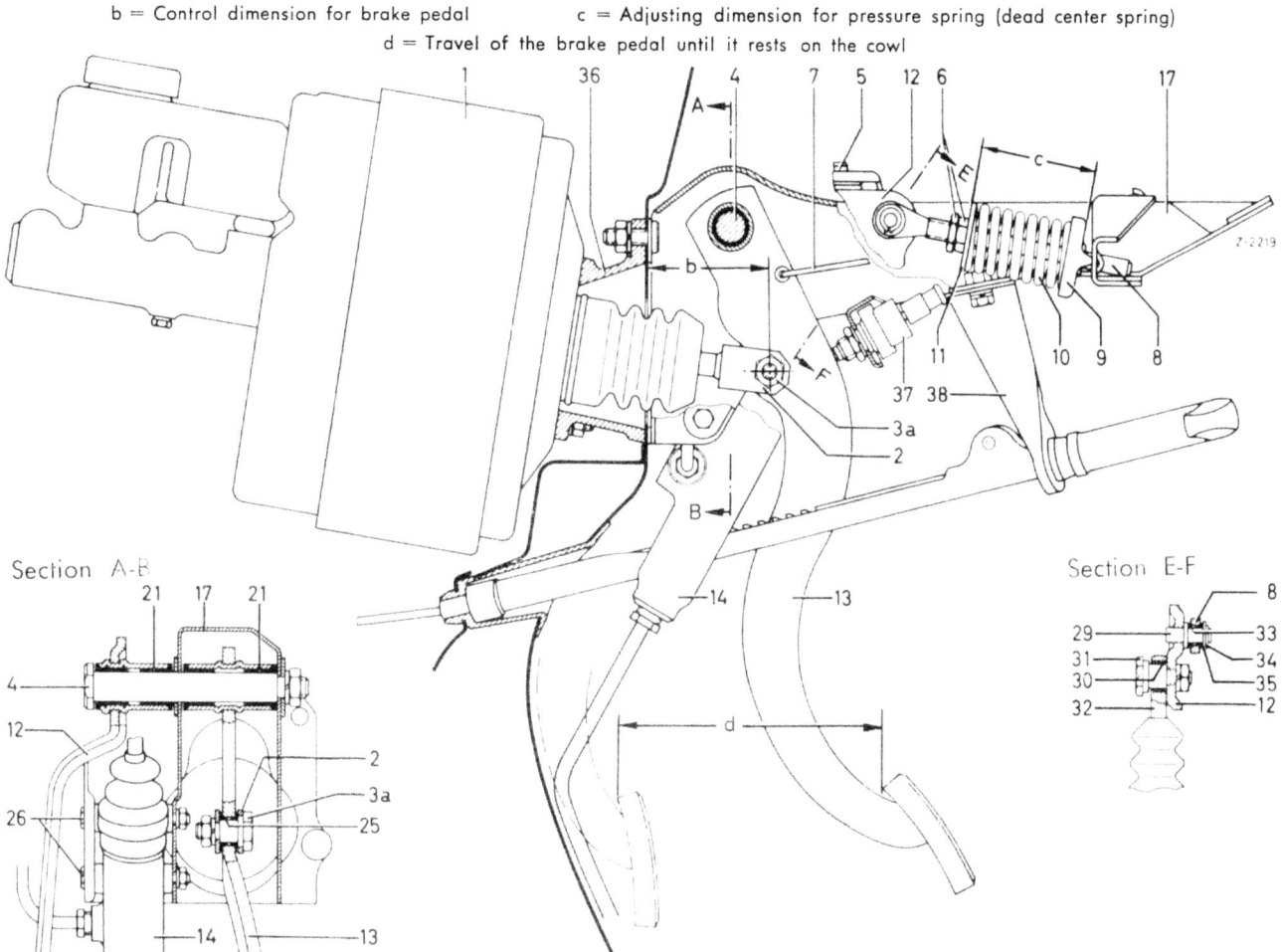

FIG 29 Arrangement of the pedals on the 230 and 230S

b = Control dimension for brake pedal c = Adjusting dimension for pressure spring (dead center spring)
d = Travel of the brake pedal until it rests on the cowl

1 Power brake T 51
2 Piston rod of power brake
3a Brake pedal adjusting screw
4 Pivot pin
5 Rubber stop for clutch pedal
6 Hexagon nut
7 Return spring for brake pedal
8 Push rod for pressure spring
9 Spring retainer
10 Pressure spring
11 Spring retainer
12 Clutch pedal
13 Brake pedal
14 Clutch master cylinder
17 Pedal support
21 Bushings for brake and clutch pedal
25 Bushings in the brake pedal
26 Hex screw with lockwasher and nut
29 Pivot pin for push rod
30 Bushing in the piston rod
31 Clutch pedal adjusting screw
32 Piston rod
33 Bushing in the push rod
34 Snap ring
35 Washer
36 Intermediate flange
37 Stop light switch
38 Bracket for ratchet

from the car in order to gain access to the parts (see **FIG 27**). Pull off the rubber boot 17 and use two small screwdrivers to lever out the silencer bracket 23. Use a hooked needle to draw the silencer 21 and filter 20 out of the unit.

Refit the parts in the reverse order of removal using a new filter. Position the silencer 21 so that its slots are at 90 degrees to the slots in the filter 20.

Take very great care not to drop the servo when it is free from the car as the control housing is made of low-impact strength plastic and will shatter at a knock.

10 Bleeding the brakes

This is not routine maintenance and is only required when air has entered the system, either by dismantling or by allowing the level in the reservoir to fall so low that air is drawn into the system.

Before starting the operation fill the reservoir as full as it will go without spilling or splashing over and then regularly check it and top up as bleeding progresses.

Use only fresh fluid to specification SAE.70.R3 for filling the reservoir and under no circumstances return fluid directly from bleeding back to the reservoir. The fluid bled through should be discarded, or stored in clearly labelled containers for use as a penetrating oil, and only if it is perfectly clean should it be kept for re-use. If the fluid is kept it should be stored in a sealed container for at least 24 hours to ensure that even the minutest air bubbles have dispersed.

The brakes are bled in the order of decreasing pipe runs, starting at the brake with the longest pipe run. If only one axle system has been dismantled then only that system requires bleeding. If both systems contain air then the system connected to the rear chamber in the master cylinder should be bled first.

Some models are fitted with a bleed nipple on the distributor of the pipe at the rear axle. This nipple is mainly for pressure bleeding but if the system has been emptied it will assist in filling the pipes if this nipple is also bled.

1 Fit a length of plastic or rubber tube to the nipple to be bled, after removing the rubber protective cover from

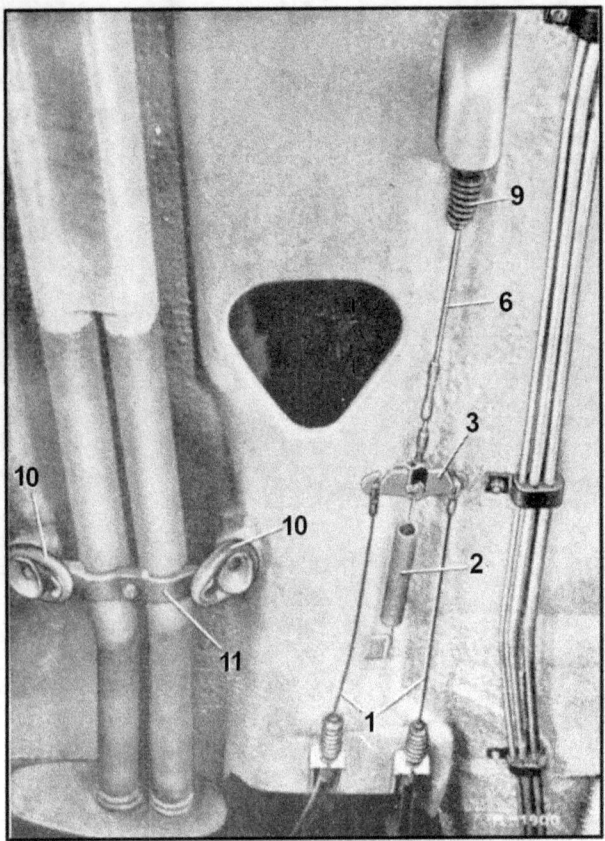

FIG 30   The handbrake cables on the 230SL

1 Rear brake cable   9 Rubber grommet
2 Return spring   10 Rubber ring
3 Equalizer   11 Lower bracket
6 Front brake cable

the nipple. Dip the free end of the tube into a little clean hydraulic fluid in a clean glass container.
2 Open the bleed nipple and have an assistant press the brake pedal right down to the floor. Close the bleed nipple before the assistant releases the brake pedal. Carry on this sequence until the fluid coming out of the tube is perfectly free from air. It will help to eject the air if slight pressure is applied to the brake pedal before opening the bleed nipple.
3 When all the brakes are bled have the assistant apply heavy pressure to the brake pedal and check through the system for leaks.
4 If the system has been previously dismantled it is advisable to rebleed the system after a few days when minute air bubbles will have coagulated into larger ones.

11 The handbrake
230SL:

The handbrake lever assembly is shown in **FIG 6** and the arrangement of the cables under the car is shown in **FIG 30**. Removal of the cables is simply a matter of freeing the ends and sliding them out through their guides. The lever assembly can be removed from the car by screwing the nut 10 off the end of the cable 9 and taking out the bolt 5. When the lever assembly is removed the ratchet 4 will remain attached to the transmission tunnel by the bolt 6.

230 and 230S:

Refer to **FIG 4** and **FIG 5**. The earlier and later systems differ only basically in the position of the butterfly adjusting nut. The rear cables are removed in a similar manner to those on the 230SL. The front cable can be removed after undoing its attachments at the equalizer lever and front pivot lever.

Pistol grip:

The pistol grip is connected to the front relay lever by a cable. On the earlier models this cable is secured to the lever by a splitpin but later a ball was used. Slacken the adjustment and turn the cable sideways so that the ball can be slipped out of its attachment on the relay lever. Remove the bracket that supports the ratchet from the pedal support. Push the ratchet right down the brake, use a suitable punch to drive out the guide pin, and then pull the ratchet out of the guide tube.

Lubricate the parts lightly with vaseline (petroleum jelly) and reassemble them in the reverse order of removal. Use a small screwdriver to lift the pawl on the guide tube so that the ratchet can be pushed in.

The cable for the pistol grip passes through a rubber sleeve. There are two version of this sleeve but only the later version is supplied as a spare part. If the old type sleeve is damaged remove it and cut down the new sleeve so that is similar to the old one before fitting it into place.

12 Fault diagnosis
(a) Spongy pedal

1 Air in the hydraulic system
2 Fluid leak in the hydraulic system
3 Gap between the lining and shoe on the rear brakes

(b) Excessive pedal movement

1 Check 1 and 2 in (a)
2 Rear brakes require adjusting
3 Excessively worn linings or pads
4 Very low fluid level in the reservoir

(c) Brakes grab or pull to one side

1 Wet/oily pads or linings
2 Cracked or distorted brake drum
3 Distorted or damaged brake disc
4 Worn out linings or pads
5 Seized handbrake cable
6 Seized wheel cylinder or piston in caliper
7 Uneven tyre pressures
8 Mixed linings or pads of different grades
9 Broken shoe return spring
10 Defective suspension or steering

CHAPTER 12 — ELECTRICAL SYSTEM

1. Description
2. The battery
3. Servicing motors
4. The starter motor
5. The alternator
6. The windscreen wipers
7. The fuses
8. The front lights
9. The rear lights
10. The direction indicators
11. The fuel gauge
12. The horns
13. Lighting circuits
14. Fault diagnosis

1 Description

All the models covered by this manual are fitted with a 12-volt electrical system, in which the negative terminal of the battery is connected to earth. The power for the system is produced by an engine driven alternator and it is stored in a 12-volt lead/acid battery. The output from the alternator is controlled by a sealed unit, which regulates the current according to the demands of the system and state of charge of the battery.

It is vital that the correct polarity is observed and that connections are correctly made. Reverse voltage will severely damage the alternator. Similarly the charging circuit must not be disconnected or reconnected while the engine is running and the alternator circuit should be disconnected when boost charging the battery or carrying out arc-welding repairs to the body.

A low-wattage test bulb and leads, or any 0 to 20 voltmeter, can be used for checking the continuity of the circuit or ensuring that the circuit is 'live' and current reaching a terminal, but cheap instruments must not be used for the testing or adjustment of components. Cheap instruments do not have the accuracy required for the calibration of components so use only high-grade, preferably moving coil, instruments for such work.

Wiring diagrams are given in **Technical Data** at the end of the manual to enable those with electrical experience to trace and rectify wiring faults.

Most of the components of the electrical system are made by Bosch and it may be found quite difficult to obtain spares, other than standard items such as brushes and bulbs, to service components. It should also be remembered that it is a waste of time and money to try to repair items which are seriously defective, either mechanically or electrically. With these factors in mind it will often be found quicker and cheaper to make use of the exchange scheme run by Bosch and fit a new or reconditioned component.

2 The battery

The whole electrical system depends on the battery being in good condition and well maintained. If the battery is in poor condition or its terminals dirty, starting will always be difficult and the performance of the remainder of the electrical system will also suffer. Out of all the

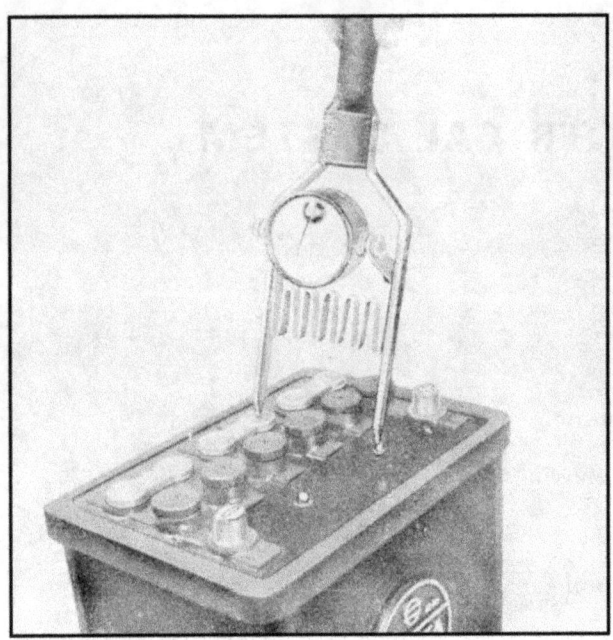

FIG 1 Checking the battery with a heavy-duty discharge tester

components in the electrical system the battery is that one that will suffer most from neglected maintenance.

In the winter the battery loses efficiency because it is cold and at the same time it has the most demands made on it. The engine is stiffer to turn, the lights are used more often and accessories such as the heater are given extensive use, so battery maintenance is even more vital in the winter. In very cold climates the battery performance can be improved by taking it out of the car and storing it in a warm room overnight. The alternator gives a higher charging current than a conventional generator but if the car is used for short-mileage journeys only, occasional charging with a trickle-charger will ensure that it is always at full capacity.

1 Always keep the top of the battery clean and dry. Moisture or dirt will form a leakage path for the charge which will drain the battery as well as causing galvanic corrosion. If the metal surrounds have become corroded, remove the battery and wash off all corrosion and spilt electrolyte with dilute ammonia or baking powder dissolved in warm water. Wash again using plenty of clean water and when the parts are dry paint them with anti-sulphuric paint.
2 Keep the battery terminals clean and tight. Wash off any corrosion with dilute ammonia followed by clean water. Before reconnecting the terminals smear them liberally with petroleum jelly (Vaseline) or a proprietary grease to prevent them from corroding again.
3 At regular intervals check the electrolyte level in the battery cells. Remove the vent plugs and top up using nothing but pure distilled water. Acid should only be added to the battery, after mixing with distilled water so that the mixture is at the correct specific gravity, when leakage or spillage has to be replaced. The correct level is 5mm (.2 inch) above the separators (15mm, .6 inch, above the level of the plates).

Charging:

The best charge rate is 10 per cent of the battery capacity, though boost chargers may go up to 75 per cent. Boost chargers should only be used in emergency and then only on batteries known to be in good condition.

Remove the vent plugs and charge until the battery is gassing freely. **Never examine the battery with a naked light as the gases given off by the battery are explosive.** If desired a hydrometer can be used to check the charge state.

Electrolyte:

Never add acid directly to the battery, always make it up into electrolyte first, and even then it should only be added to replace spillage. If electrolyte is to be

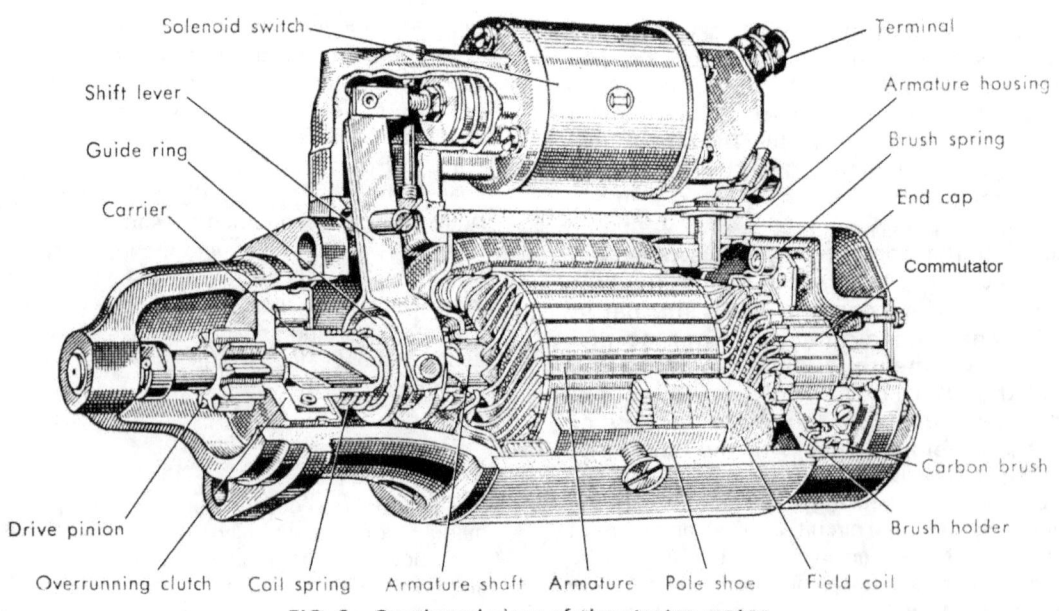

FIG 2 Sectioned view of the starter motor

made up, do so in an earthenware jar and add concentrated acid to water, **never add water to acid**. A great deal of heat is given off so allow the mixture to cool before checking its specific gravity.

Testing:

The battery should normally be tested using a hydrometer. Draw sufficient electrolyte up from the cell into the instrument so that the float is free from the bottom and sides of its chamber. Examine the electrolyte before taking a reading. If the electrolyte appears dirty or full of specks then it is likely that the cell is defective. This will be confirmed if the cell has a radically different reading from the other five cells.

Take the reading holding the instrument at eye level. If the cell has just been topped up with distilled water then the battery should be charged, or used in the car, for half-an-hour to allow the electrolyte to mix thoroughly. The specific gravity readings of the instrument give the following indications:

For climates below 32°C (90°F)
1.270 to 1.290   Cell fully charged
1.190 to 1.210   Cell half-charged
1.110 to 1.130   Cell discharged

Replace spillage with electrolyte of 1.270 specific gravity.

For climates above 32°C (90°F)
1.120 to 1.230   Cell fully charged
1.130 to 1.150   Cell half-charged
1.050 to 1.070   Cell discharged

Replace spillage with electrolyte of 1.210 specific gravity.

The figures are given assuming a standard electrolyte temperature of 16°C (60°F). To convert the actual reading to standard add .002 for every 3°C (5°F) rise above standard temperature and subtract .002 for every 3°C (5°F) fall.

The battery may also be tested using a heavy duty discharge tester, as shown in **FIG 1**. Test each cell in turn by pressing the tester into the inter-cell connectors. If the cell is in good condition it should maintain a voltage of at least 1.8 volts for 10 seconds. A poor cell will be shown by the rapid drop in voltage. **Do not use the tester on a battery known to be low in charge.** Avoid touching the resistance on the tester as it becomes extremely hot in use.

Storage:

Short term storage presents no problems, provided the battery has been correctly maintained. If the battery is to be stored for long periods it should be given a charge on a trickle charger at monthly intervals. At three monthly intervals drain the charge from the battery by connecting a lamp across it and then recharge it using a trickle charger. If this is carried out the battery plates will remain in good condition and not sulphate up. Avoid extremes of temperature for storing the battery and try to keep it somewhere where the temperature is even.

3 Servicing motors

All motors fitted to cars operate on the same principles and therefore have many similarities in design. To avoid constant repetition general instructions for motors are gathered into this one section.

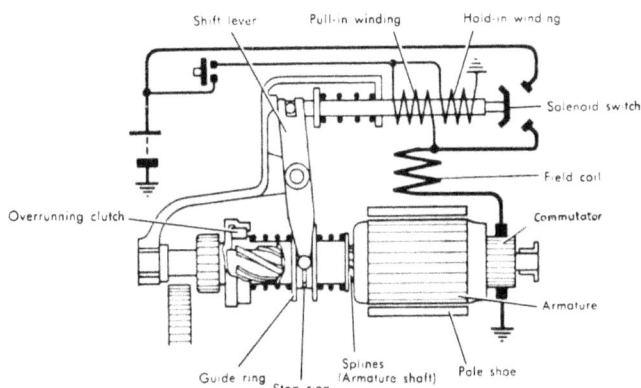

FIG 3   Schematic layout of the starter motor

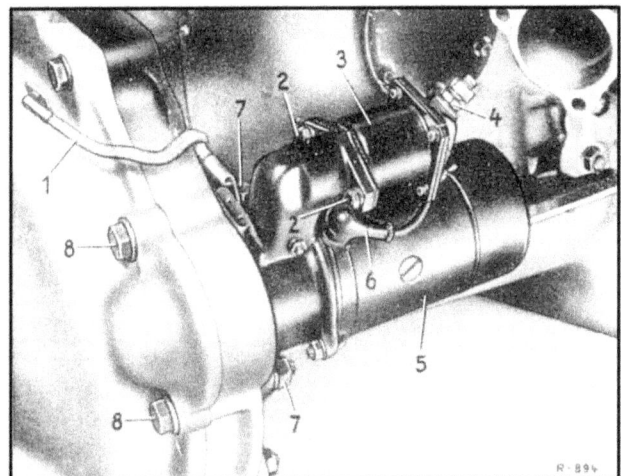

FIG 4   The starter motor attachments

1 Earth lead   5 Starter
2 Hex bolts   6 Connecting cable
3 Solenoid switch   7 Hexagon nut
4 Connecting bolt   8 Hex bolts

Some motors are sealed with the case flanged over so that they cannot be dismantled. It is possible to open the case but it must be remembered that the benefits of the exchange scheme may be lost.

The motor part of the fuel pump fitted to the 230SL must not be dismantled by the owner under any circumstances. It must be remembered that the motor on the fuel pump contains the ingredients (fuel and spark) for a major fire and that it is in close proximity to the fuel tank.

Brushgear:

Dismantle the motor sufficiently to examine the brushgear, taking care not to damage the brushes during dismantling. Renew the brushes if they are excessively worn. Check that the brushes make firm contact with the commutator and renew the brush springs if they are weak. A modified spring balance can be used to measure the actual pressure of the springs. If the brushes are fitted on arms check that the arms pivot freely.

Sticking brushes should be removed and their sides lightly polished on a smooth file. Clean the brush holder with a fuel-moistened piece of cloth, both inside and out, before refitting the brushes in their original positions.

New brushes are normally supplied with their ends ground to shape. If they require further bedding-in, wrap

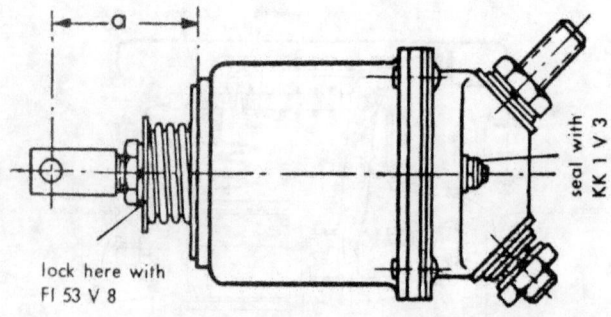

FIG 5 The starter solenoid

the commutator with a piece of fine-grade glasspaper and rotate the commutator with the brushes lightly pressing onto the glasspaper. Remove all dust and carbon before fully refitting the brushes. After a period of use the brushes bed-in very accurately so they should be refitted into their original positions if they are removed.

Commutator:

Normally this should have a slightly darkened but polished surface which is free from scoring or burn marks. Wiping with a piece of non-fluffy cloth dipped into clean fuel is sufficient cleaning. Light scoring or burn marks can be polished out using fine-grade glasspaper. **Never use emerycloth as this leaves hard particles embedded in the copper.**

On the starter motor deeper damage can be skimmed off in a lathe, providing the minimum diameter is not reached. Use the highest speed, and a very sharp tool, to remove just sufficient material to clean off the damage. Squarely undercut the insulation between the segments to a depth of .6 to .7mm (.025 to .030 inch). Take a light final skim cut of .1mm (.004 inch) using a carbide or diamond tipped tool. Clean out any dust from between the segments.

Armature:

Apart from cleaning and reconditioning the commutator very little can be done to the armature except to give it a physical examination. Check that no laminations or insulation are loose or standing proud. If they are, it is a possible sign of overspeeding and the overrun clutch on starter motors should be checked. Check the laminations for scoring or similar damage. Such damage can be caused by loose polepieces, excessively worn bearings or a bent armature shaft. **Do not attempt to machine or straighten armature but fit a new one in its place.** Electrical faults can be checked for at a garage using a 'growler'.

Field coils:

On some smaller motors a permanent magnet can be fitted in place of the field coils.

The coils should be tested for continuity, using a 12-volt test lamp and battery between the terminals. The lamp failing to light indicates a break in the circuit. The insulation should also be checked.

On the starter motor the field coils are held in place by polepieces. The polepieces are secured to the yoke (case) by large screws which are tightened to a high torque and then staked to lock them. An ordinary screwdriver should not be able to move them or tighten them to the correct torque, so if the field coils require renewing the task should be left to an agent.

Insulation:

All the insulation, including that on brush holders, should be checked using a test lamp and supply. Before testing clean the parts and wipe away any dirt, carbon or metal dust. A 12-volt test lamp and battery can be used but it is better to use a neon bulb and 110 AC supply. The lamp should not light when connected to terminals (or terminal and case) across the insulation.

Bearings:

Bushes are used on all the motors covered by this manual, though ballbearings are also used on some larger motors. On small motors self-aligning bearings may be used. These are spherical on the outside and held in place by riveted spring clips. Check that such bushes move freely in their clips as well as having the correct diameter for the shaft.

Renew any worn bearings. On the starter motor they can be pressed out and new ones pressed back into place. Make sure that the bushes are adequately, but not excessively, oiled before reassembly.

4 The starter motor

A sectioned view of the starter motor is shown in **FIG 2** and a schematic drawing of the circuit is shown in **FIG 3**. When the starter switch is operated current flows through both coils of the solenoid and the armature is drawn into the solenoid. The armature moves the shift lever so that the drive pinion is pressed into mesh with the teeth on the flywheel starter ring, and at the same time the armature closes the contacts, allowing current to flow through the motor so that it drives the engine. When the contacts close they short out the pull-in coil leaving the armature held by the weaker hold-in coil. Springs are fitted into the linkage so that it will compress, allowing

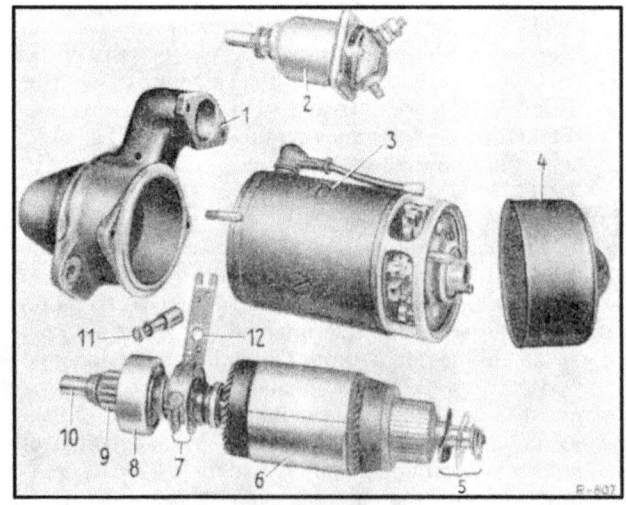

FIG 6 The earlier starter motor components

1 Drive bearing
2 Solenoid switch
3 Armature housing
4 End cap
5 Parts of armature brake
6 Armature
7 Guide ring
8 Overrunning clutch
9 Pinion
10 Armature shaft
11 Pivot pin
12 Shift lever

the motor to operate, if the teeth do not mesh but abut. The teeth will then mesh on the initial rotation of the starter motor. The overrunning clutch is fitted to prevent the engine from driving the starter motor when the engine starts and causing overspeeding of the starter motor. Brake parts are also fitted to the armature to ensure that it stops turning when the current to the motor is cut off, and they prevent the starter motor from rotating on engagement if the engine dies and has to be restarted immediately.

Starter fails to operate:

1 Check the condition and charge of the battery, paying especial attention to the cleanliness and tightness of the terminal connectors.

2 Switch on some lights and again operate the starter while watching the lights. If the lights go dim the starter motor is taking current. No drive can be caused by a defect in the starter motor, which requires removal of the motor from the engine, or else the pinion may be jammed in mesh. Select a gear and rock the car backwards and forwards to free the jammed pinion. If a pinion jams continually then it is likely that the teeth are worn or damaged and the motor should be removed for further examination. The teeth on the flywheel ring can be examined through the fitting hole for the starter motor.

3 If the lights do not go dim, there is a fault either in the wiring or the starter solenoid. The solenoid will operate with a click and, if this is heard but the motor does not turn, it is likely that the solenoid heavy duty contacts are defective. Short across the terminals of the solenoid with a heavy screwdriver or old pair of pliers. If the motor now spins freely then the solenoid is defective and must be renewed.

4 If no power is reaching the solenoid, use a test bulb or voltmeter to check through the wiring and trace defective connections or broken wiring.

Starter solenoid:

The solenoid is mounted directly onto the starter motor, as shown in **FIG 4**, and the solenoid can be removed leaving the motor in place.

Disconnect the battery and then disconnect all the cables to the solenoid. Remove the two bolts securing the solenoid to the motor, partially withdraw the solenoid so the linkage can be disconnected and the solenoid freed.

Before refitting the solenoid, energize it on a 12-volt supply and check the dimension 'a' shown in **FIG 5**. If required, slacken the locknut and adjust until the dimension is correct at 19 ± 1 mm (.75 ± .04 inch).

Refit the solenoid in the reverse order of removal taking care to correctly route and connect the cables. The thinner control cable must not be passed through the rubber boot for the main cable as it will then be liable to chafe and be made permanently live by contact with the main cable. Wind the control cable around the main cables before connecting it to its terminal.

Starter motor removal (FIG 4):

Disconnect the battery and then disconnect the cables to the starter solenoid. Take off the nuts 7, noting that the upper nut also secures the engine earth lead 1. Withdraw the starter motor and remove it from underneath the car.

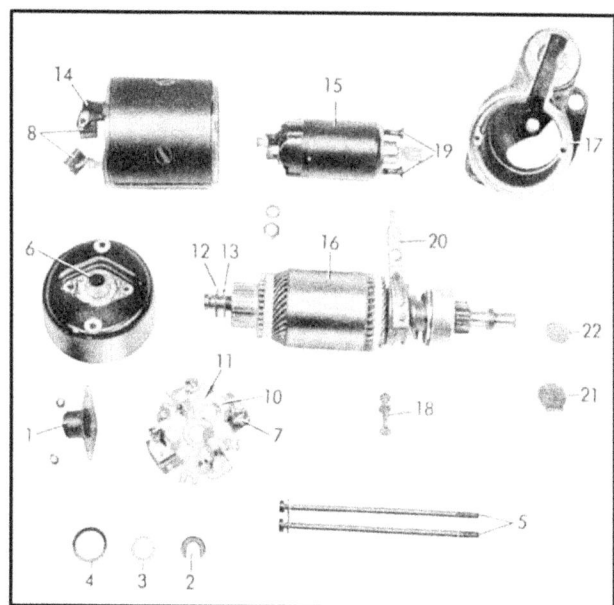

FIG 7 The later starter motor components

The lower bolt 8 is accessible from under the car, whereas the upper bolt can only be reached from inside the car (see **Chapter 7, FIG 22**).

Refit the starter motor in the reverse order of removal, making sure that all the cables, including the earth lead 1, are correctly reconnected.

Dismantling:

There are two versions of starter motor fitted which, though they are basically similar, vary in some points, especially in the mounting of the commutator end bearing. The two versions are shown in **FIG 6** and **FIG 7**. Dismantling is straightforward in both cases provided that the washers and brake washers are fitted back into their original positions. When removing the brushgear, or the commutator from under the brushes, make sure that the brushes are clear of the commutator. Lift up the springs and ease the brushes up in their brushboxes. Secure the brushes in this partially withdrawn position by resting the springs against the sides of the brushes.

Starter motor drive:

If either the drive pinion or the overrun clutch are defective they must be renewed as a complete assembly. Small burrs and light damage to the pinion teeth can be cleaned off with a smooth file. If the motor shows signs of overspeeding, the overrun clutch must be examined with particular care. The clutch must rotate quite freely in one direction and yet instantaneously take up drive in the other direction.

The parts are secured by a stop ring and snap ring. Use a suitable length of pipe to drive the stop ring up to the pinion and remove the snap ring. Slide the parts off. When fitting the drive parts make sure that the stop ring holds the snap ring in place and that the pinion moves right up to the stop ring when the solenoid is energized.

Testing:

For full performance checks, accurate and heavy duty meters are required as well as a suitable test rig. The performance figures are given in **Technical Data**.

in action. The brushes should not move up and down nor should there be excessive arcing between the brushes and commutator.

5 The alternator

The details of a typical alternator are shown in **FIG 8**. The alternator itself produces an AC current which is then rectified by diodes. As opposed to a generator the main current is produced in the stator windings which since they are not revolving can be made more substantial without the problems of balance or securing the coils against rotational forces. The excitation field is produced by the rotor and the current flow through the rotor is constant in direction. This has the double advantage of dispensing with the normal commutator and allowing the rotating coils to be made lighter as they carry less current than the rotating coils in a generator. Two slip rings and brushes are fitted in place of the commutator. The brushes carry only the low excitation current and are in constant contact with the slip rings so they will be more reliable and last longer than the brushes in a generator.

The general details of servicing motors apply to alternators, with the difference of slip rings as opposed to a commutator. When dismantling the alternator it will be necessary to unsolder the stator wires and this must be done without allowing the heat to reach the diodes. Make sure that the wires are resoldered to their original connections. The slip rings must not be machined and only lightly polished with glasspaper to remove burn marks or light scoring.

The diodes may be tested, after disconnecting them all, by connecting a test lamp and 12-volt battery across each one in turn and then reversing the polarity of the test circuit. The diode should allow current to flow in one direction but not the other. If the diode does not allow

FIG 8 Typical alternator components

The motor can be roughly tested by mounting it in a vice and connecting it to a fully charged 12-volt battery, using heavy duty leads. The motor should turn at high speed and run quite freely. On the type of motor where the commutator end bearing is not integral with the end cap, the end cap can be removed and the brushgear observed

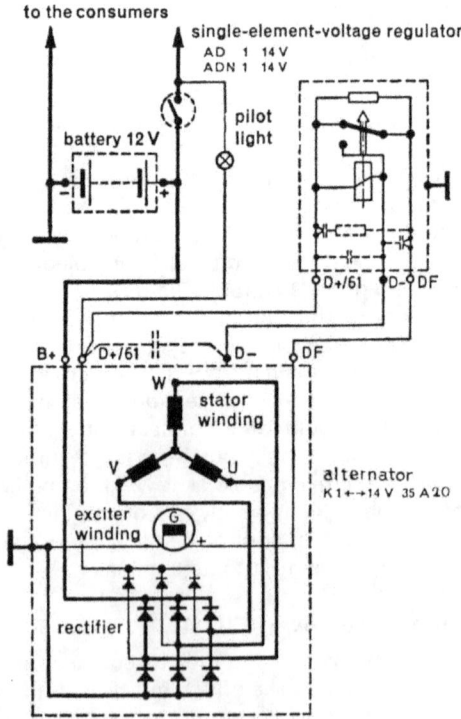

FIG 9 The charging circuit

current to flow in either direction or it allows it to flow in both directions then that diode is defective and must be renewed. When disconnecting the diode wires use a hot soldering iron and grip the pin of the diode with a pair of long-nosed pliers so they act as a heat sink. Excess heat will damage the diodes.

Checking the alternator:

1 Check the condition and tension of the driving belt (see **Chapter 4, Section 4**). Make sure that the tension is correct and renew the belt if it is defective.
2 Check through the wiring for defects or loose connections. The charging circuit is shown in **FIG 9**. Never make or break connections while the engine is running.
3 Connect into the circuit accurate meters and a variable resistance as shown in **FIG 10**. Start the engine and increase its speed so that it is running steadily at 2000 to 2500 rev/min. Adjust the variable resistance until the ammeter shows a current flow of 28 to 30 amps. If the alternator, control unit and wiring are satisfactory the voltmeter will read 13.9 to 14.8 volts. Do not connect the variable resistance into the circuit until immediately before starting the engine and disconnect it as soon as the engine is stopped, otherwise it will drain the battery.

6 The windscreen wipers

The motor and linkage on the 230SL model are shown in **FIG 11**, and the motor connected to the link on other models is shown in **FIG 12**. The motor itself is mounted in the engine compartment and secured, with its baseplate, by three screws. The linkage is shown fitted to the 230SL in **FIG 13**. The electrical connections to the motor are through a six-pin socket.

The two-speed motor has no adjustment for the parking position of the wiper arms but they should be set on their spindles so that they overlap correctly in the parked position when the motor stops. The spindles are fitted with serrations on their ends which cut into the smooth mating part on the wiper arm when the arms are tightened in position. If the park position is incorrect the serrations cut into the wiper arm should be removed and the arms reset to the correct position. Loosen the securing nuts so that the arms are partially free and move the arms across the spindles by hand with a normal wiping action so that the serrations on the spindles cut away the serrations cut into the arms. Retighten the securing nuts with the arms in the correct positions.

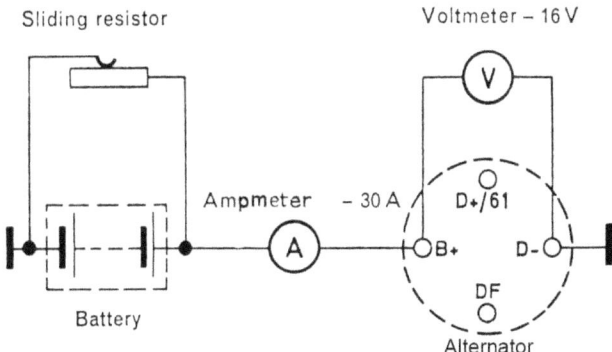

FIG 10 Circuit for testing the alternator, when fitted to the car

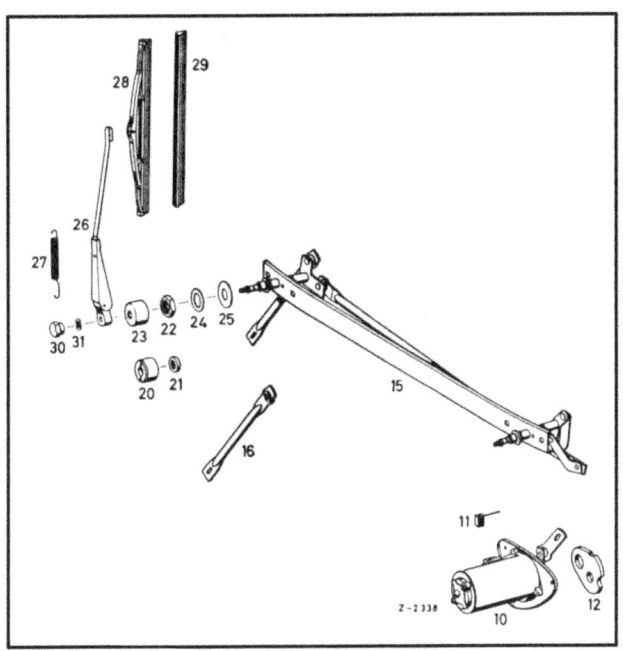

FIG 11 The windscreen wipers on the 230SL

10 Wiper motor	20 Cap nut	26 Wiper arm
11 Carbon brush	21 Sealing ring	27 Tension spring
12 Base plate	22 Hexagon nut	28 Wiper blade
15 Windshield wiper linkage with plate	23 Capsule	29 Rubber blade
	24 Washer	30 Cap nut
16 Adjustable drive rod	25 Washer	31 Corrugated washer

*First version   **Second version

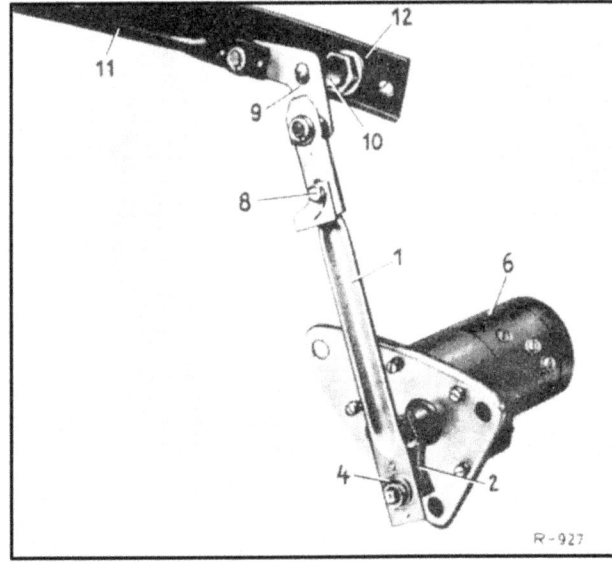

FIG 12 The windscreen wiper and motor on other models

1 Link	6 Wiper motor	10 Adjusting gage
2 Motor crank	8 Locking screw	11 Long link
4 Washer	9 Tandem lever	12 Holding plate
		13 Wiper shaft

Maintenance:

No maintenance is required apart from renewing the rubber blades at yearly intervals, or earlier if they cease to wipe the screen clean. When washing the car, lift the blades off the screen and wipe them down to remove any small particles of grit that may be sticking to them.

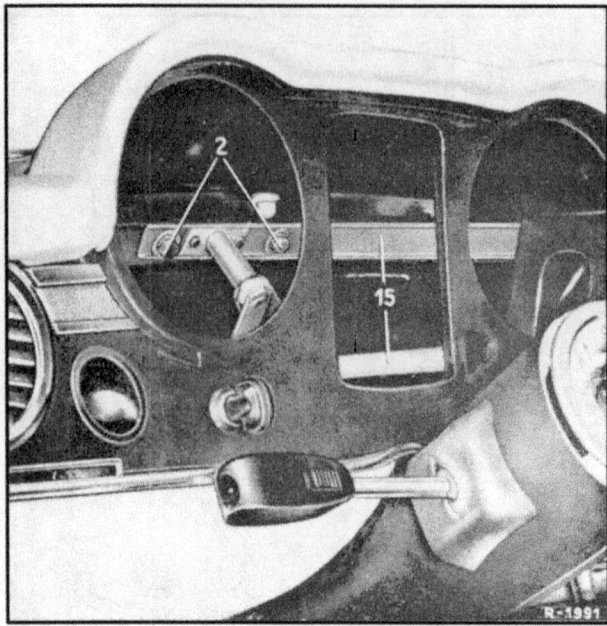

FIG 13 Wiper linkage fitted to the 230SL
2 Plate fixing screws 15 Windshield wiper linkage with plate

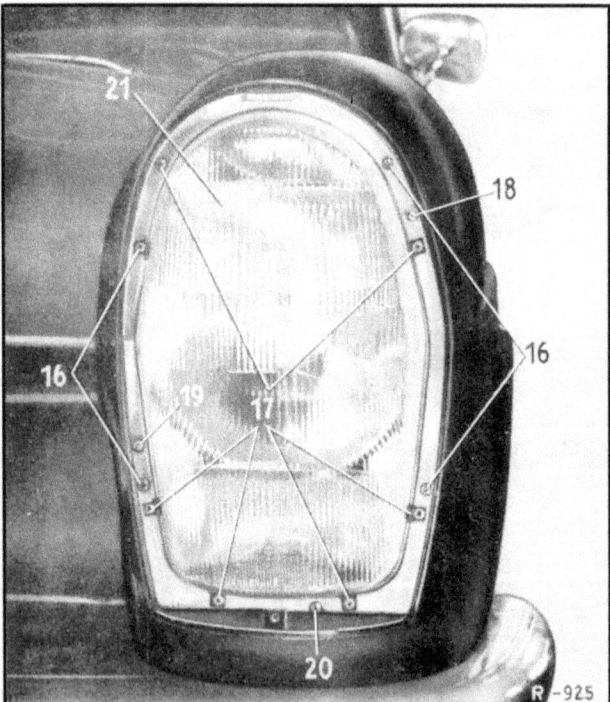

FIG 14 The standard front light unit in place, with chrome trim removed

16 Lighting unit fixing screw
17 Swivel clip
18 Vertical plane adjusting screw for main headlight
19 Lateral plane adjusting screw for main headlight
20 Adjusting screw for fog light
21 Lens

Wiper fails to operate or operates sluggishly:

Check that the appropriate fuse is not blown and if it has blown fit a new fuse after checking the circuits for faults.

Use a test lamp, or preferably a 0 to 20 voltmeter, to check that battery voltage is reaching the motor terminals. If the current is not reaching the motor trace back through the wiring until the fault is found.

If the motor feels hot after running and the wipers operate sluggishly there is either an internal fault in the motor or excessive resistance in the system. Disconnect the link from the motor. If the motor now runs freely then the fault lies in the linkage but if the motor still turns sluggishly then it has an internal fault. The blades will drag on a dry windscreen so wet it before carrying out tests.

7 The fuses

The electrical system is well protected by twelve fuses mounted in a fuse box at the rear of the engine compartment on the bulkhead. One of the fuses is not used on standard models so it is available for optional extras or accessories. The fuse box is fitted with a chart showing the circuits that the individual fuses protect.

If a fuse blows replace it with a new one of the correct rating and colour code. Operate all the circuits protected by that fuse in turn and if the fuse blows then check the circuit turned on at the time. Do not fit another fuse until the fault has been found and rectified. After long service fuses weaken and blow for no particular reason so if all the circuits are satisfactory no further action need be taken. **Never attempt to cure blowing fuses by fitting new fuses of a higher rating.**

The fuses are of the continental type using a thin strip of metal between contacts on a plastic base. The English type of fuse, with a wire inside a glass tube, will not fit into the fuse holder and as the correct type of fuse required may not be readily available it is a wise precaution to carry a selection of spare fuses.

8 The front lights

The standard front lights are all fitted into one unit on each side of the front of the car and a view of the unit with the chrome embellisher removed is shown in **FIG 14**. The unit is freed from the car by taking out the securing screws 16, **without turning the adjusting screws 18, 19 and 20.** A multi-pin connector connects all the wiring to the unit and a rear view of the unit is shown in **FIG 15**.

Some models of the 230SL are fitted with a unit of very similar appearance, shown in **FIG 16**. This type of light is mainly for the US market and uses a sealed-beam headlamp where the filaments are embodied into the unit so that the lens of the lamp is also the glass of the bulb. Removal of the headlamp is by pressing in the holding ring 'd' inwards and turning it anticlockwise so that the adjusting screws pass through the larger offset holes in the ring. The lamp is connected into the circuit by a three-pin connector. **Do not turn the adjusting screws 'a' and 'b' when removing the headlamp.** The remaining bulbs are accessible after taking off the four screws 'e', 'f', 'g' and 'h', as well as disconnecting the multi-pin connector 'e'. The adjusting screw 'c' for the foglight can be reached without removing the lamp parts from the car.

Other models may be fitted with twin headlamps to conform with US regulations and this type is shown in **FIG 17**.

Beam setting:

It is most advisable to have this done at a garage where proper setting equipment will be used, as this will ensure that the lights are set accurately and legally.

The beams can be set by standing the car squarely to, and 5 metres (16½ feet) from, a plain wall. Adjust one lamp at a time, covering the other lamp with cardboard. The car should be loaded with a weight of 70 kg (150 lbs).

For the foglights mark on the wall a horizontal line which is the same height from the ground as the centres of the foglamps. Below this line mark another horizontal line. The distance by which the second line should be below the first is marked on the lens of the lamp but it is normally 12 cm (4¾ inch). Adjust each foglamp in turn until the centre of its brightly illuminated area is centred on the lower line.

9 The rear lights

All the rear lights are contained in two units at the rear of the car. The units are removable from inside the luggage compartment and are connected to the electrical system by multi-pin connectors. Thumb screws hold the units in place.

Before fitting a unit clean out the inside of the case and the inside of the lenses with a soft cloth.

10 The direction indicators

The direction indicators are operated by a flasher unit mounted on the rear bulkhead in the engine compartment. The flasher unit uses a bi-metallic strip to make and break the current. **The unit is very delicate and will be damaged by careless handling or even connecting into the circuit when the circuit is live.** The unit is also sealed and cannot be rectified if it is damaged.

Faulty operation:

Check the appropriate fuse and check all four bulbs. A blown bulb will alter the flash rate.

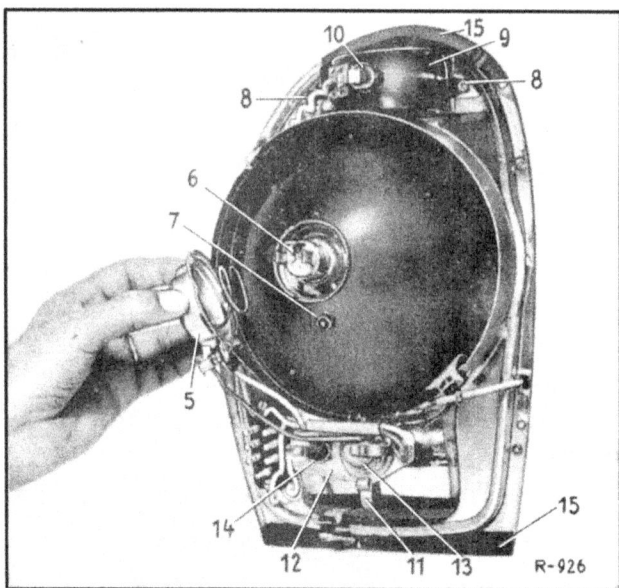

FIG 15 Rear view of the standard light unit

5 Main headlight lampholder and contact plate for parking light
6 40/45 W main headlight bulb
7 4 W parking light bulb
8 Swivel clip
9 Turn signal lampholder
10 15 W turn signal bulb
11 Retainer
12 Lampholder for fog light and clearance light
13 35 W fog light bulb
14 35 W clearance light bulb
15 Sealing frame

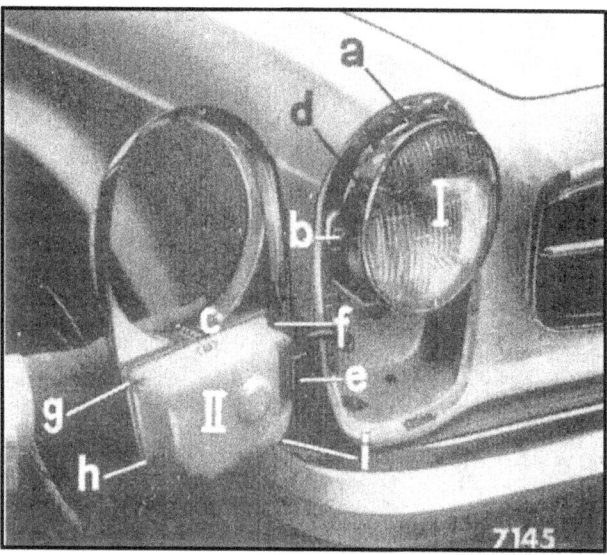

FIG 16 The front light unit fitted to the models of the 230SL in the USA

FIG 17 Twin headlamps fitted to USA models
1 Attachment ornamental frame
2 Adjusting screws, vertical
3 Adjusting screws, horizontal
4 Attachment insert

Remove the flasher unit from its socket and use a test lamp or voltmeter to check that battery voltage is reaching the terminal 15 in the socket. Connect the tester between terminal 15 and a good earth and then between terminals 15 and 31. If the reading in the second case is not as high as that in the first then the earthing of the socket is poor.

Use a jumper lead to connect the terminals 15 and 54 in the socket. Operate the direction indicator switch in both directions. The appropriate pair of lamps should light continuously with the switch selected. If the lamps do not light then there is a defect in either the wiring or the switch. If the lamp lights satisfactorily then the flasher unit is defective and must be renewed. If only one of a pair of lamps lights then either the other bulb is defective or the wiring to it is defective. Check the earth return as corrosion at the chassis often causes a high resistance at this point.

11 The fuel gauge

The fuel tank unit is fitted with an extra connection for the low-level fuel warning light. The unit contains bi-metal strips which operate over a period of 4 to 7 minutes to ensure that the warning light does not wink on and off while the car is being driven over rough roads. Sufficient fuel for approximately 30 to 35 miles further driving remains in the fuel tank when the warning light first shows.

The fuel tank unit is accessible from the luggage compartment. Lift up the rubber mat and remove the large rubber grommet from the floor. Disconnect the three leads, labelling them if required, and free the unit by taking off the ring of nuts that secure it. **When lifting the unit out of the tank take great care not to drop parts into the tank and do not bend the float arm.** Refit the unit using a new gasket. The gasket should be lightly smeared on the tank side with a petrol-resistant jointing compound.

If the gauge gives incorrect readings the wiring should be checked for defects such as loose contacts, poor insulation or broken leads. If the wiring is satisfactory either have the components tested on a special tester or renew a component and check by elimination which component is defective.

Later models may be fitted with a fuel gauge that operates from a stabilized voltage. This type may also be fitted with an electrically operated temperature gauge operating from the same supply. These instruments can be recognized, because when the ignition is first switched on the needles move slowly to the reading and once at the reading they do not fluctuate with the motion of the car. Special test equipment is essential for checking these instruments and voltage stabilizer, and under no circumstances may the battery voltage be connected across them.

12 The horns

Twin horns are fitted as standard equipment. The horns take a high operating current so it is essential that all connections are clean and tight. The spring mountings which support the horns must be bolted tightly to the frame otherwise the horns will sound weak or rough and it is also essential that the horns do not foul on any adjacent structure. After long service the contacts in the steering column may burn slightly giving erratic operation of the horns. Clean off burn marks using fine-grade glasspaper.

If the horns sound odd or weak disconnect each horn in turn and sound the other, taking great care not to allow the ends of the leads to come into contact with any metal part on the car. Renew a horn if it is defective.

13 Lighting circuits

Lamps give insufficient light:

Check, or have checked, the settings of the lamps. If the bulbs or reflectors have darkened with age, fit new ones in their place.

Lamps light when lit but gradually fade:

Check the battery as it is incapable of supplying current for any length of time. This fault will also be allied with starting difficulties.

Lamp brilliance varies with speed of car:

Check the condition of the battery as if starting is also difficult the battery may be defective. Check all the connections in the charging circuit, paying especial attention to the battery connections

14 Fault diagnosis

(a) Battery discharged

1 Terminals loose or dirty
2 Insufficient charging current
3 Shortcircuit in wiring not protected by fuses
4 Accessories left on
5 Insufficient mileage to allow the alternator to charge the battery

(b) Battery will not hold charge

1 Low electrolyte level
2 Battery plates sulphated or separators ineffective
3 Electrolyte leakage from defective case

(c) Alternator output low or nil

1 Driving belt broken or slipping
2 Control box defective
3 Defective wiring or connectors in charging circuit
4 Diodes failed in rectifier pack
5 Brushes excessively worn or slip rings dirty
6 Weak or broken brush springs
7 Defective stator or rotor coils

(d) Starter motor lacks power or will not operate

1 Battery discharged, loose or dirty battery connections
2 Starter pinion jammed in mesh
3 Defective starter switch
4 Defective starter solenoid
5 Brushes excessively worn or sticking, connectors detached or shorting
6 Weak or broken brush springs
7 Commutator dirty or worn
8 Defective armature or field coil windings
9 Starter mechanically defective
10 Engine abnormally stiff

(e) Starter motor runs but does not turn engine

1 Defective overrun clutch
2 Incorrectly assembled shift lever or maladjusted solenoid
3 Broken teeth on pinion or ring gear

(f) Starter motor rough or noisy

1 Check 2 and 3 in (e)
2 Mounting bolts loose
3 Loose polepieces
4 Excessively worn bearings

CHAPTER 13 – THE BODYWORK

1 Bodywork finish
2 Door trim and handles
3 Door windows and ventilators
4 Door locks
5 Bonnet
6 The luggage compartment lid
7 The windscreen and backlight
8 The instrument cluster
9 The 230SL hood and hardtop
10 The glovebox
11 The heater
12 The 230SL heater

1 Bodywork finish

Large-scale bodywork repairs are best left to expert panel beaters. Even small dents require careful working as too much or injudicious hammering will stretch the metal and make things worse instead of better. Filling minor dents and scratches is probably the best method of restoring the surface finish available to the owner, particularly as self-spraying cans of paint in matching colours are available for touching-up the paintwork. It must be remembered that the paint is supplied as an exact match for the new paint and that the finish on the car fades with age. Part of the original colour and gloss can be restored by removing the top filmed surface with a mild cutting compound, provided that there is still an adequate thickness of paint left.

Some models are finished in a metallic paint which will give difficulties in retouching. The colour of the metallic finish depends not only on the pigments but also the way in which the paint is sprayed.

The standard finish for all Mercedes models is a synthetic one, though some special order models may be finished in cellulose. **A cellulose finish must never be sprayed onto a synthetic one or the paint will** blister. If in doubt try a spot of paint on an area of the car where it will not show.

At regular intervals touch-in small scratches and stone chips using matching paint and a fine brush. If the small chips are left, water may work under the paint, causing the metal to corrode and the damage to spread.

Before spraying it is essential to remove all traces of wax polish. Washing with white spirits will normally remove ordinary polishes but silicone-based polishes require more drastic treatment. Unless the damage is small it is better to spray a complete wing or panel so that any mismatching in the paint will not show so badly. If possible remove any fittings or trim from the panel rather than mask them up. Lightly scuff the area to be sprayed and mask off surrounding areas with masking tape and newspaper.

Use a primer surfacer or paste stopper according to the amount of filling required. Air-drying stoppers must be built up in coats, allowing each coat to dry before the next coat is applied. When the surface is hard, rub it down using 400 grade 'Wet and Dry' paper and plenty of clean water. Spend plenty of time and patience in obtaining the best possible surface, applying more coats of filler or stopper if required. Small blemishes which hardly show

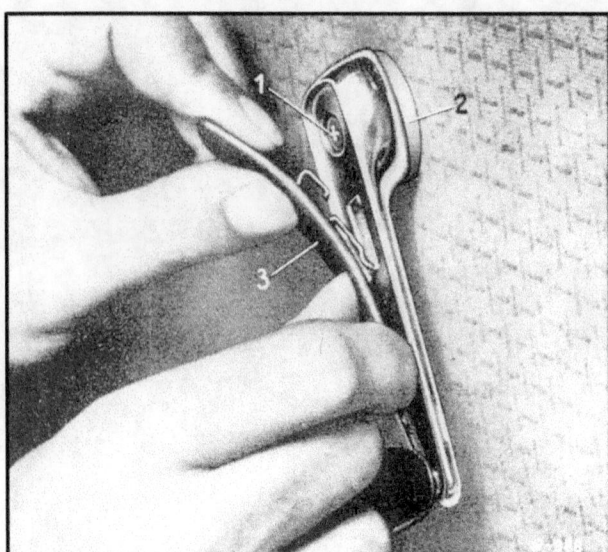

FIG 1 Removing the window regulator handle
1 Fixing screw   2 Spacer   3 Padding

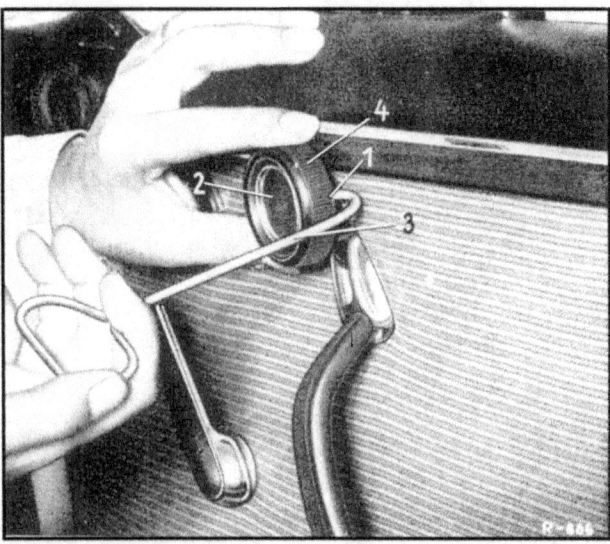

FIG 2 Removing the ventilator knob on saloon front doors
1 Notch   2 Cap   3 Wire hook   4 Control knob

Window regulator handle:

The attachment is shown in **FIG 1**. Slide a finger behind the handle and press the padding 3 out of the handle. Slide the padding towards the spindle to free it. Take out the securing screw 1 and remove the handle with the spacer 2.

Refit the handle in the reverse order of removal.

Ventilator knob (saloon front doors only):

The method of removal is shown in **FIG 2**. Find the notch 1 at the rear of the knob and insert a suitable hook 3 through the knob at this point. Use the hook to push the cap 2. Remove the securing screw now exposed and take off the knob 4.

The knob is replaced in the reverse order of removal.

Armrest and door grip:

The parts are shown in **FIG 3**. The armrest is held in place by two screws. Use a screwdriver to carefully lift and pull back the caps 1 and then take out the two screws that secure the grip. On the front doors of saloon models it may be necessary to remove the ventilator knob in order to free the caps 1.

Interior lock handle:

Open the catch and carefully use a screwdriver to prise out the insert 1 as shown in **FIG 4**. The recess can then be removed after taking out the securing screws.

The parts are refitted in the reverse order of removal.

Reveal mouldings:

The inside reveal mouldings are shown in **FIG 5**. Unscrew the lock button 4. The lower reveal moulding 5 is removed first and refitted last. Lift it up by hand to free its clips from the door. The other mouldings are secured by screws. When refitting the lower reveal moulding 5 make sure that its clips align with the mating holes in the doors.

Trim panel:

Remove all the interior door handles as well as the lower reveal moulding. Take off the trim plate from around the lock after removing its securing screws. Clips are only fitted to the vertical edges of the panels. Free the clips by sliding a blunt screwdriver or steel rule between the panel

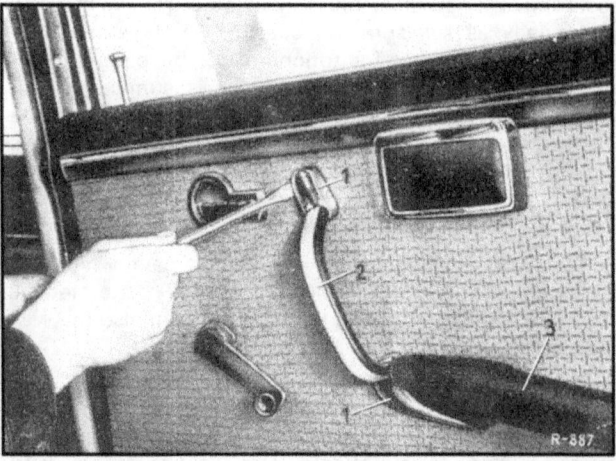

FIG 3 Removing the armrest and door grip
1 Cap   2 Grip handle   3 Arm rest

on the matt surface will stand out glaringly on the final polished finish. Wash off all slurry with plenty of clean water and when the surface is dry rub it over with a 'tacky' cloth to remove small dust particles.

Apply the paint evenly over a complete panel but for patches the edges should be thinner so that the paint is 'feathered' off. It is better to apply two thin coats, lightly rubbing down the first coat, than apply one thick coat which may run.

Leave the paint to dry for as long as possible, at least overnight, and use a cutting compound to remove spray dust and lightly polish the surface. Leave the paint to harden for at least a week before applying wax polish.

2 Door trim and handles

230SL models are only fitted with two doors and the glass does not slide in a frame around the door. However, the instructions for the saloon models apply generally to the 230SL as well.

and door, and then prise out the clips one by one. Slide the panel outwards so that it is free from the spindles, lift it up clear of the bottom channel and take it off the door.

Refit the panel in the reverse order of removal.

Exterior trim strip:

The strip is secured to the door by clips and one nut at the hinge end of the door. Open the door so that the nut is accessible and remove the nut. Slide a blunt screwdriver along under the strip, starting at the hinge end, so that the clips are freed from the door. Take great care not to scratch the paintwork in this operation.

Exterior door handle:

Two bolts secure this to the outer panel of the door. One bolt is readily accessible on the portion of the door rear of the lock, but the other bolt is only accessible after removing the trim panel. The second bolt is reached, using a socket spanner and extension, through the small circular aperture in the inner door panel just in front of the door lock. Take out the bolts and slide the handle forwards to free it; collecting the two shaped rubber sealing pads.

Before refitting the handle check the clearance between the pressure bolt on the handle and the operating lever on the lock. Press the handle, complete with sealing pads, firmly into position and visually check the gap. If the gap is incorrect, slacken the locknut and turn the pressure bolt until the clearance is correct at 1 to 2 mm (.04 to .08 inch). Tighten the locknut before refitting the handle in the reverse order of removal.

Weatherstrips:

The weatherstrips that seal the bottom of the window aperture should only be removed if absolutely essential. Removal will most likely damage them and their clips, necessitating fitting new parts on reassembly.

Take off the interior trim panel. Use a screwdriver to press the strip upwards and remove it complete with its clips. Refit the parts in the reverse order of removal, using the correct number of clips and making sure that the clips align with their holes in the door.

Weather seals:

Moulded rubber strips are fitted around the door apertures to prevent draughts and the entry of water.

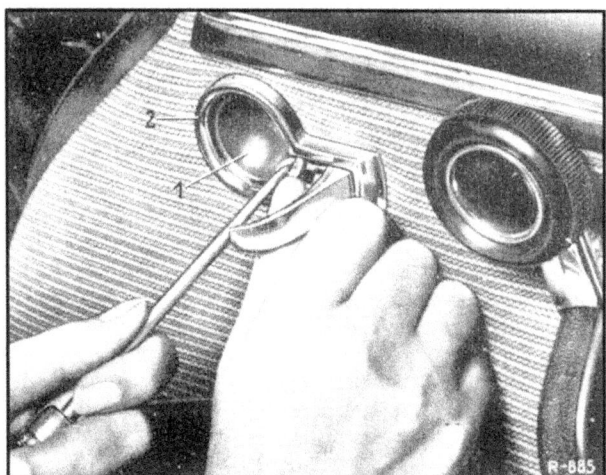

FIG 4 Removing the inside door catch
1 Insert   2 Recess

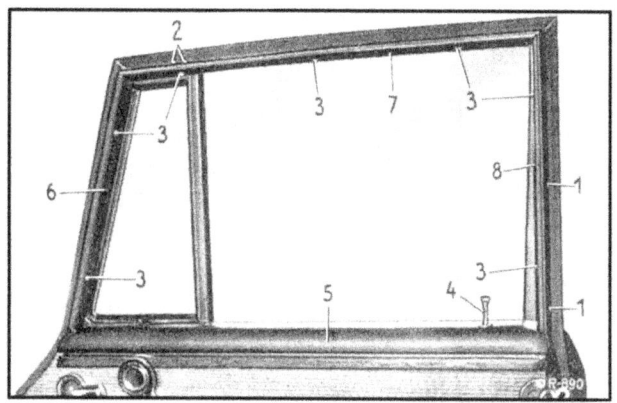

FIG 5 The window reveal mouldings

1 Fixing screws for window frame rear garnish molding
2 Fixing screws for ventilator
3 Fixing screws for reveal molding
4 Button for inside safety lock
5 Reveal molding bottom
6 Reveal molding front
7 Reveal molding top
8 Reveal molding rear

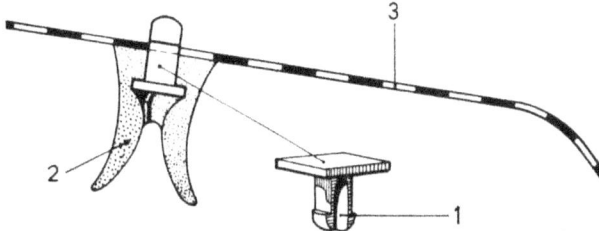

FIG 6 Attachment of the door weaher seal
1 Plastic spreader clamp 2 Weather seal 3 Door inner panel

FIG 7 Freeing the sliding window
1 Fixing screws   2 Sash channel   3 Window regulator

After long use these seals lose their shape or perish and no longer form an effective seal. They are glued into grooves and secured in places by expanding spreader clamps, as shown in **FIG 6**. A similar type of seal is fitted to the luggage compartment lid but this is secured by glue only. Remove the old seal and carefully scrape away all traces of adhesive. Coat the groove of the inner door panel with Terokal Rubber Adhesive 2 and fit the new seal into position with the adhesive still wet, fitting new spreader clamps. The new seal has already been coated with Terokal Adhesive 1 and the two parts combine to vulcanize the seal into place.

FIG 8 Freeing the regulator mechanism
1 Fixing screws for window regulator 3 Fixing screws for run channel

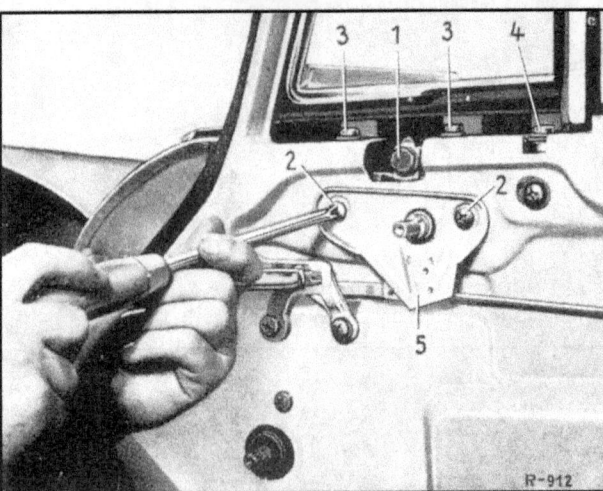

FIG 9 The quarterlight vent lower attachments
1 Hexagon bolt 3 Fixing screw 5 Mounting plate
2 Fixing screw 4 Fixing screw

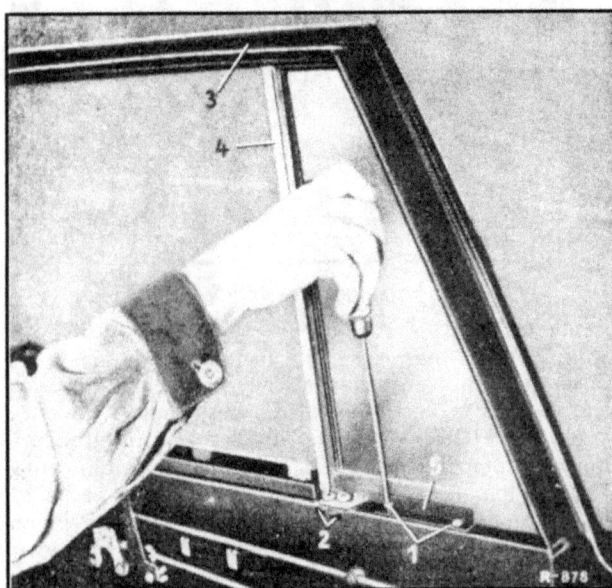

FIG 10 The rear door quarterlight attachments
1-2-3 Fixing screw 4 Window stay bar 5 Stop bracket

Window aperture trim:

Metal trim strips are fitted around the outside of the window aperture to close gaps and improve appearance. The rear strip is secured in place by two screws but the other strips are held in place by spring action. Remove the rear strip first and refit it last.

3 Door windows and ventilators

All doors are fitted with windows that open under the control of regulators mounted inside the door. On saloon models opening quarterlight vents are fitted to the front of the front doors while the rear doors each have a small fixed quarterlight at the rear. On the saloon models the glass slides inside the window aperture in a flexible window run. This flexible run is secured by clips and adhesive and it will most likely be damaged on removal. When refitting a new flexible run into position, use a wooden blade to drive it back, paying particular attention to the corners. If the run is uneven or protrudes in the corners then the glass will stick as it is opened and closed.

Sliding glass and regulator:

1 Remove the inner trim panel and interior weatherstrip (see previous section). Loosely refit the regulator handle and use it to wind the glass down to its lowest position.
2 Refer to **FIG 7** and take out the two screws 1 that secure the window to its lower sash channel 2.
3 Refer to **FIG 8**. Lift up the glass by hand and hold it in position by fitting a rubber or wooden wedge between it and the door. Remove the two screws 3 that secure the window run channel and push the channel towards the outer panel of the door. Take out the three screws 1 and remove the complete regulator assembly through the large aperture in the inner door panel.
4 Hold the glass and remove the wedge that holds it in place. Lower the glass right down to the bottom of the door and carefully turn it through 90 degrees. Lift the glass up and slide it out through the window aperture.

The parts are refitted in the reverse order of removal. Grease the regulator assembly before refitting it. The glass run channel securing screws (items 3 in **FIG 8**), should be positioned in their slotted holes so that the glass has a clearance of approximately 2 mm (.1 inch) at the sides.

Quarterlight ventilator:

Its attachments at the lower end are shown in **FIG 9**. Two screws secure the upper end to the door. The sliding glass, both weatherstrips and flexible glass run channel must all be removed before the ventilator can be taken out, and it should be remembered that new parts may have to be fitted on reassembly.

1 Remove the bolt 1 and slacken the two screws 2. Push the ventilator lock downwards so as to clear the pivot pin. The lock with its mounting plate 5 can be removed if the screws 2 are taken out.
2 Take out the screws 3 and 4 as well as the two screws that secure the upper end of the ventilator, and lift the ventilator out of the door.

The parts are refitted in the reverse order of removal. If the lock has been removed, loosely refit the knob and turn the lock until its lug aligns with the pivot of the ventilator.

Rear door quarterlight:

Again the interior trim panel, both weatherstrips and glass run channel must be removed, remembering that some of the parts will be damaged on removal and new parts will therefore be needed. The attachments are shown in **FIG 10**.

1 Remove the stop bracket 5 by taking out its two securing screws 1. Take off the stay bar 4 after removing the single screw 3 at the top and the two screws 2 from the mounting plate at the bottom.
2 The glass, complete with its rubber mounting, is removed by pulling it towards the front of the door. Refit the quarterlight in the reverse order of removal.

4 Door locks

The attachments of the lock at the front door are shown in **FIG 11**. Remove the trim panel as described in **Section 2**. Use a screwdriver to free the clip 2 and detach the rod 1. Similarly free the rod 4. Take out the four screws 3 and lift out the lock assembly.

Refit the lock in the reverse order of removal, after lightly lubricating it. The front pair of screws 3 should be fully tightened before the rear pair are tightened.

Striker plate:

This is secured in place by screws and has shims fitted under it to ensure that there is only a small clearance between the lock and striker. If the striker requires adjustment, slacken the securing screws slightly but leaving them tight enough to prevent the striker from moving easily. Gently shut the door. Never slam the door while the striker is out of adjustment. Pull or push the door until it is aligned with the body and then carefully open the door without disturbing the position of the striker. Fully tighten the striker plate securing screws and check that the door shuts correctly.

5 The bonnet (hood)

The bonnet is secured by a lock operated by a handle beside the driver. On the saloon models the front of the bonnet lifts up and an additional safety catch is fitted at the front on the righthand side. This catch must be operated separately and from outside the car in order to open the bonnet. The cable that operates the lock should be adjusted so that there is a small amount of free movement before the lock starts to open.

The striker pin on the lock can be adjusted so as to set the amount of tension in the lock. If the bonnet is difficult to shut then the striker pin should be screwed downwards so as to effectively lengthen it. Conversely if the bonnet is loose when shut, the effective length of the striker should be shortened by screwing it upwards.

Removal:

At least two people are necessary for removing the bonnet and a third person will be most useful. Pad the corners of the bonnet with rags and lay rags and sheet metal over the vulnerable points so that they will not be damaged.

All the models have the bonnet counterbalanced so that it will stay open on its own. On the earlier models a spring supplies the necessary balancing force but on later models torsion bars are used. The attachment with torsion bars is shown in **FIG 12**. Use the special tool

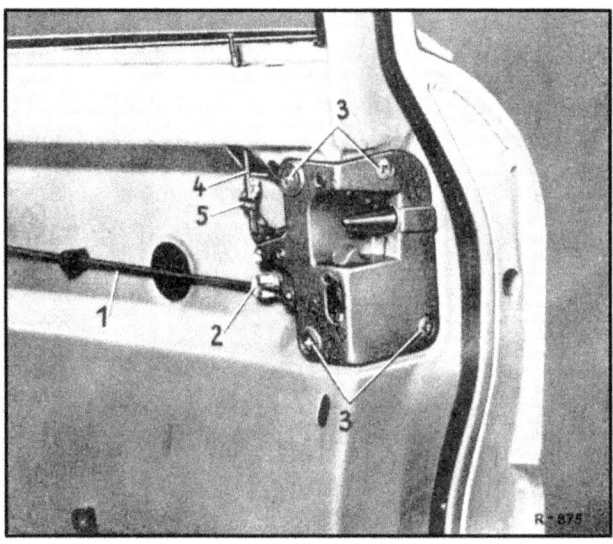

FIG 11 The door lock attachments
1 Pull rod 3 Fixing screw 5 Locking spring
2 Clip   4 Pull rod

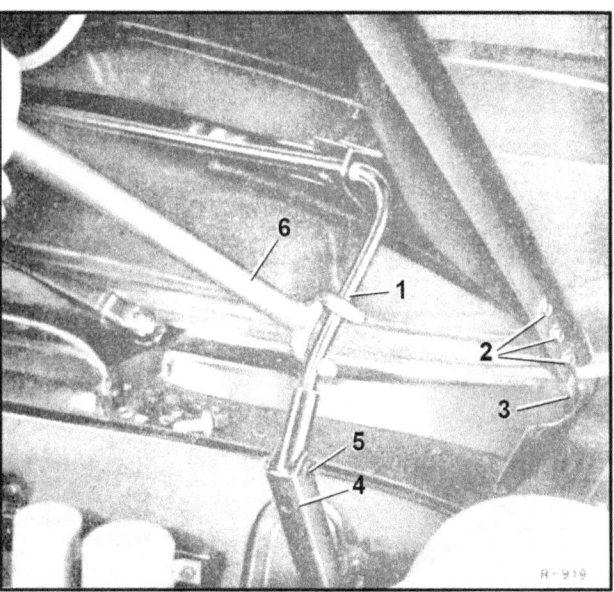

FIG 12 The bonnet attachments, using torsion bar counterbalancing

1 Torsion bar   4 Lever
2 Hexagon bolts   5 Collar bolt
3 Hinge   6 Removal Tool 111 589 02 61

No. 111.589.02.61 to take the pressure of the torsion bar and with an assistant holding open the bonnet remove the collar bolt 5. With the bonnet still supported by at least one assistant remove the two sets of three bolts 2 and lift off the bonnet.

Refit the bonnet in the reverse order of removal. Leave the securing bolts slightly slack so that the bonnet can be accurately aligned with the body and tighten the bolts fully after this has been done.

6 The luggage compartment lid

The attachments of the lid using torsion bar counterbalance are shown in **FIG 13**. A weather seal is fitted around the lid to weatherproof the luggage compartment.

FIG 13 The luggage locker lid attachments

1 Pin 3 Torsion bar 5 Rear lid hinge
2 Bolts 4 Rear compartment lid 6 Slotted hole

Backlight trim:

The strip is secured in place by two screws, one on each side by the striker for the rear door.

Windscreen trim:

A sectioned view of the windscreen is shown in **FIG 14**. Remove the two nuts that secure the lower trim moulding. The nuts are found at the bottom corners of the windscreen. Use a thin blade of wood or a very blunt screwdriver under the moulding 2 to prise out the press fasteners 6 and 7. Remove the moulding 2. Remove the rear view mirror 14 and its retaining plate 13. The upper reveal moulding can be removed after taking out their securing screws.

A sectioned view of the lower reveal moulding and instrument panel is shown in **FIG 15**. The lower reveal moulding 16 is divided into two parts, the lefthand side being secured by two nuts 6 and the righthand side by three nuts. Remove all five nuts and lift out the two parts of the moulding.

All the parts are refitted in the reverse order of removal. Before fully pushing the moulding 2 (**FIG 14**) back into position use a blunt screwdriver to lift the lip of the rubber moulding into place over the moulding 2.

Glass removal:

If the screen has broken all the broken parts should be removed, as is obvious. Less obvious is the need to ensure that the windscreen demisting ducts are free from broken glass, even if it means partially dismantling the heater to ensure that all particles are removed. **If particles are left they can be forcibly blown out by the action of the heater and may injure the passenger or driver.** If the glass is broken, strip out the trim and remove the old rubber moulding that secured the glass.

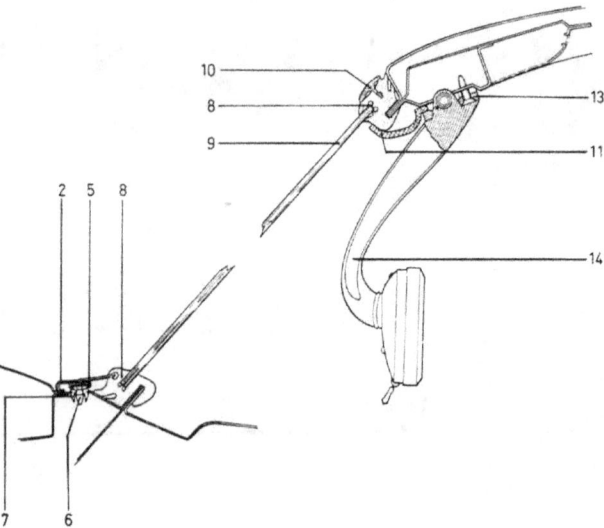

FIG 14 Section through the windscreen

2 Lower trim molding 9 Windshield glass
5 Retaining plate 10 Ornamental frame
6 Press fastener, upper part 11 Upper reveal molding
7 Press fastener, lower part 13 Rear view mirror retaining plate
8 Rubber molding 14 Rear view mirror

The seal is secured in its groove by adhesive only and is renewed using the same method as the glued portions of the door weather seal (see **Section 2**).

The lid is removed in a similar manner to the bonnet and is also refitted in a similar manner.

7 The windscreen and backlight

The method of securing the glass in place is the same in both cases though the trim differs and there are no wipers fitted to the backlight.

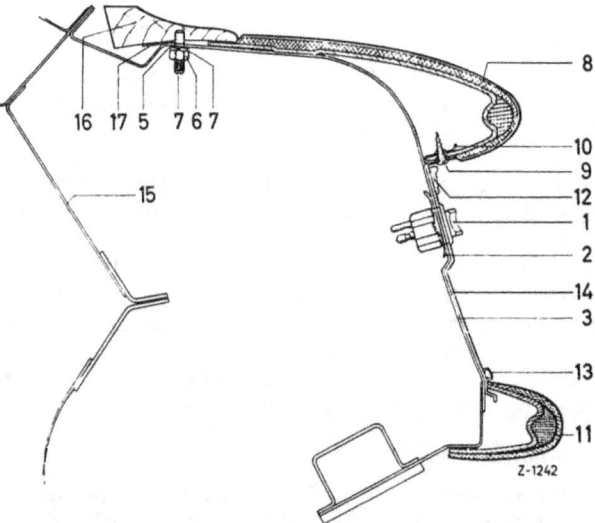

FIG 15 Section through the lower reveal moulding and instrument panel

1 Toggle switch 7 Threaded pin 12 Upper trim molding
2 Clamping springs 8 Upper padding 13 Lower trim molding
3 Instrument panel 9 Countersunk 14 Instrument panel cover
5 Washer tapping screw 15 Front wall
6 Fixing nut with 10 Clip-on nut 16 Reveal molding
  lock washer 11 Lower padding 17 Felt base

If the glass is unbroken, remove the trim as before as well as the wiper arms on the windscreen. Working from inside the car use a wooden blade or blunt screwdriver to lift the flange of the rubber moulding up and over the metal flange of the body aperture. Have an assistant outside the car to take the glass as it comes free. If need be, apply pressure with the palm of the hand, or sole of the foot (with rags to prevent the shoe from scratching the glass), at the corners of the glass to ease it out. When the windscreen is removed lay it down onto a padded bench.

The rubber moulding that secures the glass to the frame is sealed into place and as a result will most likely be damaged on removal. A new rubber moulding must be fitted if the old one is at all damaged otherwise there are likely to be constant leaks around the windscreen.

Refitting the glass:

Before refitting the glass check the flange of the aperture. Dress out any dents with a metal block and hammer and file down any protrusions. If the flange is left distorted it will either cause leaks or, more seriously, it will cause stress points in the glass which may cause it to shatter.

1 Lay the glass down onto a padded bench, convex side down. Refit the rubber moulding around the glass. Turn the glass over and fit the ornamental frame back into the rubber moulding. Before refitting the ornamental frame, open up its groove with a wooden wedge and lubricate with either soft soap or a soap solution. Turn the glass back, convex side down.

2 Lay a length of greased cord around the groove for the metal flange. The cord must be sufficiently thick so as not to cut the rubber and it must be long enough for it to meet in the middle of the screen, leaving ends of at least 30 cm (1 foot) hanging free. Lightly lubricate the lip of the rubber moulding with either tallow or glycerine.

3 Coat the flange of the body aperture with sealant BO.375/10. Pass the free ends of the cord through the aperture and have an assistant accurately position the glass against the aperture, using firm pressure. From inside the car grip the ends of the cord and pull the

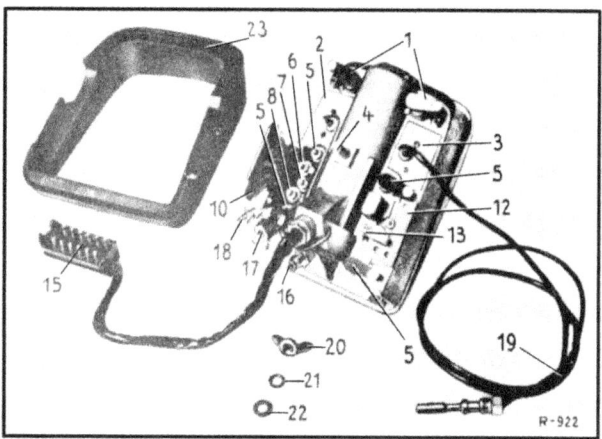

FIG 17 Rear view of the instrument cluster on saloons

1 Pilot light, flash signal
2 Oil pressure gage
3 Radiator (water temp) gage
4 Fixing bolt
5 Instrument lighting
6 Charging light
7 Pilot light, choke control
8 Pilot light, upper beam
10 Contact cover
12 Fuel gage
13 Warning light, fuel gage
15 12-pin plug
16 Speedometer connection
17 Oil pressure gage connection
18 Adjustable dimmer resistance
19 Capillary tube with heat bulb
20 Wing nut
21 Lock washer
22 Washer
23 Instrument cluster frame

FIG 18 The cables for the glove box light

1 Cable connector box
2 Cable for reading light (glove compartment)
3 Center cover
4 Water drain hose

cord out in a direction parallel to the screen, as shown in **FIG 16**, so that the lip of the rubber moulding is lifted into place over the flange.

4 Inject more sealant between the moulding and the flange as well as injecting sealant between the glass and the rubber moulding. Press the moulding firmly into place and wipe away the surplus sealant as it oozes out. The last traces of surplus sealant should be removed with a cloth moistened with methylated spirits. **Do not use excessive quantities of methylated spirits or it will soak under the moulding and remove the sealant that is meant to be there.**

5 Refit the trim in the reverse order of removal. On the windscreen correctly refit the wiper arms.

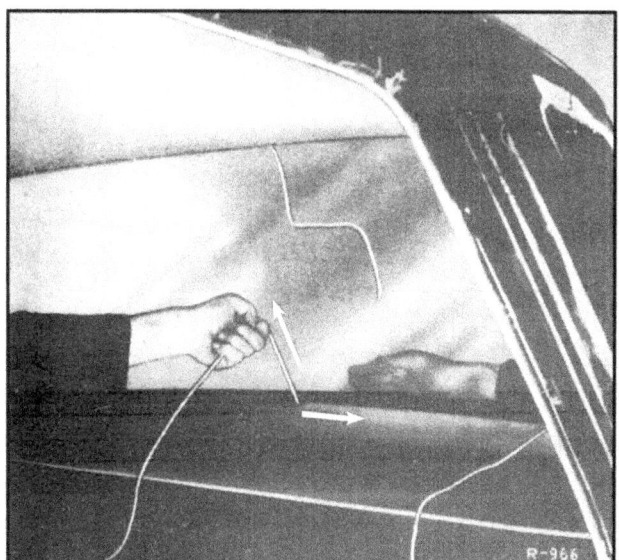

FIG 16 Refitting the glass

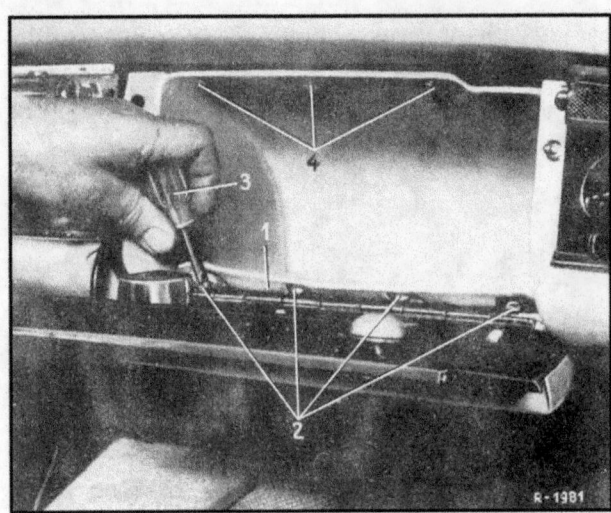

FIG 19 The glove box attachments

1 Glove compartment bottom cover
2 Countersunk screws
3 Screw driver (Dowidat 149 KPV/02)
4 Countersunk screws

2 Unscrew the temperature gauge bulb from the cooling system. Plug the aperture with a suitable cork to prevent the loss of coolant. **Take great care not to twist, bend, squash or kink the capillary tube of the gauge, as if the tube is damaged the gauge will no longer operate and a complete new assembly must be fitted.**

3 Remove the covers under the instrument panel. Disconnect the multi-pin connector for the instrument panel. Working behind the instrument panel unscrew by hand the wingnut 20 and connection 17 for the oil gauge.

4 Ease out the instrument cluster. On saloon models disconnect the speedometer drive cable before fully removing the cluster. Withdraw the instrument cluster from the car, **taking great care not to damage the capillary tube for the temperature gauge.**

Refit the instrument cluster in the reverse order of removal.

9 The 230SL hood and hardtop

This model can be fitted with either a soft-top hood or else with a hardtop which makes the car into a Coupé. The hardtop can be fitted in place without removing the hood from the car. If the hardtop is to be left on for long periods then it is advisable to remove the hood and store

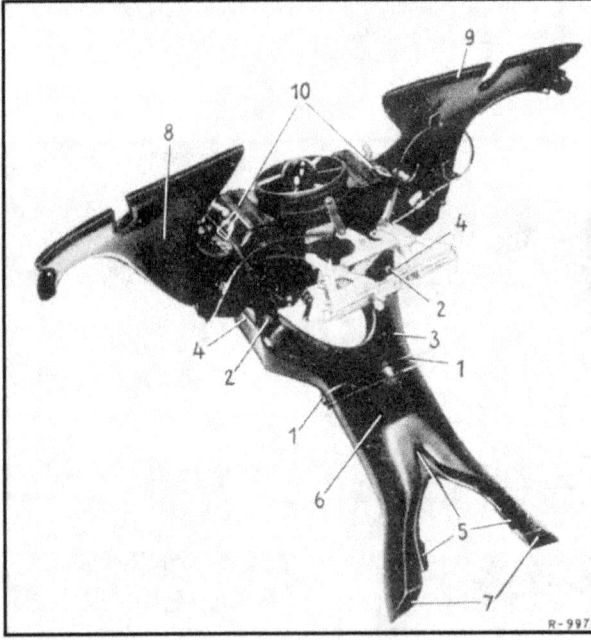

FIG 20 General view of the heater fitted to saloons

1 Self tapping screw
2 Hexagon bolt
3 Connecting duct
4 Seal
5 Self tapping screw
6 Heating duct
7 Seal
8 Left defroster nozzle
9 Right defroster nozzle
10 Clips

8 The instrument cluster

The instruments on the 230SL differ from saloon models in that the speedometer and tachometer are mounted separately on either side of the central cluster. The speedometer and tachometer are held in place by bridge pieces and knurled nuts. Partially withdraw the instruments and disconnect the drive cables so that the instruments can be removed.

A rear view of the instrument cluster fitted to saloons is shown in **FIG 17**.

1 Disconnect the battery. It is advisable to remove the steering wheel (see **Chapter 10, Section 9**).

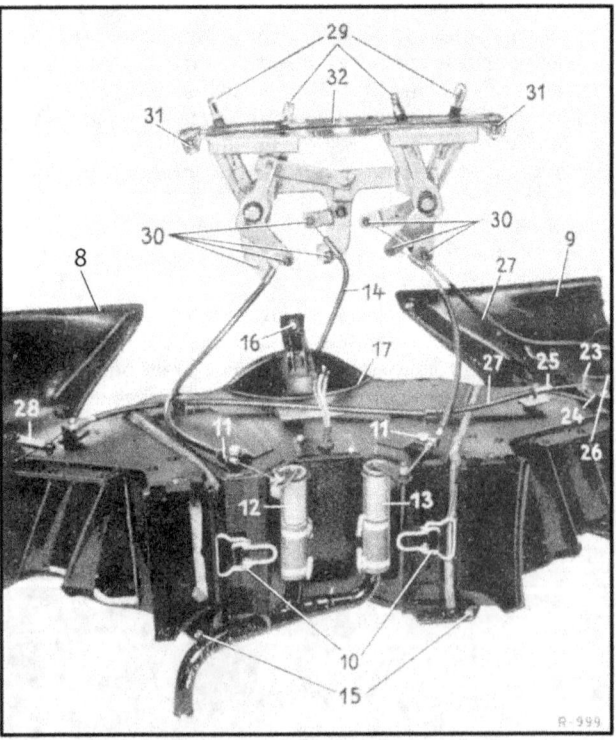

FIG 21 Underside view of the heater fitted to saloons

8 Left demister nozzle
9 Right demister nozzle
10 Cover
11 Clips for regulating valve cables
12 Left regulating valve
13 Right regulating valve
14 Wire cable for fresh-air flap
15 Bolt
16 Bolt
17 Heater box
23 Locking washer
24 Air flap lever
25 Wire cable
26 Wire cable
27 Wire cable sheath
28 Air flap lever
29 Control lever
30 Fixing screw
31 Fixing nut
32 Escutcheon

it in a container that can be obtained from an agent. **However, if the hood is left fitted the hardtop should be removed several times throughout the year and the hood erected.** Leave the hood to air, out of the direct sun, with the car windows open and restow it when it has dried out. If this precaution is not observed the hood may become mouldy and deteriorate.

Cleaning:

The hardtop is cleaned and washed normally with the remainder of the body. The hood does not require washing normally and a light brushing with a soft brush, all the strokes going rearwards, is usually sufficient cleaning. If washing is required, use a natural cleaning solution, **never fuel or solvents that will damage rubber,** and wipe with a sponge or soft brush from the front to the rear. Rinse the hood with plenty of clean water and make sure that it is absolutely dry before stowing it. Bird droppings should be cleaned off as soon as possible as they contain acids that will attack the material of the hood and cause it to leak.

After a period of time the hood will loose its full waterproof properties and start to absorb water droplets readily. If this occurs the hood should be re-impregnated with a suitable solution obtainable from an agent.

Never stow the hood in its storage locker while it is wet or damp.

10 The glovebox

Remove the cover from under the instrument panel. Refer to **FIG 18** and disconnect the cables 2 from the box 1. Refer to **FIG 19** and lift up the covering material 1 to expose the securing screws 2. Use a short screwdriver to remove the screws 2 and 4. Close the lid and draw out the glovebox.

Refit the parts in the reverse order of removal.

On the 230SL model the electric clock can be removed after the glovebox compartment has been removed. Disconnect the wires to the clock and then undo the knurled nuts that secure the bridge pieces.

FIG 22 Water connections to the heater on saloons
18 Water hose on return pipe
19 Return pipe
20 Water hose on feed pipe
21 Feed pipe
22 Rubber grommet

FIG 23 Disconnecting the mixed air control cables on the SL
1 Control cable for right mixed-air flap
2 Operating disk for right mixed-air flap
3 Operating disk for left mixed-air flap and heat exchanger

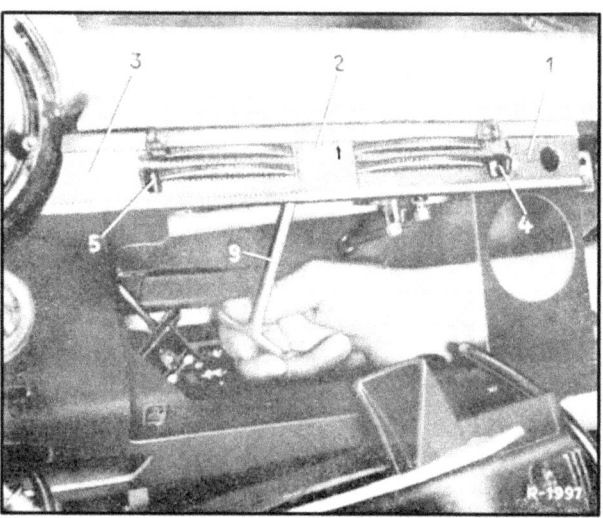

FIG 24 Removing the nuts that secure the escutcheon on the SL
1 Right escutcheon
2 Center escutcheon
3 Left escutcheon
4 Operating disk for the right mixed-air flap
5 Operating disk for the left mixed-air flap and heat exchanger
9 Articulated wrench

11 The heater

This section deals with the heater on saloon models only. The heater on the 230SL is dealt with in the next section.

A general view of the heater is shown in **FIG 20**.

Connecting duct to rear compartment:

1 Take off the cover panels under the instrument panel and remove the rubber mats and covering over the transmission tunnel.
2 Remove the connecting duct 3, complete with the rubber seals 4, after taking out the self-tapping screws 1 and bolts 2.

FIG 25 Disconnecting the control cables for the distribution box and fresh air flap on the SL

1 Operating system
2 Control cable for distribution box
3 Control cable for fresh-air flap
4 Operating disk for distribution box
5 Operating disk for fresh-air flap

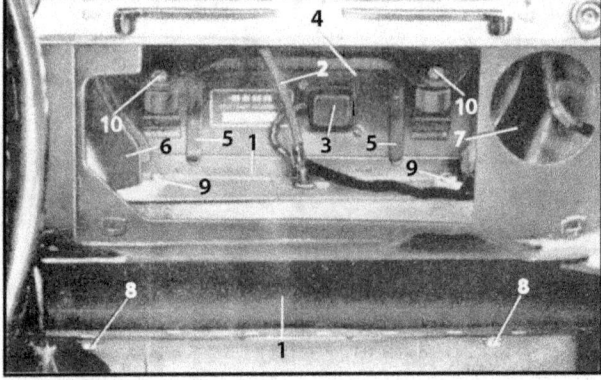

FIG 26 View of the heater with the control assembly removed from the SL

1 Distribution box
2 Control cable
3 Electric plug
4 Radial blower
5 Retaining spring
6 Left defroster nozzle
7 Right defroster nozzle
8 Fixing screw for distribution box
9 Fixing screw for defroster nozzle
10 Fixing screw for radial blower

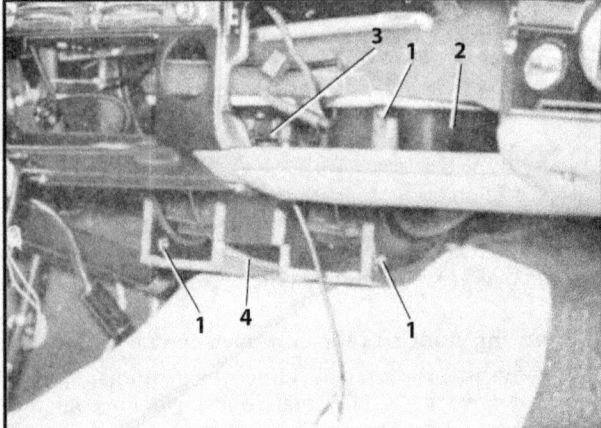

FIG 27 Blower motor connections on the SL

1 Fixing screw for cap
2 Right cap
3 Electric plug
4 Radial blower

3 The rear duct 6 can now be removed. Take out the self-tapping screws 5 and remove the duct with the seals 7 out of the crossmember.

Refit the parts in the reverse order of removal. Take care not to damage the seals 4 and 7 and make sure that they are snugly in place.

Righthand side demister nozzle:

1 Remove the connecting duct 3. Open all the clips 10, as shown in **FIG 20**. Refer to **FIG 21** remove the locking washer 23 and pull the cables 25 and 26 off the air flap lever 24. Free the outer cable sheaths 27 from their clips.
2 Remove the locking washer and disconnect the link from the wiper motor arm (see **Chapter 12, Section 6**). The nozzle 9 can now be removed downwards. Refit the parts in the reverse order of removal.

Heater box and blower motor:

1 Remove the righthand side demister nozzle as just described and use the same procedure to remove the lefthand side demister nozzle 8.
2 Free the clips 11 from the regulating valves 12 and 13 and also free the cable 14 from the fresh-air flap.
3 Take out the two bolts 15 and the bolt 16 on the water tank. Only a socket spanner on an extension will reach these three bolts and the lefthand side demister nozzle 8 should be pulled to the left to gain access to the lefthand bolt 15.
4 Disconnect the blower motor leads from the connector. Drain the cooling system.
5 Refer to **FIG 22** and disconnect the water hoses 18 from the return pipe 19. Also disconnect the water hose from the feed pipe 21 and remove the three rubber grommets 22. The heater box assembly can now be withdrawn rearwards and removed from the car.

Refit the parts in the reverse order of removal.

Lefthand side demister nozzle:

This can only be removed after the heater box assembly has been removed. It may also be necessary to disconnect the choke control cable at the instrument panel and push it through into the engine compartment. Free the cable 25 and sheath 27 from the lever 28 and remove the nozzle downwards.

Refit the parts in the reverse order of removal.

Control assembly:

Remove the covers from under the instrument panel. Disconnect all the cables and sheaths from the assembly, labelling them for reassembly. Remove the blower switch and pull the control levers out from their spring-loaded holders. Take off the two nuts 31 and remove the escutcheon rearwards. Slide the control unit forwards to remove it.

Cable adjustments:

The cables are set with the flaps closed and the controls just moved a fraction away from their closed positions.

When the cables have been adjusted operate the controls several times to ensure that they are working satisfactorily and that the valves or flaps close fully without undue strain being put on them.

12 The 230SL heater

To gain access to the parts the trim and panels must be removed from the instrument panel. Remove the glove compartment and electric clock. From underneath the panel pull out the reading lamp and disconnect its leads. Take out the securing screws and remove the padding from under the instrument panel. Ease the top edge of the panel with the model number on it outwards using a blunt screwdriver, and press the panel upwards to remove it. Disconnect the cigar lighter and remove the centre cover from the instrument panel.

Control assembly:

1 Remove the padding and trim. Disconnect the operating cables 1 for the mixed air flaps from the operating discs 2 and 3, as shown in **FIG 23**.
2 Remove the blower switch and unscrew the nuts securing the escutcheon parts 1, 2 and 3, as shown in **FIG 24**. Note that a socket spanner and universal joint will be required for undoing the nuts and the operating discs 4 and 5 must be moved in the opposite direction from that of the nuts when being removed. Take off the escutcheon parts in the order 1, 2 and 3 as they are toothed together.
3 Tilt the control assembly and disconnect the cables 2 and 3 as shown in **FIG 25**. When the cables are disconnected ease the assembly out through the aperture in the instrument panel.

Refit the parts in the reverse order of removal.

Distributor box:

1 Remove the control assembly and take off the cover under the centre of the instrument panel.
2 Take out the screws 9 that secure the demister nozzles 6 and 7 to the distribution box, shown in **FIG 26**. Disconnect the control cable 2 from the operating disc.
3 Take out the screws 10 and slide the distributor box downwards so that it clears the springs 5 and can be removed.

Refit the parts in the reverse order of removal.

Blower assembly:

1 Remove the distributor box as described earlier.
2 Refer to **FIG 27**. Disconnect the plug 3 from the blower 4. Remove the screw 1 and caps 2 from the blower.
3 Disconnect the hose that leads to the righthand side window demister nozzle. Without altering the adjustment disconnect the link from the wiper motor crank. Remove the righthand side demister nozzle.
4 Take out the nut and bolt that secure the blower to the bracket on top of the transmission tunnel. An assistant is needed for this operation. The assistant should stand at the left of the engine and reach down with his left

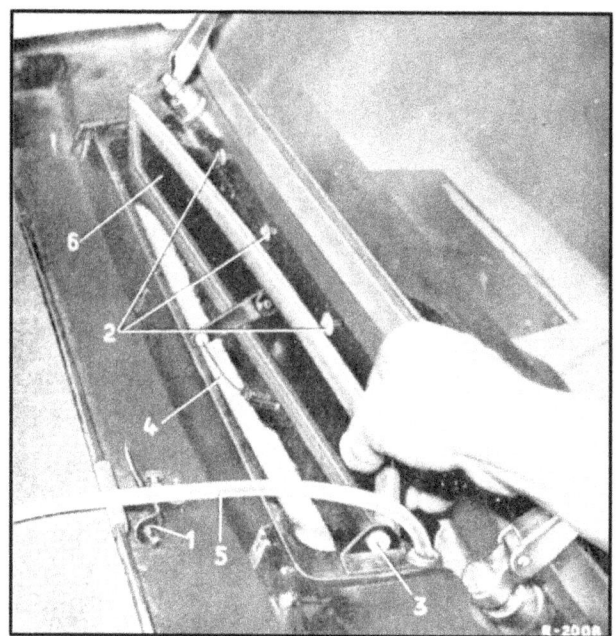

FIG 28 Freeing the fresh-air flap on the SL

1 Fresh-air flap hinge
2 Fixing screw for scoop
3 Bearing bushing for fresh-air flap
4 Control cable for fresh-air flap
5 Windshield washer hose
6 Fresh-air flap

FIG 29 Disconnecting the link on the SL

1 Scoop
3 Bearing bushing for fresh-air flap
4 Control cable for fresh-air flap
5 Hose
8 Left mixed-air flap
9 Ball cup for operating heat exchanger

hand into the transmission tunnel for the nut. **Make sure that the engine is cold before attempting this.**
5 Loosen the carpet on the righthand side of the transmission tunnel and remove the blower towards the right.

Refit the parts in the reverse order of removal.

Heat exchanger:

1 It will be necessary to remove the blower motor assembly.
2 Drain the cooling system and disconnect the water hoses from the heat exchanger. Remove the ornamental grille from the scoop. Unscrew the ends of the scoop from the cowl, take out the four securing screws and lift out the scoop.
3 Refer to **FIG 28**. Unscrew one of the hinges 1 for the fresh-air flap 6 and lift the other end of the flap out. Remove the fresh-air cleaner element from the orifice. (Renew the element at regular intervals.)
4 Refer to **FIG 29**. Disconnect the ball cup 9 of the operating linkage at the mixed air flap 8, and lay the link on top of the heat exchanger and still attached to the heat exchanger.
5 Remove the securing screws and lower the unit out of the car taking great care not to damage the hose unions.

Refit the parts in the reverse order of removal.

TECHNICAL DATA

Unless otherwise stated the dimensions are given in millimetres and inches, the first figure being millimetres and the figure in brackets being inches. The metric figures are always the accurate ones and are official, so if there is any doubt as to the accuracy of the conversion from one to the other the metric figures should be taken as the correct figure.

A conversion table can be found at the end of this section so that the owner may confirm the accuracy of the metric equivalents.

ENGINE

Type:	Six-cylinder in-line, OHV with single overhead camshaft, watercooled
Compression ratio:	
230, 230S	
Standard	9:1
Low	7.2:1
230SL	9.5:1
Maximum speed:	
230, 230S	6000 rev/min
230SL	6500 rev/min
Firing order:	1–5–3–6–2–4
Cubic capacity:	2306 cc (140.71 cu in)
Bore (standard):	82 (3.23)
Stroke:	72.8 (2.86)
Tappet clearance (cold):	
Inlet	.08 (.003)
Exhaust	.15 (.006)
Compression test pressure (with engine hot and throttle fully open):	
230, 230S with standard compression	
Normal	10 to 11 kg/sq cm (142 to 156 lb/sq in)
Minimum	8.5 kg/sq cm (125 lb/sq in) approx
230, 230S with low compression	
Normal	7.8 to 8.8 kg/sq cm (111 to 125 lb/sq in)
Minimum	6.5 kg/sq cm (92.5 lb/sq in) approx
230SL	
Normal	11 to 12 kg/sq cm (156 to 170.6 lb/sq in)
Minimum	9.0 kg/sq cm (128 lb/sq in) approx.
Maximum variation between cylinders	1.5 kg/sq cm (21 lb/sq in)
Crankshaft:	
Type	4 main bearings, integral balance weights, and damper mounted at front end
End float	.1 to .175 (.004 to .007)
Maximum end float	.3 (.012)
Radial play	.045 to .060 (.0018 to .0024) but aim at .050 (.002)
Standard journal diameter	59.965 to 59.955 (2.3606 to 2.3598)
Undersize main bearing shells	4 overhaul stages, two wall thicknesses for all sizes
Standard crankpin diameter	47.715 to 47.755 (1.8882 to 1.8874)
Undersize big-end bearings	4 overhaul stages, two wall thicknesses for all sizes
Minimum journal diameter	58.965 to 58.955 (2.3213 to 2.3205)
Minimum crankpin diameter	46.965 to 46.955 (1.8488 to 1.8480)

Maximum ovality, crankpins and journals
  New ... ... .005 (.0002)
  Run-in ... ... .01 (.0004)
Maximum taper, crankpins and journals
  New ... ... .01 (.0004)
  Run-in ... ... .015 (.0006)

Camshaft:
End float ... ... .050 to .128 (.002 to .005)
Radial play ... ... .025 to .057 (.001 to .002)
Standard sizes   *Front bearing*   *2nd and 3rd*   *Rear bearing*
  Journal ...   34.975 to 34.959   47.975 to 47.959   48.975 to 48.959
  Bearing ...   35.000 to 35.016   48.000 to 48.016   49.000 to 49.016
Undersizes ... ... Intermediate bearings (Grey) are .1 mm undersize and are for journals which are .1 mm undersize.
Overhaul stage bearings (Red) are also available

Cylinder bores:
Standard bore ... ... 82.000 to 82.022
Intermediate ... ... +.25
Overhaul ... ... Two stages each +.500 larger than standard

Maximum taper and ovality
  New ... ... .013 (.0005)
  Worn ... ... .04 (.0016)
Maximum wear ... ... .12 (.005)
Piston clearance ... ... .04 (.0016)

Cylinder head:
The compression ratio of the engine is counted as 9.0:1 but on 230 and 230S models the front two cylinders have a lower compression ratio.
Front cylinder ... ... 8.6:1, compression space 49.3 to 52.6 cc
Second cylinder ... ... 8.8:1, compression space 48.0 to 51.2 cc
Remainder ... ... 9.0:1, compression space 47 to 49.2 cc
Valve seats ... ... Renewable
  Seat angle ... ... 90 deg.—30 sec.
  Seat width ... ... 1.25 to 2.0 (.049 to .079)
  Backing-off ... ... 120 deg. cutter to prevent lower edge of valve sealing face from resting on valve seat
Valve guides ... ... Renewable, one intermediate and two overhaul stages
Valve guide internal diameter
  Exhaust valves ... ... 11.000 to 11.0018
  Inlet valves ... ... 9.000 to 9.015
Height of cylinder head ... ... 84.8 to 85.0
Maximum stock removal ... ... .8 (.031)

Piston rings:
Clearance in groove
  Top compression ring ... ... .060 to .092 (.0024 to .0036)
  Other rings ... ... .040 to .072 (.0015 to .003)
Fitted gap
  Top compression ring ... ... .55 to .70 (.022 to .028)*
  Second compression ring ... ... .45 to .60 (.018 to .024)*
  Oil control ring ... ... .30 to .45 (.012 to .018)

Molybdenum-filled rings are fitted with a gap .15 to .20 (.006 to .008) less than the gap given

Chain tensioner spring:
Free length	91 (3.583)
External diameter	11.3 (.445)
Loaded length	50 mm at 4.2 kg
Fitted length	44 mm at 4.5 to 5.3 kg

Valve springs: *(Wear limit 10 per cent)*

	Inner	Outer
230SL		
Part No.	180.053.08.22	180.053.08.20
External diameter	21.8 (.859)	32.8 (1.291)
Free length	40.5 (1.594)	52 (2.047)
Loaded length	31.5 mm at 8.8 to 11.2 kg	40 mm at 26.6 to 30 kg
Fitted length	21.5 mm at 19.8 to 22.2 kg	30 mm at 56.4 to 63.6 kg
230, 230S		
Part No.	108.053.00.22	108.053.00.20
External diameter	22.2 (.835)	32.8 (1.291)
Free length	45 (1.772)	52 (2.047)
Loaded length	31 mm at 12.8 to 15.2 kg	40 mm at 26.6 to 39 kg
Fitted length	21 mm at 22.8 to 25.2 kg	30 mm at 56.4 to 63.6 kg

Valves:

All exhaust valves are sodium-cooled and care must be taken in their disposal.

Seat angle	90 deg. + 30 ft	90 deg. + 30 ft
Head diameter	*Inlet*	*Exhaust*
230SL	39.3 to 39.1 (1.547 to 1.539)	35.25 to 34.95 (1.388 to 1.376)
230, 230S	41.3 to 41.1 (1.626 to 1.618)	37.25 to 36.95 (1.466 to 1.455)
Stem diameter		
All models	8.970 to 8.948 (.3531 to .3523)	10.950 to 10.928 (.4311 to .4302)
Length	128 (5.039)	112.7 (4.437)
Height of unmachined portion above seat		
New	1.5 (.059)	2.4 to 2.6 (.094 to .102)
Minimum	1 (.039)	1.5 (.059)

Valve timing:

	230SL	*230, 230S*
Inlet opens	10 deg. BTDC	11 deg. BTDC
Inlet closes	58 deg. ATDC	53 deg. ATDC
Exhaust opens	51 deg. BTDC	47 deg. BTDC
Exhaust closes	23 deg. ATDC	21 deg. ATDC

Lubrication:

Minimum oil pressure	.6 kg/sq cm (8.5 lb/sq in)
Operating oil pressure	2 to 6 kg/sq cm (28 to 85 lb/sq in)

Relief valve springs

	Crankcase	*Oil filter*
Part No.	127.993.02.01	181.993.06.01
External diameter	8.7 to 9 (.343 to .354)	12.25 (.482)
Free length	43.6 (1.73)	49 (1.93)
Loaded length	39 mm at 2 kg	32 mm at 2.26 kg
Fitted length	30.5 mm at 5.25 to 5.95 kg	24 mm at 3 to 3.6 kg
Release pressure of valve	5.5 to 6.5 kg/sq cm (78 to 82.5 lb/sq in)	2.2 to 2.5 kg/sq cm (31 to 35.5 lb/sq in)

FUEL SYSTEM

Type:
Carburetters:

230	Twin Solex 38.PDSI
230S (and later 230)	Twin Zenith 35/40.INAT
230SL	Bosch six-cylinder fuel injection pump PES.6.KL.70/120.R.11

Fuel pump:
Type

Carburetter models	DVG diaphragm pump, mechanically operated from engine
230SL	Bosch feed pump FP/ESB.5.RC.25/12.A1 electrically operated

Mechanical pump
Delivery pressure	.12 to .16 kg/sq cm (1.7 to 2.3 lb/sq in) at starter speed
	.15 to .20 kg/sq cm (2.1 to 2.8 lb/sq in) at idling speed
Suction	230 to 320 mm Hg (4.3 to 5.7 lb/sq in)

Electrical pump
Delivery pressure	.6 to .8 kg/sq cm (8.5 to 11.4 lb/sq in) measured behind fine fuel filter
Discharge pressure	Minimum 1.2 kg/sq cm (17 lb/sq in) measured behind damper unit in fuel line with dummy plug on line

Idling speed (given in revs/min):

	Manual transmission	Automatic transmission O, N or P	2, 3, 4 or R
230, 230S	750 to 800	850 to 900	650 to 700
230SL	750 to 800	700 to 750	700

Carburetter jet details:

	Solex 38.PDSI	Zenith 35/40.INAT Stage 1	Stage 2
Air horn 'K'	26	24	28
Main jet 'Gg'	135	115	120
Air correcting jet 'a'	180	100	130
Mixing tube 's'	Not replaceable	4S	4N
Emulsion chamber vent bore	.5	—	—
Idle fuel jet 'g'	50	45	—
Build-up fuel jet	—	—	60
Idle air bore	1.6 mm	1.3 mm	—
Build-up air bore	—	—	1.0 mm
Accelerating pump injection	1.0 to 1.3 cc/stroke*	.7 to 1.0 cc/stroke	—
Fuel level	21 to 23 mm	Correct with 1 mm washer under valve	
Float needle valve	2.0	2.0	2.0

*.6 to .9 cc/stroke on front carburetter on models fitted with automatic transmission

IGNITION SYSTEM

Firing order: 1–5–3–6–2–4

Distributor points gap: ... ... .3 to .4 (.012 to .016)

Distributor dwell angle: ... ... $38 ^{+3}_{-1}$ deg. Tolerance is ± 3 deg. at 4000 rev/min

Sparking plugs:
Gap
  230, 230S
    Normal plugs ... ... .7 to .8 (.027 to .031)
    Radio-suppressed ... ... .9 to 1.0 (.035 to .039)
  230SL ... ... .5 (.0196)
Type
  230, 230S
    Normal ... ... Beru D.225/14/3
                                                            Bosch W.225.T.28
    Radio-suppressed ... ... Beru ED.225/14/3
                                                            Bosch W.225.RT.28
    City driving only ... ... Beru D.200/14/3 or ED.200/14/3
                                                             Bosch W.200.T.27 or W.200.RT.27
  230SL ... ... Beru 250/14/3
                                                            Bosch WG.250.T.28

Static ignition settings:*

	Standard compression	Low compression
230, 230S	1 deg. BTDC	4 deg. BTDC
230SL		
IFUR.6		
0.231.116.046		
0.231.116.050		
0.231.116.051	6 deg. BTDC	—
0.231.116.047	3 deg. BTDC	—
VJUR.6.BR49T	2 deg. BTDC	—

Stroboscopic ignition settings:*

Set at 4500 rev/min with vacuum disconnected, check at other speeds. All figures given with the vacuum control disconnected and they are degrees BTDC.

Engine speed (rev/min)	Starter	800	1500	3000	4500
230, 230S—standard compression	3	5 to 15	20 to 27	25 to 31	37
230, 230S—low compression	6	8 to 18	23 to 30	28 to 34	40
230SL					
IFUR					
0.231.116.046	8	8	10 to 12	30	30
0.231.116.050					
0.231.116.047	5	—	13 to 20	30	30
0.231.116.051	8	—	12 to 19	30	30
VJUR.6.BR.49.T	4	4 to 7	15 to 19	30	30

Advance at 4500 rev/min with vacuum control connected:*

	Standard compression	Low compression
230, 230S	10 ± 3	10 ± 3
230SL with VJUR.6.BR.49.T	11 ± 3	—

*The part numbers given following the model are the Bosch designation of the distributor.

COOLING SYSTEM

Normal operating temperature:	70 to 95°C
Inhibitor:	Castrol 7016, Gulfcut soluble oil
	Houghton Phosphatal
	Mobil Solvac 1535.G, Shell Donax C
	Veedol Anorust 50
	This list is not fully inclusive but does give those most readily obtainable. All to be used at 2.5 to 5 cc/litre
Antifreeze:	BP Anti-Frost, Caltex Anti-Freeze
	Castrol Antifreeze
	Gulf Antifreeze and Summer Coolant
	Mobil Permazone
	Shell Antifreeze (or Antifrost)
	Veedol Frostfree
	This list is not fully inclusive. Quantities required are given in **Chapter 4, Section 7**
Pump lubricant:	Hypoid SAE.90 oil

CLUTCH

Operation:	Hydraulic
Hydraulic fluid:	Must meet specification SAE.70.R.3 Amongst the recommended fluids are: ATE Blue, Lockheed HD.1, HD.12, HD.31
Pressure plate:	Fichtel and Sachs TK.228.KX, Part No. 000.250.68.04
Earlier pressure plate:	TK.228.KV, Part No. 128.250.02.04 (000.250.29.04 for 230SL)
Driven plate:	Fichtel and Sachs 228.SD, Part No. 001.250.11.03
Early 230SL driven plates:	Part No. 000.250.87.03
	Part No. 000.250.72.03
Clutch springs:	
Part No.	000.252.18.20
Quantity	9
Identification colour	Yellow and Gold
Free length	55.1
Fitted length	37.2 mm at 61.5 ± 2.5 kg

GEARBOX

Type: Four forward speeds with synchromesh engagement on all forward speeds
Lubricant: ATF type A fluid
Ratios:

	First	Second	Third	Fourth	Reverse
230	4.09:1	2.25:1	1.42:1	1:1	3.62:1
230S	4.05:1	2.23:1	1.40:1	1:1	3.58:1
230SL	4.42:1	2.28:1	1.53:1	1:1	3.92:1

AUTOMATIC TRANSMISSION

Type ... Four forward-speed DB transmission
Lubricant ... ATF Type A fluid
Operating temperature ... 80°C (176°F)

Shift points:

Shifting Selector lever position	Accelerator pedal position	Regulator type	1st/2nd gear up	1st/2nd gear down	2nd/3rd gear up	2nd/3rd gear down	3rd/4th gear up	3rd/4th gear down	Max. speed in gears km/h
4	little partial throttle	1	—	—	28	23	40	30	
		2	—	—	28	23	40	30	
		3	—	—	25	18	40	30	
		4	—	—	25	18	45	30	
	full throttle	1	18*	—	48	23	76	30	
		2	18*	—	40	23	85	30	
		3	18*	—	40	18	100	30	
		4	—	—	15	18	120	30	
	kick-down	1	28	10-12	48	30	76	66	
		2	28	10-12	54	30	85	75	
		3	25	10-12	48	30	100	85	
		4	25	10-12	75	30	120	105	
3	little partial throttle	1	—	—	28	23	—	—	
		2	—	—	28	23	—	—	
		3	—	—	25	18	—	—	
		4	—	—	25	18	—	—	
	full throttle	1	18*	—	48	23	—	—	86
		2	18*	—	54	23	—	—	86
		3	18*	—	58	18	—	—	115
		4	18*	—	75	18	—	—	130
	kick-down	1	28	10-12	48	38	—	—	
		2	28	10-12	54	44	—	—	
		3	25	10-12	58	46	—	—	
		4	25	10-12	75	64	—	—	
2	little partial throttle	1	15	10	—	—	—	—	
		2	15	10	—	—	—	—	
		3	15	10	—	—	—	—	
		4	15	10	—	—	—	—	
	full throttle	1	15	10	—	—	—	—	55
		2	15	10	—	—	—	—	55
		3	40	10	—	—	—	—	70
		4	45	10	—	—	—	—	80
	kick-down	1	28	23	—	—	—	—	
		2	28	23	—	—	—	—	
		3	40	30	—	—	—	—	
		4	45	30	—	—	—	—	

Note: All values are approximate
*Applies only if 1st gear was previously engaged by kick-down

Transmission ratios:

Gear	Transmission	Transmission ratio
First	In front and rear planetary gear set	3.93:1
Second	In front planetary gear set	2.52:1
Third	In rear planetary gear set	1.58:1
Fourth	No transmission	1:1
Reverse	In front and rear planetary gear set	4.15:1

REAR AXLE

Ratios:
230, 230S ... 4.08:1
230SL
   Standard ... 3.75:1
   Optional and USA ... 4.08:1

SUSPENSION

There are combinations of road springs and dampers to suit all conditions and a local agent should be consulted for the most advantageous combination.

The positioning and geometry of the steering requires special gauges for accurate checking and this work should be left to a local agent.

Following data is given for standard springs only and with the car in kerb condition.

Camber:
Front wheels
   230, 230S ... +0 deg. 30 sec.
   230SL ... 0 deg. 10 sec. + 20 sec.
Rear wheels, without level control
   230 ... +1 deg. 30 sec. ± 30 sec.
   230SL ... +1 deg. 45 sec. ± 30 sec.
Rear wheels, with level control
   230 ... +0 deg. 30 sec. ± 1 deg.
   230S ... 0 deg. ± 1 deg.

Castor:
Power steering ... 4 deg. ± 15 sec.
Mechanical steering ... 3 deg. 30 sec. ± 15 sec.

Kingpin inclination ... 5 deg. 30 sec. ± 10 sec.

Front wheel alignment ... 2 ± 1 mm (.08 ± .04 in)
0 deg. 20 sec. ± 10 sec.

STEERING

Type ... Recirculating ball
   Power assisted as an optional extra

Wheel lock: ... Controlled by stops on suspension unit, safety stops internal in steering box

Lubricant: ... Hypoid SAE.90 oil (ATF for power assisted)

Turning circle diameter:
230 ... 11.4m (37.4 feet)
230S ... 11.5m (37.7 feet)
230SL ... 10.35m (33.6 feet)

Overall steering gear ratio:
Manual ... 1:21.9 or 1:22.8
Power assisted ... 1:17.2 (Approximately 3 turns lock to lock)

BRAKES

Hydraulic fluid: ... ATE Blue, or fluid meeting SAE.70.R.3 (same fluids as for clutch)

Type: ... Hydraulically operated disc brakes on front wheels. Hydraulically and mechanically operated Simplex drum brakes on rear wheels.

Hydraulic system: ... Master cylinder mounted onto servo unit in engine compartment. Tandem master cylinder

Adjustment:	Two mechanical adjusters per rear brake
Disc brakes:	
230, 230S	Girling type 17/2 or Teves S.2/57
230SL	Girling type 17/3
Disc thickness	12.7 (½)
Disc reconditioning limit	11.7
Minimum pad thickness	2 (.08)
Drum brakes:	
Type	Simplex with 65mm malleable-iron brake shoes and Alfin or grey cast iron drums
Drum internal diameter	230 + .2 (9.055)
Reconditioning limit	
Alfin drums	232 (9.134)
Cast iron drums	231 (9.094)
Minimum lining thickness	1.5 (.06)
Friction pads:	**Do not intermix grades of pads**
Teves and Girling 17/2	Fadil 77-79 (Green-white)
	Fadil 77-79 N7 (Green-green-white)
	Textar TP.25.D (Green-yellow)
	Textar V.1431 (Green-yellow-green)
Girling 17/3	Ferodo DS.5.S (Blue-blue-blue)
	Ferodo DS.31 (Blue-white)
	Textar TP.25.D (Green-yellow)
Vacuum assisted servo	
230, 230S	ATE 51/100
230SL	ATE.T.51/200

ELECTRICAL SYSTEM

Polarity:	Negative earth
Voltage:	12-volts
Battery:	Lead/acid
Capacity	
230, 230S	44 amp/hr
230SL	55 amp/hr
Acid level	5 (.2) above separators
	15 (.6) above plates
Starter motor:	Bosch type AL/EEF 0.8/12.R.2 or AL/EEF 0.8/12.R.7
Alternator:	
230, 230S	Bosch 14V 35A
230SL	Bosch K.1/14V 35A 20
Maximum output	490 watts maximum

WEIGHTS AND DIMENSIONS

Weight:	
Kerb condition	
230	1305 kg (2880 lb)
230S	1350 kg (2980 lb)
230SL	1295 kg (2855 lb)
Maximum all-up	
230	1805 kg (3980 lb)
230S	1850 kg (4080 lb)
230SL	1650 kg (3638 lb)
Dry and empty	
230	1235 kg (2723 lb)
230S	1280 kg (2820 lb)

Overall length:
230 .. .. 4730 mm (186.5 in)
230S .. .. 4875 mm (191.9 in)
230SL .. .. 4285 mm (168.69 in)
Overall width:
230 .. .. 1795 mm (70.7 in)
230S .. .. 1795 mm (70.7 in)
230SL .. .. 1760 mm (69.28 in)
Overall height (unloaded):
230 .. .. 1495 mm (58.8 in)
230S .. .. 1500 mm (59.09 in)
230SL
  Hood .. .. 1320 mm (51.96 in)
  Hardtop .. .. 1305 mm (51.37 in)

WHEELS AND TYRES

Rim size:
230, 230S .. .. 5JK x 13.HB
230SL .. .. 6J x 14.HB
Tyre sizes:
230 .. .. 7.00.S x 13 (tubeless)
230S .. .. 7.25.S x 13 (tubeless)
230SL .. .. 185.HR x 14
Tyre pressures (all checked cold):
  Pressure is given in kg/sq cm, figure in brackets is lb/sq in
  A drop in pressure of more than .2 (3) per week indicates a puncture.

230		*Front*	*Rear*
1 to 4 passengers		1.5 (21)	1.8 (26)
Heavy loads		1.7 (24)	2.1 (30)
Winter tyres		1.7 (24)	2.2 (31)
230S			
1 to 4 passengers		1.6 (22.8)	1.8 (25.6)
Heavy loads		1.6 (22.8)	2.1 (29.9)
Winter tyres		1.7 (24.2)	2.2 (31)
230SL			
Winter tyres		1.8 (25.6)	2.2 (31)

CAPACITIES

Automatic transmission:
From dry (including cooler) .. .. .. 4¾ Litre (8¼ Imp pints) 10 US pints
Refill .. .. 3¾ Litre (6½ Imp pints) 7.9 US pints
Brakes: .. .. ½ Litre (.9 Imp pint)
Cooling system:
230 .. .. 14 Litre (3.1 Imp gall) 3.7 US gall
230S .. .. 11.4 Litre (2.5 Imp gall) 3.0 US gall
230SL .. .. 10.8 Litre (2.37 Imp gall) 2.85 US gall
Engine:
Maximum .. .. 5½ Litre (9.7 Imp pint) 11.6 US pint
Minimum .. .. 3½ Litre (6.2 Imp pint) 7.4 US pint
Oil filter .. .. .5 Litre (.9 Imp pint) 1 US pint
Fuel tank: .. .. 65 Litre (14.3 Imp gall) 17.2 US gall
Gearbox: .. .. 1.4 Litre (2½ Imp pint) 3 US pint
Hubs: .. .. Total 65 to 80 grammes (2.3 to 2.8 ozs)
Power steering: .. .. 1.4 Litre (2½ Imp pint) 3 US pint
Rear axle: .. .. 2½ Litre (4 Imp pint) 5 US pint
Steering box: .. .. .3 Litre (½ Imp pint)
Water pump: .. .. 10 cc

TORQUE WRENCH SETTINGS

Engine

	lb f ft	Nm
Cylinder head bolts (cold)	58	80
(hot)	65	90
Rocker ball pivots	72	100
Connecting rod big-end cap bolts	44	61
Main bearing cap bolts	58	80
Flywheel (or driveplate) bolts	50	69
Sump bolts	6	8
Spark plugs	25	35
Oil filter centre bolt	30	41
Oil cooler drain plug	18	25
Camshaft sprocket bolt	58	80
Fuel injection pipe unions	25	35
Crankshaft pulley bolt	150	207
Crankshaft damper socket screws	25	35
Engine rear plate bolts	36	50
Oil pump mounting bolts	36	50
Chain tensioner plug	42	58
Sump drain plug	30	41
Clutch or torque converter housing to engine	36	50
Driveplate to torque converter bolts	25	35

Fuel

	lb f ft	Nm
Fuel injection valves to cylinder head	25	35
Fuel injection pressure valve (Stage 1)	29	40
(Stage 2)	25	35
Carburettor mounting nuts	15	21

Clutch

	lb f ft	Nm
Clutch bellhousing bolts to engine	36	50
Clutch pressure plate cover bolts	25	35
Clutch slave cylinder bolts	22	30
Clutch master cylinder bolts	26	36

Manual Transmission

	lb f ft	Nm
Output flange nut	108	150
Drain and filler plug	43	60
Side cover bolts	11	15
Front cover bolts	11	15
Rear cover bolts (large)	32	45
Rear cover bolts (small)	11	15
Countershaft front and rear nuts	108	150
Mainshaft front nut	58	80
Clutch bellhousing to engine bolts	36	50

Automatic Transmission

	lb f ft	Nm
Drive plate to torque converter bolts	25	35
Output flange nut	87	120
Oil pan bolts	5	7
Torque converter housing to engine bolts	36	50

Propeller Shaft

	lb f ft	Nm
Intermediate bearing carrier bolts	15	21
Sliding sleeve nut	22 to 28	30 to 39
Flexible coupling plate self-locking nuts	30	41
Coupling flange bolts to rear axle drive pinion	32	44

Rear Axle

	lb f ft	Nm
Enclosed type axleshafts		
Differential suspension carrier upper mounting bolt	87	120
Differential suspension carrier mounting plate bolts to floor pan	32	45
Locating strut to bodyframe nuts	65	90
Locating strut bolts to differential housing	144	200
Front plate to differential housing bolts	25	35
Universal joint to side gear of differential	47	65
Left-hand axle tube to differential bolts	36	50
Differential carrier pivot bolt pinch bolt	87	120
Brake backplate bolts	18	25
Axleshaft bearing ring nut	144	200
Open type axleshafts		
Flexible mounting to differential end cover	94	130
Flexible mounting (rear) to floor pan	18	25
Front flexible mounting plate to floor pan	29	40
Front flexible mounting to differential carrier	87	120
Axleshaft to flange bolt	69	95
Differential end cover bolts	32	45

Brakes

	lb f ft	Nm
Front disc to hub bolts	82	113
Caliper securing bolts	82	113
Master cylinder mounting nuts	15	21
Fluid line unions	12	16
Master cylinder stop bolt	6	8
Vacuum line union to servo unit	22	30

Suspension & Steering

	lb f ft	Nm

Cars with king pin and bush type stub axle carrier and enclosed type axleshafts

Front suspension

	lb f ft	Nm
Shock absorber lower mounting bolt	18	25
Crossmember flexible mounting bolt	72	100
Upper control arm pivot to crossmember bolts	72	100
Lower control arm pivot to crossmember bolts	94	130
Stabiliser bar leaf springs to bodyframe	87	120
Stabiliser bar flexible mounting clamps	18	25
Control arm threaded pivot bushes	130	180
King pin lower nut	65	90
Lateral positioning rod bolts	44	60
Lower control arm to stub axle carrier bolt	130	180
Upper control arm cam bolt	32	45

Cars with king pin and bush type stub axle carrier and enclosed type axleshafts *(continued)*

	lb f ft	Nm
Rear suspension		
Shock absorber lower mounting bolt	32	45
Rear axle compensating spring right-hand carrier	87	120
Rear axle hydro-pneumatic strut left-hand balljoint	58	80
Rear axle hydro-pneumatic strut right-hand balljoint	87	120
Steering		
Steering box to bodyframe	43	60
Steering drop arm nut	144	200
Idler arm shaft self-locking nut	87	120
Track rod end and drag rod balljoint nuts	25	35
Steering coupling pinch bolts	18	25
Steering wheel to shaft nut	36	50
Steering wheel to hub (boss) nut	11	15
Roadwheels		
Roadwheel bolts	72	100

Cars with swivel balljoint type stub axle carriers and open type axleshafts

Torque wrench settings as foregoing except for:

	lb f ft	Nm
Lower control arm bearing cam bolts	87	120
Upper control arm bearing bolts	44	60
Front wheel bearing clamp pinch bolt	10	14
Steering arm to stub axle carrier bolts	58	80
Upper and lower control arm swivel balljoint nuts	58	80
Suspension rear link to rear axle carrier	87	120

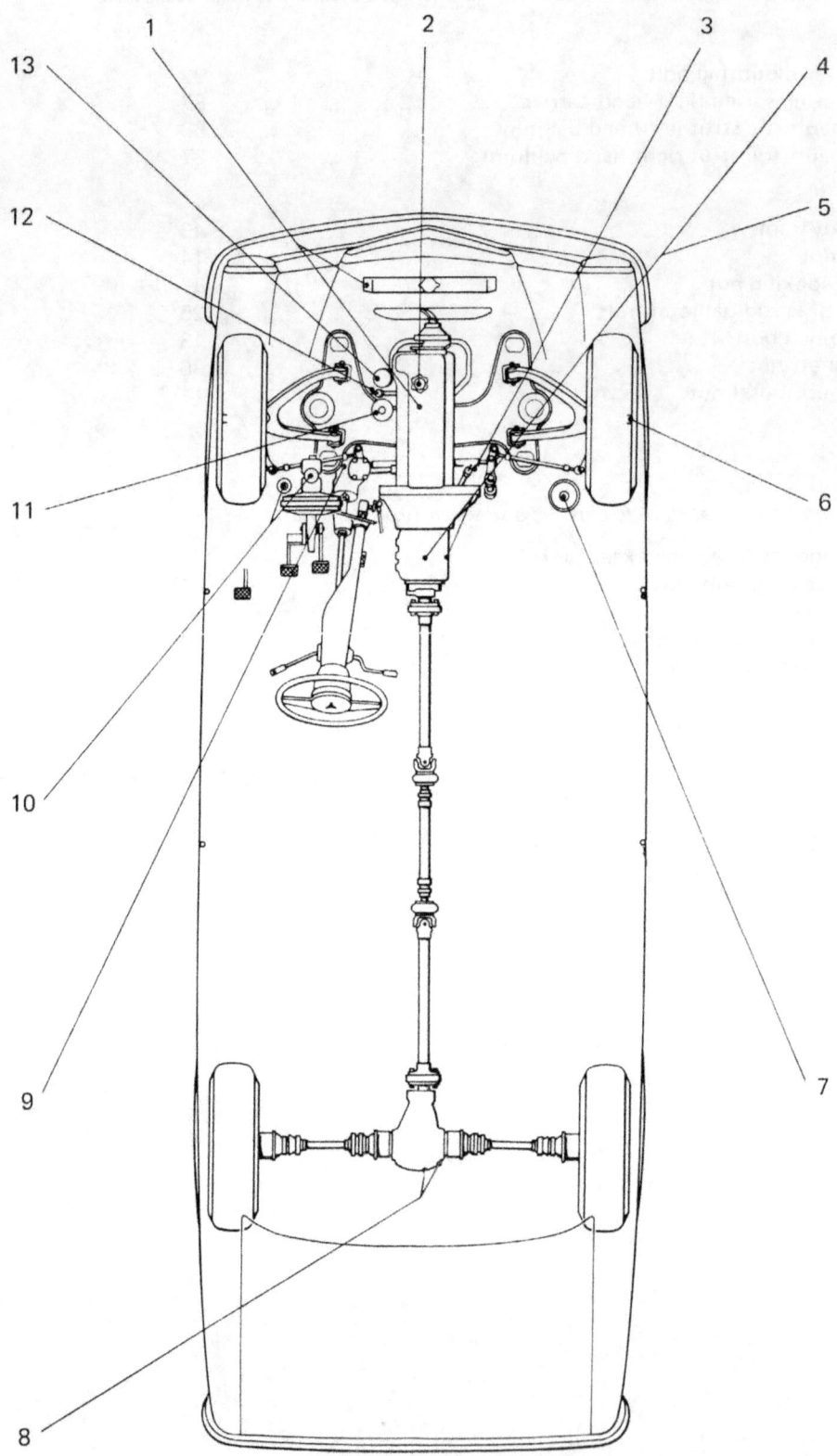

Lubrication points—230/8, 250/8 engine and running gear.

1. Crankcase drain plug (1) Oil cooler drain plug (2)
2. Oil fill cap
3. Automatic transmission dipstick
4. Automatic transmission drain plugs
5. Manual transmission drain and fill plugs
6. Front wheel bearings
7. Leveling device reservoir
8. Rear axle drain and fill plugs
9. Steering box oil fill plug
10. Brake and clutch reservoirs
11. Power steering reservoir
12. Engine oil dipstick
13. Distributor cam felt

Lubrication points—230/8, 250/8 engine and running gear.

230 WIRING DIAGRAM - PART 1

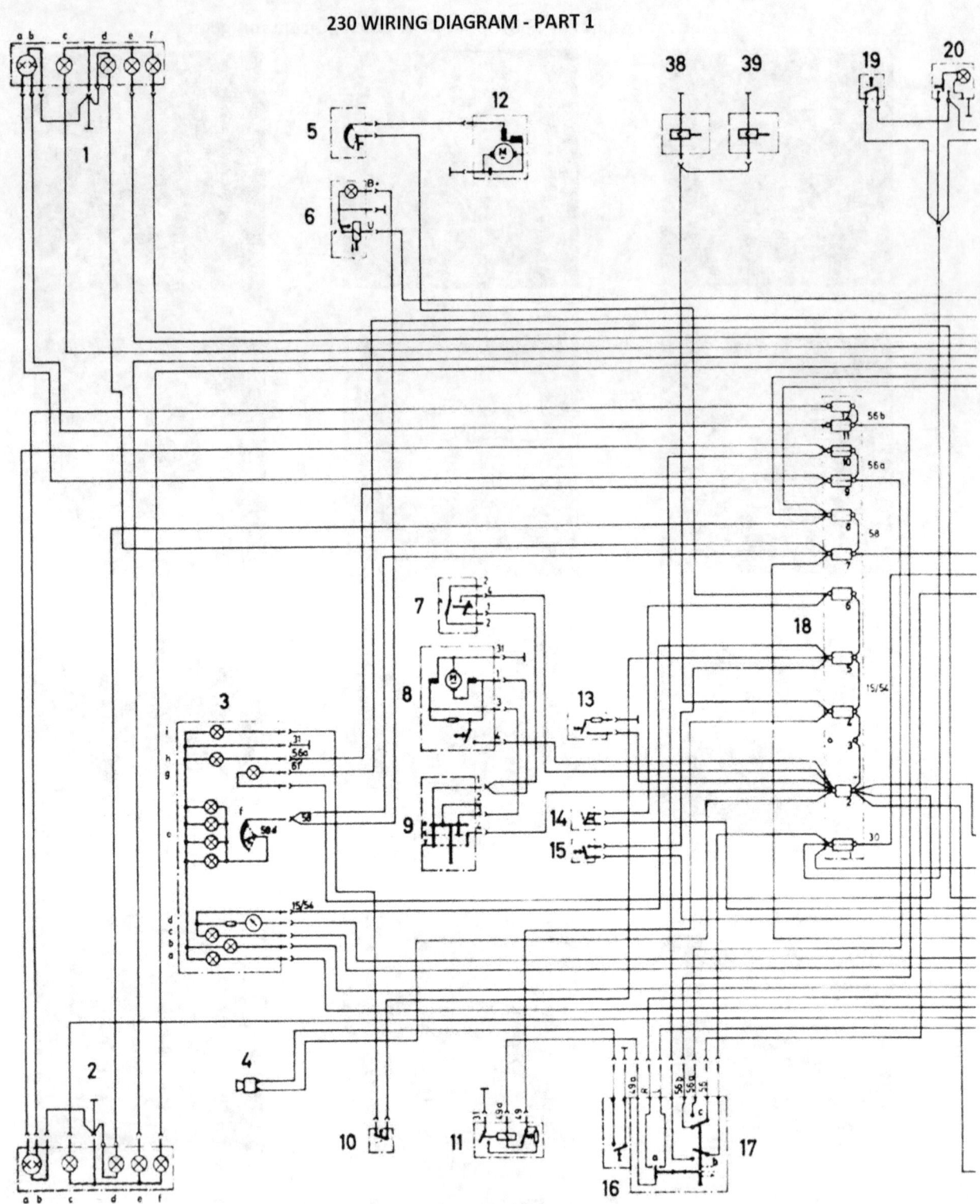

1 Headlight, right
2 Headlight, left
  a High beam
  b Low beam
  c Blinker
  d Parking light
  e Foglight
  f Clearance light
3 Instrument cluster
  a Blinker pilot light, left
  b Blinker pilot light, right
  c Fuel reserve warning light
  d Fuel gauge
  e Instrument lighting
  f Regulating resistor for instrument lighting
  g Generator control
  h High beam pilot light
  i Handbrake pilot light
4 Signal horn
5 Heater fan switch
6 Electric clock
7 Foot pump windshield washer
8 Windshield wiper motor
9 Windshield wiper switch
10 Handbrake pilot switch
11 Blinker transmitter
12 Heater fan motor
13 Cigar lighter
14 Brake light switch
15 Reversing light switch
16 Signal ring
17 Instrument cluster switch
  a Blinker switch
  b Passing signal switch
  c Hand dimmer switch
18 Fuses
19 Courtesy light, left

230 WIRING DIAGRAM - PART 2

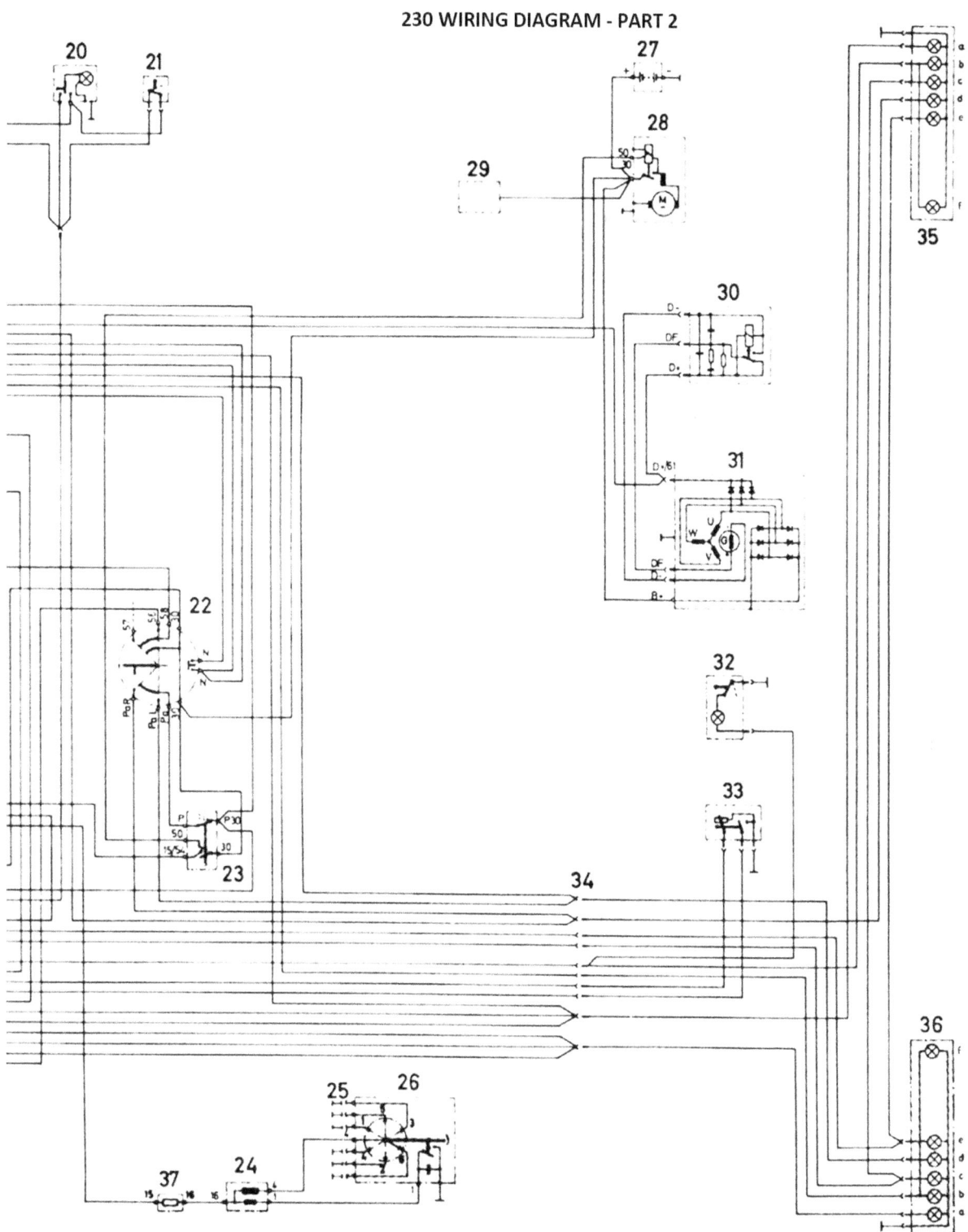

20 Reading light
21 Courtesy light, right
22 Light turn switch
23 Ignition starter switch
24 Ignition coil
25 Spark plugs
26 Distributor
27 Battery
28 Starter
29 Line for special request (radio)
30 Voltage regulator
31 Generator
32 Trunk light
33 Fuel gauge transmitter
34 Plug connection for tail lights line set
35 Tail light, right
36 Tail light, left
  a Blinker
  b Tail light
  c Reversing light
  d Clearance light
  e Brake light
  f License plate light
37 Series resistance
38 Auto starting device on rear carburetter
39 Auto starting device on front carburetter

230/8 WIRING DIAGRAM (Carburettor) – PART 1

1		Right lighting unit
2		Left lighting unit
	a	Upper beam
	b	Lower beam
	c	Flash signal
	d	Parking light
	e	Fog light
	f	Clearance light
3		Instrument cluster
	a	Left signal indicator
	b	Right signal indicator
	c	Fuel reserve warning light
	d	Fuel level indicator
	e	Electric clock
	f	Control resistance for instrument lighting
	g	Instrument lighting
	h	Charging light
	i	Upper beam control
	k	Brake control
4		Two-tone horn mechanism
5		Blower switch (air intake)
6		Blower motor (air intake)
7		Stop light switch
8		Reversing light switch
9		Foot pump windshield washer
10		Wiper motor
11		Control switch for brake fluid
12		Control switch for parking brake
13		Flash signal mechanism
14		Horn ring
15		Combination switch
	a	Flash signal switch
	b	Flash approach signal switch
	c	Hand dimmer
	d	Windshield wiper switch
	e	Wiper speed switch
16		Cigar lighter
17		Front left door contact
18		Reading light
19		Front right door contact
20		Roof-light switch (on model 250 only)
21		Rear roof light (on model 250 only)
22		Battery
23		Starter
24		Lead for optional extra (radio)
25		Automatic start mechanism on rear carburettor
26		Automatic start mechanism on front carburettor
27		Fuses
28		Rotary light switch
29		Ignition starter switch
30		Series resistance
31		Ignition coil
32		Spark plugs
33		Distributor
34		Sleeve union for tail light wiring harness
35		Fuel level indicator
36		Generator
37		Voltage regulator
38		Trunk compartment light
39		Right tail light
40		Left tail light
	a	Flash signal
	b	Tail light
	c	Reversing light
	d	Clearance light
	e	Stop light
41		License plate light

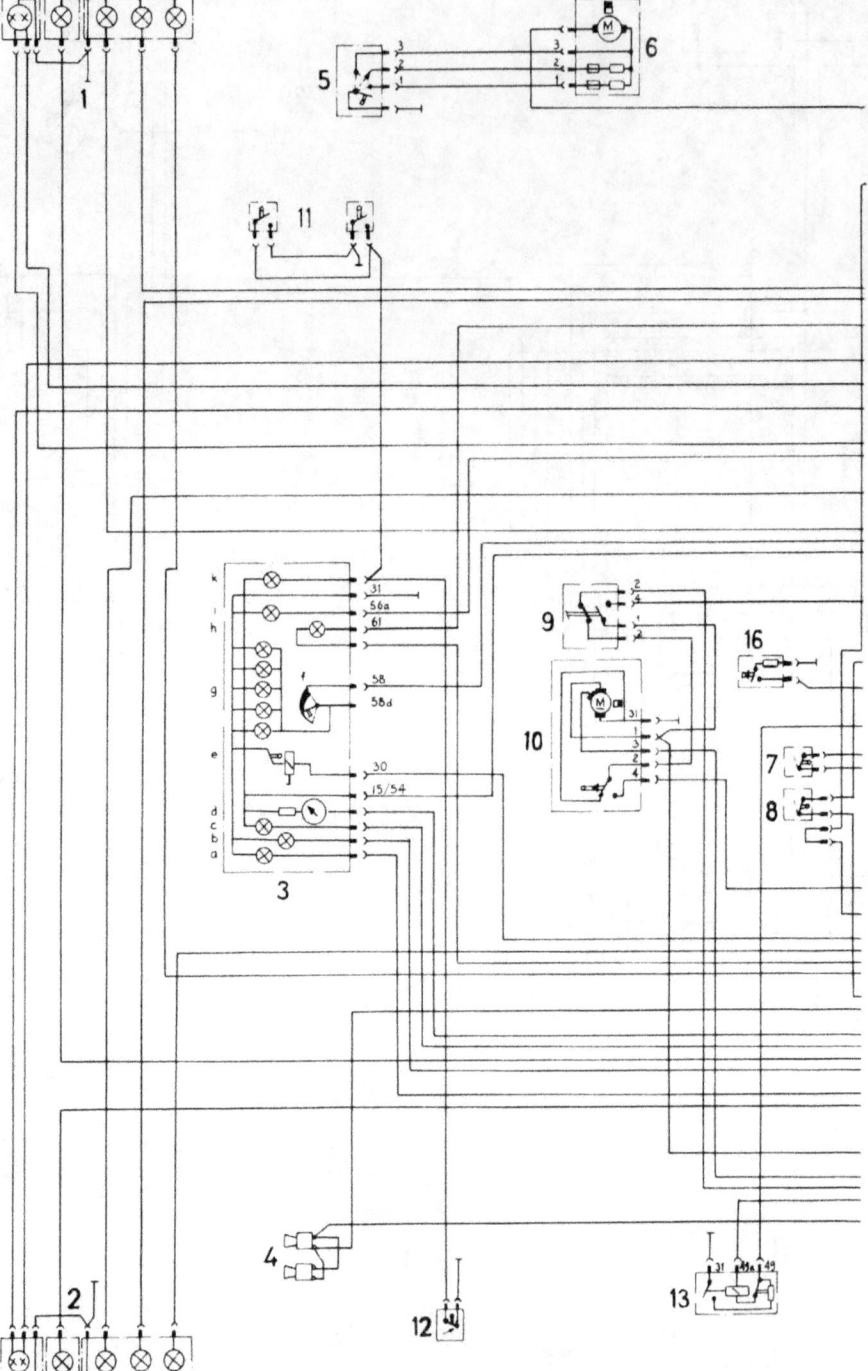

230/8 WIRING DIAGRAM (Carburettor) - PART 2

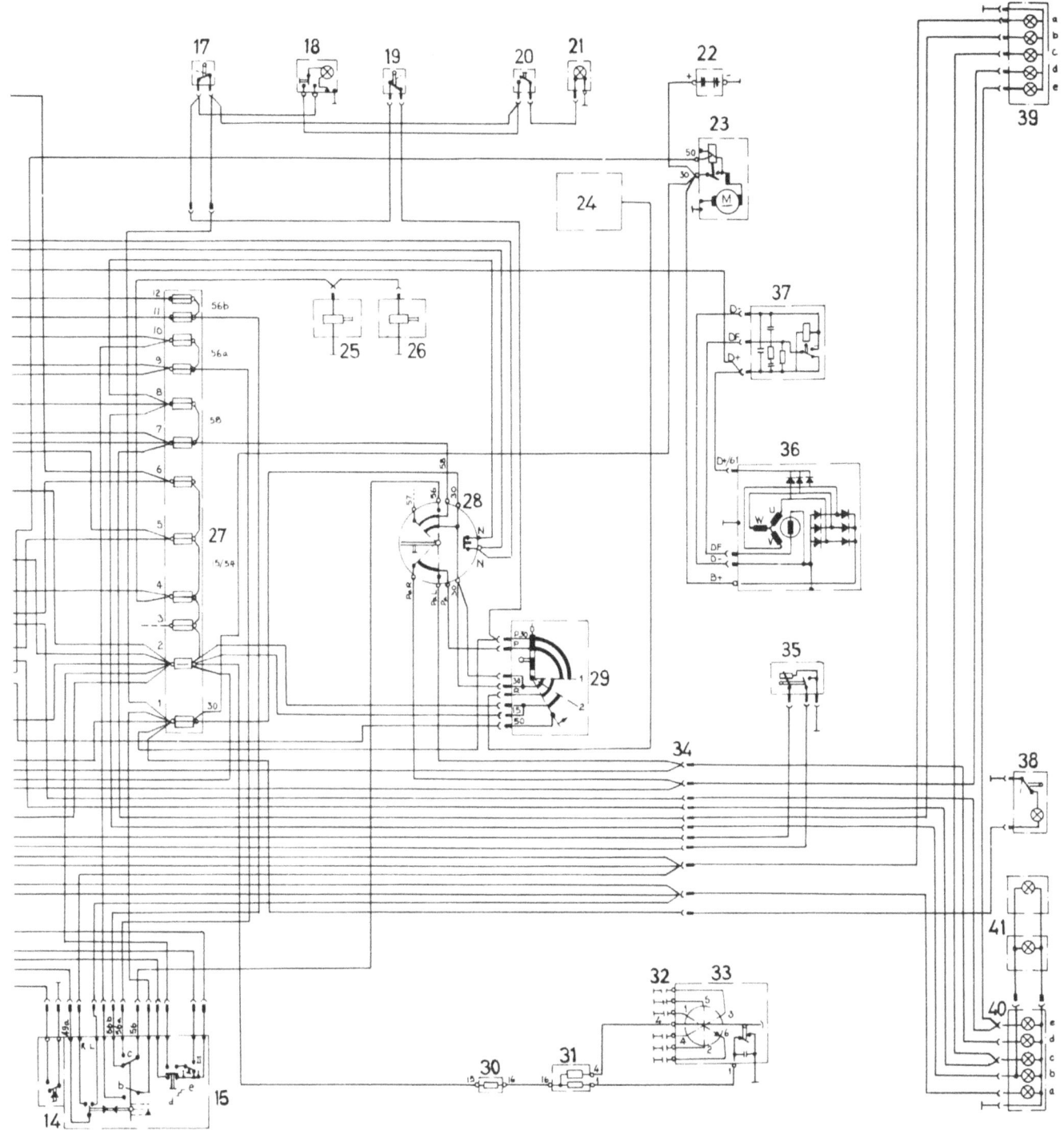

230SL WIRING DIAGRAM - PART 1

1. Lighting unit, right
2. Lighting unit, left
   a. High beam
   b. Low beam
   c. Direction signal light
   d. Parking light
   e. Fog light
   f. Clearance light
3. Glove compartment and reading light
4. Glove compartment light switch
5. Heater blower switch
6. Electric clock
7. Courtesy light and switch
8. Speedometer light
9. Revolution counter light
10. Instrument cluster
    a. Flasher control light, left
    b. Flasher control light, right
    c. Fuel reserve warning
    d. Fuel level indicator
    e. Instrument light
    f. Regulating resistor for illumination
    g. Ignition warning light
    h. High beam control light
11. Dual tone horns
12. Heater blower motor
13. Illumination, heating control
14. Door contact switch, right
15. Door contact switch, left
16. Windshield wiper motor
17. Relay for wiper motor
18. Flasher unit
20. Time switch

230SL WIRING DIAGRAM - PART 2

21 Mixture control solenoid relay	29 Steering column switch	33 Solenoid for mixture control	45 Transmitter for fuel gauge
22 Windshield washer pump	a Flasher switch	35 Dimmer switch	46 Plug connection tail light leads
23 Brake light switch	b Headlight flash switch	36 Rotary light switch	47 Distributor
24 Back-up light switch	c Windshield washer switch	37 Ignition starter switch	48 Tail light, right
25 Cigarette lighter	d Windshield washer switch	38 Spark plugs	49 Tail light, left
26 Horn ring	e Switch for wiper speed	39 Ignition coil	a Direction signal light
27 Socket	f Plug connection,	40 Battery	b Tail light
28 Fuses	steering column switch	41 Starter	c Back-up light
	30 Series resistance	42 Voltage regulator	d Clearance light
	31 Electromagnetic starter valve	43 Generator	e Brake light
	32 Thermo time switch	44 Fuel feed pump	f Identification light

Inches	Decimals	Milli-metres	Inches to Millimetres Inches	mm	Millimetres to Inches mm	Inches
1/64	.015625	.3969	.001	.0254	.01	.00039
1/32	.03125	.7937	.002	.0508	.02	.00079
3/64	.046875	1.1906	.003	.0762	.03	.00118
1/16	.0625	1.5875	.004	.1016	.04	.00157
5/64	.078125	1.9844	.005	.1270	.05	.00197
3/32	.09375	2.3812	.006	.1524	.06	.00236
7/64	.109375	2.7781	.007	.1778	.07	.00276
1/8	.125	3.1750	.008	.2032	.08	.00315
9/64	.140625	3.5719	.009	.2286	.09	.00354
5/32	.15625	3.9687	.01	.254	.1	.00394
11/64	.171875	4.3656	.02	.508	.2	.00787
3/16	.1875	4.7625	.03	.762	.3	.01181
13/64	.203125	5.1594	.04	1.016	.4	.01575
7/32	.21875	5.5562	.05	1.270	.5	.01969
15/64	.234375	5.9531	.06	1.524	.6	.02362
1/4	.25	6.3500	.07	1.778	.7	.02756
17/64	.265625	6.7469	.08	2.032	.8	.03150
9/32	.28125	7.1437	.09	2.286	.9	.03543
19/64	.296875	7.5406	.1	2.54	1	.03937
5/16	.3125	7.9375	.2	5.08	2	.07874
21/64	.328125	8.3344	.3	7.62	3	.11811
11/32	.34375	8.7312	.4	10.16	4	.15748
23/64	.359375	9.1281	.5	12.70	5	.19685
3/8	.375	9.5250	.6	15.24	6	.23622
25/64	.390625	9.9219	.7	17.78	7	.27559
13/32	.40625	10.3187	.8	20.32	8	.31496
27/64	.421875	10.7156	.9	22.86	9	.35433
7/16	.4375	11.1125	1	25.4	10	.39370
29/64	.453125	11.5094	2	50.8	11	.43307
15/32	.46875	11.9062	3	76.2	12	.47244
31/64	.484375	12.3031	4	101.6	13	.51181
1/2	.5	12.7000	5	127.0	14	.55118
33/64	.515625	13.0969	6	152.4	15	.59055
17/32	.53125	13.4937	7	177.8	16	.62992
35/64	.546875	13.8906	8	203.2	17	.66929
9/16	.5625	14.2875	9	228.6	18	.70866
37/64	.578125	14.6844	10	254.0	19	.74803
19/32	.59375	15.0812	11	279.4	20	.78740
39/64	.609375	15.4781	12	304.8	21	.82677
5/8	.625	15.8750	13	330.2	22	.86614
41/64	.640625	16.2719	14	355.6	23	.90551
21/32	.65625	16.6687	15	381.0	24	.94488
43/64	.671875	17.0656	16	406.4	25	.98425
11/16	.6875	17.4625	17	431.8	26	1.02362
45/64	.703125	17.8594	18	457.2	27	1.06299
23/32	.71875	18.2562	19	482.6	28	1.10236
47/64	.734375	18.6531	20	508.0	29	1.14173
3/4	.75	19.0500	21	533.4	30	1.18110
49/64	.765625	19.4469	22	558.8	31	1.22047
25/32	.78125	19.8437	23	584.2	32	1.25984
51/64	.796875	20.2406	24	609.6	33	1.29921
13/16	.8125	20.6375	25	635.0	34	1.33858
53/64	.828125	21.0344	26	660.4	35	1.37795
27/32	.84375	21.4312	27	685.8	36	1.41732
55/64	.859375	21.8281	28	711.2	37	1.4567
7/8	.875	22.2250	29	736.6	38	1.4961
57/64	.890625	22.6219	30	762.0	39	1.5354
29/32	.90625	23.0187	31	787.4	40	1.5748
59/64	.921875	23.4156	32	812.8	41	1.6142
15/16	.9375	23.8125	33	838.2	42	1.6535
61/64	.953125	24.2094	34	863.6	43	1.6929
31/32	.96875	24.6062	35	889.0	44	1.7323
63/64	.984375	25.0031	36	914.4	45	1.7717

UNITS	Pints to Litres	Gallons to Litres	Litres to Pints	Litres to Gallons	Miles to Kilometres	Kilometres to Miles	Lbs. per sq. In. to Kg. per sq. Cm.	Kg. per sq. Cm. to Lbs. per sq. In.
1	.57	4.55	1.76	.22	1.61	.62	.07	14.22
2	1.14	9.09	3.52	.44	3.22	1.24	.14	28.50
3	1.70	13.64	5.28	.66	4.83	1.86	.21	42.67
4	2.27	18.18	7.04	.88	6.44	2.49	.28	56.89
5	2.84	22.73	8.80	1.10	8.05	3.11	.35	71.12
6	3.41	27.28	10.56	1.32	9.66	3.73	.42	85.34
7	3.98	31.82	12.32	1.54	11.27	4.35	.49	99.56
8	4.55	36.37	14.08	1.76	12.88	4.97	.56	113.79
9		40.91	15.84	1.98	14.48	5.59	.63	128.00
10		45.46	17.60	2.20	16.09	6.21	.70	142.23
20				4.40	32.19	12.43	1.41	284.47
30				6.60	48.28	18.64	2.11	426.70
40				8.80	64.37	24.85		
50					80.47	31.07		
60					96.56	37.28		
70					112.65	43.50		
80					128.75	49.71		
90					144.84	55.92		
100					160.93	62.14		

UNITS	Lb ft to kgm	Kgm to lb ft	UNITS	Lb ft to kgm	Kgm to lb ft
1	.138	7.233	7	.967	50.631
2	.276	14.466	8	1.106	57.864
3	.414	21.699	9	1.244	65.097
4	.553	28.932	10	1.382	72.330
5	.691	36.165	20	2.765	144.660
6	.829	43.398	30	4.147	216.990

VELOCEPRESS MANUALS – AUTOMOBILE BY MAKE

ALFA ROMEO GIULIA WORKSHOP MANUAL 1300 TO 2000cc 1962-1975
ALFA ROMEO GIULIA TECH MANUAL CARBURETED CARS FROM 1962
ALFA ROMEO GIULIA TECH MANUAL FUEL INJECTED CARS FROM 1969
ALFA ROMEO GIULIETTA & GIULIA 750 & 101 SERIES 1955-1965 WSM
AUSTIN-HEALEY SPRITE & MG MIDGET WORKSHOP MANUAL 1958-1971
BMW 600 LIMOUSINE FACTORY WORKSHOP MANUAL
BMW 600 LIMOUSINE OWNERS HAND BOOK & SERVICE MANUAL
BMW 2000 & 2002 1966-1976 WORKSHOP MANUAL
BMW 2500, 2800, 3.0 & BARVARIA WORKSHOP MANUAL
CORVAIR 1960-1969 WORKSHOP MANUAL
CORVETTE V8 1955-1962 WORKSHOP MANUAL
FERRARI HANDBOOK ROAD & RACE CARS (SERVICE/SPECS) 1948-1958
FERRARI 250GT SERVICE & MAINTENANCE by JIM RIFF 1956-1965
FERRARI 250GT & 250GTE FACTORY PARTS AND REPAIR MANUALS
FIAT 500 FACTORY WORKSHOP MANUAL 1957-1973
FIAT 600, 600D & MULTIPLA FACTORY WORKSHOP MANUAL 1955-1969
JAGUAR E-TYPE 3.8 & 4.2 SERIES 1 & 2 WORKSHOP MANUAL
JAGUAR MK 7, 8, 9 & XK120, 140, 150 WORKSHOP MANUAL 1948-1961
MERCEDES-BENZ 230 SERIES 1963-1968
MERCEDES-BENZ 280 SERIES 1968-1972
METROPOLITAN FACTORY WORKSHOP MANUAL
MGA & MGB OWNERS HANDBOOK & WORKSHOP MANUAL
MG MIDGET TC, TD, TF & TF1500 WORKSHOP MANUAL
PORSCHE 356 1948-1965 WORKSHOP MANUAL
PORSCHE 911 2.0, 2.2, 2.4 LITRE 1964-1973 WORKSHOP MANUAL
PORSCHE 911 2.7, 3.0, 3.2 LITRE 1973-1989 WORKSHOP MANUAL
PORSCHE 912 WORKSHOP MANUAL
PORSCHE 914/4 & 914/6 1.7, 1.8, 2.0 LITRE 1970-1976 WSM
TRIUMPH TR2, TR3, TR4 1953-1965 WORKSHOP MANUAL
VOLKSWAGEN TRANSPORTER, TRUCKS & WAGONS 1950-1979 WSM
VOLVO 1944-1968 ALL MODELS WORKSHOP MANUAL

VELOCEPRESS TECHNICAL BOOKS - AUTOMOBILE

HOW TO BUILD A FIBERGLASS CAR
HOW TO BUILD A RACING CAR
HOW TO RESTORE THE MODEL 'A' FORD
MASERATI OWNER'S HANDBOOK
PERFORMANCE TUNING THE SUNBEAM TIGER
SOUPING THE VOLKSWAGEN
SOLEX CARBURETORS (EMPHASIS ON UK & EU AUTOMOBILES)
SU CARBURETORS (EMPHASIS ON UK AUTOMOBILES)
WEBER CARBURETORS (EMPHASIS ON ALFA & FIAT)

VELOCEPRESS BOOKS & GUIDES - AUTOMOBILE

COMPLETE CATALOG OF JAPANESE MOTOR VEHICLES
FERRARI 308 SERIES BUYER'S AND OWNER'S GUIDE
FERRARI BROCHURES AND SALES LITERATURE 1968-1989
FERRARI SERIAL NUMBERS PART I - ODD NUMBERS TO 21399
FERRARI SERIAL NUMBERS PART II - EVEN NUMBERS TO 1050
HENRY'S FABULOUS MODEL "A" FORD
MASERATI BROCHURES AND SALES LITERATURE

VELOCEPRESS BOOKS – AUTO RACING

BOOK OF THE 1950 CARRERA PANAMERICANA - MEXICAN ROAD RACE
DIALED IN - THE JAN OPPERMAN STORY
VEDA ORR'S NEW REVISED HOT ROD PICTORIAL
LIFE OF TED HORN – AMERICAN RACING CHAMPION

www.VelocePress.com

VELOCEPRESS MANUALS – MOTORCYCLE BY MAKE

AJS 1932-1948 SINGLES & TWINS 250cc THRU 1000cc (BOOK OF)
AJS 1945-1960 SINGLES 350cc & 500cc MODELS 16 & 18 (BOOK OF)
AJS 1955-1965 SINGLES 350cc & 500cc (BOOK OF)
AJS 1957-1966 FACTORY WSM - ALL SINGLES & TWINS
AJS 1959-1969 FACTORY WSM G80CS G85CS & P11 OFF ROAD
ARIEL UP TO 1932 (BOOK OF)
ARIEL 1932-1939 PREWAR MODELS (BOOK OF)
ARIEL 1933-1951 (WORKSHOP MANUAL)
ARIEL 1939-1960 4 STROKE SINGLES (BOOK OF)
ARIEL 1958-1964 LEADER & ARROW FACTORY WSM & PARTS LIST
ARIEL 1958-1964 LEADER & ARROW (BOOK OF)
BMW R26 R27 (1956-1967) FACTORY WORKSHOP MANUAL
BMW R50 R50S R60 R69S (1955-1969) FACTORY WORKSHOP MANUAL
BMW R50/5 R60/5 R75/5 (1969-1973) FACTORY WORKSHOP MANUAL
BRIDGESTONE 90 SERIES FACTORY WSM & PARTS CATALOGUE
BRIDGESTONE 175 SERIES FACTORY WSM & PARTS CATALOGUE
BRIDGESTONE 350 SERIES FACTORY WSM & PARTS CATALOGUES
BSA SERVICE SHEETS MASTER CATALOGUE ALL MODELS 1945-1967
BSA BANTAM D1 TO D7 1948-1966 FACTORY SERVICE SHEETS MANUAL
BSA BANTAM ALL MODELS FROM 1948 ONWARDS (BOOK OF)
BSA BANTAM D14 FACTORY SERVICE MANUAL
BSA DANDY FACTORY WORKSHOP MANUAL (COMPILATION)
BSA SINGLES & V-TWINS UP TO 1926 inc. 1927 SUPPLEMENT (BOOK OF)
BSA SINGLES & V-TWINS UP TO 1930 (BOOK OF)
BSA SINGLES & V-TWINS UP TO 1935 (BOOK OF)
BSA SINGLES & V-TWINS 1936-1939 (BOOK OF)
BSA C10, C11 & C12 1945-1958 FACTORY SERVICE SHEETS MANUAL
BSA OHV & SV SINGLES 250-600cc 1945-1959 (BOOK OF)
BSA C15 & B40 1958-1967 FACTORY SERVICE SHEETS MANUAL
BSA OHV & SV SINGLES 250cc (ONLY) 1954-1970 (BOOK OF)
BSA B31, B32, B33 & B34 1945-60 FACTORY SERVICE SHEETS MANUAL
BSA OHV SINGLES 350 & 500cc 1955-1967 (BOOK OF)
BSA M20, M21 & M33 1945-1963 FACTORY SERVICE SHEETS MANUAL
BSA TWINS A7 & A10 1948-1962 FACTORY SERVICE SHEETS MANUAL
BSA TWINS A7 & A10 1948-1962 (BOOK OF)
BSA TWINS A50 & A65 1962-1965 FACTORY WORKSHOP MANUAL
BSA TWINS A50 & A65 1962-1969 (SECOND BOOK OF)
DOUGLAS 1929-1939 PREWAR ALL MODELS (BOOK OF)
DOUGLAS 1948-1957 POSTWAR ALL MODELS FACTORY SHOP MANUAL
DUCATI 160cc, 250cc & 350cc OHC MODELS FACTORY SHOP MANUAL
HONDA 50cc ALL MODELS UP TO 1970 INC MONKEY & TRAIL (BOOK OF)
HONDA 90cc ALL MODELS UP TO 1966 (BOOK OF)
HONDA TWINS & SINGLES 50cc THRU 305cc 1960-1966 (BOOK OF)
HONDA TWINS ALL MODELS 125cc THRU 450cc UP TO 1968 (BOOK OF)
HONDA C100 50cc SUPER CUB O.H.C. 1959-1962 FACTORY WSM
HONDA C110 50cc SPORT CUB O.H.C. 1960-1962 FACTORY WSM
HONDA 50-65-70-90cc O.H.C. SINGLES 1959-1983 WSM
HONDA 100-125cc SINGLES CB/CD/CL/SL/TL 1970-1984 FACTORY WSM
HONDA 125-150cc TWINS C/CS/CB/CA 1959-1966 FACTORY WSM
HONDA 125-160-175-200cc TWINS 1965-1978 WORKSHOP MANUAL
HONDA 250-305cc TWINS C/CS/CB 1961-1968 FACTORY WSM
HOHDA 250-350cc TWINS CB/CL/SL 1968-1973 FACTORY WSM
HONDA 250-360cc TWINS CB/CL/CJ 1974-1977 FACTORY WSM
HONDA 350F & 400F 4-CYLINDER 1972-1977 FACTORY WSM
HONDA 450cc TWINS CB/CL 1965-1974 K0 TO K7 WORKSHOP MANUAL
HONDA 500cc & 550cc 4-CYL 1971-1978 FACTORY WORKSHOP MANUAL
HONDA 750cc SHOC 4-CYL 1969-1978 K0~K8 WORKSHOP MANUAL
INDIAN PONYBIKE, BOY RACER & PAPOOSE ILL PARTS LIST & SALES LIT

VELOCEPRESS MANUALS – SCOOTERS BY MAKE

BSA SUNBEAM SCOOTER WORKSHOP MANUAL 1959-1965
BSA SUNBEAM SCOOTER 1959-1965 (BOOK OF)
LAMBRETTA 1947-1957 ALL 125 & 150cc MODELS (BOOK OF)
LAMBRETTA 1957-1970 LI & TV MODELS (SECOND BOOK OF)
NSU PRIMA 1956-1964 ALL MODELS (BOOK OF)
TRIUMPH TIGRESS SCOOTER WORKSHOP MANUAL 1959-1965
TRIUMPH TIGRESS SCOOTER (BOOK OF)
VESPA 1951-1961 (BOOK OF)
VESPA 1955-1963 125 & 150cc & GS MODELS (SECOND BOOK OF)
VESPA 1955-1968 GS & SS (BOOK OF)
VESPA 1963-1972 90, 125 & 150cc (THIRD BOOK OF)

VELOCEPRESS MANUALS – MOPEDS & MOTORIZED BICYCLES

CYCLEMOTOR (BOOK OF)
NSU QUICKLY 1953-1963 ALL MODELS (BOOK OF)
PUCH MAXI N & S MAINTENANCE & REPAIR (3 MANUAL COMPILATION)
RALEIGH MOPEDS 1960-1969 (BOOK OF)

J.A.P. ENGINES 1927-1952 & MOTORCYCLES 1934-1952 (BOOK OF)
MATCHLESS 1931-1939 ALL MODELS 250cc THRU 990cc (BOOK OF)
MATCHLESS 1945-1956 350 & 500cc SINGLES (BOOK OF)
MATCHLESS 1955-1966 350 & 500cc SINGLES (BOOK OF)
MATCHLESS 1957-1966 FACTORY WSM - ALL SINGLES & TWINS
NEW IMPERIAL ALL SV & OHV FROM 1935 ONWARDS (BOOK OF)
NORTON 1932-1939 PREWAR MODELS (BOOK OF)
NORTON 1932-1947 (BOOK OF)
NORTON 1938-1956 (BOOK OF)
NORTON 1945-1963 MODELS 16H, Big4, ES2, 19 & 50 WSM'S & PARTS
NORTON 1955-1963 MODELS 19, 50 & ES2 (BOOK OF)
NORTON 1948-1970 DOMINATOR TWINS FACTORY WSM'S & PARTS
NORTON 1955-1965 DOMINATOR TWINS (BOOK OF)
NORTON 1960-1970 TWIN CYLINDER FACTORY WORKSHOP MANUAL
NORTON 1970-1975 COMMANDO 850 & 750cc FACTORY WSM
NORTON 1975-1978 MK 3 COMMANDO 850 cc FACTORY WSM
PANTHER 1932-1958 LIGHTWEIGHT MODELS 250 & 350cc (BOOK OF)
PANTHER 1938-1966 HEAVYWEIGHT MODELS 600 & 650cc (BOOK OF)
PENTON-KTM-SACHS 1968-1975 100cc & 125cc WORKSHOP MANUAL
RALEIGH MOTORCYCLES 1919-1933 (BOOK OF)
ROYAL ENFIELD 1934-1946 SINGLES & V TWINS (BOOK OF)
ROYAL ENFIELD 1937-1953 SINGLES & V TWINS (BOOK OF)
ROYAL ENFIELD 1946-1962 SINGLES (BOOK OF)
ROYAL ENFIELD 1948-1962 350cc & 500cc PRE-UNIT BULLET WSM
ROYAL ENFIELD 1948-1963 500cc TWINS FACTORY WORKSHOP MANUAL
ROYAL ENFIELD 1952-1963 700cc TWINS FACTORY WORKSHOP MANUAL
ROYAL ENFIELD 1956-1966 250cc CRUSADER & 350cc NEW BULLET WSM
ROYAL ENFIELD 1958-1966 250cc & 350cc SINGLES (SECOND BOOK OF)
ROYAL ENFIELD 1962-1970 INTERCEPTOR WSM'S & PARTS (Compilation)
RUDGE 1933-1939 (BOOK OF)
SACHS 1968-1975 100cc & 125cc ENGINES WSM & M/CYCLE PARTS LIST
SUNBEAM 1928-1939 (BOOK OF)
SUNBEAM 1946-1957 S7 & S8 (BOOK OF)
SUZUKI 50cc & 80cc UP TO 1966 (BOOK OF)
SUZUKI T10 1963-1967 FACTORY WORKSHOP MANUAL
SUZUKI T20 & T200 1965-1969 FACTORY WORKSHOP MANUAL
SUZUKI TWINS 1962 ONWARDS 125-500cc WORKSHOP MANUAL
TRIUMPH 1935-1949 SINGLES & TWINS (BOOK OF)
TRIUMPH 1937-1961 SINGLES SV & OHV 250cc-600cc + TERRIER & CUB
TRIUMPH 1945-1955 PRE-UNIT 350cc, 500cc & 650cc TWINS WSM No.11
TRIUMPH 1945-1959 TWINS (BOOK OF)
TRIUMPH 1956-1969 TWINS (BOOK OF)
TRIUMPH 1956-1962 PRE-UNIT 500cc & 650cc TWINS WSM No.17
TRIUMPH 1957-1963 UNIT CONSTRUCTION 350-500cc WSM No.4
TRIUMPH 1963-1974 UNIT CONSTRUCTION 350-500cc FACTORY WSM
TRIUMPH 1963-1970 UNIT CONSTRUCTION 650cc FACTORY WSM
TRIUMPH 1968-1974 TRIDENT T150 & T150V FACTORY WSM
TRIUMPH 1971-1973 650cc OIL-IN-FRAME FACTORY WSM
TRIUMPH 1973-1978 750cc BONNEVILLE & TIGER FACTORY WSM
TRIUMPH 1979-1983 750cc T140, TR7 & TR65 FACTORY WSM
VELOCETTE 1925-1970 ALL SINGLES & TWINS (BOOK OF)
VELOCETTE 1933-1952 MOV-MAC-MSS RIGID FRAME FACTORY WSM
VELOCETTE 1953-1960 MAC SPRING FRAME WSM & ILL PARTS LIST
VELOCETTE 1954-1971 MSS-VENOM-THRUXTON-VIPER FACTORY WSM
VILLIERS ENGINE UP TO 1959 INC. 3 WHEELERS (BOOK OF)
VILLIERS ENGINE UP TO 1969 (BOOK OF)
VINCENT 1935-1955 (WORKSHOP MANUAL)
YAMAHA 1961-1967 YA5 & YA6 (WORKSHOP MANUAL & ILL PARTS LIST)
YAMAHA 1968-1971 DT1 & MX SERIES Inc. GYT WORKSHOP MANUAL
YAMAHA 1971-1972 JT1& JT2 (WORKSHOP MANUAL & ILL PARTS LIST)

VELOCEPRESS MANUALS - THREE WHEELER'S

BOND MINICAR THREE WHEELER 1948-1967 (BOOK OF)
BMW ISETTA FACTORY WORKSHOP MANUAL
BSA THREE WHEELER (BOOK OF)
RELIANT REGAL THREE WHEELER 1952-1973 (BOOK OF)
VINTAGE MORGAN THREE WHEELER (BOOK OF)

VELOCEPRESS TECHNICAL BOOKS – MOTORCYCLE

1930'S BRITISH MOTORCYCLE CARBS & ELEC COMPONENTS (BOOK OF)
1930'S BRITISH MOTORCYCLE ENGINES (OVERHAUL & MAINTENANCE)
1930'S BRITISH MOTORCYCLE GEARBOXES & CLUTCHES (BOOK OF)
CATALOG OF BRITISH MOTORCYCLES (1951 MODELS)
LUCAS ELECTRONICS BRITISH M/CYCLES REPAIR & PARTS (1950-1977)
MOTORCYCLE ENGINEERING (P.E. Irving)
MOTORCYCLE ROAD TESTS 1949-1953 (Motor Cycle Magazine UK)
SPEED AND HOW TO OBTAIN IT (Motor Cycle Magazine UK)
TUNING FOR SPEED (P.E. Irving)
WIPAC (COMBO) MANUAL NUMBER 3 + M/CYCLE & SCOOTER MANUAL